August-Wilhelm Scheer

Principles of Efficient Information Management

Second, Completely Revised Edition

With 166 Figures

Springer-Verlag

Berlin Heidelberg New York
London Paris Tokyo
Hong Kong Barcelona
Budapest

Professor Dr. August-Wilhelm Scheer
Director of the Institut für Wirtschaftsinformatik
and the CIM Technology Transfer Center
University of Saarland
Im Stadtwald, Gebäude 14
D-6600 Saarbrücken 11, FRG

The first edition appeared under the title "Computer: A Challenge for Business Administration"

ISBN-13: 978-3-642-46744-8   e-ISBN-13: 978-3-642-46742-4
DOI: 10.1007/978-3-642-46742-4

2142/7130-543210

Preface

The first edition of this book appeared in the Federal Republic of Germany in 1984, and in English translation as "Computer: A Challenge for Business Administration" in 1985. This book, which is a translation of the fourth German edition, has been comprehensively revised. As a result both the character and the expected audience of the book have changed, which is reflected in the alteration to the title.

This book adresses itself to issues arising from the research areas of both information systems and computer science. Computer science departments are primarily concerned with the development of EDP techniques, and the business economics aspects remain largely ignored. The emphasis in information systems departments is placed on the investigation of the business economic impact of the use of already existing systems. This strongly empirical approach is accompanied by a disinclination to consider actual system design; this is considered the responsibility of the software houses.

This partitioning, however, leaves untapped the considerable potential which could be realized by an interdisciplinary approach from computer science and business economics. An isolated approach neglects both the effects that business economics can have on the implementation of EDP techniques, and the structural impact of EDP on business economics.

Consequently, this book investigates the interdependences between business economics and EDP in both directions:

- What implications can business economics draw from EDP techniques for its problem solving approaches?
- How can business economics ensure that EDP techniques and their implementations are more efficiently structured?

The material is extended by many practical examples and is also aimed at practitioners from both business economics and EDP departments.

I would like to thank Irene Cameron for her careful translation ot the German original, and my employees Ruth Bartels and Carmen Kächler for their dedicated support in the technical preparation of the manuscript.

Saarbrücken, West Germany

March 1991   August-Wilhelm Scheer

Contents

X

Chapter 1: EDP-Orientation of Business Economics

A. Business Economics and EDP

The areas of emphasis within business economics have changed several times in the last 40 years. In production theory factors of production and the ways of combining them occupy the foreground; in decision-oriented business economics the stress is on the analysis and optimization of decision processes; system-oriented business economics considers business processes as interdependent feedback loops; and the empirically-based research approach emphasizes the necessity of establishing the empirical foundations for theoretical statements.

None of these approaches can be expected to provide comprehensive coverage of the practical field of "business economics". Rather, these approaches should be regarded as complementary.

In this sense, therefore, the proposed EDP-orientation of business economics should be understood as a further area of emphasis within this field. Reflecting the renaming of "computer science departments" as departments for "information systems" or "information management", the term "information-oriented business economics" is equivalent to the term "EDP-oriented business economics", as long as "information-oriented" is understood as closely linked with the possibilities of information processing techniques. This conceptual development is reflected in the title **"Principles of efficient information management"**.

The collective term **"electronic data processing" (EDP)** comprises the information and communication techniques for the electronic processing of data, that is the entry, storage, transformation, transfer and output of data. For simplicity, the term "information and communication techniques" will often be replaced by the term "information techniques".

This includes both hardware and software technology as well as concrete implementations, e.g. in the form of specific hardware configurations and application programs.

The relationships between business economics and EDP are manifold:

-     **EDP makes possible the use of corporate planning methods that are costly in processing and data terms. This in turn facilitates the introduction of**

    organizational processes which would be uneconomical or infeasible without EDP.

- **The economic advantages of EDP can only be fully exploited if suitable business application concepts for its use are available.**

- **EDP application programs have an increasing effect on fundamental business processes within the enterprise**. It has been asserted, for example, that an industrial concern whose EDP system fails becomes functionally incapacitated within about 10 days (see *Anselstetter, Nutzeffekte der Datenverarbeitung 1986, p. 19*). With increasing levels of penetration this interval will become considerably shorter. **Widely used standard application programs for financial accounting, production planning, etc. have a large multiplier effect on the business concepts they contain.**

These three aspects form the basis for the close interdependences between business economics and EDP:

- **EDP support for processing-intensive or data-intensive business methods,**
- **the need for EDP-oriented business models to improve data processing efficiency,**
- **the considerable organizational effects of applications software.**

EDP know-how did not find its way into business economics until the mid '60s with the establishment of business informatics. **Business informatics is defined as the science of designing and implementing computerized information and communication systems**.

Because the use of information techniques has largely developed in the practical sphere, the theoretical foundations for business applications were only developed subsequently. For a long time, therefore, the business informatics literature mainly consisted of predominantly instrumental textbooks. Here descriptions of hardware and software basics and techniques for designing EDP systems were predominant. Systematic presentations of computerized business applications have only started to appear more recently.

For this reason the EDP-technical publications provide little motivation for specialists in the classical business disciplines to become more involved with the possibilities of electronic data processing. In fact they exacerbate the prejudice that business informatics is principally concerned with "technical" problems. As a result the existing uncertainty with regard to EDP is increased, and defensive attitudes towards this supposedly "alien" discipline are strengthened.

On the other hand, business informatics would be severely overstretched were it to attempt to provide computer application designs for all business functions. Its main task, in addition to establishing fundamental principles, should rather be one of developing **general** formulations and methods of EDP application and solution procedures which enable the classical business disciplines to take greater account of aspects of EDP applications. This development is increasingly under way.

Even business organization theory, which has close links with information processing, has so far not involved itself adequately with this area. For example, research is aimed at specifying the techniques needed in organizational practice for the achievement of concrete goals, the criteria for implementing a new information technique (see *Picot, Bürokommunikation 1982, p. 10*), or the effects of the use of EDP on the organizational structure of enterprises (see *Leavitt, Whisler, Management 1958; Kieser, Kubicek, Organisation 1983*). This approach, however, pays too little attention to the more important question of how business procedures and decision processes can or must be restructured in light of the new techniques.

The decision theory school of business economics also considers only a minimal subset of the problem area relevant to any EDP solution. For example, the implementation of a re-ordering algorithm (e.g. Andler formula, s-S-rule, etc.) within an ordering policy software system constitutes only 0.1% of the program code, while the greater part of the software controls the data flow to and from preceding and subsequent processes, error handling, and user guidance in the organizational treatment of diverse cases. In executing a concrete purchase order the EDP functions are certainly of greater significance than the re-order algorithm. **In other words: a software system for order handling can certainly be effective without a highly complex re-order algorithm; the most sophisticated re-order rule without links to the information base and the organizational framework is useless.**

In some specialist branches of business economics approaches which take EDP techniques into account already exist, e.g. in marketing (see *Meffert, Marketing-Informationssysteme 1975; Zentes, EDV-gestütztes Marketing 1987*), in industrial economics (see *Heinen, Industriebetriebslehre 1985, p. 1039 ff.; Jacob, Industriebetriebslehre 1972; Hahn, Lassmann, Produktionswirtschaft 1986*), and in personnel management (see *Domsch, Personalarbeit 1980*). Some new publications also systematically consider the possibilities for restructuring business processes by using EDP techniques. Nevertheless, many classical business economics texts display a considerable lack of EDP-orientation, sometimes even ignorance.

The concept of information resource management discussed in the USA (see *Synott, Gruber, Information Resource Management 1986; Horton, Information Management Workbook 1981*) interprets information as an independent factor of production which, analogous to the other factors of production, must be effectively employed and optimally combined with other factors of production in order to achieve optimal productivity. This concept also generates the demand that all information-processing activities should be unified in **one** organizational unit. Hence, this concept offers the basis for a comprehensive organizational integration of information and communication techniques in an information management sense.

The mutual influence described between EDP and business economics applies not only in theory, but also to the practical use of EDP within the enterprise. This book is therefore aimed at both students and business specialists in the academic and the practical environment.

B. Concept of EDP-Oriented Business Economics

B.I. Definition and Objectives

EDP-oriented business economics is justified by the close links between business economics and electronic data processing resulting from:
- EDP support for processing-intensive or data-intensive business methods,
- the need for EDP-oriented business models to improve data processing efficiency,
- the considerable organizational and multiplier effects of EDP systems for business functions.

The subject matter of EDP-oriented business economics is therefore the reciprocal effects between information technology and business economics. These relate to the entire spectrum of business problem configurations and extend the explanatory and structuring functions of business economics.

As in every new approach within a discipline, specific representational forms are required to fulfil the explanatory function. In the case of EDP-oriented business economics it is necessary to check the existing EDP terminology and representational forms used in data processing as to their suitability for adoption into the business economics sphere.

The structuring function needs to develop approaches which allow the further development and solution of the tasks and problems arising from the new orientation. Here too the suitability of the methods used in the context of EDP system design for the support of problem-solving needs to be assessed.

B.II. EDP-Oriented Business Economics and Business Informatics

It has been stated that EDP has such a great impact on the structure of business economics problems that their treatment cannot solely be the responsibility of business informatics. Attempting to provide a single-handed treatment of computer applications would not only overburden business informatics with an excess of content, but, more importantly, it would give rise to the false conclusion that the content of the general and specialist business economics theories could remain unchanged. But this is not possible, instead the classical business economics disciplines need to become more strongly EDP-oriented. Even the development of specialist business economics chairs of business informatics, such as "business informatics in production" or "business informatics in banking" has diverse perspectives. On the one hand this indicates a recognition of the significance of information techniques in this sector and the specialization ensures a competent treatment of applications, on the other hand the danger exists that the classical disciplines of production economics and banking remain unchanged alongside. If there is a balanced division of labour between these specialist areas, however, this does not conflict with the concept of EDP-oriented business economics. In this case a specialized business informatics for a sub-area of business economics is then identical with the special EDP-oriented business economics for that sub-area. The problem is thereby reduced merely to one of institutional organization: the specialist area "business informatics in production" could be a parallel chair to both business informatics and production economics.

Each specialist area within business economics should therefore consider the question of how their issues are affected by the use of information techniques and how the business decision models and processes can be restructured under the influence of data processing in an organization-independent sense. General business economic theory should provide a basic overview of these problems.
As long as EDP issues are not considered by the classical business economics disciplines, business informatics should lay its emphasis on the EDP-related business applications, so that alterations to the enterprise resulting from EDP do not have to be effected without scientific accompaniment and support (see Figure 1.B.II.01).

Stronger EDP-orientation within business economics would allow business informatics to concentrate more upon the development of methods of structuring computerized information systems. The results of this research can then be taken over by EDP-oriented business economics and used as tools for representing EDP-suited solutions to business problems. The basic EDP knowledge, which includes the structure and operation of

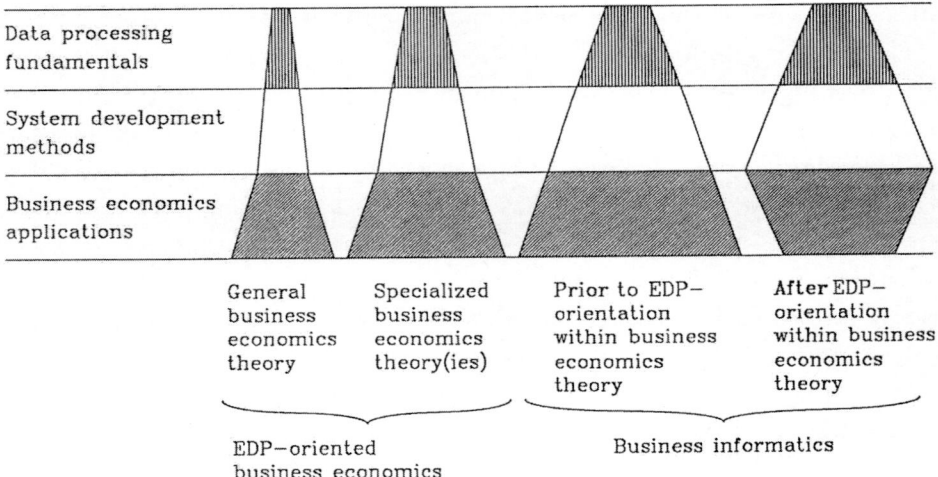

Fig. 1.B.II.01: Points of emphasis in EDP-oriented business economics and business informatics

hardware systems, the architecture and effects of operating and database systems, programming languages, and programming techniques, then carries more weight in the content of business informatics once the EDP-orientation of business economics has been achieved.

It is to be expected that an EDP-oriented business economics will make new demands on the research and training work of business informatics. This impetus within business informatics would then be an indication of a genuine integration of EDP content into business economics.

B.III. Information System Components Relevant to Business Economics

The components of a computerized information system that are relevant to business economics are the database and functions that are linked together and with the user via process control (see Figure 1.B.III.01). The hardware and system software needed for operation are only of significance in so far as they influence these components.

The **database** is of overwhelming importance because the enterprise's centrally or decentrally stored data and their structural relationships determine the evaluation possibilities using application programs and free query languages.

Business knowledge, whose transformation into EDP systems is effected by programming into applications software, is included in the **functions** components. The programs also

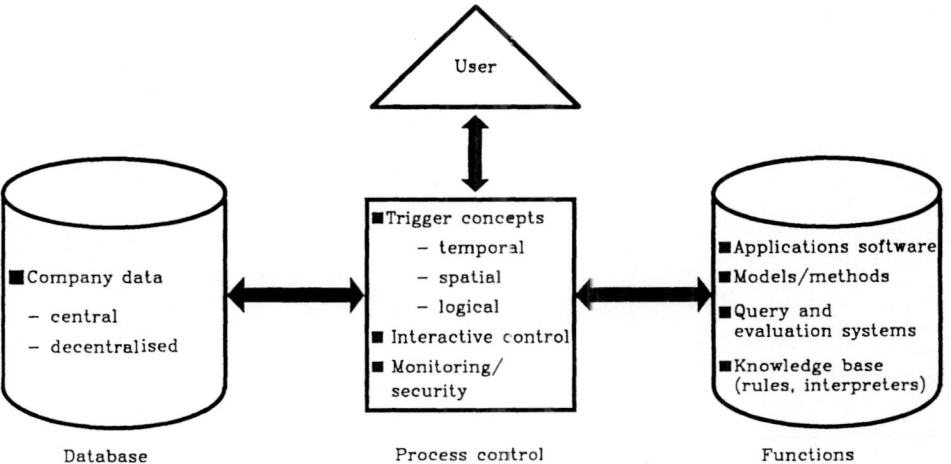

Fig. 1.B.III.01: Computerized information system

include business decision rules, such as lot sizing formulae, and organizational processes. The concept of functions is interpreted very broadly to cover the application programs handling classical business applications, as well as model and method banks, query languages and evaluation systems such as are made available by database systems or planning languages, and the knowledge-based interactive systems of artificial intelligence.

Process control links database and applications software, in that it provides temporal, spatial and logical control of the sub-tasks and transactions. The business subject matter is also established in these three dimensions. At the same time, by managing the interactive steps (interactive control), process control provides the user interface.

The elements of an information system presented here are constructed from the viewpoint of their business impact. Concrete EDP techniques can therefore be effective in several of the three elements. For example, the use of a database system affects the structuring possibilities for the database, the associated query language is part of the applications software, and the trigger concept and interactive software it contains are part of process control.

Although the hardware and software system of an information system play only a subordinate role in this book, the structure of a typical EDP configuration is explained in order to introduce some essential terminology and to facilitate the subsequent treatment of related application issues.

Figure 1.B.III.02 provides a schematic representation of the essential hardware components of an EDP system.

Central processing unit   Channels   Controls   Peripherals

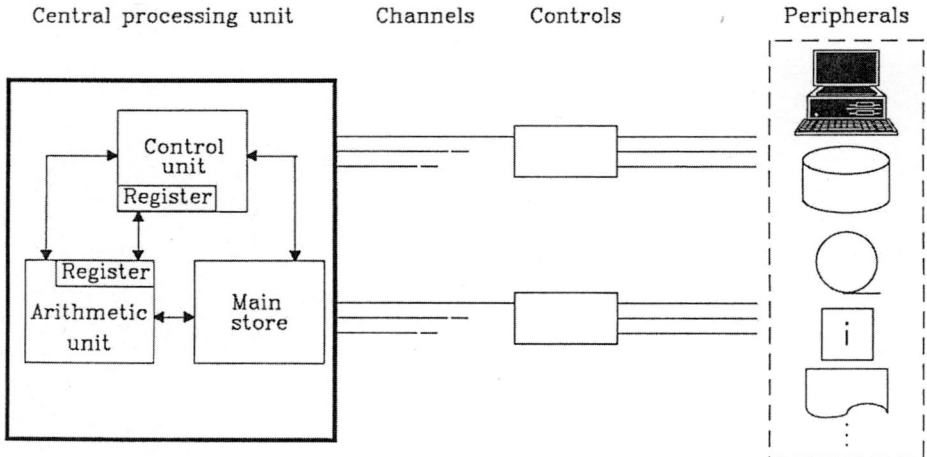

Fig. 1.B.III.02: Hardware components of an EDP system

The essential hardware component is the **central processing unit (CPU)** which consists of the control unit, the arithmetic unit and the main store. The control unit and arithmetic unit are often referred to collectively as the processor. In some publications the main store is also included within the term CPU.

In the CPU so-called **registers** and other fast stores (e.g. cache memory) are provided for the speedy storage and processing of small data segments.

The **main store** contains both programs and part of the associated data. All storage locations of the main store are directly accessible by specification of the address.

The function of the **control unit** is to control the execution of the operations in the CPU. It loads the commands from the main store and interprets the operating code they contain. According to the type of command this is done either by the control unit alone, or with the support of the arithmetic unit, or by accessing additional data from the main store.

The task of the **arithmetic unit** is to execute the arithmetic and logical operations. It is initiated and supplied with the appropriate data by the control unit. The arithmetic unit makes use of the registers to carry out its operations.

The **peripherals** of an EDP system, i.e. all those system components concerned with **input, output** and **external storage**, also constitute part of the hardware. Here external storage means that the data are not located in the main store. The external devices are linked with the CPU via so-called **channels**. In general, several identical or diverse devices are linked to the processor via a **controller**, to which several channels can be assigned. The storage devices (e.g. magnetic tape units, diskette units, magnetic disk units) are generally located near the processor, whereas input and output devices can be more remote. In this case a telecommunication link is required.

With regard to **software** it is necessary to distinguish between applications software and system software (see Figure 1.B.III.03).

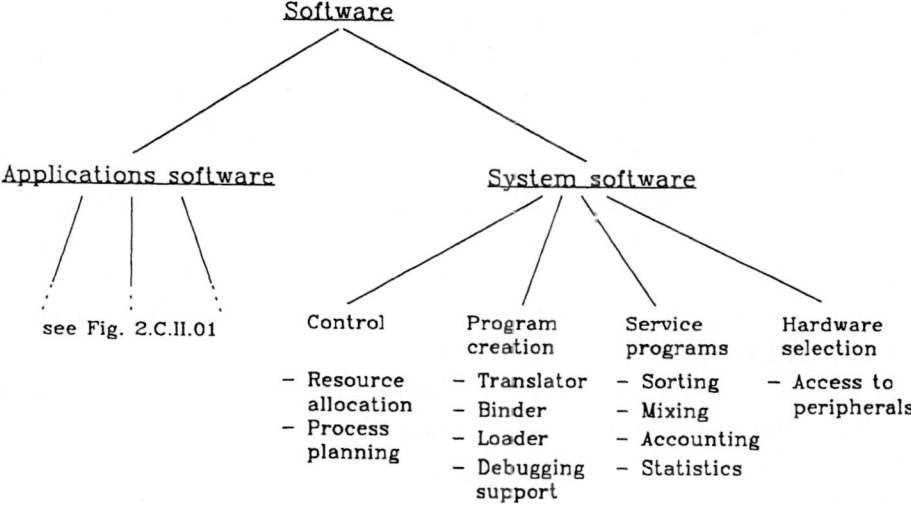

Fig. 1.B.III.03: Software classification

In the context of commercial EDP installations **applications software** supports the solution of business problems.

System software (system programs), along with the hardware, forms the basis for the functioning of the EDP system. The **operating system** is constituted by the system programs in their entirety. Operating systems are generally tailored to the available hardware. They handle the administration of the EDP system, program creation (software creation), the execution of frequently required auxiliary functions (service programs) and hardware selection.

Control programs control the processes in the EDP installation, in that they allocate the required resources to users and plan the execution sequence of the queue of tasks.

Programs supporting **program creation** are editors, translators, binders, loaders and debuggers.

The **service programs** are made up of sorting and mixing programs as well as programs for administering the EDP installation (accounting functions, statistics).

The **hardware selection software** handles the transformation of logical functions into the physically-oriented instructions for accessing peripherals.

C. Structure of the Book

The essential developmental and application trends that are currently visible in the EDP field relate to the intensified use of database systems and interactive processing, the development of user-friendly languages and expert systems, the development of tools for software development, graphical data processing, networking of diverse hardware systems and the development of powerful microcomputers and computerized control systems for production facilities. The so-called "new media", particularly videotex and office technology, are generating the impetus for establishing local networks and communication via electronic mail and electronic conferencing.

The manufacturers and researchers involved in these developments are aware of the close interdependences between these technologies. As a result, the aggregation of essential techniques relevant to sector-specific models is generating application architectures. For example, the CIM concept (computer integrated manufacturing) relates to a general model for integrating technical and business applications in an industrial firm, and the term electronic banking to the integrated use of computers in the banking context. The "office automation" concept, which is sector-independent, combines electronic mail, text and data processing, and other elements, to provide a total system for office automation.

The Japanese Ministry for International Trade and Industry (MITI), in collaboration with Japanese industry, has produced a model for producing 5th generation computer systems, which incorporates the recognizable developments of very large scale integration (VLSI), artificial intelligence (expert systems) and user-friendly language interfaces. This program has meantime given rise to corresponding efforts in the USA and Europe (ESPRIT).

The use of these techniques will profoundly alter the nature of business problem issues, solution concepts and organizational processes, and thereby the entire nature of the enterprise. Indicating the direction of these influences occupies the foreground of this book.

Chapter 2 analyses the nature and extent of the influences on business problem issues resulting from developments in the components of an information systems: database, process control and applications software. Both directions of influence will be investigated: the implementation of techniques by business economics and the structuring of the application of techniques by business economics. The use of databases, interactive processing, networking of computer systems, expert systems and computer aided software engineering (CASE) will be individually analysed.

In **Chapter 3** the EDP-oriented business economics problem solutions will be compared with the familiar business economics approaches. The strategic significance of EDP-oriented solutions will be given particular emphasis. This applies not only to production planning and control, which has been accorded an independent planning model in many EDP systems, but also to the information and control system in retailing, whose strict computerized application has already given rise to new types of company. In banking and insurance comprehensive data processing concepts for payments and correspondence have also been developed. New approaches to linking the customers' EDP systems with those of the banking sector extend the possibilities considerably. The business economics approaches to supra-branch functions, such as financial accounting, cost accounting, marketing, personnel management, enterprise planning and office automation are increasingly influenced by the use of EDP.

Chapter 4 summarizes the important results of the book and incorporates them in a EDP-oriented business economics model of an information system, which can then provide the perspective for the future generation of business economics application solutions.

The important basic concepts will be explained in the text. Unexplained concepts are largely understandable from the context. The discussion will be supported by many examples and illustrations.

Chapter 2: Business Economics Implementation and Structuring of EDP Techniques

The EDP system is part of the non-economic environment of an enterprise, and must be taken into account in the structuring of operations and decision processes.

For example, the processing speed of the EDP system puts a limit on the use of extensive planning models. Advances in EDP developments relax these limitations, such that business economics models that were previously unusable can now be implemented. This applies, for example, to the solution of large sets of simultaneous equations which are capable of replacing heuristic procedures in the context of internal costing procedures. The integrated management information system model (MIS) which was developed in the '60s and which could not be implemented given the inadequacy of the existing EDP possibilities, can also be realised with more advanced EDP techniques.

Of course, these limitations are primarily relevant to the management of real enterprises and not to the development of business economic theories; however, applied business economics must also take them into account. If there is too great a discrepancy between the requirements of business economic theory and the possibilities of EDP implementation, there will be a tendency to develop independent models that are more suited to EDP implementation. This has happened in the production planning and control area, for example, where the EDP-oriented planning model has been developed in the practical context. This model is presented in **Chapter 3, Section B.I.1.**

EDP techniques can also open up new possibilities for theoretically interesting business economics problem solutions, e.g. man-machine communication in interactive decision making. This is an important EDP contribution to business economics.

Given the speed of development of EDP techniques their business potential has not yet been fully exploited in practice. In general, no new business models have been available, so that manual processes have simply been "programmed up" (see *Mertens, Rechnungswesen 1983, pp. 23-36*).

Any practical introduction of radical changes to a business economics model will involve drastic alterations to the organizational and operational structure. In (large) enterprises, however, such alterations are often extremely difficult to effect. For this reason EDP producers have also held back in their development of new EDP-oriented business economics models, for fear of generating too much organizational resistance.

The development of new organizational-business concepts is becoming increasingly urgent, however, since the high costs of using databases, interactive processing and networks demand the exploitation of all possibilities for using them efficiently. Having completed the first rationalization wave, which mainly related to the execution of simple mass procedures, complex information systems need differentiated adaptation to the individual organization.

The breakdown of the EDP techniques to be discussed follows the components of an information system as they have already been introduced: database, process control and functions.

The discussion of the EDP techniques follows the same pattern.

In the first section each technique is described in as much detail as is needed for an understanding of the business implications.

The second section provides an analysis of how they can be implemented as new business processes or decision structures. This also relates to the question: **What inferences can business economics draw from EDP techniques?**

The third section then considers the ways in which business economics might restructure the technique or its implementation. This relates to the question: **How can business economics provide a more efficient structure for the technique or its implementation?**

A. Database: Database Systems

A.I. Description of Database Systems

In the early years of EDP the foreground in application system development was occupied by the program. This meant that the data needed by each program were individually prepared on some data medium. Since many applications used the same data, the result was a large number of files with overlapping (redundant) contents. For example, the "order processing" represented in Figure 2.A.I.01 required master data from the article and customer files. During order processing an order file would be created. The application "customer and article statistics' would then need the master data in a different sequence e.g. the customer files sorted by name instead of by customer number. As a result a subset of the data in question would be prepared as a newly created customer and article file in the altered sequence required. The same would apply to the order file.

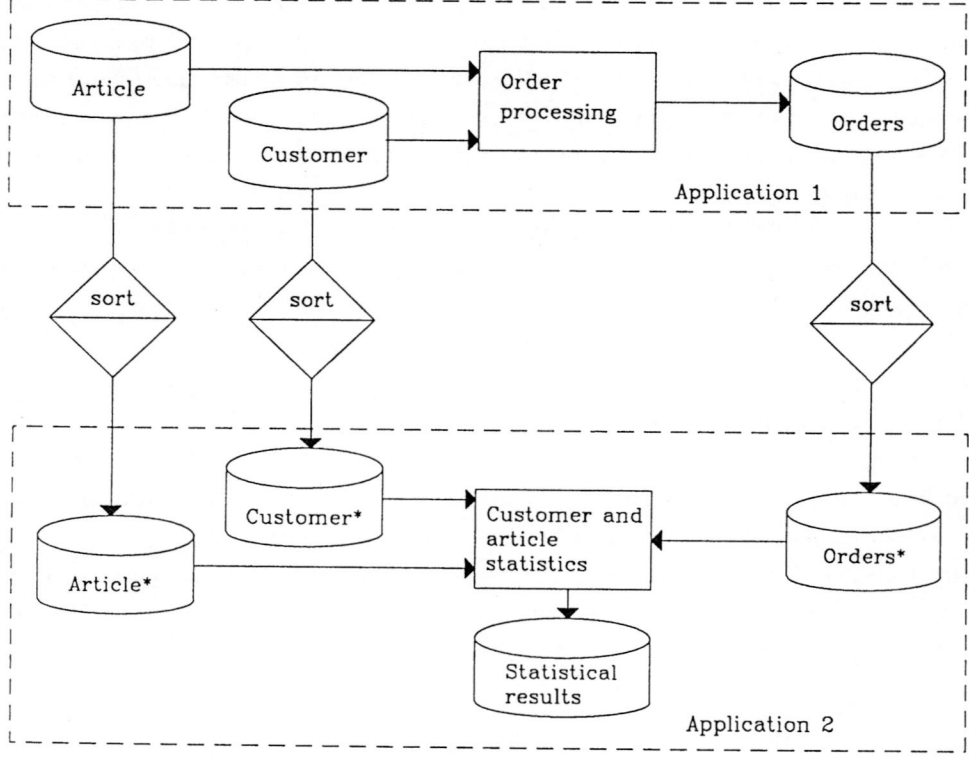

Fig. 2.A.I.01: Conventional data processing

The files prepared for order processing would therefore be set up a second time. This data redundancy not only implies higher storage costs, but above all much higher costs of documenting the data structures, updating the data, and protecting them against system breakdown. Furthermore, the storage and access techniques of classical data management systems (direct addressing, sequential storage, index-sequential storage) were in any case incapable of storing complex data structures without redundancy.

These difficulties gave rise to the concept of treating data, not as adjuncts to programs, but as a separate organizational element independent of the individual applications. For this purpose **database systems** were developed. Database systems are software systems related to the operating system, which perform the task of managing an enterprise's data such that individual users without knowledge of the physical storage form can access these data (see Figure 2.A.I.02). The **database management system** provides powerful commands for storing, amending, reading and deleting data, in which no special details concerning the physical storage of the data arise. The optimization of the physical storage structures as regards ease of access and storage space management is the task of the **database administrator**, who performs this function centrally for the enterprise's data.

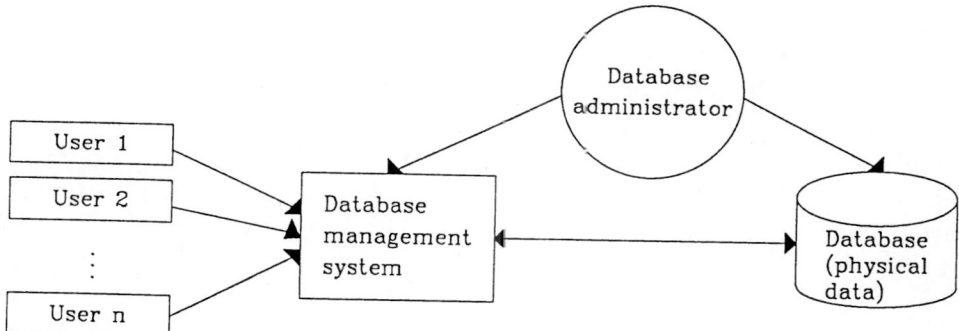

Fig. 2.A.I.02: Use of a database system

With program-independent data organization diverse applications can access the same database. Figure 2.A.I.03 represents this for the example of order processing and sales statistics.

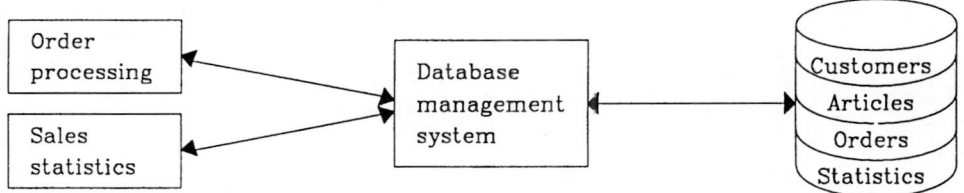

Fig. 2.A.I.03: Program-independent data organization

In order for a user (this may be a person with an ad-hoc query from a terminal or an application program) to be able to work with the data in the database he needs to know both the data and the data relationships within the database. However, this knowledge of the logical contents of the database is different from knowledge of the physical storage.

The development and use of database systems have increased in importance considerably in recent years. All the big computer manufacturers and many large software houses offer database systems. Some well-known products are shown in Figure 2.A.I.04.
Some database systems are capable of running both on mainframe and microcomputers. There are also special database systems offered for microcomputers, e.g. dbase IV from Ashton Tate.

Product	Supplier	Type	Host computer	Microcomputer Workstation
ADABAS	Software AG	Relational–oriented	x	
CLIPPER	Nantucket Coorp.	Relational–oriented		x
DB 2	IBM	Relational	x	
dbase IV	Ashton Tate	Relational		x
DMS	Unisys	Network	x	
IDMS/SQL	Cullinet	Relational	x	
IMAGE/3000	Hewlett Packard	Network	x	
IMS/VS–DB	IBM	Network–oriented	x	
INFORMIX	INFORMIX Coorp.	Relational	x	x
INGRES	Relational Technology	Relational		x
ORACLE	ORACLE	Relational	x	x
PISA	infodas	Relational	x	x
PROGRESS	PROGRESS	Relational		x
SESAM	Siemens	Relational	x	
SOKRATES	gft	Relational		x
StarBase	COGNOS	Relational		x
TOTAL	NCR	Network	x	
UDS	Siemens	Network	x	
VAX Rdb/VMS	Digital Equipment	Relational	x	x

Fig. 2.A.I.04: Summary of several database systems

The acquisition of a database system is binding on an enterprise for a considerable period, since the data structures created are used in many application programs and can only be altered on changing database systems at considerable cost. In addition each database system used in the enterprise requires the acquisition of specialized know-how, which can lead to considerable capacity requirements in the personnel sphere. For these reasons the selection of a database system must be based not on the needs of a single application, but on the entire information processing strategy of the enterprise. Given the long-term significance of this decision it should also be reconciled with the general strategic enterprise plan. This requires the involvement and insight of the enterprise's top executives.

Before data can be stored in a database the logical conformation of the database, that is the **data structure** to be used, needs to be determined (see *Wedekind, Datenbanksysteme I 1981*).

Data structures are designed in several steps (see Figure 2.A.I.05). First they are conceived at an abstract level without reference to concrete database systems. These structures are referred to as the **logical-conceptual data model**. In the next step this is transformed into the schema of a **data model**, which is already related to the characteristics of specific database systems. In the third step the schema is described in a special **data description language** as the schema of a specific database system. Using this schematic description the database system can set up and later access all data and their relationships.

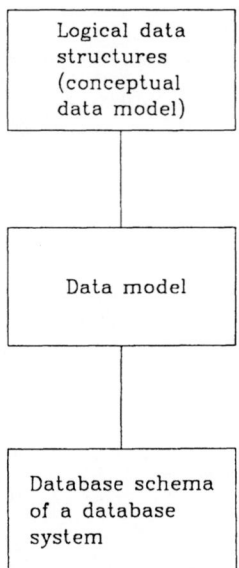

Fig. 2.A.I.05: Data description levels

In designing the logical data model, technical demands on the database's ability to provide information are formulated. Since specialist knowledge must be incorporated at this stage it is, from the application viewpoint, the most important. In the two subsequent steps the logical data structures are simply restructured without altering their technical content. Tools are already available which, given the description of the logical data structure, can automatically produce the other formulations (e.g. ER/Designer from Chen, MastER System from GESI srl, msp easy from msp, Information Engineering Workbench (IEW) from Knowledge Ware and STRATOS from SIEMENS).

The conceptual data model presents a data-oriented picture of reality. It records the objects of interest, their characteristics, and the relationships existing between them.
The individual concrete objects are referred to as **entities**. These might be the enterprise's individual employee "Müller", the individual customer "Schmidt", or the

individual article "No. XYZ". Entities of the same kind are consolidated as higher level (collective) concepts, or **entity types**. These will then comprise all employees, all customers, all articles of the enterprise.

Entities are described by their characteristics (**attributes**), e.g. customers by their customer number, their name, address, etc.

Logical assignments between entity types are referred to as **relationships**. Figure 2.A.I.06 creates the relationship between the entity types CUSTOMER and ARTICLE using the word "PURCHASE", i.e. the relationship indicates which customers purchase which articles, or which articles are purchased by which customers. Analogous to the entities, the same kinds of relationships are consolidated into **relationship types**.

Entity types are represented by rectangles, relationships by rhombi. The representation in Figure 2.A.I.06 follows the entity-relationship model (ERM) (see *Chen, Entity-Relationship Model 1976*) which is widely used as design support.

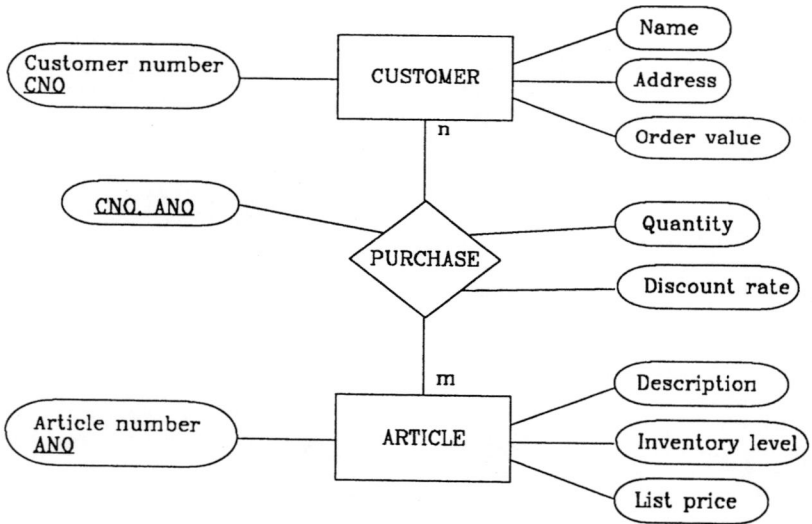

Fig. 2.A.I.06: Representation of entity and relationship types

Relationships, as well as entity types, can also have attributes, e.g. for the relationship "PURCHASE" this could be the total quantity of a particular article bought by one customer, or the discount rate relating to customer **and** article.

The **ranges (domains)** of the attributes are also sets and are represented graphically by bubbles. The specific assignments between elements of the domains and elements of the entity and relationship types are themselves in turn relationships and are represented by edges.

In the context of the entity-relationship model 1:n, m:n, m:1, and 1:1 relationships between two or more entity types can be represented (see Figure 2.A.I.07). In a 1:1 relationship each element of the first set is assigned to precisely one element of the second set and vice versa. In a 1:n relationship each element of the first set is assigned to n elements of the second set, each element of the second set, however, is assigned to only one element of the first set. The n:1 relationship expresses the same idea in reverse.

In a n:m relationship each element of the first set is assigned to several elements of the second set and vice versa.

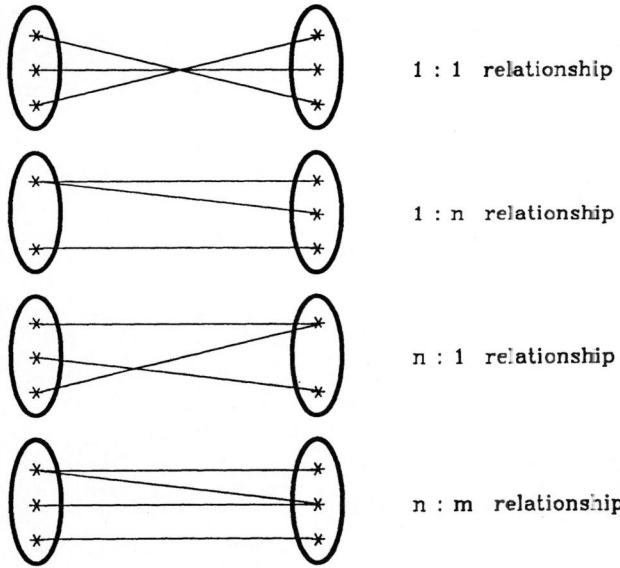

1 : 1 relationship

1 : n relationship

n : 1 relationship

n : m relationship

Fig. 2.A.I.07: Relationship types between sets

The complexity of the relationship type is indicated on the edges of the entity relationship diagram (see Figure 2.A.I.06). A 1:1 relationship must exist between one entity type and at least one domain. The values of this domain can then identify the instances of an entity; in the example these are the customer number CNO and the article number ANO. They are referred to as **key attributes**.

Relationships are identified by combining the key values of the entitytypes concerned - in this case the PURCHASE relationships by specifying the customer **and** article number.

Key attributes are indicated by underlining.

In the course of the design procedure a factor initially defined as a relationship type can provide the starting point for further design considerations. In Figure 2.A.I.08 this is represented for the order header, which was initially characterized as a relationship type, and has been "reinterpreted" as an entity type by being enclosed in a rectangle.

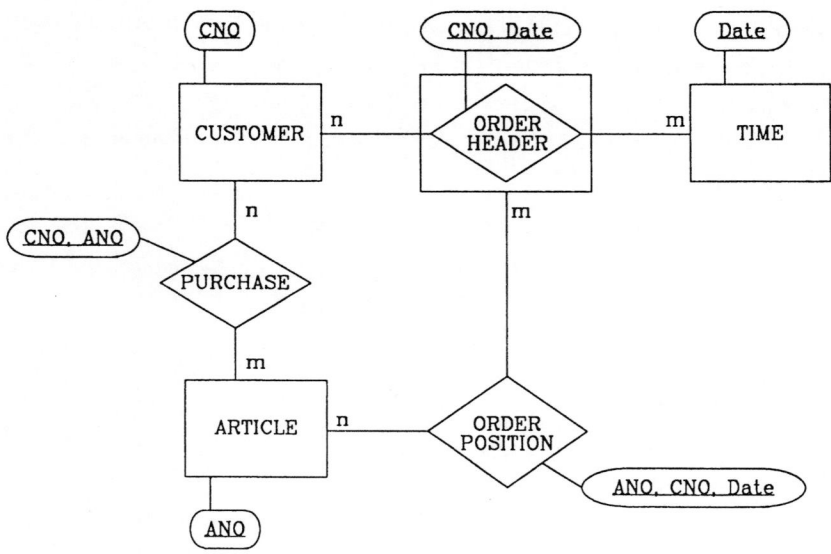

Fig. 2.A.I.08: Re-interpretation of a relationship type

For the creation of further relationships to other entity types this reinterpreted factor is used like a normal entity type. Graphically the procedure is made clear as follows: the development of the relationship type with the entity types involved is expressed by the fact that the connecting lines are joined to the points of the rhombus. The lines leading from the reinterpreted entity type, however, do not touch the rhombus but lead only from the edge of the rectangle.

The example is interpreted as follows: The data structure of Figure 2.A.I.06 is extended by the n:m relationship ORDER HEADER between CUSTOMER and TIME. The entity type TIME is identified by the attribute Date. Each order is identified by specifying the customer number CNO and Date. Since an order can have several positions, each of which relates to a different article ordered, a n:m relationship exists between the ORDER HEADER and the entity type ARTICLE. In addition, the original relationship type ORDER HEADER is now regarded as an entity type.

Once the conceptual data model has been designed the data structure is translated into the notation of a specific data model. This data model also describes the entity types and their relationship to each other. The description, however, is orientated towards the philosophies of concrete database systems. In addition to the hierarchical data model, which is now only of historical interest, network-oriented and relational data models are at present being discussed; for so-called non-standard applications in engineering and the office area the object-oriented data model is of increasing significance. This will not be considered in more detail here, however. The last three models are capable of describing the essential data structures arising in reality. Given its huge applications significance the relational model occupies the foreground of the following discussion.

In a simple interpretation of the relational model entity and relationship types of type n:m are represented by tables. Each line in a table represents an instance which is identified by the key attribute. The tables of the relational model can be derived directly from the ERM model, whereby the underlined key attributes are extended by several non-key attributes. For each table one instance (line) is shown. In Figure 2.B.I.11 the database is extended to several lines.

R.CUSTOMER (CNO, Name, Location, ...)
           4711 Müller   Hamburg
           ...   .

R.ARTICLE (ANO, Description, ...)
           223   Table lamp XII
           ...   ...

R.PURCHASE (CNO, ANO, Quantity, ...)
           4711 223   5
           ...   .

R.TIME (Date, ...)
         4.11.90
         ...

R.ORDER HEADER (CNO, Date,   Handled by, ...)
           4711 4.11.90 Meier
           ...   .

R.ORDER POSITION (CNO, Date,   ANO, Quantity, Price, ...)
           4711 4.11.90 223   2   320.00
           ...   .

The relational model has no graphical representational form and does not distinguish between entity and relationship types.

Given its simple structure and mathematical definition the relational model is a suitable basis for user friendly query languages and the 4th generation programming languages based on them, whereby the "generations" of languages are as follows:

1st generation: (machine code),

2nd generation: assembler (machine-oriented language),

3rd generation: problem-oriented language,

4th generation: user-oriented language.

In the third step the data description for a concrete database system is derived from the data model and formulated using the database system's data description language (DDL). This is then referred to a database schema.

Figure. 2.A.I.09 shows an excerpt from the data description for the example introduced above. The complete schema is shown in Figure 2.C.I.09c.

```
CREATE TABLE Customer
    (CNO                INTEGER           NOT NULL,
     Name               CHAR (30)         NOT NULL);


CREATE TABLE Time
    (Date               DATE              NOT NULL);


CREATE TABLE Order header
    (CNO                INTEGER           NOT NULL,
     Date               DATE              NOT NULL,
     Handled by         CHAR (30)         NOT NULL);
```

Fig. 2.A.I.09: Data description excerpt

This completes the description of the three stages of development of a data structure. It imposes limits on the evaluation possibilities of the database, since only those informational relationships provided for in the schema can be used in evaluation programs or ad hoc queries.

The design of the conceptual data model from which the conceptual database schema is ultimately derived is therefore of fundamental significance. It must be undertaken in such a way that the numerous present and planned future applications can use the database.

From the **conceptual schema**, which describes all the logical data structures in a concrete database in the data description language of a database system, each application is provided with an extract of only that information which it requires. These extracts are referred to as **external schema** (sub-schemata). These relationships are represented in Figure 2.A.I.10.

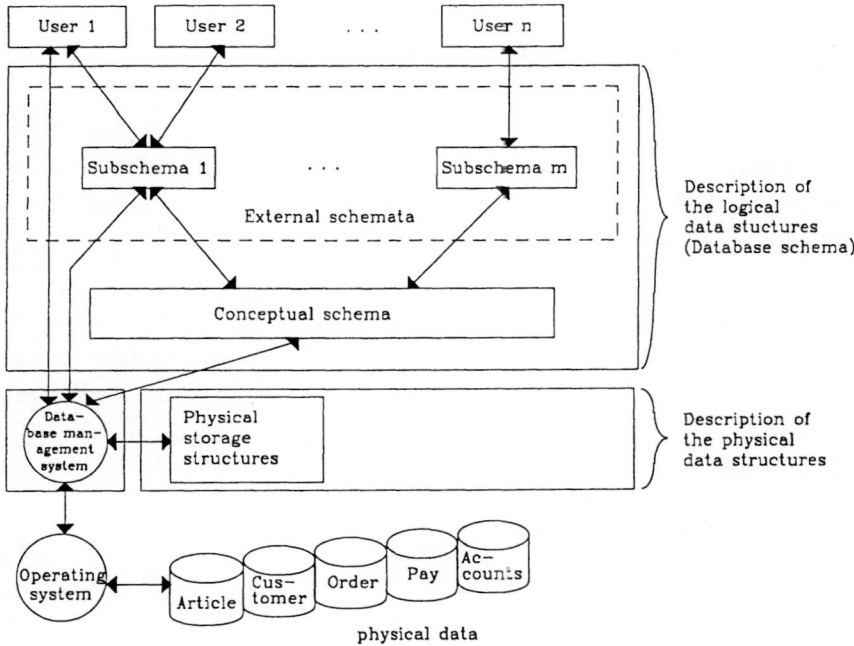

Fig. 2.A.I.10: The relationship between database schema and physical data structures

Figure 2.A.I.10 also shows the interplay between the **database management system (DBMS) and the operating system (OS)** of a computer installation. To store and search for physically stored data the database management system also uses the storage and access routines of the operating system.

A.II. Business Economics Implementation of Database Systems

The use of database systems makes it possible to use new organizational models of the operational and organizational structure and to achieve up-to-date, information-oriented control of the enterprise. An enterprise's data are therefore increasingly being recognized as one of its most important resources which also necessitates an adequate description in business economics terms.

24

The use of the resource "database system", however, does not automatically generate these changes, but rigorous exploitation of the potential of this resource can succeed in realizing these effects.

A.II.1. Supporting Process Chains (Operational Integration)

At present the operational structure of processes is largely dominated by the principle of functional specialization. This means that a homogeneous process is broken down so that sub-processes can be performed at functionally specialized workplaces. The advantage of this organizational form lies in the increased speed of processing the sub-functions.

The principle of functional organization also influences the organizational structure, in that departments, areas, etc. are formed by the consolidation of functionally similar units. Since these units of the enterprise are responsible for their own organization, the information systems, which are the most important organizational tool, are also functionally structured.

Figure 2.A.II.01 shows the functional breakdown of an enterprise's information system. At the lowest levels the **quantitative systems** which relate to the operative functions of production, engineering, purchasing, sales and personnel management are shown horizontally. The quantitative processes are then entered vertically into the **evaluative**

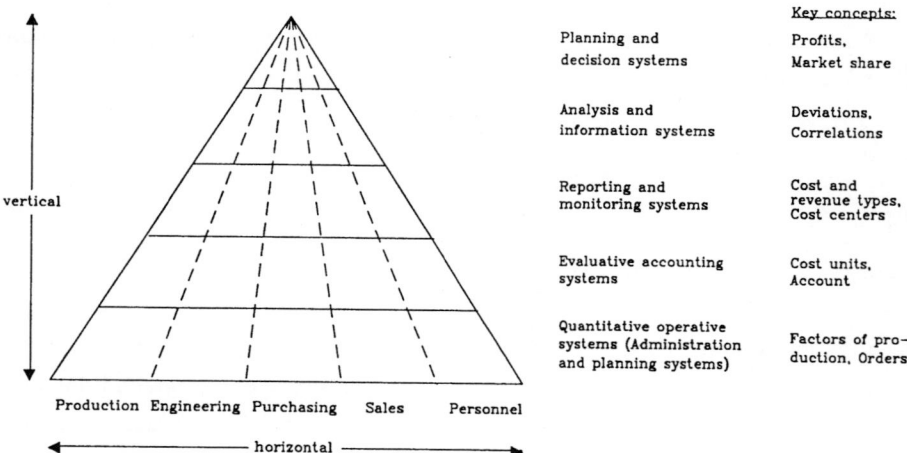

Fig. 2.A.II.01: Functionally-oriented information systems

systems within financial accounting. Examples are accounts payable for purchasing, accounts receivable for sales, and pay-roll accounting for personnel management. At the third level **reporting and monitoring systems** are derived from the quantitative and evaluative systems.

A further level of consolidation generates **analysis and information systems**, which include data from external sources as well as the consolidated data. Examples are marketing, purchasing and production information systems. The highest level of consolidation then generates the **planning and decision systems**, which are designed to provide support especially for long-term decisions.

A.II.1.1. Operational Effects of Horizontal and Vertical Data Integration

Strict functional divisions give rise to the construction of isolated information systems which may provide good support within the functions, but which provide inadequate support between the horizontal and vertical functions.

The enterprise's operations, however, are typically not fully processed within one individual function, but pass through several horizontal and vertical functional areas.

This is clear from the simplest examples. Figure 2.A.II.02 presents the execution of a purchasing procedure.

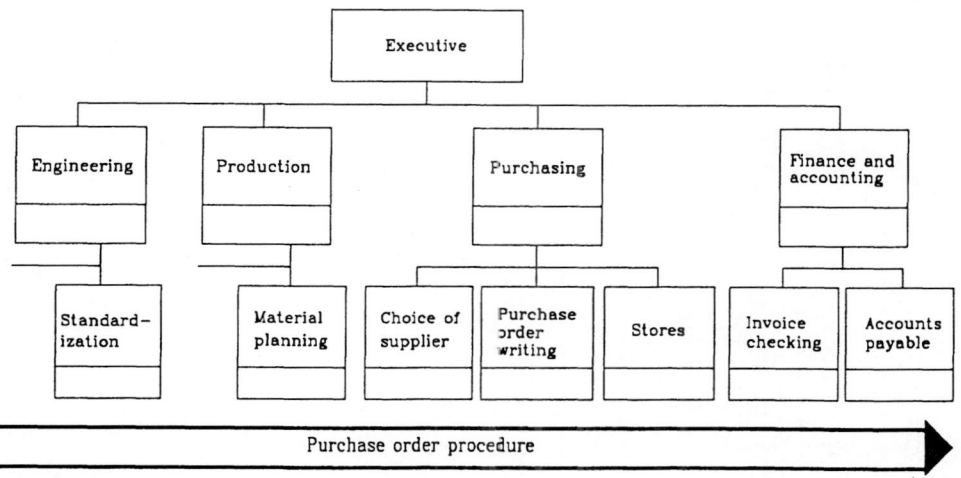

Fig. 2.A.II.02: Execution of a purchasing procedure

26

From the decision in favour of a bought-in part by the standardization department, through determination of requirements (material planning), choice of suppliers, order writing, receipt of goods, invoice checking to accounts payable, the procedure passes through several functional areas of the organizational structure. As well as involving several horizontal operative areas it is also processed in the evaluative information system of financial accounting.

Figure 2.A.II.03 examines an excerpt from this procedure (material planning, choice of supplier and order writing) with the aim of establishing what new operational possibilities could be generated by the use of an integrated database. Case (a) shows a functionally specialized organization in which each individual sub-process has its own data management. Each sub-process within the entire process involves a lead-in period which is indicated by the shaded areas. To be able to perform a subsequent job operation information from the previous job operation must be passed on to the next workplace.
As well as information transfer, waiting times arise before an operation can be processed at the workplace.

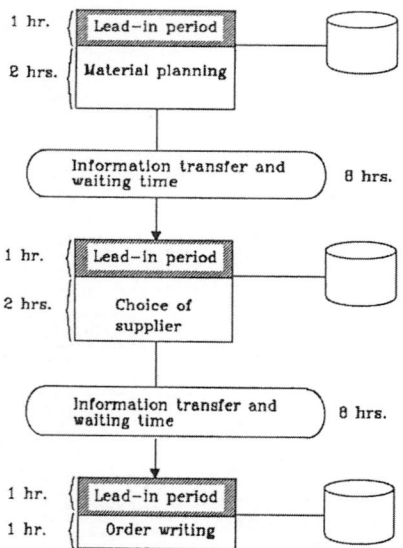

Process chain with functionally specialised data management

Throughput time = 24 hrs. = 3 days

Fig. 2.A.II.03a: Processing in a traditional, functionally-specialized organization

The numerical values used in the example have been chosen arbitrarily, the effects they demonstrate however are realistic.

In a traditional, functionally-specialized organization the entire process of the example requires 24 hours, i.e. with an assumed working day of 8 hours three working days will be required.

With the use of an integrated database in case (b) all information that arises at one workplace is placed in the database and immediately becomes available to all the other workplaces. This means that the material planning figures generated at the end of sub-process 1 can be applied in the choice of supplier without incurring any further information transfer times. Of course, waiting times will in general still arise here before actual processing. However, the reduction in information transfer times generates a reduction in throughput time to 16 hours (two working days).

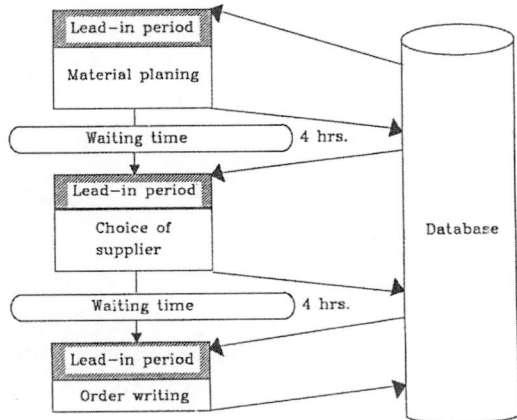

Process chain with an integrated database

Throughput time = 16 hrs. = 2 days

Fig. 2.A.II.03b: Processing with the support of an integrated database

If load profiles are available for each of the workplaces, improvements in the policy for distributing tasks to workplaces can eliminate waiting times between the individual processes (case c). The throughput time is then reduced to 8 hours (one working day).

The transport and distribution of sub-processes to be executed can be supported by the use of **action databases**. Action databases contain information about processes to be performed, e.g. in the form of process numbers which are held in electronic mailboxes and assigned to the workplaces.

28

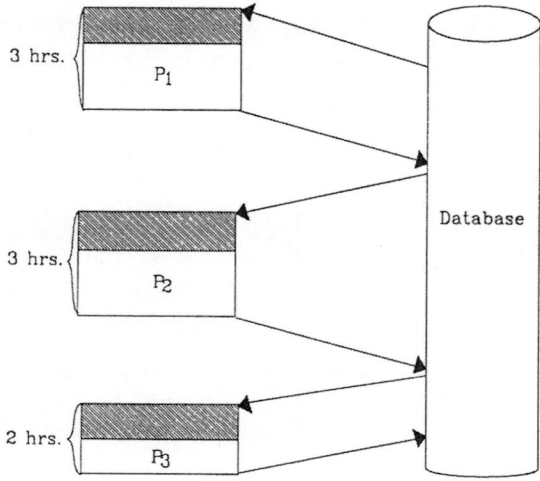

Throughput time = 8 hrs. = 1 day
no waiting time

Fig. 2.A.II.03c: Effects of optimizing distributional policy

So far it has been assumed that a sub-process represents a self-contained task. However, a sub-process can often be broken down into further operational steps, e.g. if a material planning process has to be carried out for several article numbers, or the choice of suppliers for several articles. Case (d), therefore, breaks down the first two sub-processes into one lead-in period and two operational steps, whereas the third sub-process is carried out after the lead-in period in one operational step.

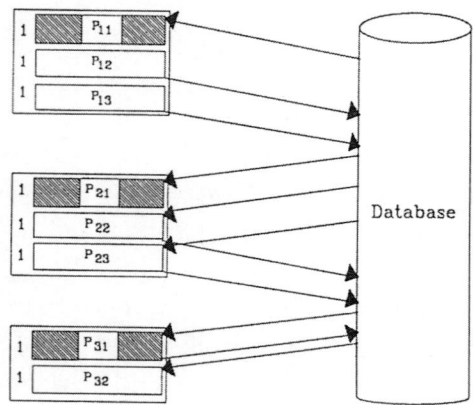

Throughput time = 6 hrs. P_{22} requires P_{12}
                             P_{32} requires P_{22}

Fig. 2.A.II.03d: Breakdown of sub-processes

If the results of the individual operational steps are placed directly in the database, as is the case with strict interactive processing, the next workplace can begin further processing even before the entire sub-process is completed. These overlapping activities achieve a further reduction in throughput time for the entire process to 6 hours.

The individual temporal effects, **shown to scale**, are summarized in Figure 2.A.II.03e.

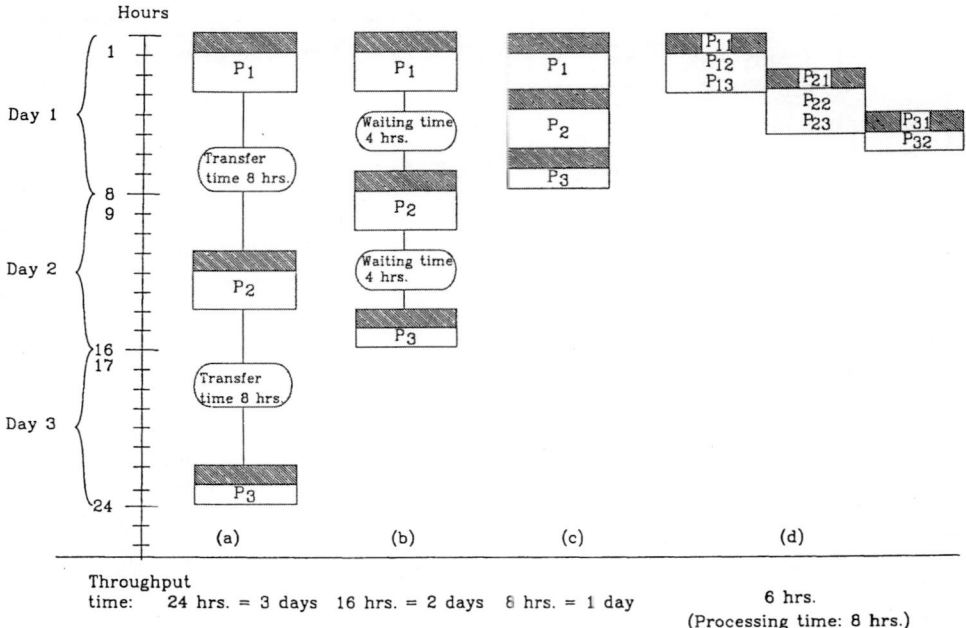

Fig. 2.A.II.03e: Summary of the temporal effects

The reduction in throughput times achieved for a closed process organization indicates the rationalization potential. The extent of the reduction shown in the example is, if anything, an underestimate. There are cases of implementations in which strict data integration and exploitation of overlapping potential has reduced the processing time for a design amendment, for example, from over 50 days to 2 days. Whereas previously the design amendment (e.g. replacing one material with another) passed sequentially through the departments quality assurance, inventory management, pay-roll recording, production planning, operational data collection, cost accounting and stores, and could only be processed further once it had been released by the previous department, in each case involving information transfer times and waiting times, integrated processing allowed these steps to be executed almost in parallel.

A strict operational organization of process chains means that data are always entered at the point they arise in the process chain and subsequently need only be modified or extended. This means that even those data that are not needed by the sub-function also need to be recorded as they arise.

The data flow for the material management example is presented in Figure 2.A.II.04. At the very start of the process chain data relating to the quantity needed, parts number, required quality, conditions, the cost center responsible for the order, cost type, and the relevant cost unit are already known. The evaluative data cost center, cost type, cost unit, and conditions are of no immediate significance for the quantitative (horizontal) process of order handling, but later become relevant in the context of invoice checking and the further (vertical) processing in financial accounting. If these data are recorded at the start of the process chain, however, a so-called pro-forma invoice can be created at order writing and placed in the database to provide a basis for later invoice checking thereby considerably simplifying this process, sometimes even rendering it fully automatic.

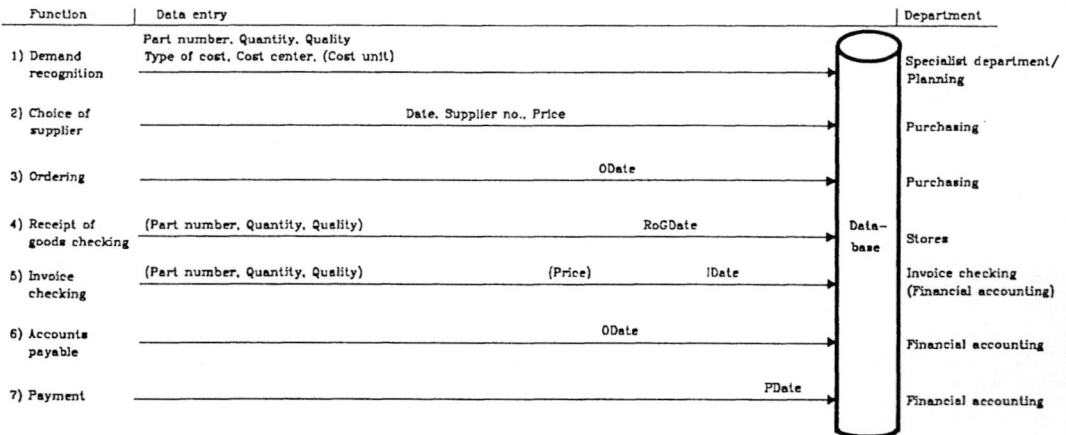

Data in brackets are only entered where they differ from the previously recorded data

Fig. 2.A.II.04: Data flow in material management

The burden imposed by data entry at the start of a chain thereby generates a simplification of subsequent operational steps. In a functionally-specialized enterprise organization in which the organization is always based on sub-processes, however, this relocation is not in the interest of the function carrying the burden, but can only be appreciated by looking at the process in its entirety.

The two arrows in the information pyramid of Figure 2.A.II.05, therefore, indicate the directions of database integration to support process chains.

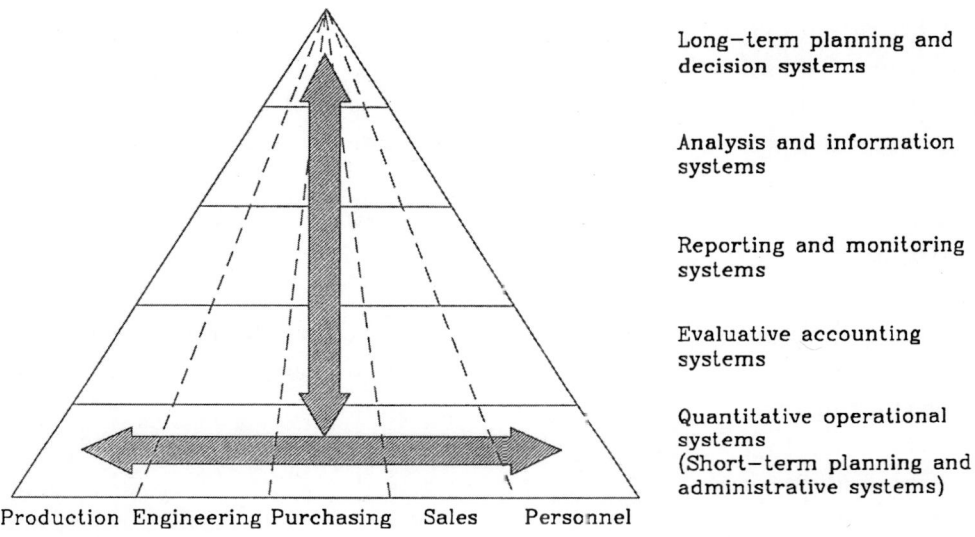

Long—term planning and decision systems

Analysis and information systems

Reporting and monitoring systems

Evaluative accounting systems

Quantitative operational systems
(Short—term planning and administrative systems)

Production Engineering Purchasing   Sales   Personnel

Fig. 2.A.II.05: Integrated information systems

The horizontal arrow at the operative system level depicts the perspective of the integration of functional information systems into a total integrated system (horizontal integration). The vertical arrow describes the consolidation/breakdown process whereby consolidated data are derived from operative data up to the level of global decision support for the entire enterprise; in the reverse direction global objectives can be broken down into detailed operative objectives.

A.II.1.2. Typical Process Chains

The terms operational chain, process chain and business process are regarded as equivalent. Alongside material logistics, **sales logistics** also constitutes a unified process chain if a unified database is used from order acceptance through order management, production planning and material planning to dispatch management. This perspective again goes beyond traditional departmental boundaries, since the process chain runs through the sales, production planning, stores, material planning, production control, dispatch and accounts receivable departments. At the same time the process chain is further processed vertically in the sales and marketing information systems.

Further process chains that also have a unified and hence integrated character are:

Product development from the initial idea generated by marketing through the technical development (design), work scheduling, quality assurance to preliminary costing (see *Scheer, CIM 1990, p. 91*).

Production control as the overall term for current production support. Here the functions of order scheduling, quality assurance, storage and transport control have to be integrated before a production order can be executed (see *Scheer, CIM 1990, p. 97*).

In a trading firm **retail management**, i.e. the up-to-date and article-specific monitoring of the flow of goods, constitutes a process chain.

In insurance firms **customer acquisition** and **processing of claims** are examples of process chains.

The basic principle of **data modelling** is to depict the broadest spectrum of interdependences. As a result knowledge of the fundamental processes is needed to design the database.

To implement the specific processes that build on this foundation using computer programs requires further breakdown. Integrity is then ensured by the up-to-dateness of the unified database.

Data interdependences are often obvious not only for links of the process chain that are closely linked temporally, but also for temporally disjoint applications. This applies particularly to the vertical integration direction, since the higher levels generally produce periodic evaluations, whereas the operative levels are event-controlled. Nevertheless, the data interdependence is indicated by the same object.

For example, in the context of its annual planned cost estimation, cost accounting needs bills of materials, work schedules and equipment data. At the same time these are master data for production planning and control (PPC) and are normally managed there.

If cost accounting and PPC are handled as independent functional areas with different EDP systems the master data from the production area need to be made available to the cost accounting programs with the help of a **bridge program** (see Figure 2.A.II.06). This bridge program re-formats the data from the production area into the form needed by the cost accounting program system.

Since the quantity of data in question can be extremely large this procedure can take a considerable amount of time. For the cost estimation information needed in the offer creation context, therefore, additional simplified cost estimation procedures are included in the EDP system for production planning and control. The operational interdependences here have thus given rise to the situation in which up-to-date cost

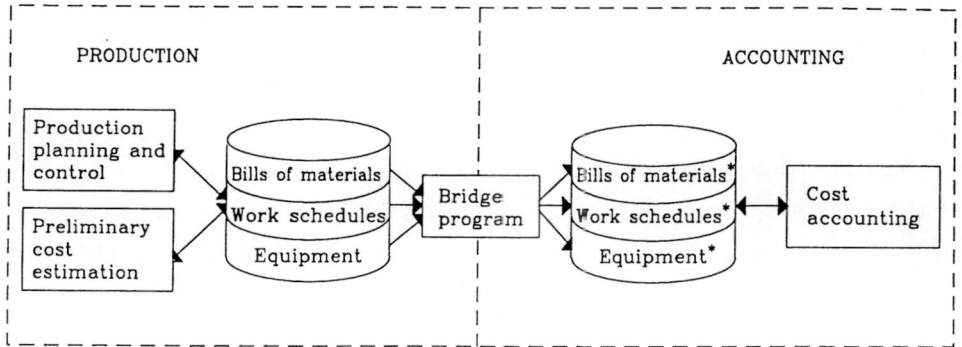

Fig. 2.A.II.06: Bridge program linking production planning and cost accounting

estimation applications of the application "cost estimation" have followed the data proximity to production planning.

Since strictly speaking both bill of materials and work schedule data and cost estimation data describe the same object - the product, this should give rise to a unified organization, as represented in Figure 2.A.II.07.

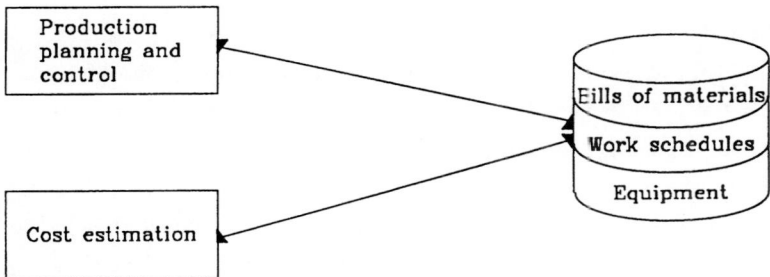

Fig. 2.A.II.07: Integrated database for production and cost accounting

A.II.2. Effects on the Organizational Structure of the Integration of Functional Business Areas

Examination of processes encourages an overlapping view of functional business areas. The close interdependence between processes resulting from common data demands comprehensive cooperation between the functional areas in designing the data structures, and forces an integrated examination of the operative functions. The definition of the bills of materials, i.e. the end products, assemblies and components of a company, also defines the cost units and, along with the construction of the data structure for an operational data collection system, establishes the entry points for performance and actual cost recording.

Data integration considerations link operational areas which up to now have had only slight contact with each other. In the computerized design context, for example, bill of materials and work schedule data are required and produced, which are also relevant for production planning and control and for cost accounting. Close cooperation in the work of data design is therefore essential.

This supra-functional cooperation in designing information systems is not only needed in the development of new information systems, but also in the choice of standard software. If the integration of data structures occupies the foreground, the selection procedure cannot be tailored to the functional requirements of a single area of the enterprise, but must at the same time also consider the data relationships with neighboring functional areas. This has given rise to the situation where enterprises are increasingly using so-called software families which provide consistent support for the concept of data integration. A consequence of this is that the individual functional areas of an enterprise (see here Figure 2.A.II.08) can no longer construct its own information system in isolation from the other functional areas.

On the other hand, since the use of EDP has an increasing effect on the quality of the work within a functional area the head of a functional area thereby loses part of his responsibility and creative control. This issue becomes even more important when sub-areas of the enterprise are controlled using a profit center philosophy. This philosophy presumes that the sub-area has control of the relevant instruments so that it can influence its own results. The tendency towards integrative cooperation in constructing information systems means that changes are needed here.

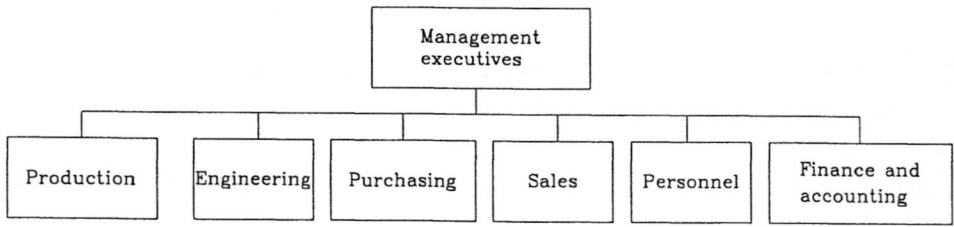

Fig. 2.A.II.08: Functional areas of an enterprise

If examination of processes also takes issues of organizational structure into account this leads to a more strongly object-oriented breakdown, in that, for example, uniform processes for certain product groups are constituted as independent units. Examples are production islands in the production area or the creation of product areas in the sales, material management and material planning areas.

For important processes units of organizational structure can be formed whose responsibility runs at right angles to the functional breakdown. An example might be a central department for logistics, order control or quality assurance.

The streamlining of operations and their consolidation into independent organizational units generates a flattening of the organizational structure. Coordination activities are eliminated by the data and process integration, so that the area of control can become greater and the organizational pyramid flatter.

A.III. Business Economics Structuring of Data Integration

A.III.1. Structuring of Process Chains

The rationalization effects of the process chain organization normally arise only when they are effected consistently; support for only some sub-processes within the chain can be ineffectual in its overall impact.

The data integration generated by implementing a database system allows the consistent structuring of process chains. Conversely, the exposure of these operational sequences is a prerequisite to the design of the integrated database schema.

Since in reality the individual processes to be handled are often very complex, the perspective needed for a unified organization is frequently impeded. For this reason, a careful analysis of a process needs to be undertaken before the planned model for a suitable EDP process can be created.

This will be demonstrated using a practical example. The example is based on an actual case. To represent the procedures **process chain diagrams** (see Figure 2.A.III.01a and Figure 2.A.III.01b) are employed, which have proven extremely useful in many practical system analyses that have been undertaken by the Institut für Wirtschaftsinformatik (IWi) in Saarbrücken.

The left column indicates the individual **sub-processes** (underlined) and **operational steps** in a process chain.

The following columns indicate whether an activity is **computerized** or receives only **manual** processing. A distinction is drawn between the processing support and the kind of database used. In the case of computerized processing **batch** and **on-line processing** are distinguished.

36

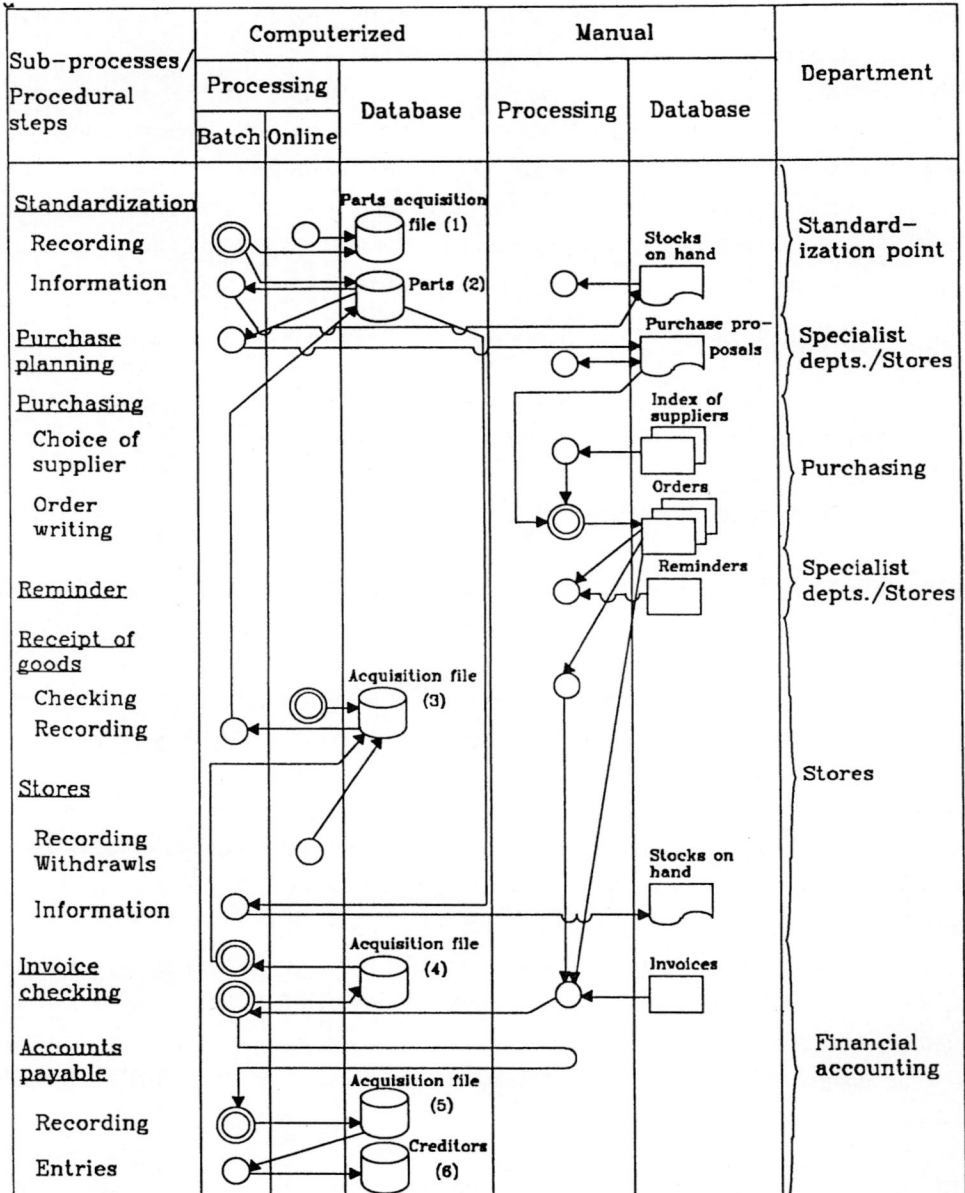

Sub-processes/ Procedural steps	Computerized			Manual		Department
	Processing		Database	Processing	Database	
	Batch	Online				
Standardization			Parts acquisition file (1)			Standard- ization point
Recording					Stocks on hand	
Information			Parts (2)			
Purchase planning					Purchase pro- posals	Specialist depts./Stores
Purchasing					Index of suppliers	
Choice of supplier						Purchasing
Order writing					Orders	
Reminder					Reminders	Specialist depts./Stores
Receipt of goods						
Checking			Acquisition file (3)			
Recording						Stores
Stores						
Recording Withdrawls						
Information					Stocks on hand	
Invoice checking			Acquisition file (4)		Invoices	
Accounts payable			Acquisition file (5)			Financial accounting
Recording						
Entries			Creditors (6)			

Fig. 2.A.III.01a: Largely departmentally specialized data processing

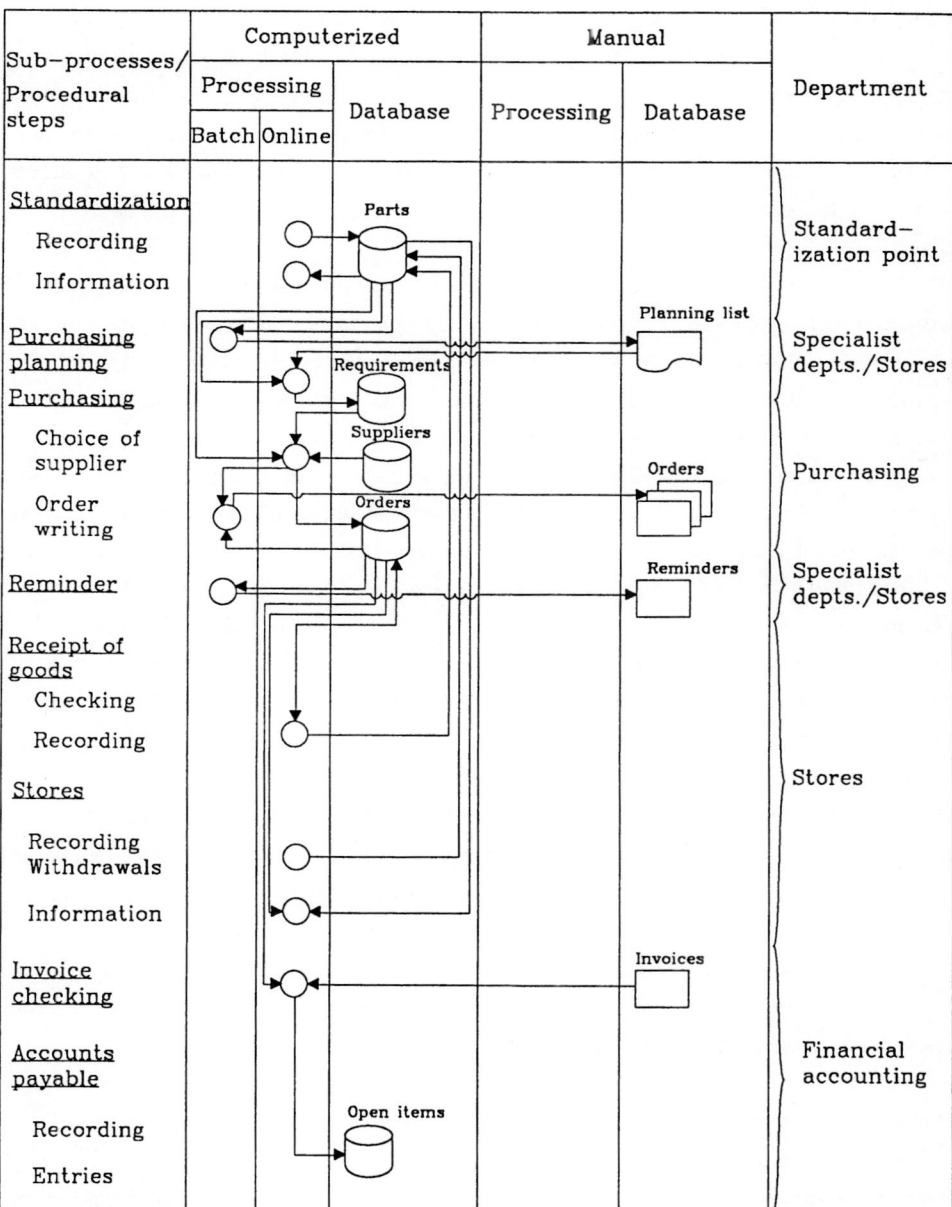

Sub-processes/ Procedural steps	Computerized			Manual		Department
	Processing		Database	Processing	Database	
	Batch	Online				
Standardization			Parts			Standard- ization point
Recording						
Information						
Purchasing planning					Planning list	Specialist depts./Stores
Purchasing			Requirements			
Choice of supplier			Suppliers			Purchasing
Order writing			Orders		Orders	
Reminder					Reminders	Specialist depts./Stores
Receipt of goods						
Checking						
Recording						Stores
Stores						
Recording Withdrawals						
Information						
Invoice checking					Invoices	
Accounts payable						Financial accounting
Recording			Open items			
Entries						

Fig. 2.A.III.01b: Process with data integration

The last column gives the names of the **departments** which carry out the sub-processes. This makes it clear once more that the processes are examined from beyond the departmental perspective.

In the columns simple, self-explanatory symbols from process diagram or data flow techniques are used. The arrows indicate the direction of the data flow. Specialist processing is indicated by a circle, redundant recording functions by a double circle.

Figure 2.A.III.01a shows the initially unintegrated material management process. EDP processes which are based on largely isolated file concepts are linked using manual processing procedures. Some EDP functions are performed on-line, others as batch jobs. The individual activities are assigned to the departments which perform them, so that the (isolated) department-specific organization is obvious.

The standardization point establishes specifications such as parts number, description, etc. for parts to be introduced. Recording is via terminal to an acquisition file (1). This is transferred to the parts master file (2) in a (redundant) batch run. From here information is made available in the form of lists which are processed manually. Material planning, i.e. establishing requirements, is carried out manually by the specialist departments and stores on the basis of purchase proposal lists generated in batch runs. The purchasing department then makes purchases on the basis of these material planning lists, whereby suppliers are chosen from a manually kept index file. Duplicates of the manually generated purchase orders are sent to receipt of goods, invoice checking and those specialist departments which generated the orders. The specialist departments then handle reminders decentrally without informing the purchasing department, which is then not in a position to record the reminders in its supplier file.

In stores goods received are recorded online in an acquisition file (3) on the basis of the delivery notes and then transferred to the parts master file in a (redundant) batch run. Withdrawals from stores are also recorded in the acquisition file. Lists for informational purposes are created in batch runs from the parts master file.

The financial accounting department records the incoming invoices (4) at invoice checking and compares them manually with the purchase orders, and in a batch run with the quantities delivered recorded at receipt of goods.

Finally, the vouchers are manually entered into preliminary accounts, then recorded on magnetic tape (5) at bookkeeping data entry stations without the support of computerized plausibility checks, and final entries are made in a batch run of the accounts payable program.

It is obvious that the essential data organization is based upon the applications perspectives of the individual departments. This leads to multiple recording of identical data. Thus, requirements data (article number, quantity, etc.) are recorded by the specialist departments in the course of material planning and again by purchasing in the course of order writing. In the stores area incoming quantities of goods are recorded once more from the delivery note. At invoice checking, article data is recorded yet again from the incoming invoices.

Figure 2.A.III.01c outlines a data-integrated solution for this example. Via a unified program system all functions can access the same database for parts, requirements, purchase orders, suppliers and open items. The data structure of the database is represented as an ERM, although the specification of relationship types (n:m or 1:n) is omitted. The operational sequence which is possible with this database is represented in Figure 2.A.III.01b.

In the process chain diagram of Figure 2.A.III 01b only those real and reinterpreted entity types which are shown within bold frames in Figure 2.A.III.01c are included.

The relationship type REQUIREMENT-PURCHASE ASSIGNMENT assigns a purchase order to the requirements which generated it, and a requirement to the purchase orders resulting from it. Via the relationship type ORDER-OPEN ITEMS open items can be assigned to the purchase order from which they originate, and the purchase order can be assigned to the open item which it has generated.

Via the SUPPLIERS-PARTS RELATIONSHIP the supplier relevant to a particular part and the parts supplied by a particular supplier can be identified.

Purchase orders are broken down into ORDER HEADER and ORDER POSITIONS.

By reformulating relationship types as entity types the data structure design process is once again highlighted.

The conceptual data model is static and indicates all the data structures needed.

All functions can now access the same data stocks and at data entry the existing information needs only to be extended to include those data that are missing.

At the standardization point the specification of new parts is recorded online directly into the parts file, and the entire file is then available for information purposes.

Material planning lists are generated in a batch run. Requirements are written to the requirements file, whereby details such as parts description, etc. do not need to be recorded but can be transferred directly from the parts file.

Information concerning suppliers is available interactively to the purchasing department, so that the order records can also be set up interactively. Orders are printed from the order file in a batch run.

Reminders are also created from the order file.

40

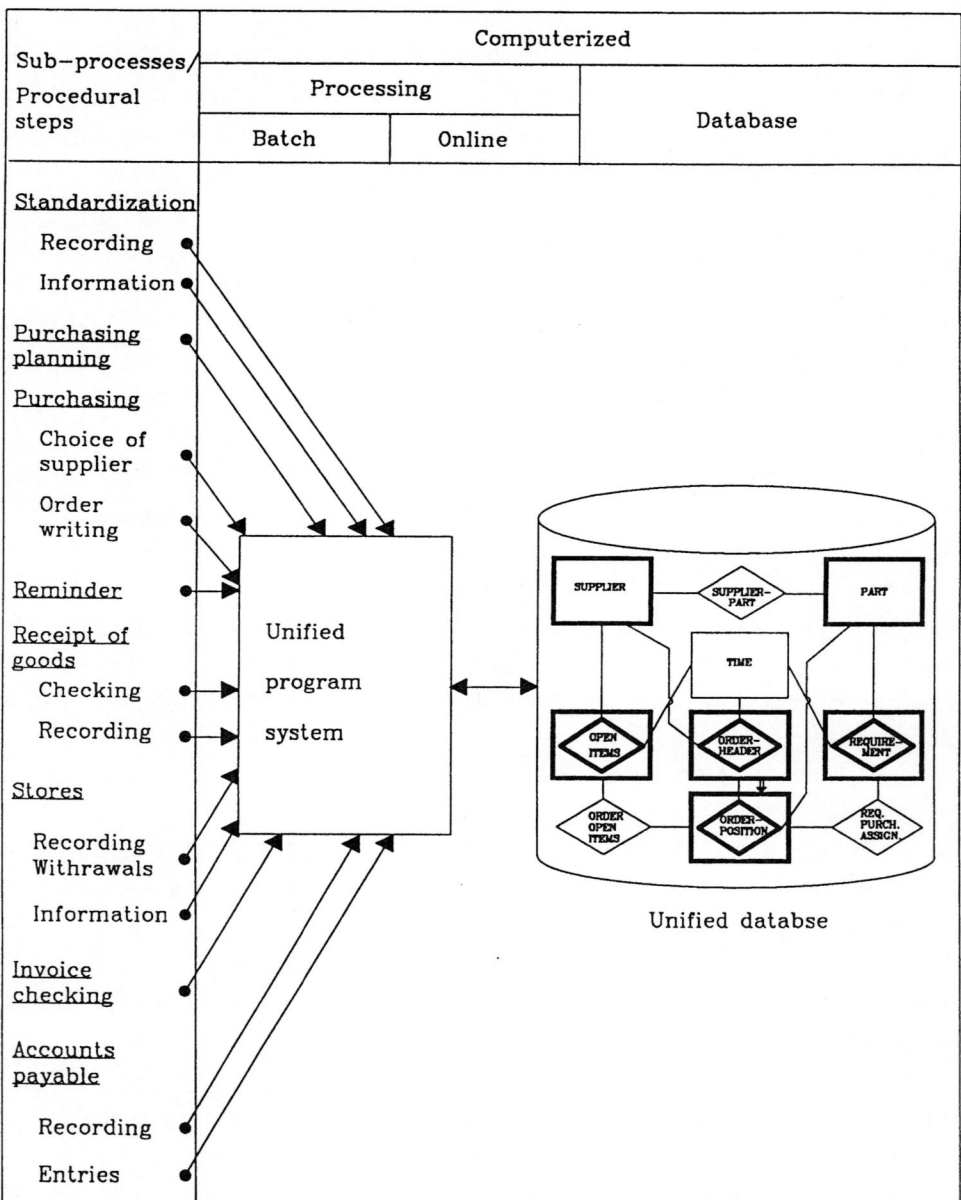

Sub−processes/ Procedural steps	Computerized		
	Processing		Database
	Batch	Online	

Standardization
  Recording
  Information

Purchasing planning

Purchasing
  Choice of supplier
  Order writing

Reminder

Receipt of goods
  Checking
  Recording

Stores
  Recording Withrawals
  Information

Invoice checking

Accounts payable
  Recording
  Entries

Unified program system

Unified databse

Fig. 2.A.III.01c: Unified database

At receipt of goods the order data are available online for the receipt of goods checks; at the same time the receipts are recorded in the parts file. Stock withdrawals are also entered in the parts file. Invoice checking accesses the order file and adds information concerning invoice details so that entry records can be created in accounts payable for the open items.

The interweaving of the data flow lines highlights the data integration.

As well as reduced redundancy in the storage and recording of data, the advantage of data integration lies in reduced information transfer times between the links in the process chain. As a result the throughput time for the entire process can be cut dramatically.

The business theoretic structuring of process chains constitutes an optimization problem in which the operational steps to be executed are distributed between the individual workplaces, taking data requirements, capacity loads and personnel qualifications into account. The objectives being pursued might be the optimization of throughput times, costs, revenue or profit. At the Institut für Wirtschaftsinformatik (IWi) in Saarbrücken the simulation system CAPSIM has been developed for the task of defining process chains and their optimal allocation to workplaces. The system CAPSIM represents a tool for solving these allocation problems (see *Brandenburg, Simulation von "Computer-am-Arbeitsplatz"-Systemen 1983; Krcmar, Gestaltung von "Computer-am-Arbeitsplatz"-Systemen 1983*). It consists of a GPSS-F generator which represents processes using a description language.

A CAPSIM example is shown in Figure 2.A.III.02 for order processing. The boxes represent processes, with both the process name and the processing department indicated. Once a process is completed it can either be divided into several diverse processes or it can progress as a unit to the next processing stage. A transfer to preceding processes is also possible, if reworking is required, for instance.

Using the process description the software system CAPSIM generates a simulation program in the language GPSS-F. With the simulation program diverse assumptions can be made regarding structural assignments, transfer probabilities, process durations and distributions of the arrival of elements to be processed. The output of the model is the effect on the objective variables such as departmental throughput times and capacity exploitation.

Additional description languages for modelling office systems are given by Wißkirchen and others (see *Wißkirchen et al., Bürosysteme 1983, Krallmann et al., Kommunikationsstrukturanalyse 1989*).

42

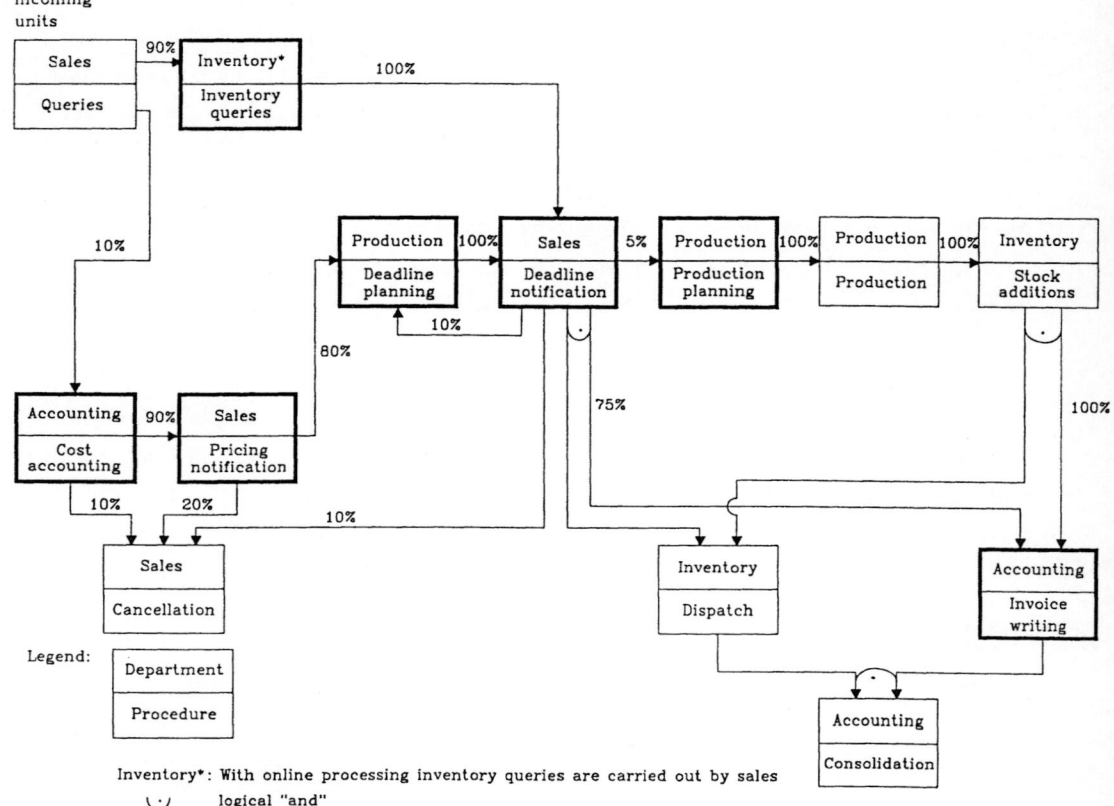

Fig. 2.A.III.02: Graphical representation of order processing in CAPSIM

The derivation of optimal process chains and their logical data structures is the task of EDP-oriented business economics. However, not only the optimization of process chains but also determining the optimal degree of database integration constitutes an optimization problem. With increasing levels of integration the benefits in terms of accelerated processing increase at a diminishing rate - at least beyond a certain level of integration. The costs of integration, in terms of maintaining system security, system management and the higher qualifications required from employees with the increasing complexity of the information system, increase beyond a certain level of integration at an increasing rate (see Figure 2.A.III.03). The optimal level of integration is determined where the vertical distance between the two curves is maximized. Hübner provides another definition of the optimal level of integration in terms of the accordance between internally integrated sub-systems (see *Hübner, Integration 1979, p. 381*). A comprehensive assessment of these cost and benefit components is therefore a further task of EDP-oriented business economics.

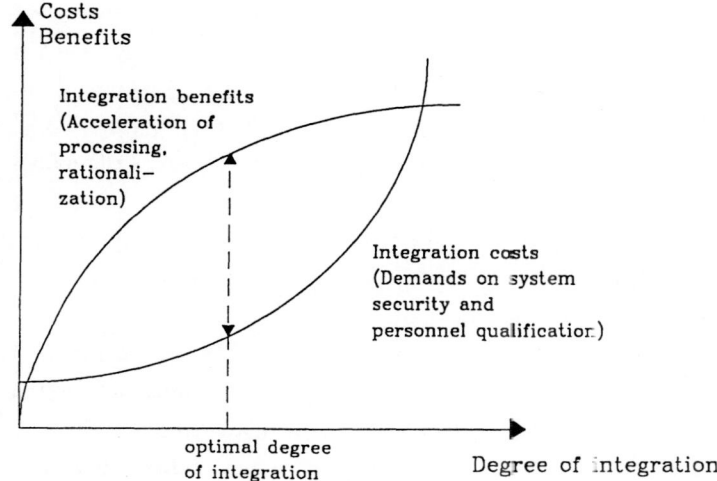

Fig. 2.A.III.03: Optimal degree of integration

A.III.2. Data Modelling: The Enterprise-Wide Data Model

An application-independent design of a data model for an enterprise is impossible. It must be based on a thorough business understanding of the decision complexes and organizational processes. Only then can the informational interdependences between entity types from diverse application areas be incorporated in the data structure.

Business economics concerned itself extensively in the '60s and '70s with decision interdependences between operational problem areas, and derived integrated planning models. However, this integration approach is different from the concept of data integration developed here.

Integrated planning takes account of interdependences between operational decisions, in that a simultaneous approach or reconciliation procedure is used to allow for the effects of one decision variable on other decision variables and vice versa (see e.g. *Bleicher, Organisation 1987, p. 38*).

A data-related integration of business functions, however, analyses which data are used in common by the various functions, and how these data can be structured, so that they can fulfil these requirements with low-redundancy and easy access. The common use of data stocks is, therefore, the basis of the integration principle used here (see *Emery, Integrated Information Systems 1975, p. 108*).

For this reason it is necessary to establish very carefully from an enterprise-wide standpoint which informational interdependences are necessary for the success of the

44

enterprise in the context of an enterprise strategy, so that they can be supported either by an in-house developed information system or one made up of standard software. The specification of an enterprise-wide data model provides a systematic approach to the design of such an integrated database. This can be derived in a top-down approach with close links to other enterprise models in business economics. Typical business economics enterprise models are:

-   The factors of production system developed by Gutenberg allows the description of the procedures required in the output creation process of industrial enterprises (see *Gutenberg, Betriebswirtschaftslehre 1951*).
-   External accounting, with its concepts of accounts and entries, has achieved a highly commendable level of abstraction which allows diverse processes in an enterprise to be represented in a simple, uniform description language.
-   Internal accounting, with the concepts of cost type, cost center, and cost unit, has also developed a simple description language for representing a variety of business processes.
-   The aggregate enterprise models developed in the operations research context (see *Rosenkranz, Modell- und computergestützte Unternehmensplanung 1981* and the literature references contained therein) provide a detailed description of supra-functional decision interdependences.

The concepts of the business economics models can be assigned to the various levels of Figure 2.A.II.05. The Gutenberg model relates to the operative level, financial accounting to the evaluative accounting systems, the cost accounting model to the controlling level and the enterprise planning model to planning and decision systems level.

In order to design an enterprise-wide data model of the operative levels, therefore, the ideas arising from the theory of the firm, that the output creation process of an enterprise is characterized by the combination of factors of production and that an enterprise maintains business relationships with market partners are of importance. Figure 2.A.III.04 represents this factual information using the entity types MARKET PARTNER, OUTPUT, and FACTORS OF PRODUCTION. The term MARKET PARTNER covers partners in both the buying and selling markets, the term OUTPUT covers self-produced and bought-in outputs. The terms will be specified in more detail below. BUSINESS RELATIONS form an n:m relationship type between OUTPUT and the world outside the enterprise, represented by the entity type MARKET PARTNERS. An instance of this relationship might describe, for example, the conditions negotiated between a customer and an article. The output creation process is described by the relationship type PRODUCTION INSTRUCTIONS. This indicates how an output can be produced by using the factors of production equipment, human labor and material. Since a particular output can often be created using different production instructions, and factors of productions are used in various outputs the relationship here is also of type n:m.

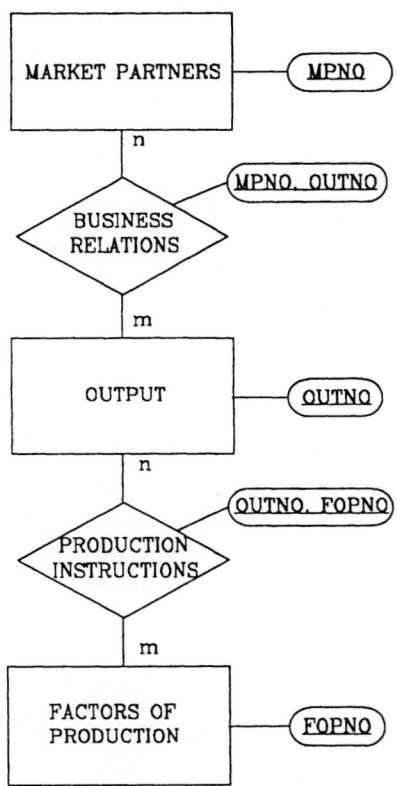

Fig. 2.A.III.04: Elementary entity types and their temporally-independent relationships

The structure presented is static, i.e. only temporally-independent data structures are considered. These are referred to in computer language as **master data**. In addition to these static structures, there arise procedures that are executed in time. Typical examples are orders from (or to) an external partner or for in-house products to the own production department. By specifying the time reference (date) it is possible to identify (repeat) orders. Furthermore, the implication is that these procedures, in contrast to the static data, are of interest for data storage only until the processing is completed.

To represent these procedures the general entity type TIME is first introduced (see Figure 2.A.III.05). EXTERNAL ORDERS form a relationship between MARKET PARTNERS, OUTPUT, and TIME. Similarly, INTERNAL ORDERS can be interpreted as the combination of TIME and the OUTPUT to be produced.

The term OUTPUT can then be interpreted in the MARKET PARTNER direction as output to be sold or bought, and in the FACTORS OF PRODUCTION direction as in-house products.

In the next step these data structures are refined by sub-dividing the terms that have been introduced. This process is referred to within the context of the data structure design process as **specialization**.

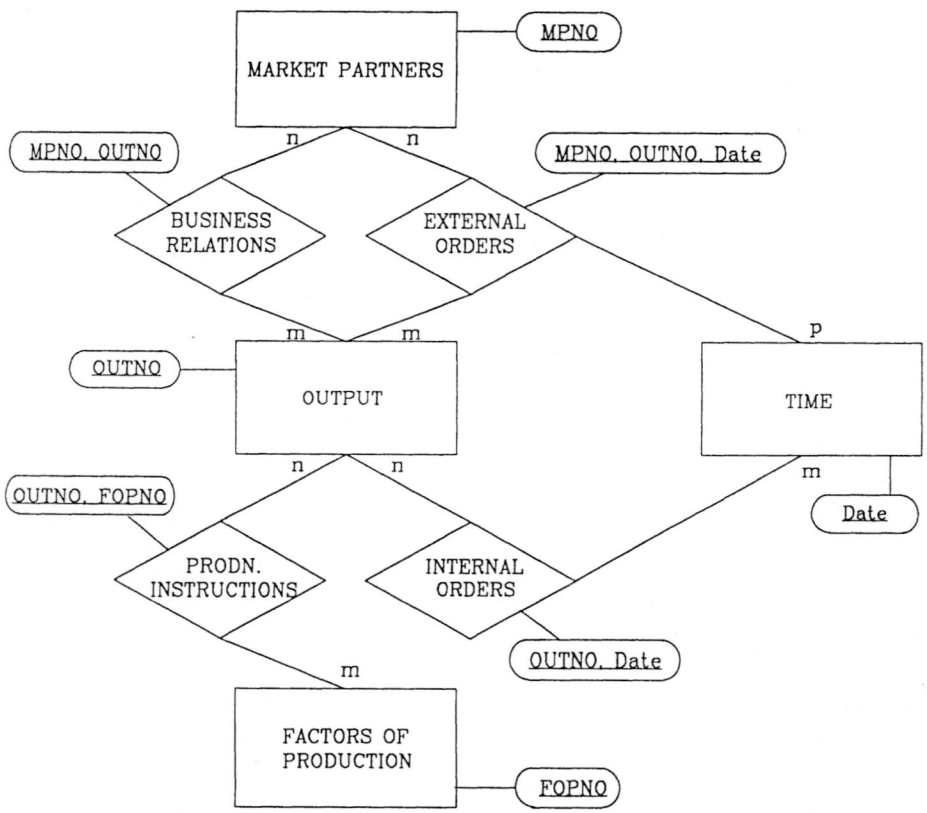

Fig. 2.A.III.05: Extension to Fig. 2.A.III.04 to include temporally-dependent relationships

The entity type MARKET PARTNER is broken down into the sub-concepts CUSTOMERS and SUPPLIERS. Similarly, FACTORS OF PRODUCTION are sub-divided into MATERIAL, EQUIPMENT, and EMPLOYEES. This is expressed graphically in Figure 2.A.III.06 by the introduction of an "is a" relationship, which indicates the specialization of a general concept into sub-concepts. At the same time OUTPUT is broken down into SALEABLE OUTPUT, EXTERNAL OUTPUT and INTERNAL OUTPUT. Whereas the entity type EXTERNAL OUTPUT is a specialization viewed from the OUTPUT standpoint, because only raw materials and assemblies are specified here, it is a generalization with respect to the factors of production MATERIALS and EQUIPMENT, since EQUIPMENT is not recorded in the bill of materials, but is itself an external output and hence the subject of purchase orders.

Differentiated relationship types also result from this specialization of the entity types. Whereas in Figure 2.A.III.05 EXTERNAL ORDERS cover both purchase and customer orders, these are now introduced as independent relationships. Correspondingly, BUSINESS RELATIONS between SUPPLIERS and EXTERNAL OUTPUT now relate to the conditions pertaining to suppliers, while the BUSINESS RELATIONS between CUSTOMER and SALEABLE OUTPUT record data relating to customers.

The specification of attributes is omitted from Figure 2.A.III.06 for reasons of clarity.

The specialization process has far-reaching significance for the design of information systems. By breaking down MARKET PARTNERS into SUPPLIERS and CUSTOMERS a formerly unified application area, namely the handling of external orders with unspecified partners, has generated two separate application areas "purchasing" and "sales".

However, the mirrored data structures for the two areas highlight the close connections between them.

It follows from this that carrying out the specialization process too early leads to splittering of information systems. Whereas looking at Figure 2.A.III.05 the processing of external orders could still be handled using a single application software system, Figure 2.A.III.06 suggests that it is appropriate to develop two separate application systems for purchasing and sales.

The lower part of Figure 2.A.III.06 represents output creation. The PRODUCTION INSTRUCTIONS contain the information as to how in-house products can be created using MATERIALS, EQUIPMENT and EMPLOYEES. PRODUCTION ORDERS are transaction data which are therefore linked with the entity type TIME. The important data in a production order are the output to be produced (indicated by a part number, for example), the completion date, and the quantity to be produced. If the order is scheduled to the resources this generates a relationship between the PRODUCTION ORDERS and the PRODUCTION INSTRUCTIONS assigned to it. This relationship is referred to as RESOURCE ALLOCATION. To carry out this procedure the production order is first "reinterpreted" as an entity type. Although it was designed as a relationship type, the introduction of the relation RESOURCE ALLOCATION has now conferred on it the character of an entity type. This distinction is indicated graphically by the fact that on introduction of the PRODUCTION ORDERS the edges are connected to the points of the rhombus, whereas the edges leading to the relationship RESOURCE ALLOCATIONS proceed only from the edges of the rectangle.

48

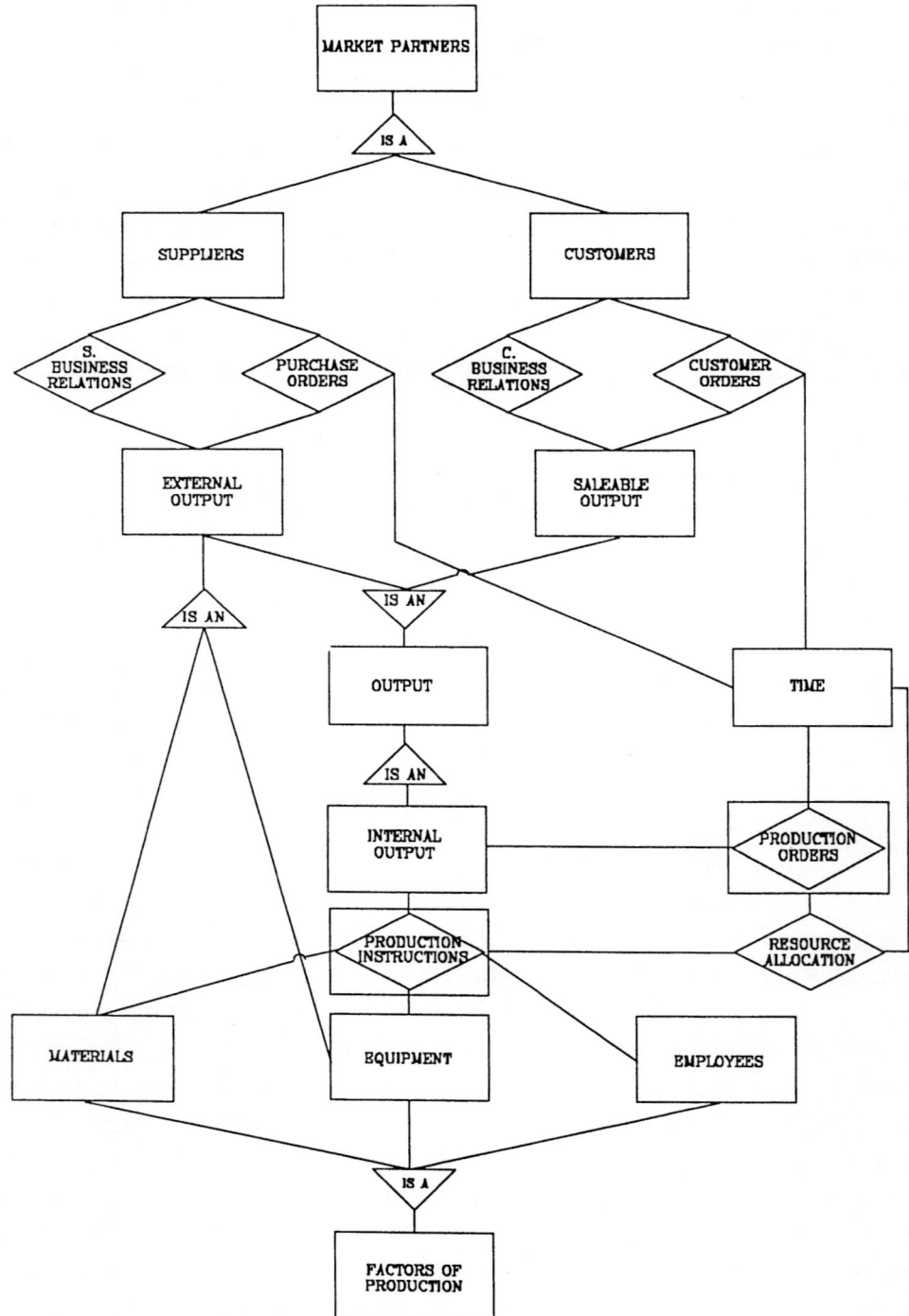

Fig. 2.A.III.06: Using the "specialization" operation to differentiate the data structure of
Fig. 2.A.III.05

The enterprise-wide data model presented in Figure 2.A.III.06 is still at a very high level of abstraction. For practical purposes it needs to be refined by further specialization of

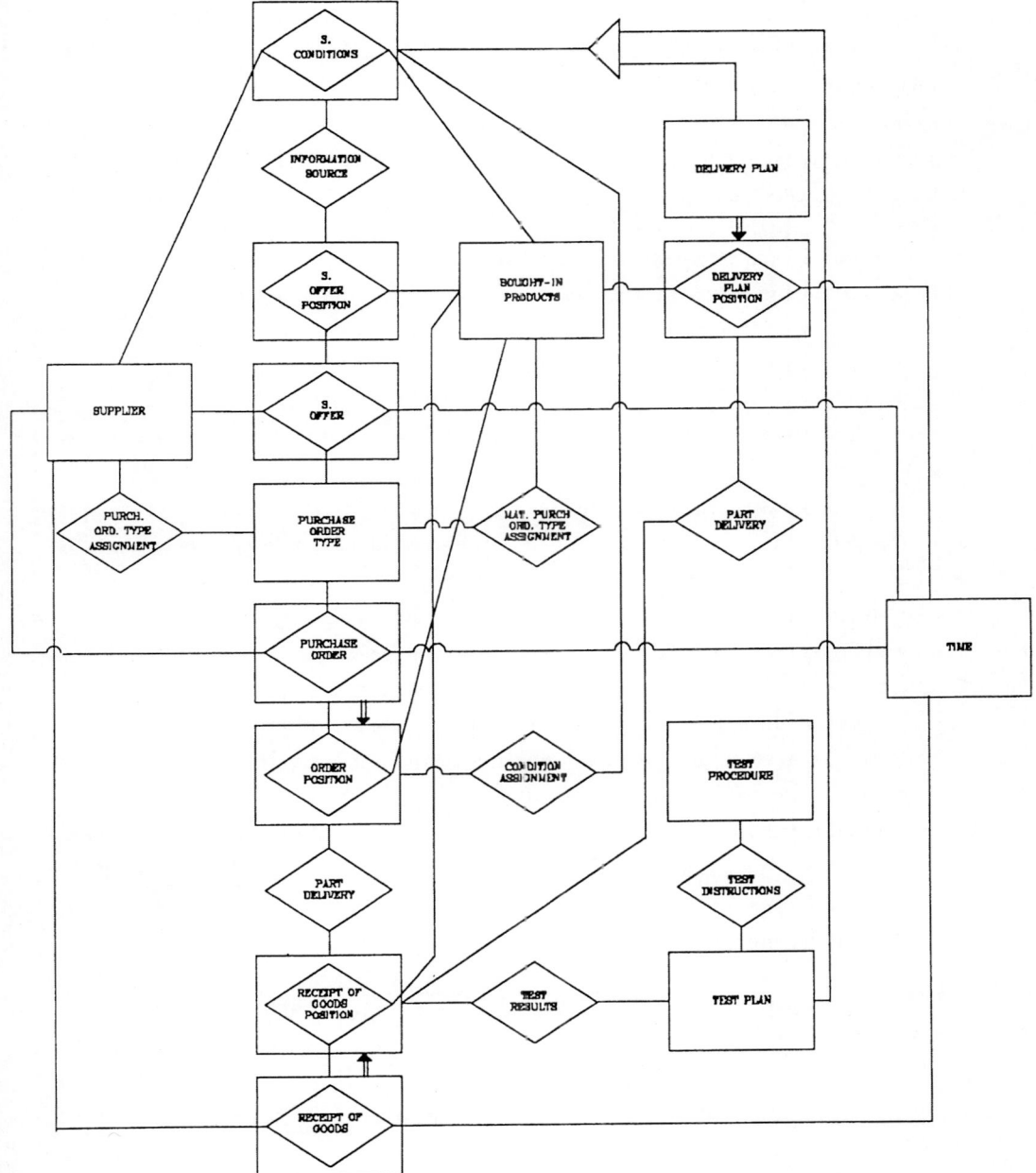

Fig. 2.A.III.07: ERM: ordering and receipt of goods

the concepts. This has been undertaken for an industrial firm (see *Scheer, Enterprise-Wide Data Modelling 1989*). The model developed comprises about 300 entity and relationship types from the operative areas of production, purchasing, sales, personnel, and design. The model has already been employed as a reference model for several practical applications. An indication of the degree of specialization of the model is given in Figure 2.A.III.07, which presents an excerpt from the purchasing area. It, therefore, represents a further specialization of the connectivities indicated by the entity and relationship types SUPPLIERS, S.BUSINESS RELATIONS, PURCHASE ORDERS and EXTERNAL OUTPUT in Figure 2.A.III.06.

In addition to the management of master data relating to suppliers, supplier conditions, external output and purchase order types, purchase order handling from the request to submit offers through allocation of orders to receipt of goods is represented. The delivery and test plans are shown as specializations of the conditions.

The following are typical and important application areas within an enterprise-wide data model:

1. Documentation of the important enterprise resource "data".
2. Condensed representation of the integrational interdependences as a basis for training and familiarization with the enterprise's information processing.
3. A fundamental starting point for the design of new information systems.
4. Additional documentation of existing information systems.
5. A basis for comparison with standard software data structures.
6. A basis for classifying sub-projects for implementing an integration model,
    in this context redundant data structures within sub-projects and data interfaces can be particularly well identified.
7. A basis for monitoring methods for top management in the information processing area, since the graphical presentation and condensed lucidity can identify an effective project framework.
8. The identification of the implications of procedural changes.

B. Process Control

B.I. Temporal Control: Interactive Processing

B.I.1. Description of Interactive Processing

In **batch processing**, which dominated until the end of the '70s, instances to be processed were collected together as jobs and processed by computer program without the intervention of the user.

In **interactive processing**, however, the entire processing is effected via interaction between man and computer.

A dialogue between man and the EDP system is always beneficial when one partner alone (in monologue) cannot solve the problem, or cannot do so as effectively.

Interactive programming is not only of significance for terminal applications of large EDP systems, but is also the dominant, sometimes even the only possible, processing form for workplace-oriented EDP systems (workstations and personal computers). The American news magazine TIME already expressed this close relationship between the user and the EDP system visually in its cover picture for the selection of the computer as "Machine of the Year 1982" where not simply an isolated EDP system was to be seen, but a user interacting with the computer.

In order to communicate with an EDP system a **user-friendly system interface**, which generates the contact with the technical hardware functions, and a **programming language** for handling business problems are necessary.

The demands made on the system interface and the programming language will depend on the possibilities and expectations of the user.

To distinguish between these demands different classifications for groups of users have been discussed (see e.g. *Martin, Application Development 1982, pp. 102-106; Davis, Olson, Management Information Systems 1984, pp. 503-533*).

Davis and Olson propose four criteria for classifying users:

1. Developers as opposed to non-developers: developers develop their own systems, whereas non-developers use systems developed by others.
2. Lay users as opposed to experts.
3. Frequent as opposed to occasional users
4. Direct as opposed to indirect users: Direct users employ the system for their own evaluations, indirect users enter data which are then employed by other (direct) users.

The different classifications emphasize above all the distinction between skilled and unskilled users. This gives rise to the goal of increasing the "simplicity" of user interfaces and programming languages.

The screen can be broken down into several areas (**windows**). Several different processes can then be assigned to the windows. This makes it possible for the user to communicate quasi-simultaneously with several processes. This also makes the transmission of data from one process to another possible, by transferring them from one window to the other.

As regards data entry the trend is moving away from digital towards analog functions. So, as well as digital keyboards, **light pens** and **mouse techniques** are used to activate functions by means of analog cursor positioning functions which are shown on the screen. **Touchscreens** require only the touching of the screen in the appropriate place. Execution and data entry can be effected using **commands, menu techniques, screen form control** and **prompting**.

With **command control** the user is provided with certain commands, whereby calling up the command COPY can produce a copy of a file, or SORT can sort a file on the basis of some further specified criterion, for example. Command control is very flexible, but it assumes the corresponding EDP knowledge on the part of the user.

For unskilled users, therefore, **menu control** is more suitable. Here, the user is provided with a list of possible choices. In the main menu very global functions are suggested which, once chosen, are then broken down into more specialized functions in sub-menus.

The individual options within a menu can be indicated using either words or symbols (**icons**). For example, the option "delete" can be represented using the symbol of a trash can. If this symbol is activated by a cursor using mouse techniques the area of the screen or the file indicated is deleted.

Menu hierarchies give rise to **tree structures**; if a sub-menu can be accessed via several higher level nodes then **net structures** are also plausible. For example, the menu control in the German Bildschirmtext (videotex) system represents a net structure.

Tree structures are made obvious by **pull down** and **pop up menus**. Both these kinds of menu allow the transfer from one level to the next level down.

With **screen form control** the user is provided with a kind of form on the screen in which he can make entries in the vacant fields. This offers greater variability than menu control, but with rigid sequencing of screen forms the processing becomes rather cumbersome.

With **prompting control** the system poses questions to the user which he must answer. For example, the system can demand a password as user identification at the start of an interaction.

Further interactive processing support is provided by **help keys**, which, when pressed, provide the user with information concerning the current state of his interaction and possible continuations. Using **function keys** the user can freely define and call up a wide range of processing commands.

In the development of **computer languages** there is also a strong tendency towards user-orientation. This is particularly clear in the fourth generation languages. The emphasis is no longer on describing the derivation of results - the **"how"** - but on describing the results themselves - the **"what"**. To carry out an evaluation the user simply needs to specify the desired variables with the corresponding formatting details. The fourth generation languages then translate these requirements into a procedure which generates the evaluation. To distinguish them from the earlier **procedural languages** these fourth generation languages are also referred to as **non-procedural**.

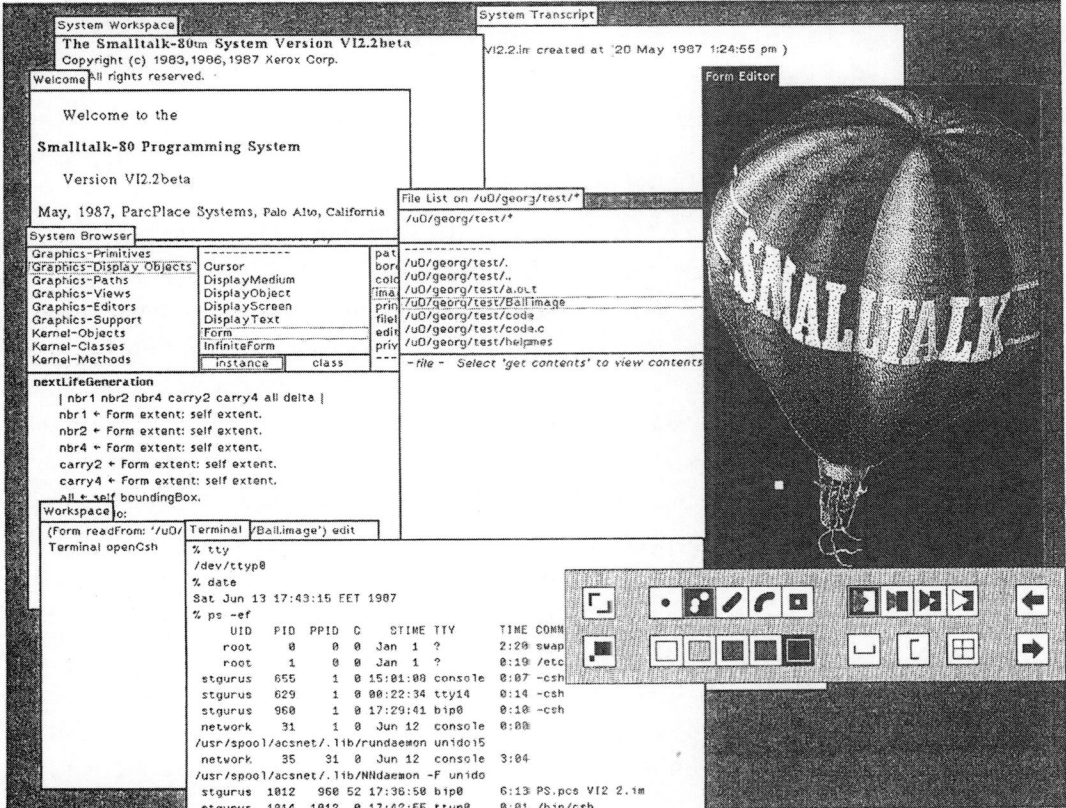

Fig. 2.B.I.01: Smalltalk example

(from *Gansinger et al., Smalltalk 80 1987, p. 241*)

The system Smalltalk 80 (see Figure 2.B.I.01) combines a user-friendly interface and programming language (see *Gansinger et al., Smalltalk 80 1987*). It is based on an **object-oriented programming language** approach. It also makes extensive use of window and mouse-cursor techniques. The user can identify objects on the screen by pointing at them with the mouse. Messages can then be exchanged between these objects by menu selections which activate the system.

Interactive processing offers new approaches to problem-solving in business economics. This applies especially to event-oriented planning, increased integration between business processes and workplaces (functional integration), and support for interactive decision-making.
For specific applications these factors often apply collectively and provide mutual support for the advantages of interactive programming.

B.I.2. Business Economics Implementation of Interactive Processing

B.I.2.1 Event-Orientation

Interactive processing improves **data currency**. Data amendments are entered at a display as soon as they are known and are thereby made available immediately to subsequent applications.
However, the same degree of currency is not needed for all the enterprise's data. If data are merely needed at some previously appointed evaluation deadline, they only need to be "up-to-date" at this deadline. If data are needed without foreknowledge or continuously they need to be up-to-date at all times. This applies especially to **master data** such as article, customer, supplier and employee data, which are accessed by many applications. Master data refers to those data which need to be held up-to-date by the enterprise at all times. The storage duration of a master data entity cannot be limited in advance. In contrast, **transaction data** such as orders, purchase orders, bookkeeping entries, etc., are subject in advance to a temporally limited storage and updating duration.
Given the need for considerable up-to-dateness the management of master data has become largely interactive and has almost completely replaced batch processing with its complex error-handling runs.

The currency issue is not only of interest as regards the data, however, but also with respect to planning procedures. **Batch-oriented planning runs** are carried out at previously appointed timepoints (e.g. at the end of the week or month) for the coming planning period (see the timepoints T1, T2 and T3 in the upper part of Figure 2.B.I.02). With rolling planning the planning periods can overlap, for example period (T2, T3) which is planned both at points T1 and T2. Using the **re-optimization principle** variables which have already been planned in a previous planning run for the overlapped planning periods are specified anew freely and without restrictions.

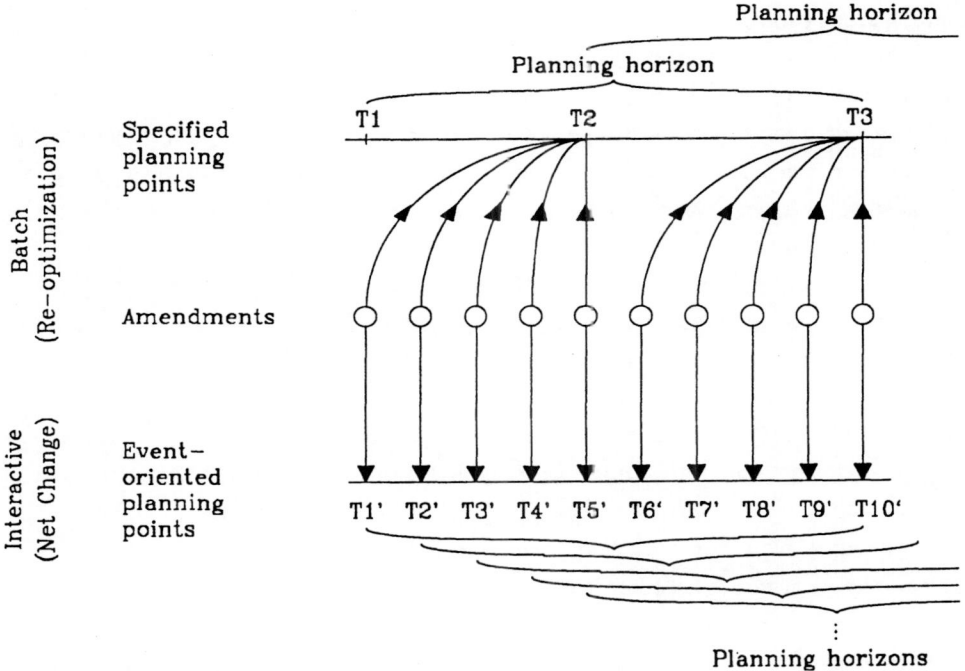

Fig. 2.B.I.02: Re-optimization and net change principles

A considerable disadvantage of the batch-oriented planning principle is that data amendments which arise after planning has been carried out (e.g. new sales forecasts, breakdown of production facilities, cancellation of an important customer order, etc.) cannot generate amendments to the current plan, but are accumulated and processed at the next planning point insofar as they have effects on subsequent planning periods. So, data amendments that arise in the time period (T1, T2) are only taken into account at T2. The planning principle is based on fixed planning points and fixed planning periods. At the point of plan creation there exists a large number of degrees of freedom, especially when the re-optimization principle is applied. Many of the planning models developed by quantitative business economics largely follow this planning approach. As a result there is a close correspondence between this aspect of business economics planning theory and the batch processing aimed at planning periods and points.

However, with an **interactive-oriented planning philosophy** the planning procedure is not carried out at a prescribed planning point, but in response to an event which makes planning amendments or re-planning desirable. Such an event might be a substantial data change, e.g. receipt of a rush order, breakdown of a production facility, cancellation of an important customer order or delay of a delivery. As soon as a data change of this kind is recognized it is incorporated in the planning procedure and processed in all the planning areas concerned.

In concrete terms this means that when a customer order has been cancelled, for example, the order file is immediately amended and in response to the requirement breakdown production and purchase orders are reduced. In this way the order change that has arisen is immediately taken into account in all planning files. If at any point both positive and negative data amendments arise only the difference (**net change**) is taken into account in updating the planning.

This procedure is indicated in Figure 2.B.I.02 by the planning points T1', T2', ..., T10' arising from data amendments. If the same planning periods are assumed as for the batch processing, the overlap now becomes very pronounced.

Where planning is based on planning periods in accordance with the re-optimization principle the objectives for the entire planning period must be known at the plan creation point. When the net change principle is followed, however, new objectives can be applied at any change of plan. (see *Kazmeier, Ablaufplanung 1984*).

The net change principle accepts from the outset that plan amendments are possible. As a result it is not necessary to carry out a complete optimization run, in which in principle all planning variables can be altered, every time there is a change. Rather, it makes sense for organizational reasons to handle only strictly necessary changes, in order to ensure greater stability of the planning results. In contrast to re-optimization, therefore, this means that not all degrees of freedom are used.

This approach explicitly accepts a certain sub-optimality of planning. The question remains, though, whether an approach based on planning periods and planning points with its assumption of data constancy during the planning period is not capable of being attacked more profoundly.

The same applies to stochastic models which require knowledge of the probability distribution of the data at the planning point. Even the flexible planning principle presents a strategy in which an optimal procedure is made possible for all data situations conceivable at the point of planning. (see *Hax, Laux, Flexible Planung 1972*). As soon as the assumed probabilities or alternatives change in the course of the process this approach ceases to be valid.

A planning approach in the interactive processing context which follows the net change philosophy must take into account the processing times needed. Interactive processing is only appropriate for tasks that can be handled interactively, i.e. in a dialog in which both the user and the computer system can respond to queries within a reasonable time span. This requirement supports the use of the simpler planning procedures provided in connection with interactive decision processes, which will be discussed in the next section.

The net change philosophy has already been implemented in computerized planning systems, especially in the production area (see *Scheer, Produktionsbereich 1983, p. 82 ff.; Berthold, Aktionsdatenbanken 1983; Hoffmann, Aktionsorientierte Datenverarbeitung 1988*).

The transition from periodic to interactively-controlled, event-oriented planning has far-reaching consequences for the handling of problems in business economics. For example, considerable parts of business cost accounting, which have up to now been carried out on a very strongly periodic basis, could be modified. For instance, EDP systems chiefly carry out cost estimations for the entire production program only once a year, since transferring data from prior production areas precludes more frequent processing. Given the strong fluctuations in exchange rates, raw material prices, etc, more up-to-date cost estimation may be desirable (see e.g. *Langer, Kosteninformationssystem 1980*). In this case it would be possible to calculate the costs for certain end products interactively, as soon as this kind of data change arises. The same also applies to cost estimation in the order negotiation area.

Despite the advantages of interactive processing that have been mentioned batch processing runs are still useful. The capacity load on the EDP system can rule out the immediate updating of all known amendments. But batch processes are also still suitable for planning or calculation functions which relate to certain periods over a long term, and where data amendments are only taken into account at certain established monitoring times. For example, the analysis of planned/actual deviations in standard costing relates to periodic values and their calculation is, therefore, only carried out in batch runs at the end of these periods (e.g. months). If this organizational principle is maintained the introduction of event-oriented interactive processing is not appropriate here. However, if the plan relates to variables other than periods this assertion may need to be altered. For example, it may be that the standard costing relates to production orders and continuous actual costs are recorded by up-to-the-minute operational data collection. Then it would be possible by way of ad-hoc queries at arbitrary points to give instructions for corrective intervention. It is also possible for the EDP system to give independent (event-controlled) information regarding cost deviations whenever certain warning limits are exceeded.

The net change principle is of particular significance for short-term planning considerations, where it is necessary to react to data amendments immediately.

In order to combine the degrees of freedom offered by re-optimization with the currency of the net change principle, therefore, a graduated approach is suggested (see Figure 2.B.I.03).

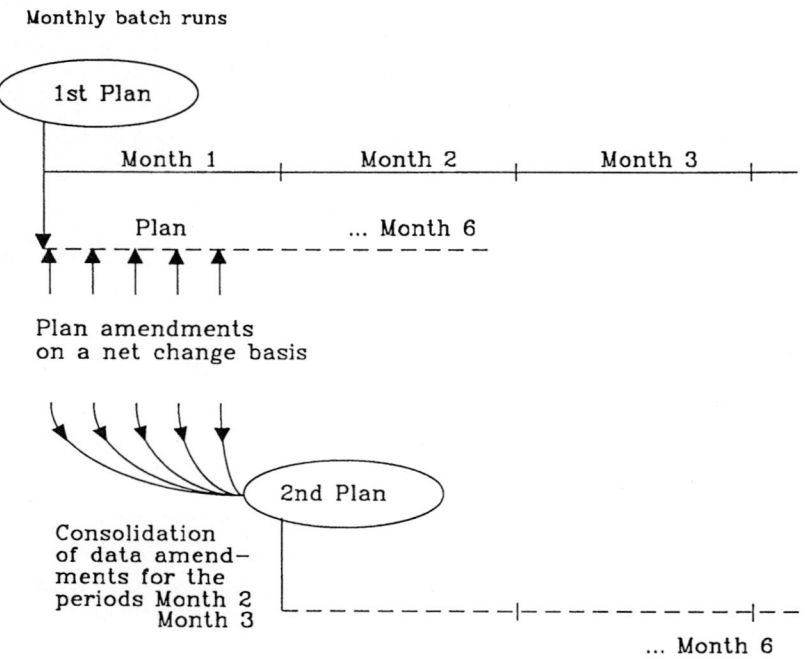

Fig. 2.B.I.03: Combining re-optimization and net change

For a certain planning task, e.g. establishing the production program, the production program for the next six month period is planned at specified planning points, e.g. at monthly intervals. This planning procedure can be carried out either in batch runs or in an interactive decision process. The important point is that the planning procedure is undertaken at a specified date. Given that the procedure is not very up-to-date and the potentially considerable computational costs, e.g. in using an LP model, a batch solution might be desirable.

In the course of the following month important data amendments are incorporated immediately in accordance with the net change principle. The existing production plan is changed as little as possible and only adjusted to the data amendments to the extent that impermissibilities and gross efficiency violations can be avoided. The data amendments are also assembled and incorporated in a completely new plan at the next planning run in accordance with the re-optimization principle.

Batch processing and immediate online or realtime processing are the two extremes of an entire range of temporal processing forms, with other possibilities existing between them. In **asynchronous online processing**, for example, the processes are recorded interactively but the data are then placed in a queue from which they are processed in accordance with the load on the EDP system. The control between immediate online processing, asynchronous processing through to batch processing is implemented in a computer-technical sense using **trigger concepts** (see Figure 2.B.I.04). This is illustrated using the example of order processing.

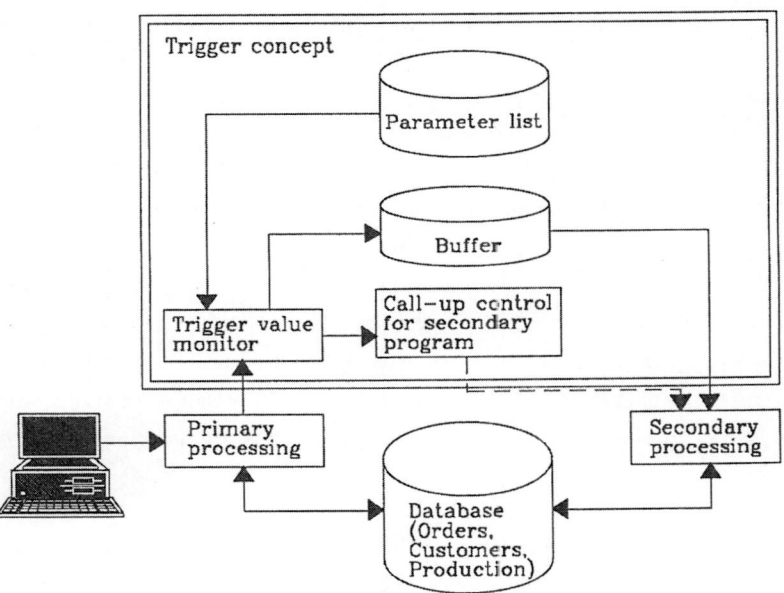

Fig. 2.B.I.04: Trigger concept for order processing

On acceptance of a customer order the primary processing of the trigger control is effected. The order data are thereby placed in the database by the order recording program. Thereafter, the system passes the data to a checking mechanism which decides whether secondary processing needs to be undertaken immediately on the basis of this primary processing, e.g. reservation of the stocks needed for the order, or whether several orders should first be accumulated in a **buffer**, before being processed together (in a batch run). The initiation of secondary processing is controlled by **parameter lists** or can be effected at specified times. With the help of the trigger concept it is, therefore, also possible to carry out batch processing.

Trigger concepts also control the communication between terminal workplaces and online programs, as well as between online programs and other online programs (see *Berthold, Aktionsdatenbanken 1983*). The trigger functions thereby control not only the temporal process but also ensure that the interactive chains remain logically consistent. To do this the predecessor-successor relationships between the interactive steps (transactions) are specified, e.g. in transaction matrices. Thus, they contain not only the technical delimiter functions but also substantial portions of the business process logic.

B.I.2.2. Functional Integration

In the batch processing context data recording, handling by specialists, and data processing are kept strictly separate. This is physically evidenced in special data recording workplaces, separate workplaces for handling staff in the specialist departments, and the closed-shop operation of the computer center.

In contrast, in the interactive programming context these functions are integrated in a single display workplace. The specialist records data, carries out monitoring functions at the terminal, and controls the processing procedure. An instructive example (see *Reblin, Stapel- oder Dialogverarbeitung 1980, p. 50*) shows in Figure 2.B.I.05 that the nineteen steps needed for a financial accounting procedure in batch processing can be consolidated into five steps at a terminal workplace in interactive processing. In particular, costly transport operations between data recording, the computer center and the specialist staff can be eliminated, so that a considerable acceleration of the process is also achieved.

By consolidating data entry and specialist handling into combined workplaces data processing is rescued from an organisational dead end.

In addition to the integration of data entry and data processing, interactive processing also allows those tasks that needed to be separate in manual processing for reasons of functional specialization to be united at a single workplace. The procedural simplification resulting from EDP support reduces the advantages of specialization, and the disadvantages of increased coordination costs and temporal delays resulting from transfer and lead-in times can be avoided by functional reintegration.

An important motive for dividing up processes is also the difficulty in providing the up-to-date information needed for a comprehensive handling of the process at a single workplace. Whereas, if the process is split up only that information needed for the sub-process to be handled needs to be provided at each workplace. With a computerized,

Batch processing

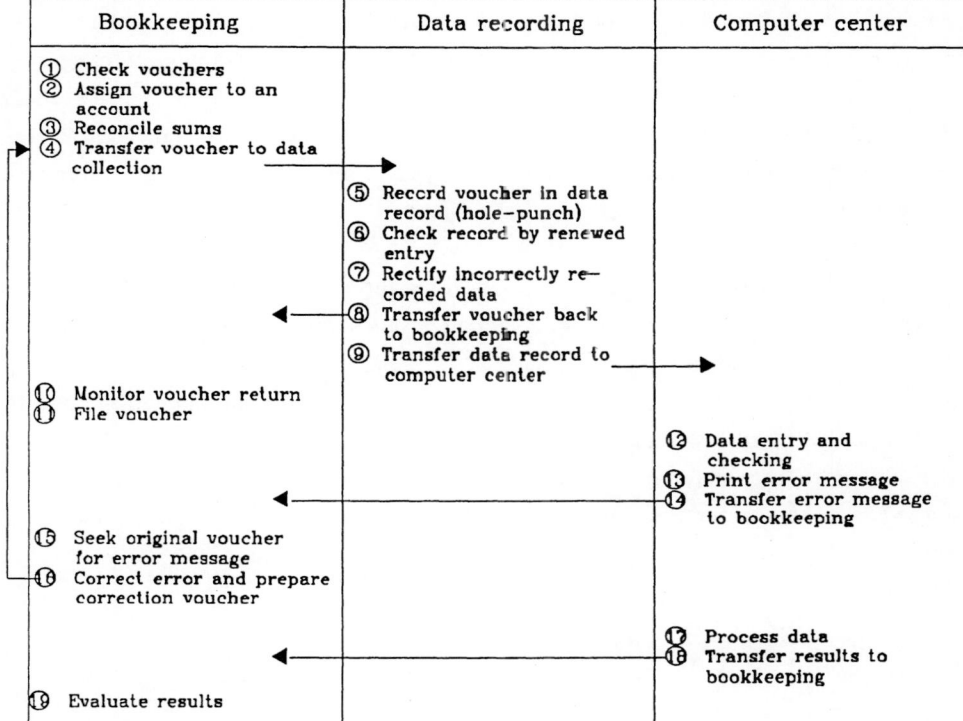

Interactive processing

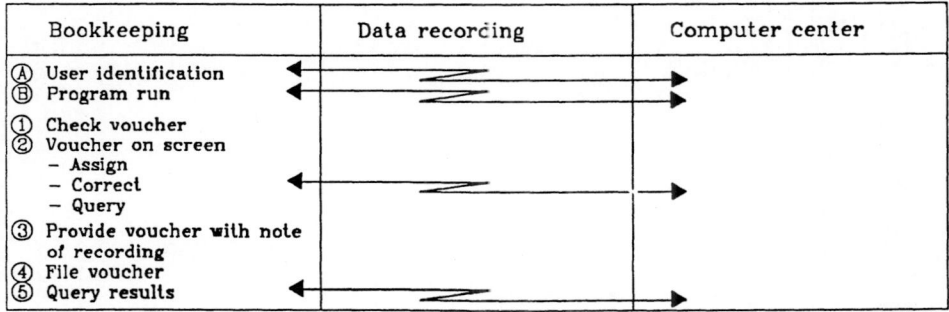

Fig. 2.B.I.05: Functional integration in the transition from batch to interactive
programming

integrated database the employee can access comprehensive current information from his
workplace, so that this argument in favour of a functionally specialized process
breakdown loses its force.

62

Figure 2.B.I.06 shows the example of the process chain already presented in Figure 2.A.II.03. It has already been pointed out for cases (c) and (d) that the considerable throughput time reduction can only be achieved by the combined use of integrated databases and interactive processing. Only in this way can the updated database become immediately available for further processing on completion of a (sub-) process. To this extent the reduction in throughput times achieved is also a result of the interactive approach.

By combining processes into larger work lots throughput and processing times can be further reduced, since transfer (and/or waiting) times and lead-in times are either eliminated or shortened.

If the functionally specialized procedure through P1 (material planning), P2 (choice of supplier) and P3 (order writing) is newly structured, such that choice of supplier and order writing are carried out at one workplace the transfer/waiting time between them is eliminated and the lead-in time applies only once for the combined (P1 + P2).

The four cases in the example generate the processes shown in Figure 2.B.I.06.

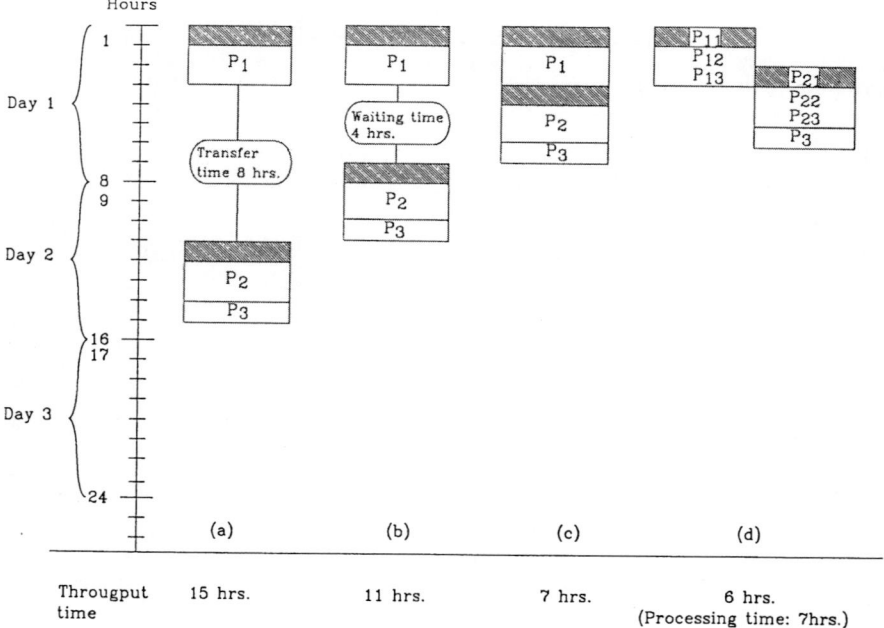

Fig. 2.B.I.06: Reducing throughput time

This **holistic process handling** leads to functional enrichment at the workplace. EDP is, therefore, not the cause of impoverishment of the human work content, but rather of its enrichment. This is indicated, for example, by the demand for multiple qualifications. It also appears that the introduction of EDP-related integration concepts such as CIM (Computer Integrated Manufacturing, see Chapter 3, Section B.I.2.) could increase the demands on employees qualifications to the extent that this could become a decisive bottleneck. This point has been made emphatically by Shunk (see *Shunk, CIM in den USA 1988*) in his ordering of the most important success factors for the enterprise: personnel, technology, capital.

Even the more holistic process handling must take the capacity limits of the workplaces into account. This may necessitate distributing work lots to several workplaces, but the distribution is no longer made on a functional basis but on the basis of the work objects.

In Figure 2.B.I.07 case (a) first shows a functional breakdown in which for each processing function groups of workplaces are formed, consisting in the case of material planning of two workplaces and in the other functions of one workplace each. All four processes for the articles A to D are processed by these groups.

In case (b) the choice of supplier and order writing functions are consolidated, but two work groups are formed each of which is responsible for specific article groups. The work lot is therefore broken down according to objects. In this way the specialization is more strongly object-oriented.

With functional breakdown, in contrast, a broad spectrum of objects are handled within a narrow function - with object-oriented breakdown, in contrast, a narrower spectrum of objects is subject to total processing.

The advantage of functional integration lies in the reduction of lead-in times for specialist employees, reduction of transfer times and improved information provision at the workplace. Functional specialization, in contrast, despite the possible rationalization achievements, has led to a considerable deterioration of customer service in many areas. For example, in banks separate counters have often been set up for savings, giro, customer advice and cash services. As a result the customer has had to queue at several counters. In addition, personnel providing information often have not had access to up-to-date listings. With interactive processing several functions (at least savings and giro business) can be integrated at one workplace. This eliminates considerable waiting times for the customer (see *Scheer, Wirtschaftlichkeitsanalyse 1978, p. 305 ff.*). The customer can also be provided with comprehensive and up-to-date information about his various accounts from a single workplace.

64

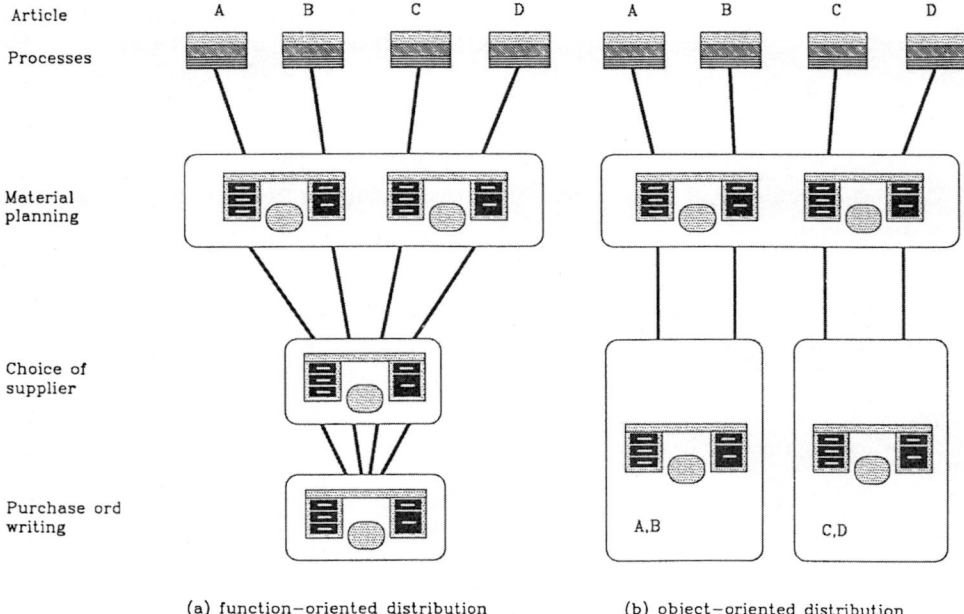

Article
Processes

Material
planning

Choice of
supplier

Purchase ord
writing

(a) function—oriented distribution   (b) object—oriented distribution

Fig. 2.B.I.07: Distribution of tasks to workplaces

Figure 2.B.I.08 presents a further example: that of functionally integrated order processing. On receipt of an order the order processor first checks the credit standing of the customer by accessing the customer file (1). Then he checks the availability of the article by accessing the article/inventory files (2). If stocks are available he instigates a reservation (3). If there are insufficient articles in store he establishes the earliest date for new articles by accessing the production plan (4). He determines the current delivery date by accessing the dispatch and itinerary plan (5). Finally he prints an order confirmation for the customer and effects storage of the customer order.

In traditional functionally specialized processing these functions would each be carried out by different departments (order acceptance, stores, production and dispatch) in sequence. Each employee would have to familiarize himself with the case in hand, and considerable transfer times would accrue between the processing steps. Practical observations indicate that integrated processing makes it possible to reduce the throughput time from several days to a few minutes (see also Figure 3.B.IV.01).

The special feature of functional integration, as compared with the data-oriented integration described above under the use of database systems, is that all functions are effected from a _single workplace_. However, it presupposes data integration since the same data must be available for diverse functions.

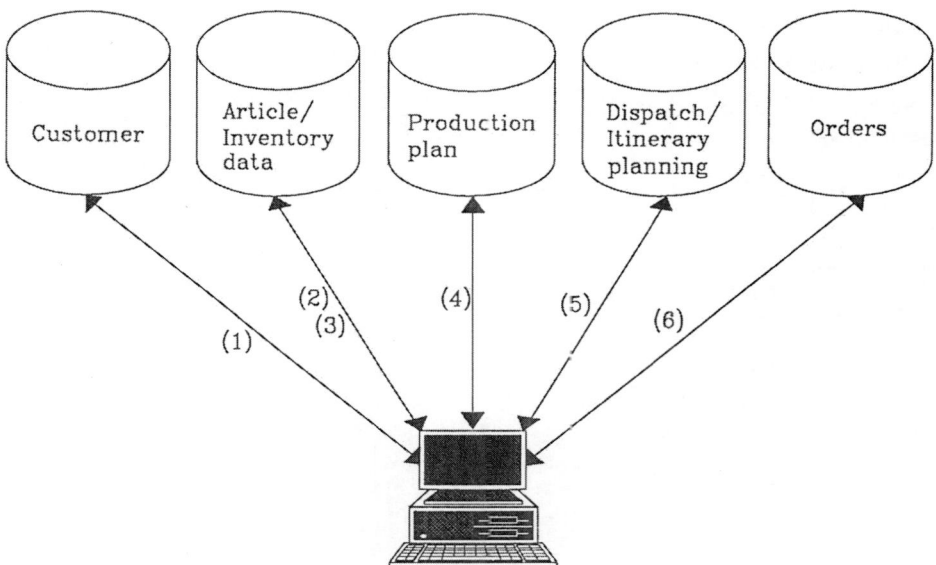

Fig. 2.B.I.08: Integrated order processing from a single workplace

The integration of interconnecting functions at one workplace demands higher personnel qualifications than specialization in a single segment of the processing sequence. At the same time direct access to data maintained by other specialist departments involves the danger of misinterpretation since, in passing on information at the request of other departments, the filter provided by the specialist department responsible for the data no longer exists. Training is then needed to promote awareness of responsible data utilization.

With increased interactive interdependences the complexity of the EDP system also increases and therewith its sensitivity to technical and user errors. For this reason, those parts of the operating system controlling interactive processing (**teleprocessing monitors**) possess comprehensive systems for restarting after system breakdown (see *Reuter, Fehlerbehandlung 1982*).

Given the numerous possibilities for accessing various data from one workplace there arises the problem of defining clear accession classes, so as to exclude as far as possible unauthorized data access. Here too, teleprocessing monitors provide suitable tools via table controls.

For example, Figure 2.B.I.09 indicates that a certain employee can only read file A, can alter file B and can make new entries in file C. This kind of approach can be applied at the file level, the record level, the field level down to the field contents level (see *Scheer, Wirtschaftsinformatik 1978, p. 485 ff.*).

	Objects		
User	File A	File B	File C
1	read	amend	write
2	write	. . .	. . .
3			
.			
.			
.			

Fig. 2.B.I.09: Access authorization table

Highly integrated software systems are sensitive to errors, since the breakdown of a central system component usually affects entire application groups. However, these disadvantages must be weighed against the considerable advantages of eliminating multiple processing, acceleration of process handling, improved provision of information resulting in better customer service, and improved planning quality.

The integration trends indicated can have a lasting impact on classical occupation descriptions. It is to be expected that many business functions will be temporally relocated nearer the start of the process chain. For example, in the case of a customer-specific one-off product critical path materials could already be determined in the course of the design procedure. The designer could immediately specify the purchase order entries (see also Chapter 3, Section B.I.). In traditional processing these purchase order records would only be created by material management after the entire bill of materials had been established and hence considerably later. Models of office automation are also based on the exploitation of these integration principles (see Chapter 3, Section C.V.).

The problem for business economics is, therefore, one of developing suitable operational structuring concepts for the amalgamation of traditionally distinct functions, thereby reversing the high level of functional specialization by means of reintegration.

B.I.2.3. Interactive Decision Process

The interactive solution of decision problems is a particularly intensive interactive form with many interactions between the user and the EDP system. The user defines alternatives which are evaluated by the EDP system. On the basis of these results the user can develop new alternatives whose effects are again evaluated by the EDP system. The process ends when the user has found a satisfactory solution.

In this interaction the capabilities of both partners - the specialist knowledge, fantasy, and creativity of the user and the storage capacities and computational speed of the EDP system - should provide mutual support.

This idea is also pursued in the concept of "**decision support systems**". A decision support system (DSS) is an interactive system which helps managers to make decisions (see *Awad, Management Information Systems 1988, p. 37*). They are used to handle so-called **semi-structured decision problems**.

Structured decision problems can be unambiguously represented by a model and are thus programmable. Examples of programmable decision rules are lot sizing formulae, or linear programming models for production planning. **Unstructured decision problems**, however, are not admissible to programmable decision rules since the objectives are not clearly defined, the alternative space is unlimited, or no procedural methods are available which can provide solutions within finite computational capacities. Such problems require heuristic methods as well as human intuitive judgement. Semi-structured decisions possess a programmable component, but at the same time still require a certain input of human judgement.

The suitability of the interactive approach is then immediately obvious: the computer takes over the provision of information or the evaluation of alternatives in the structured categories, whereas the unstructured parts, that is the addition of further qualitative objective criteria or the provision of new alternatives, is left to the user.

Building on the work of Gorry and Morton (see *Gorry, Morton, A Framework for MIS 1971*) Awad has developed a table in which the three decision types are listed against examples from different management levels (**operational control, management control, strategic planning**).

Whereas in the case of structured EDP applications the economic exploitation of the EDP system in the application configuration occupies the foreground, decision support systems aim to achieve the greatest possible benefits for the user in terms of service and the speedy provision of information. It is not the most economic use of EDP that is central, but the greatest possible benefit to the decision maker. For this reason, decision support systems employ costly graphics and colour support for output. A decision

Types of decision \ Management activity	Operational control	Management control	Strategic planning	Support needed
Structured	Inventory reordering	Linear programming method	Plant location problems	EDP or management science models
Semistructured	Bond trading; Production scheduling	Setting market budget for consumer products	Capital acquisition analysis; Mergers	DSS
Unstructured	Selecting a cover for LIFE	Hiring managers	R & D portfolio development	Human intuition

Fig. 2.B.I.10: Decision types for management activities

(from Awad, Management Information Systems 1988, p. 270)

support system consists of a **database**, a **programming language** for formulating queries to, and simple evaluations from, the database, tools for preparing input and output data (**report generators**), the **mathematical statistical methods** of regression analysis, risk analysis and simulation, and **languages** supporting model construction.

Given their great flexibility relational database systems are employed. In addition to managing its own data, the decision support system must also be able to access the general enterprise data. This can be achieved either by using a common database or by importing data into the decision support system via an interface. Since DSS applications are not in general time critical, the import of data is adequate in many cases, especially if data consolidation from the operative data stocks can be undertaken at the same time.

Suitable programming languages are non-procedural languages such as SQL (Structured Query Language). Using the three key words **SELECT**, **FROM** and **WHERE** wide-ranging evaluations can be undertaken, which can also involve linking several databases (tables). For the relational database in Chapter 2 Section A.I. the following query can be formulated, for example:

"List all customer numbers with the corresponding customer names and those article numbers and descriptions on which the customers in question has spent more than 1,000 $"

CUSTOMER

CNO	Name	Location	....
4711	Müller	Hamburg	
4853	Bauer	München	
4869	Fischer	Stuttgart	
5112	Weber	Frankfurt	
5247	Schulz	Hannover	
5328	Wagner	Mainz	
⋮	⋮	⋮	

ARTICLE

ANO	Description	....
223	Table lamp X11	
274	Kitchen light M2	
389	Office lamp 520	
541	Cristal chandalier 3115	
575	Ceiling light V12	
⋮	⋮	

ORDER POSITION

CNO	Date	ANO	Quantity	Price	....
4711	11−04−90	223	2	320,00	
4869	11−17−90	541	15	598,00	
5112	11−18−90	575	5	249,00	
5247	11−18−90	541	1	598,00	
5328	11−19−90	389	250	198,00	
⋮	⋮	⋮	⋮	⋮	

TABLE OF RESULTS

CNO	Name	ANO	Description
4869	Fischer	541	Cristal chandalier 3115
5112	Weber	575	Ceiling light V12
5328	Wagner	389	Office lamp 520

Fig. 2.B.I.11: Example of a database for SQL query

by means of the following expression

SELECT	CNO, Name, ANO, Description
FROM	CUSTOMER, ARTICLE, ORDER POSITION
WHERE	Quantity * Price > 1,000
	AND CUSTOMER.CNO = ORDER POSITION.CNO

The result of the query constitutes another table which can then be used as input for further evaluations (see the database with examples of line entries in Figure 2.B.I.11).

Special programming languages as well as model and method banks are available for incorporating model calculations in the decision procedure (see Chapter 2, Section C.III.). Since many plans exhibit a tabular structure **spreadsheet programs**, which are particularly available in microcomputer systems, are also suitable for developing a DSS model.

The spreadsheet representation of a processing problem takes the form of a table. Each line may contain constants (character strings, numbers) or formulae for encoding processing functions. Information is filed in lines (see *Nastansky, Tabellenkalkulations-programme 1987, p. 329*). Figure 2.B.I.12 represents a spreadsheet application for cost estimation (see *Haberstock, Kostenrechnung 1987, p. 177*).

Whereas spreadsheets primarily provide a framework for data manipulation in tabular form, special **planning languages** are more concerned with the requirements of formulating typical models.

Figure 2.B.I.13a presents the model of an earnings plan in the language FCS (Financial Control System) from the firm EPS Consultants (see *EPS, FCS-EPS 1982*). Each variable is defined by a name given in inverted commas and can then be identified by the corresponding line number. So the variable revenue is generated by multiplying the unit price by the number of units, indicated by the respective line numbers 20 and 25.

The system informs the user immediately of any input errors, for example, the missing apostrophe in line 35. In Figure the 2.B.I.13b the abbreviated model is provided with data. The third step in Figure 2.B.I.13c involves the calculation and output of results.

The commands that have been presented are largely self-explanatory. The separation of model definition, data entry, and computation and output preparation is of particular significance, since this means that the three components can be amended independently of each other.

Column numbering

Line numbering

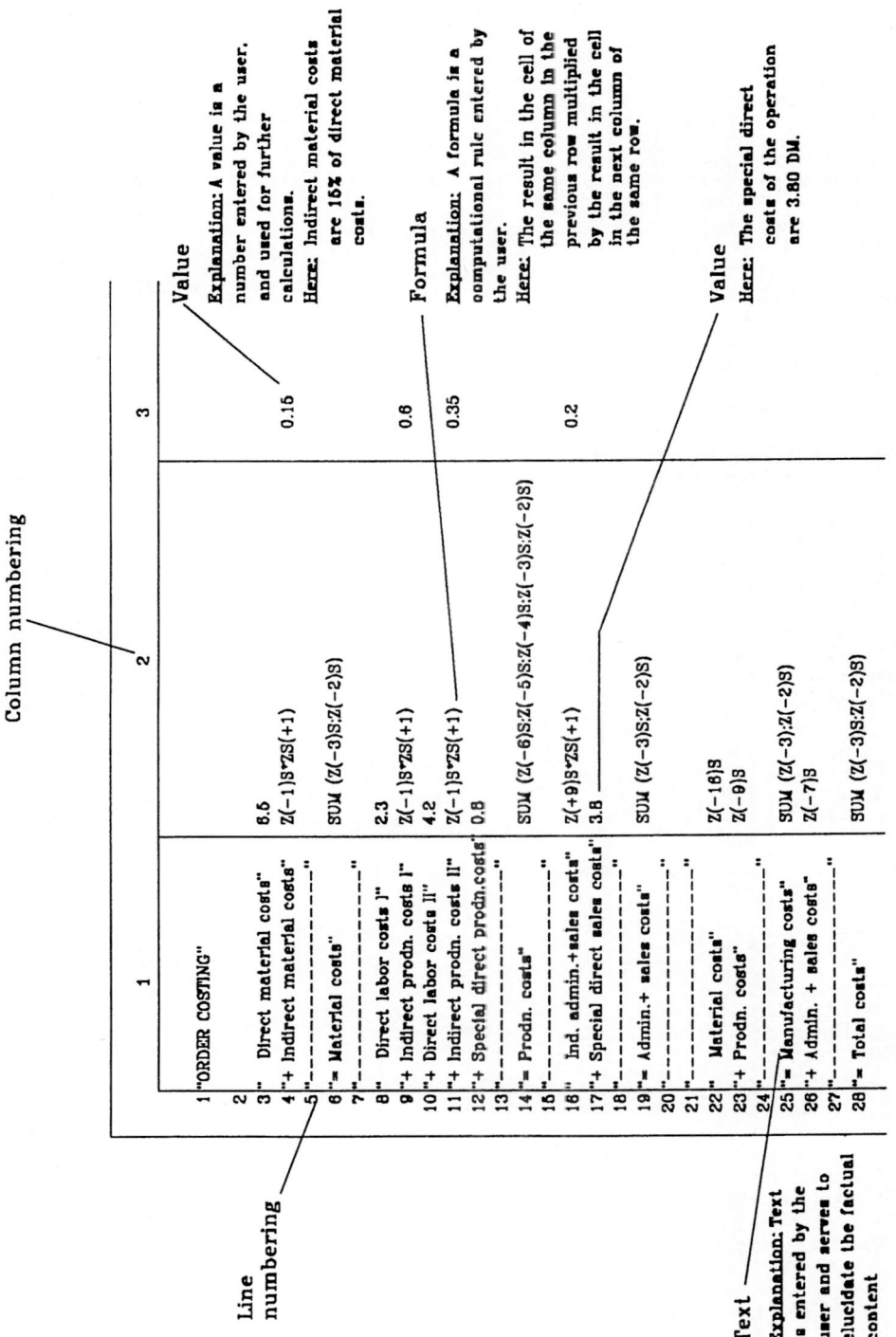

	1	2	3
1	"ORDER COSTING"		
2			
3	" Direct material costs"	8.5	
4	"+ Indirect material costs"	Z(-1)S7ZS(+1)	0.15
5	" ------------"		
6	"= Material costs"	SUM (Z(-3)S:Z(-2)S)	
7	" ------------"		
8	" Direct labor costs I"	2.3	
9	"+ Indirect prodn. costs I"	Z(-1)S7ZS(+1)	0.6
10	"+ Direct labor costs II"	4.2	
11	"+ Indirect prodn. costs II"	Z(-1)S7ZS(+1)	0.35
12	"+ Special direct prodn.costs"	0.8	
13	" ------------"		
14	"= Prodn. costs"	SUM (Z(-6)S:Z(-5)S:Z(-4)S:Z(-3)S:Z(-2)S)	
15	" ------------"		
16	" Ind. admin.+sales costs"	Z(+9)S7ZS(+1)	0.2
17	"+ Special direct sales costs"	3.8	
18	" ------------"		
19	"= Admin.+ sales costs"	SUM (Z(-3)S:Z(-2)S)	
20			
21			
22	" Material costs"	Z(-18)S	
23	"+ Prodn. costs"	Z(-9)S	
24			
25	"= Manufacturing costs"	SUM (Z(-3):Z(-2)S)	
26	"+ Admin. + sales costs"	Z(-7)S	
27	" ------------"		
28	"= Total costs"	SUM (Z(-3)S:Z(-2)S)	

Value

Explanation: A value is a number entered by the user, and used for further calculations.
Here: Indirect material costs are 15% of direct material costs.

Formula

Explanation: A formula is a computational rule entered by the user.
Here: The result in the cell of the same column in the previous row multiplied by the result in the cell in the next column of the same row.

Value

Here: The special direct costs of the operation are 3.80 DM.

Text

Explanation: Text is entered by the user and serves to elucidate the factual content

a) Inputs

	1	2	3
1	ORDER COSTING		
2			
3	Direct material costs	6.50	
4	+ Indirect material costs	0.98	15%
5	-------------------		
6	= Material costs	7.48	
7	-------------------		
8	Direct labor costs I	2.30	
9	+ Indirect prodn. costs I	1.38	60%
10	+ Direct labor costs II	4.20	
11	+ Indirect prodn. costs II	1.47	35%
12	+ Special direct prodn. costs	0.80	
13	-------------------		
14	= Prodn. costs	10.15	
15	-------------------		
16	Indirect admin. + Sales costs	3.53	20%
17	+ Special direct sales costs	3.80	
18	-------------------		
19	= Admin. + Sales costs	7.33	
20	-------------------		
21	-------------------		
22	Materialcosts	7.48	
23	+ Prodn. costs	10.15	
24	-------------------		
25	= Manufacturing costs	17.63	
26	+ Admin. + Sales costs	7.33	
27	-------------------		
28	= Total costs	24.95	

b) Results

Amounts in DM

Fig. 2.B.I.12: Example of a spreadsheet application

```
SYSTEM > LOGIC

+20 'Unit price'
+25 'No. of units'
+30 'Revenue'=20*25
+35 'Discount %
 35 'Discount %
       §
+35 'Discount %'
+40 'Discounts'=30 at 35
+45 'Net revenue'=30-40
+50 'Unit costs'
+55 'Variable costs'=25*50
+60 'Fixed costs'
+65 'Profit'=45-55-60
```

Fig. 2.B.I.13a: Model formulation in FCS

```
SYSTEM > DATA

* 20 U 1.2 1.2 1.25 1.3 1.33
* 25 G 5000,6
* 35 U 3*5,*6
* 50 I 0.7,0.05
* 60 A 900,10
* END
```

Explanations:

U = Units
G = Geometric growth
    on a base of 5000 at a
    rate of 6% (5000, 5300, 5618, ...)
I = Constant growth at a rate of
    0.05 units (Increment=0.05),
    (0.7, 0.75, 0.8, 0.85, ...)
A = Arithmetic growth on a base of
    900 with a 10% growth rate (900,
    990, 1080, ...)

Fig. 2.B.I.13b: Data entry in FCS

The distinction between model creation, data provision and preparation of output gives the language a particular flexibility, whereby for example, a model, once created, can easily be generated with diverse data sets and diverse output forms.

```
SYSTEM > CALCULATE
SYSTEM > LIST
COLUMNS?  1- 3
ROWS?     20-65
```

Results plan

	1988	1989	1990
20 Unit price	1.20	1.20	1.25
25 No. of units	5000.00	5300.00	5618.00
30 Revenue	6000.00	6360.00	7022.50
35 Discount %	5.00	5.00	5.00
40 Discounts	300.00	318.00	351.13
45 Net revenue	5700.00	6042.00	6671.37
50 Unit costs	0.70	0.75	0.80
55 Variable costs	3500.00	3975.00	4494.40
60 Fixed costs	900.00	990.00	1080.00
65 Profit	1300.00	1077.00	1096.97

Fig. 2.B.I.13c: Calculation and presentation of results in FCS

Typical analyses which make the incorporation of the programmable parts visible in the higher-level interactive decision process are:

-       "what if" analyses,

-       "what to do to achieve" analyses,

-       risk analyses.

Figure 2.B.I.14 applies a **what if** analysis to the financial plan, whereby it is asked how the plan would change if the variable "number of units" in line 25 is altered from -5% to +5% in steps of 5%. Only the columns 1 to 3 and lines 25, 30 and 65 of the financial plan which are of interest are generated.

74

```
SYSTEM > STEP
ROW?, FROM%, TO%, STEPS%? 25,-5.5,5
COLUMNS TO LIST? 1-3
ROWS TO LIST? 25,30,65
```

-5.00 % SENSITIVITY ON NO. OF UNITS

	1988	1989	1990
25 No. of Units	4750.00	5035.00	5337.10
30 Revenue	5700.00	6042.00	6671.37
65 Profit	1190.00	973.65	988.13

.00 % SENSITIVITY ON NO. OF UNITS

	1988	1989	1990
25 No. of Units	5000.00	5300.00	5618.00
30 Revenue	6000.00	6360.00	7022.50
65 Profit	1300.00	1077.00	1096.97

5.00 % SENSITIVITY ON NO. OF UNITS

	1988	1989	1990
25 No. of Units	5250.00	5565.00	5898.90
30 Revenue	6300.00	6678.00	7373.62
65 Profit	1410.00	1180.35	1205.82

Fig. 2.B.I.14: "What if " analysis in FCS

"What if" queries are concerned with the speedy recognition of the effects of data alterations on a given starting position. For example, the query might concern how the financial plan would be affected by a certain percentage fall in the exchange rate for an important export market.

"What if" queries can also be answered using spreadsheet programs. By using formulae to link data items a specific data alteration can be used to update the entire spreadsheet, including the output variables of interest, in accordance with the new value.

A "**what to do to achieve**" query, which is often referred to as "goal-seeking", investigates the opposite case. Here it is asked what value a certain variable needs to take in order to achieve a specified goal. For example, for a given liquidity plan showing under-coverage the question is how many extra units of an end product would need to be sold to eliminate this under-coverage.

In **risk analysis** probability distributions are defined for certain parameters, for example, in the case of a capital investment project for income, outgoings, or the rate of interest. With the help of Monte Carlo simulations probability distributions for the objective variables of interest (net present value or internal rate of return) can be calculated (see the example in Chapter 3, Section C.IV.).

Planning languages, which are suited to the construction of decision support systems, are available both on microcomputer systems and on HOST computers and combinations of both. Typical systems are the already mentioned FCS (Financial Control System), IFPS (Interactive Financial Planning System) and MSA (Management Science America)-Expert. Spreadsheet systems are increasingly being further developed into integrated systems with data management, data dictionary, graphics and documentation. Where micro- and HOST computers are combined, model formulation and output preparation are largely performed on the microcomputer, in particular taking advantage of the typical user-friendly graphics. The management of large stocks of data and the access to the operative databases is then handled by the HOST interface.

The possibilities of interactive problem-solving mean that problems that have up to now only been inadequately soluble by EDP systems using programmed decision rules can now be newly structured. A typical application example is capacity scheduling in the context of a computerized production planning and control system. Previously, extensive EDP systems, such as CAPOSS (IBM), attempted to eliminate capacity bottlenecks by temporal rescheduling of orders with the help of priority rules. However, the considerable complexity of the problem resulting from the large number of interdependent orders and the complexity of the sometimes inconsistent objectives (high capacity utilization, short throughput times, accurate deadlines, low capital tie-up) mean that this problem is not programmable. As a result, for large scale problems these approaches have basically failed or led to unacceptable computation times. For this reason more recent EDP systems aim merely to present the user with graphical representation of capacity bottlenecks indicating the production orders affected. Using simulations the user can then delay the orders or assign them to alternative equipment until the bottleneck is eliminated. The simulation can incorporate optimization models or simpler heuristic decision rules to ensure the admissibility of a solution or to allow easier evaluation of alternatives. Monitoring of the entire process, however, is carried out by the human planner.

In decision support systems, providing information to the decision-maker occupies the foreground. The decision-maker is not to be replaced, merely assisted. This distinguishes them from **expert support systems (ESS)** in which problem-solving strategies are stored in the form of rules that distance the user from the decision process to a greater extent.

The system, rather than the user, generates and proposes the alternatives (see Chapter 2, Section C.IV. on expert systems).

The decision calculus approach developed by Little represents a special form of interactive problem-solving. It is based on the fact that decisions often have to be made on the basis of assumptions concerning the behaviour of market partners which affect the impact of certain advertising expenditures on forecasts of consumer behaviour. Such intuitive behavioural hypotheses in the heads of decision-makers are quantified in the course of the interaction and their consequences for the decision-maker are indicated. If the results are plausible the hypothesis can be maintained, if not the user is prompted to amend them (see *Little, Decision Calculus 1977*).

B.I.3. Business Economics Structuring of Interactive Applications

Event-orientation, functional integration and interactive decision processes have been elaborated as characteristics of interactive processing of importance to business economics. The possibility of avoiding work peaks by continuous data recording and the simplification of procedures through the use of user-friendly screen forms and support routines extend the arguments.

Figure 2.B.I.15 indicates how these characteristics affect goals such as time-saving, personnel saving, improved information potential and simplification of organizational procedures. Event-orientation is illustrated by the improved up-to-dateness of the data and functional integration by plausibility checks. For example, recording procedures with integrated plausibility checks lead to time savings in error correction and hence simultaneously to the potential for personnel savings.

Given the grounds for interactive processing, business functions can be broken down into individual steps and checked as to their suitability for interactive processing. Figure 2.B.I.16 shows this for a part of a production planning and control system.

In the transfer to interactive processing it is also necessary to take into account whether the elements of a task are suited to the interaction. Both user and computer must be capable of reacting to the partner's results within a reasonable response time.

Goals \ Characteristics	Event–orientation (Currency)	Function integration (Plausibility)	Interacvtive decision–making	Avoidance of bottle–necks	Handling improve–ments	Qualitative improve–ments
Time savings	x	x	x	x	x	
Personnel savings		x		x	x	
Informational gains	x		x			x
Job satisfaction	x	x		x	x	x
Simplification of organizational procedures		x	x		x	

Fig. 2.B.I.15: Criteria and goals for interactive programming

Since the concept of up-to-dateness relates not only to data changes but also to the scheduling and execution of processes the tasks need to be analysed with regard to their suitability for interactive processing or batch-related evaluation. It is precisely this investigation that is linked with the development of new planning concepts for operational function areas.

The development of interactive decision systems is already well advanced (see *Meffert, EDV im Marketing 1980, p. 52 ff.; Dinkelbach, Entscheidungsmodelle 1982, p. 200 ff.*). Nevertheless, the incorporation of computationally efficient algorithms in the interactive environment remains an area with a lot of scope for many issues in business economics.

Trigger concepts handle the control between batch and interactive environments and especially between diverse forms of interactive processing (see Figure 2.B.I.04 above). These are to some extent already implemented in database systems. Establishing the parameter list for the trigger level monitor requires knowledge of the business content. For example, in the financial accounting system it can make sense to update the VAT account only on a daily basis, while managing the open items in accounts receivable interactively, since these are continually being used for decision-making in the credit investigation context.

Tasks	Sub-tasks	Grounds for interactive processing			
		Event-based (Currency)	Function-integration (Plausibility)	Iterative modification	Interactive decision process
Primary data management	Creation of BOMs			x	
	BOM breakdown	(x)			
	Creation of work schedules			x	
Master production scheduling	Forecasting				x
	Program planning				x
Material requirement planning	Requirement breakdown	(x)			
	Determination of lot sizes				x
Capacity planning	Process scheduling	(x)			
	Capacity overview	(x)			
	Load leveling				x
Detailed scheduling	Availability check		x		
	Sequencing				x
	Progress control	x			
Purchase planning	Material planning	(x)			
	Lot sizes				x
Order scheduling	Enquiries	x			
	Order acceptance		x	x	
	Reservation (Allocation)				x
Purchasing	Purchase ordering				x
	Receipt of goods checking		x		
Storage	Additions		x		
	Withdrawals		x		

x = applies
(x) = applies within limits

Fig. 2.B.I.16: Interactive applications for production planning and control systems

In the interactive processing context the concept of the **transaction** is of great importance. It refers to the sequence of operational steps (in interactive programming) which, when effected, transform the database from one consistent state to another. The database is inconsistent, for example, when in the course of a bookkeeping procedure the debit entry has been made but the credit entry has not. Hence, a transaction is the smallest unit which must be either carried out in full or not at all in order to ensure that elementary consistency requirements on the database are fulfilled. The definition of transactions as self-contained procedures can therefore not be carried out without the relevant business understanding.

In designing an interactive system close cooperation between the users and the system developers is essential. This applies both to the logic of the interactive process and to the design of the screen forms.

The cooperation between the specialist business department and the system developer demands a unified description language. In particular, the sequence of screen forms (terminal states) needs to be agreed with the user. Here, **interaction diagrams** can be used, whose graphical representational form has the advantages of being largely self-explanatory and being applicable at various levels of the design hierarchy (see *Budde, Schnupp, Schwald, Software-Produktion 1980, p. 109 ff.*).

Figure 2.B.I.17 shows the interactive process for handling an order at the highest hierarchy level. The start and end of the interaction are indicated by triangles. A circle represents the state in which an EDP process is awaiting the response of an interactive partner. Interactive partners in the process might be, in addition to the terminal (and hence the user), a database or a peripheral device such as a printer. Complex functions in which further interactions may arise are shown within double lines.

In Figure 2.B.I.17 the EDP process first prepares the screen form with the basic menu and displays it at the terminal. Then the process waits for a response from the terminal, i.e. entry of the identification of the desired function. When the function is completed the screen form is displayed once more, and on entry of the end identification the interaction is terminated.

Figure 2.B.I.18 represents the interactive process for order recording in greater detail. The database and printer are introduced as further interactive partners in the EDP process. Each box represents one step in the application program which is interrupted to await responses from the terminal, database and printer. When the customer number is entered the program prepares for database access to the customer record. The process then awaits response from the database, indicated by the circle with DB. If the customer number does not exist an error message is prepared and the terminal returns to the initial screen form. Otherwise the customer data is taken from the customer record and displayed at the terminal. The process then awaits entry of the article number. Thereafter, the process accesses the article file, and after a successful search the article data are displayed at the terminal. On entry of the order quantity the article line of the order confirmation is prepared complete with price. When all article items have been processed the order confirmation is printed.

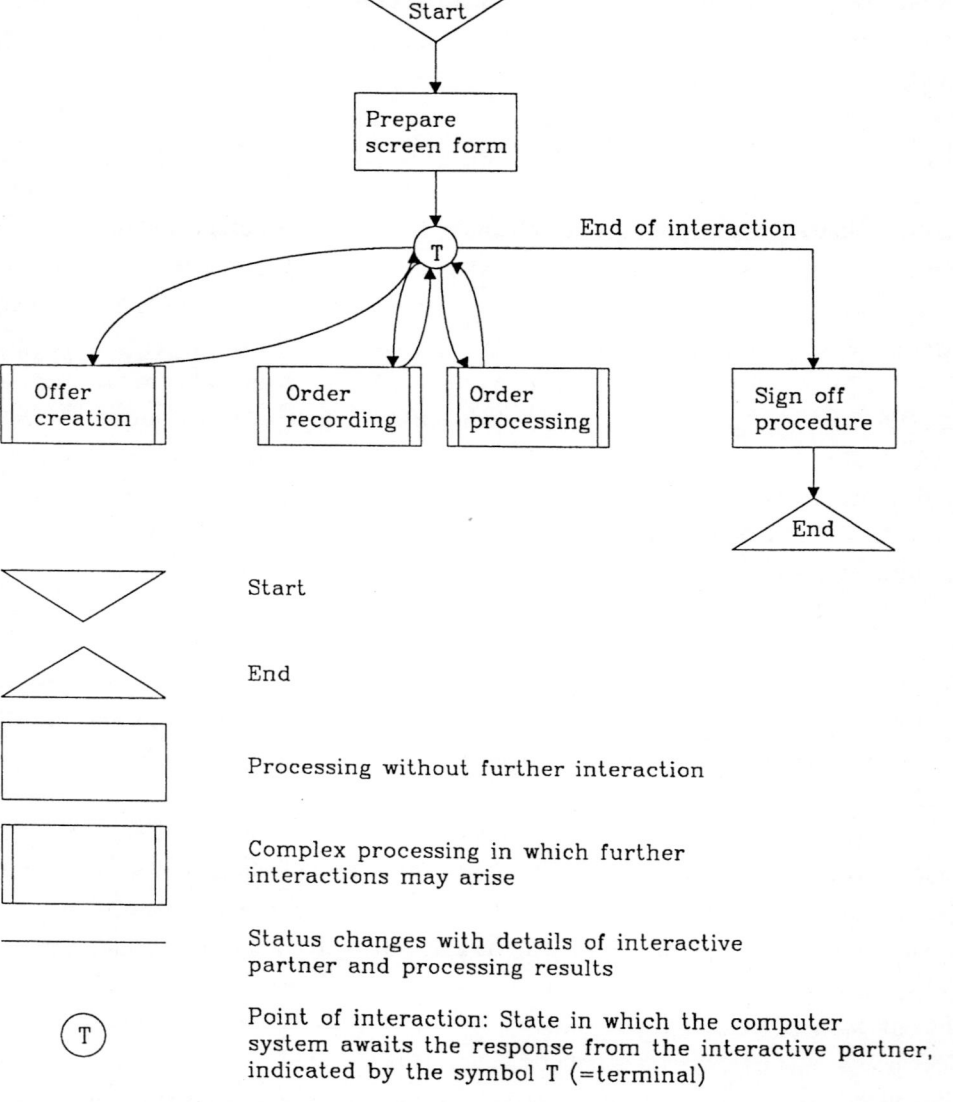

Fig. 2.B.I.17: Interaction diagram (outline) for order processing and elucidation of symbols

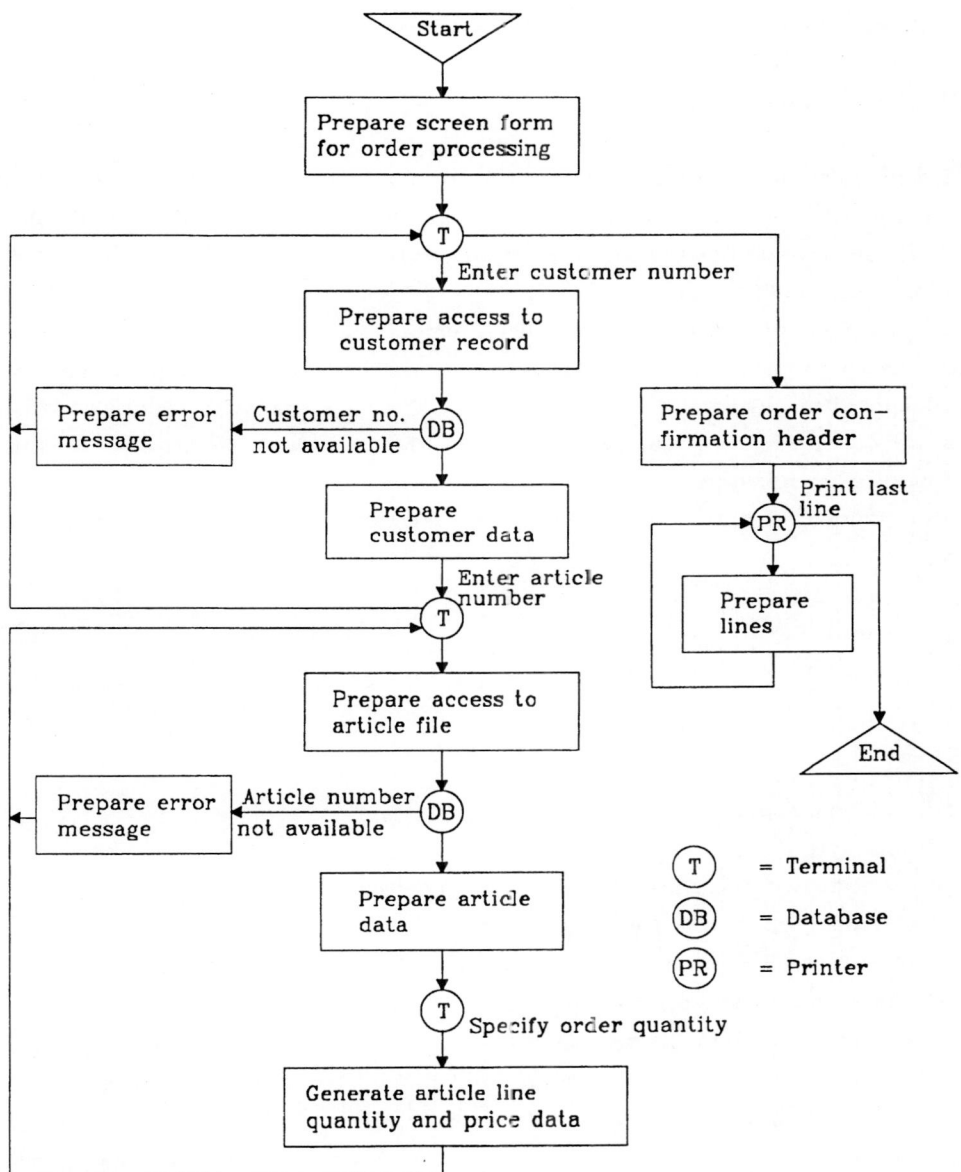

Fig. 2.B.I.18: Interaction diagram (detailed) for order processing

B.II. Spatial Control: Networking of EDP Systems

B.II.1. Description of Networks

If computers are linked together such that data can be exchanged between them this is referred to as a **computer network**. Where the physical distances are greater the public network services of the German Bundespost (HfD = Hauptanschluß für Direktruf, DATEX-L, DATEX-P) are used.

Since computers process digital information, whereas many public networks can handle only analog signals, the signals need to be transformed using a **modem** (modulator/demodulator) (see Figure 2.B.II.01). The data transfer is controlled by a special **communication sub-system (CSS)**. The **front-end processors** of this communication sub-system control the transfer of data to and from the public network, assign priorities, make decisions concerning alternative routes, encode and decode messages.

Fig. 2.B.II.01: Computer links

Computers are linked together (see *Schnupp, Rechnernetze 1982, p. 17*) in order to

- even out capacity peaks (**capacity network**),
- make special hardware available in several places without it needing to be physically located there (**equipment network**),
- make data stored in diverse locations available to other locations (**data network**),
- coordinate several sub-tasks assigned to individual computers into a single overall task (**intelligence network**),
- provide postal-type services for communication between physically distant human users (electronic mail, electronic conferencing) via computer systems (**communication network**).

Of these network forms, data networks, intelligence networks (often linked with equipment networks) and communication networks are of the greatest business significance, whereby in specific applications several network forms are generally implemented together.

B.II.1.1. Types of Network

Networks can be distinguished according to their
- topology,
- transfer medium and
- transfer protocol (network access rules).

As regards the **topology** of computer network systems four possibilities can be distinguished (see Fig. 2.B.II.02).

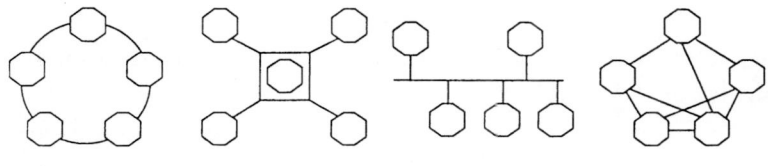

Ring network   Star network   Bus structure   Direct−link network

Fig. 2.B.II.02: Computer network topologies

In a **ring network** all nodes have equal status, i.e. the network can be controlled by any node. Each station is "active", since a message is checked by each station on its route, to determine whether the message is to be received there or merely passed on. If one station is down the entire network is interrupted. On the other hand, this topology leads to low cabling costs. It is therefore also used for PC networks.

In a **star network** there is an unambiguous hierarchy, whereby network control is effected by the central node. This topology is typical of terminal networks in which many terminals are linked by a HOST computer. If one terminal is down this has no effect on the other stations, but if the host computer is down the entire network fails. It is sometimes claimed that a star network is particularly suitable for business organizations, since it reflects the typical hierarchical organizational structure. Organizational theory, however, stresses the independence of information system and enterprise structure (see *Hedberg et al., Organizational Power Structures 1975, p. 131 ff.; Millington, Systems Analysis 1981, p. 84*).

A **bus** is capable of transporting large quantities of data on a bus cable. The stations, however, have no control functions, they are merely "passive". As a result, if one station is down this has no effect on the others.

This topology has become particularly predominant for **LANs (Local Area Networks)**. LANs are networks with a very high throughput rate, to which the most diverse hardware systems, from diverse producers, with diverse interfaces (terminals, printers, microprocessors, plotters and mainframe computers) can be connected. They are restricted to some limited physical space, e.g. a building. They have the advantage that, for networks of this type, the monopoly restrictions of the Bundespost for network and transfer structures do not need to be adhered to.

LANs are of particular importance in connection with office automation, since within spatially limited organizations text processing, data processing, graphical output and word processing can be linked with each other.

In a **network with direct links** there may be a control center, but the network links need not necessarily run via this center.

The reason for installing a network with direct links, and hence with redundant data paths, is greater protection against breakdown. A star network, for instance, has only one path between two points, a ring network has two, a network with direct links has several paths, so that if one route is down there is a variety of alternatives.

As regards the **transfer media**, a distinction is drawn in networks between broadband and baseband cables. A **broadband cable** has a high throughput capacity. The frequency range can be subdivided into various areas (channels), each of which handle separate links. Broadband cable is suitable for high transfer speeds (48,000 baud; baud = bit per sec.) and is implemented in new technology with glass fibres.

Baseband cable is currently used principally for telephone links. It has a transfer rate of 4,800 or 9,600 baud and is therefore suitable for moderate data transfer requirements.

For network accessing (especially for LANs) two transfer protocols, CSMA/CD (Carrier Sense Multiple Access with Collision Detection) and token passing, are of particular significance.

In **CSMA/CD** a station "listens in" to the network to see if it is free for a transfer, i.e. whether any other message is currently being handled. If the network is free the station then transmits. This can give rise to "collisions" if another station transmits at the same moment. In this case a random algorithm determines the network access sequence. This accessing principle is implemented in the ETHERNET network system developed by XEROX, and has also been adopted by other suppliers such as DEC (DECNET).

In the **token passing** principle a bit pattern (token) wanders around the network. A station wishing to transmit waits for a free token and then attaches the message to be sent to it. The receiving station removes the message and the token is then free again.

Since this principle implies that a message can only be sent when the network is free there is no danger of collision. The token passing procedure is available particularly for PC networks in token ring form.

In a modern EDP system diverse network topologies can be implemented in accordance with differing requirements as is shown in Figure 2.B.II.03.
Financial accounting is linked to the HOST computer in a star network of "dummy" terminals for a central bookkeeping program.

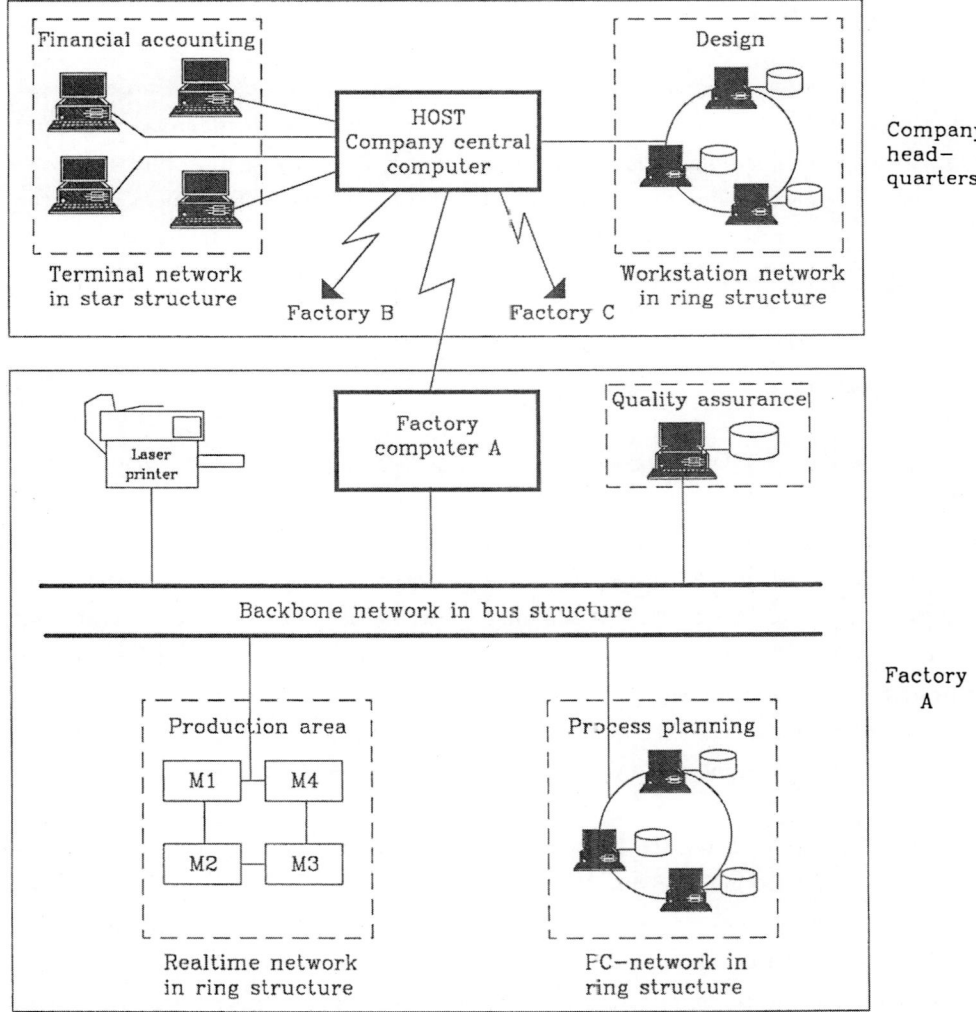

Fig. 2.B.II.03: Computer network for an enterprise

Design handles its CAD applications on workstations which are linked together in a ring network.

The factory computers are linked with the central computer in a star network.

A bus network forms the backbone of the aggregate information flow within the factory, since large quantities of data have to be handled.

The PC in quality control is a direct participant in the bus network.

For production areas with critical applications realtime networks with a ring structure are set up, which allow particularly speedy data transfer. The PCs in process planning are linked together in a PC ring network with a relatively low transfer rate which is linked to the bus network.

Computer networks can nowadays be of global proportions and can link an enterprise with branches, customers and suppliers. However, despite all the standardization efforts, there are still considerable compatibility problems in linking diverse hardware. For global communication links satellite networks, which support services such as tele-conferencing and video-conferencing, are increasing in importance (see Chapter 3, Section C.V. on office automation).

B.II.1.2. Distributed Data Processing

The term **distributed data processing** refers to the EDP-technical possibility of breaking down a logically integrated task into sub-tasks and distributing them within a computer network to several computers. Similarly, **distributed database** refers to the possibility of distributing a logically integrated database between several storage locations. Both processing forms are closely related. Although they have been discussed for several years, at first euphorically, and then, recognizing the considerable technical difficulties, more cautiously, the comprehensive implementation of these kinds of systems can be expected in the near future. A detailed summary of the requirements on a distributed database is given by Date, for example (see *Date, Database Systems 1983*).

Figure 2.B.II.04 represents the principle of a distributed database. The sub-databases DB_A, DB_B and DB_C are stored at their respective locations. However, they constitute a logical entity, that is, the user working at a display in any of the locations can access the combination of these data sets from these three databases without knowing at which location they are to be found. Reasons for assigning data to a specific storage location arise from the optimization between storage space and data transfer costs, and the fulfilling of conditions relating to response time and network security. For this reason, redundant data storage within a computer network is also sometimes desirable.

For example, in an industrial firm it may be advisable to store all customer data and customer orders in the head office computer, at the same time holding subsets of the customer order data decentrally in the computers of the individual production plants. It should also be possible for the head office to obtain information relating to the production status of customer orders by accessing the current decentralized data records.

The ability of one computer to access another depends on whether the computers use the same transfer protocol and the same operating system, or whether the computers to be linked are heterogeneous, e.g. from different manufacturers.

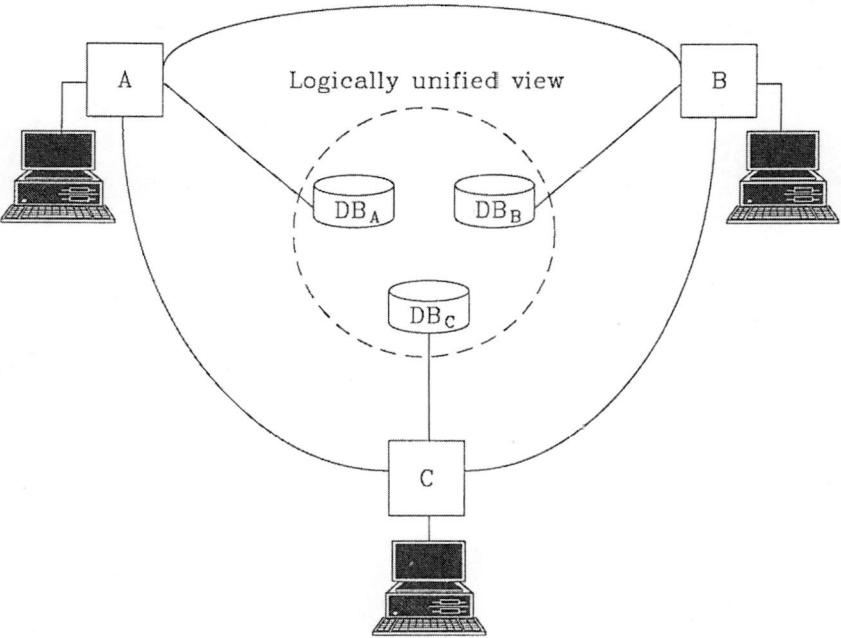

Fig. 2.B.II.04: Distributed database

A computer network form that is already widely implemented is file transfer. This makes it possible to transfer an entire file from one computer to another. Direct access from an application program on one computer to an application program on the other computer is not possible, however. This kind of **inter-application link** is necessary, though, if one program needs to start up an application program on the other computer, whose results need to be further processed by the application in the first program. For example, if order processing is being handled on computer A and the order of a customer whose data are stored on computer B needs to be processed, the program could interrupt the customer processing on computer A and send a message to computer B. Here investigation of the credit standing of the customer in question is initiated and the results are sent back to computer A, which can then resume the interrupted processing of the relevant customer order. All these steps should occur at the transaction level, that is interactively, without the user being aware of, or having to control, the underlying data transfer process.

This approach can also be applied to decentralized stores. A transaction is initiated on computer A to check whether there are stocks on hand of a given article in response to a customer query. If sufficient stocks are available in the database of computer A, an appropriate message is sent and the transaction is terminated. If not, computer A automatically generates a new transaction, which transfers the original query to computer B. The same process can then be carried out in the storage information system there as in computer A. In such a multi-level transaction processing system a query can pass through a maximum of as many computers as are linked together in the network.

Figure 2.B.II.05 represents an inter-application link. The user at the terminal at location A communicates only with his processing program PP and his commands to the database management system DBMS$_A$ and can thereby access the computer at location B, even though its database might be managed by another (different) database management system DBMS$_B$. All the necessary code and command translations are undertaken by the communication sub-system.

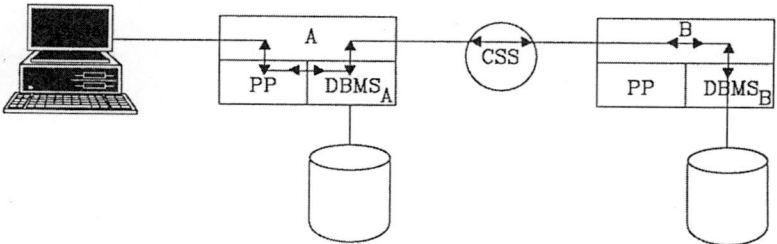

Fig. 2.B.II.05: Inter-application links between computers

B.II.1.3. Bildschirmtext as Open Network

The Deutsche Bundespost's Btx system (Btx = Bildschirmtext = Videotex) is also a computer network (see Figure 2.B.II.06).

It provides EDP services not only to commercial EDP users, but also to private households. It became obvious very soon after the introduction of Btx in 1984, however, that its use in the private sphere would not become widespread in the short term, as a result of acceptance problems in the household.

But given the level of standardization it has achieved and its easy accessibility Btx is of great significance for business applications of trading users and suppliers.

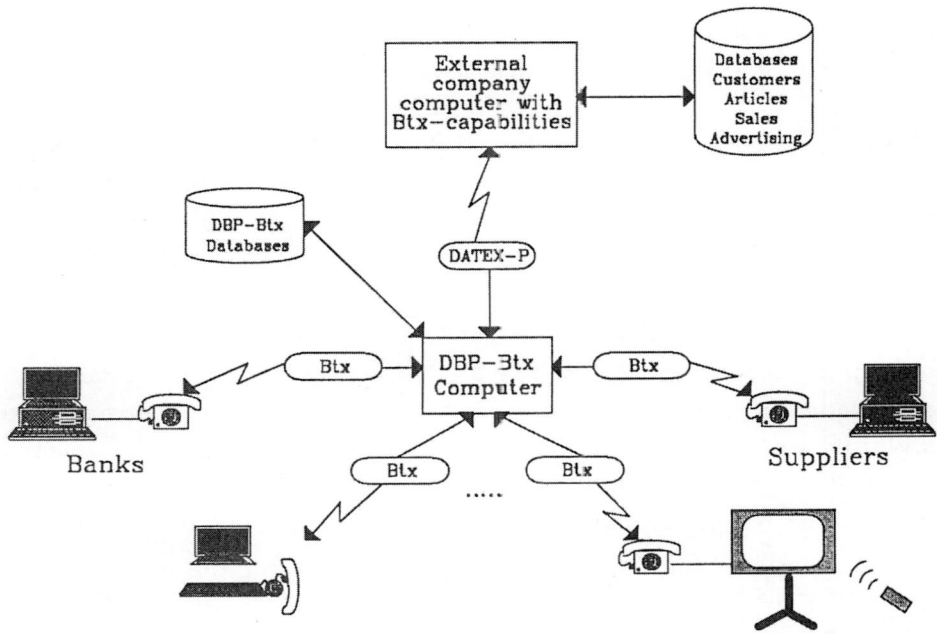

Fig. 2.B.II.06: Btx Network

A prerequisite for using Btx is data terminal equipment capable of handling Btx as well as a keyboard, telephone connection and a modem. It is the task of the **modem** to convert the digital signals from the data terminal equipment into analog signals for the telephone network. The Btx network distinguishes between connections to Btx users and Btx suppliers. For users the necessary data terminal equipment can consist in the simplest case (private households) of a television and an integrated decoder. In every Btx terminal the **decoder** has the task of transforming the signals received into Btx format (generally 24 lines * 40 characters/line) and presenting them on the screen.

In professional use the participating station consists of either **Btx terminals**, **microcomputers** with hardware and software decoders, or **screen telephones**. The latter consist of user-friendly handsets with Btx components such as a decoder, small screen and keyboard.

Btx supplier connections also have the possibility of creating Btx pages (editor devices) which can be entered into the Btx mail system. The Btx pages in the mail system contain information available to all Btx participants. One supplier connection variant is the Btx computer network.

This enables suppliers of information to link up an EDP installation with Btx capabilities (external computer) via Datex-P to the Btx network. The considerable degree of standardization of the Btx network is hereby of significance. Btx is an **open network** as defined in the recommendations of the CCITT (Commission Consultatif Internationale de Télégraphie et Télécommunication), which enables access by any hardware from diverse manufacturers.

Particularly suitable applications within the computer network are spare part ordering systems in the automobile industry, e.g. as used by BMW AG (see *Vorteile im Wettbewerb 1987*) or in the electronics industry.

In addition to ordering systems for industry, retail ordering systems are also widespread. The fresh produce ordering system used by the REWE retailing group has been in use successfully for years (see *Seibt, Btx im geschäftlichen Bereich 1986*). This makes it possible for individual retailers in the REWE group to place orders for their daily fresh produce requirements in the greengrocery line via Btx to a central order point. The delivery of the fresh produce can then be effected before opening hours. An advantage of the use of Btx in the retail industry is that Btx orders can be placed outside opening hours, and hence employees are freed from these administrative tasks during opening hours.

Other widespread applications are transport planning systems or agent control systems (insurance). For example, from a hotel room equipped with a Btx device, a representative can call up his firm's external computer via the Deutsche Bundespost's exchange computer, access the order processing program, and enter those orders taken during the day. The order processing program checks the plausibility of the data and draws the representative's attention to erroneous entries, logical inconsistencies or unavailability of the desired goods. This program may be the same one used for order acceptance within the firm, although its user interface must be amended. On completion of order entry the representative receives information concerning the customers he is to visit the following day.

The basic point is that Btx is of considerable benefit wherever distances needs to be bridged expediently. This is particularly the case for affiliated or cooperating firms (see *Leismann, WWS mit Btx 1990*).

However, Btx is not well-suited to data transfer functions for larger volumes of data, since the transmission speed of 1200 bit/sec. leads to considerable transfer times. However, this will be improved considerably by the fast communication lines being generated by the use of ISDN.

In addition to the examples already mentioned from the industrial, retailing, and service sectors, Btx has also given rise to new applications in the banking sector. The new services providing payment transactions for commercial users, home banking for private customers and cash management systems should be mentioned. Finally, Btx-supported access to retrieval systems is also an important application aspect. Since the Btx system can be linked via gateways with other international computer networks (especially other Videotex systems abroad) the user has almost unlimited informational possibilities from a multiplicity of databases at his disposal.

B.II.2. Business Economics Implementation of Networks

Organizational theory recognized the significance of the EDP systems networking possibilities for organizational adjustments at an early stage.

At first this development was discussed with respect to the possible advantages of decentralized or centralized use of EDP systems (see *Grochla, Zentralisationswirkungen 1969; Grochla, Organisationstheoretische Ansätze 1978; Grochla, Dezentralisierungs-Tendenzen 1976; Grochla, Konsequenzen 1982; Poensgen, Zentralisation und Dezentralisation 1967*). The starting point here is the realization that, in the question of organizational centralization, not only issues of tasks, objects, space, time and persons are decisive, but also the formation of units of action according to their content, in this case the EDP system.

However, this investigation was merely concerned with how the information system itself could be organizationally distributed considering technological developments, especially networking and the appearance of mini- and microcomputers. Data processing tasks are broken down into data recording, data transformation, data output and data storage. The result of this appraisal is that the first three functions tend in the direction of decentralization, whereas for data storage there is still a tendency towards centralization (as in large systems) (see *Grochla, Dezentralisierungs-Tendenzen 1976, p. 516*). The possibility of altering the entire organizational structure by the adoption of information techniques has been mentioned, but not considered further (see *Grochla, Dezentralisierungs-Tendenzen 1976, p. 511; Grossenbacher, Verteilung der EDV 1985, p. 9 f; Emery, Integrated Information Systems 1975 p. 95 ff.*).

The concept of the integration effects of communication techniques which is occasionally used is also usually interpreted as the integration of various information techniques into a complete system (e.g. a data and text processing system), but not the integration effects on businesses processes.

When EDP systems started to be introduced the organizational literature derived a trend towards centralization from the fact that all data are stored in a central EDP system, and therefore, decisions should also be taken in the vicinity of this system (see *Lucas, Information Systems 1981, p. 55 f.*). However, with distributed data processing it is possible to access all enterprise data from decentralized locations, so that this general tendency cannot be upheld.

Another approach within organizational theory investigates empirically the effects of the new communication technology on human communication forms. In the empirical project undertaken by Reichwald and Picot (see *Picot, Reichwald, Kommunikationstechnologien 1978; Reichwald, Bürotechnik 1982; Schellhaas, Schönecker, Kommunikationstechnik 1983*) only the tools of Telefax and Teletex were examined, more recent tools - such as Videotex, computer networks, etc. - which allow more powerful EDP use, were not included. The result of these investigations was that the communication forms via Telefax and Teletex are suitable for only a fraction of the contact possibilities between managers, and therefore, face-to-face communication remains necessary for a large proportion of contacts.

In addition, an empirical investigation was undertaken to determine the extent to which the communication possibilities of computer network systems might generate new forms of work organization. This is concerned with the possibilities of working at home, whereby specialist activities can be carried out at home or at offices in the immediate neighbourhood by using a computer system network (see *Olson, Remote Office Work 1983*). The prerequisites for this kind of use are based on the employee, the firm, and the kind of tasks available. The employee must possess considerable self-motivation and self-discipline. The firm must be able to monitor the work performed on the basis of results. Suitable tasks are characterized by low communication requirements, low resource requirements and clear demarcation (see also *Heilmann, Heilmann, Telearbeitsplatz 1983; Korte, Robinson, Telearbeit 1988; Lenk, Telearbeit 1989*).

The contributions from organizational theory that have been cited have a common concern with the effects of computer networks but leave the business procedures and decision processes largely unchanged. No suggestions are made concerning the structuring of business processes and the handling of problems based on the possibilities of computer networking. Elucidating these possibilities is the task of EDP-oriented business economics as it is interpreted here. Consequently, the following treatment will consider three possibilities for structural alteration of the issues in business economics by the use of computer network systems.

These are:

- redistribution of decision-making power,
- unification of business procedures between business associates,
- redistribution of functions between firms via inter-company process chains.

B.II.2.1 Redistribution of Decision-Making Power

One reason for decentralization of the enterprise given in the organizational literature is the limited ability of top management to absorb and process information (see *Poensgen, Zentralisation und Dezentralisation 1967, p. 377*).

The extension of information processing capabilities at headquarters by computer network links relaxes this limitation. As a result, the business advantages resulting from centralization can again be exploited more extensively.

On the other hand the headquarter's ability to make up-to-date inspections of the data records and processes of decentralized units via computer network allows greater functional delegation, since headquarters can more easily make coordinating and monitoring interventions.

In this way the introduction of computer networks increases the degrees of freedom in how the organization is structured, and increases the urgency of a new and differentiated assignment of decision-making responsibilities within the organizational structure of an enterprise.

The following discussion uses several examples to illustrate the possibilities for a redistribution of decision-making responsibilities and their consequences for business economics.

Computer network systems make it possible to communicate stock levels and sales data from decentralized branches to the retail organization headquarters on an up-to-date basis. The headquarters can then place orders and make purchases for the branch or affiliated outlets. This has the advantage that larger order quantities can be achieved, and more sophisticated economic techniques can be used for making sales forecasts and determining order quantities. Such procedures demand a higher level of business economic competence, which is not usually available at the decentralized branch level.

This means that economic modelling and techniques can achieve more widespread application than previously. At the same time, however, they need to be modified so that they also apply to the distribution between different locations within such a planning system. These developments are of particular importance in connection with retail information and control systems (RICS) (see Chapter 3, Section B.II.).

Within a hierarchical retail information and control system articles can be handled in differing ways, i.e., depending on their importance or on characteristics such as perishibility the requirements for specific goods can be determined either centrally or decentrally. Figure 2.B.II.07 indicates the distribution of material planning functions

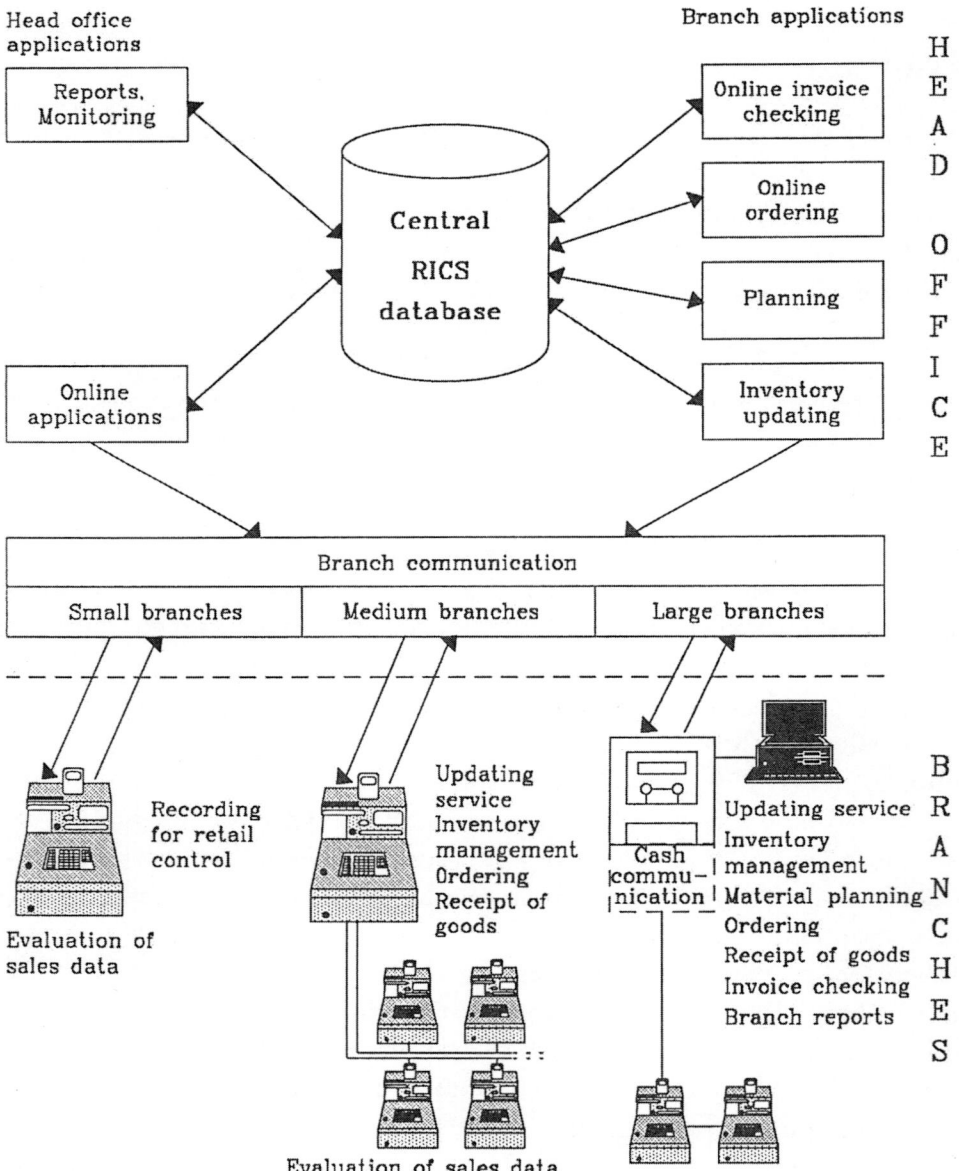

Fig. 2.B.II.07: Assignment of tasks between head office and branches in a retail information and control system (RICS)

within a retail information and control system between branches of various sizes. Small branches are largely controlled by headquarters (push system). The branch merely records sales data and transfers them to headquarters for evaluation; stock records, etc, are managed by headquarters alone.

In medium-sized branches parts of the range are planned at the branch level.

In larger branches the material planning functions at branch level can be further extended.

Delimitation problems demand appropriate economic problem-solving approaches. Similar considerations also apply in the area of physical stock-keeping. Using networks requirements can be communicated from subsidiary locations to higher-level areas of the enterprise, so that supplies from a centralized warehouse can be effected expediently. Such a system makes it possible to hold the planned inventories at a relatively high level of the hierarchy, since here random variations in actual requirements tend to cancel each other out far more than at lower levels. In concrete terms this means that within a hierarchical storage system a given level of availability at lowest cost with safety stocks is achieved at the highest level of the hierarchy (see *Zacharias, Lagerverbundsysteme 1982, p. 17*). In practice this kind of development can be observed within the automobile retailing organization, for example. The supply of spare parts to Volkswagen AG retailers is largely carried out centrally (see *Seitz, Warenbewirtschaftung 1982*).

But the trend towards centralization of planning applies not only to physical goods, but also to capital stocks. For example, in larger enterprises the transfer of current bank balances and cash holdings from subsidiary to parent company allowed current capital planning, in which the interest savings covered the costs of the entire network (see *Schnupp, Rechnernetze 1982, p. 45*). Meanwhile even banks offer their customers the use of networks to consolidate their separate accounts. This generates the possibility of central and up-to-date cash management.

Support for the optimal determination of planning functions within a network and their integration into a decision system requires the development of hierarchical business economics modelling approaches. Such models are already partially developed for certain application areas, such as production program planning (see *Hax, Golovin, Hierarchical Production Planning 1978; Kistner, Switalski, Hierarchical Production Planning 1987*) even if they do not expressly incorporate the issues arising from computer network systems.

In an industrial enterprise with several production works sometimes producing the same products, the sales program and the rough production programs for the works need to be

96

established at the central level (see Figure 2.B.II.08). To do this sales forecasts, inventory levels, and the capacities of the works are needed as important and up-to-date information at the time of planning. If necessary this planning can also be undertaken with consolidated data, e.g. at the article group level (see *Wittemann, Produktionsplanung 1984*).

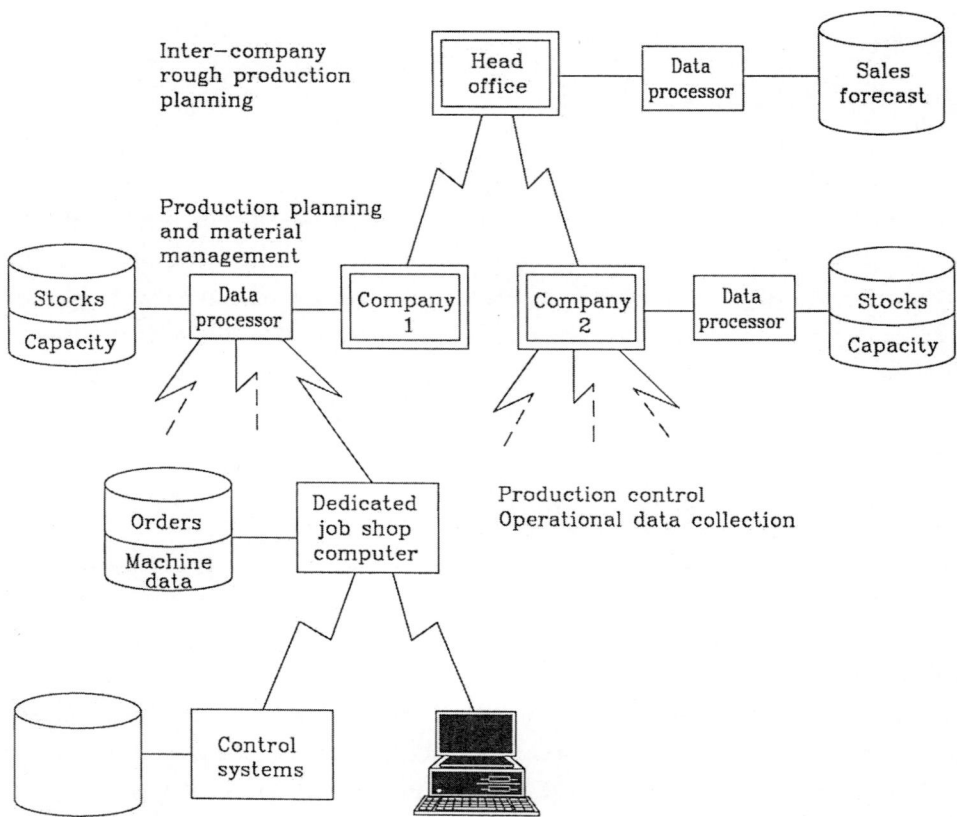

Fig. 2.B.II.08: Hierarchical production planning and control

The data resulting from the production program constitute the master production schedules for the works, where production planning, in the usual sense of the term, is now initiated, and breaks down the production program for end products to the assembly and material level and allows for more detailed time scheduling in capacity planning.

These planning steps then link up with production control and operational data collection at the job shop level. Further computer hierarchies and diverse functional allocations can then arise at this level.

An intelligent network of diverse computers may be desirable for the production planning and control functions, since special problems of up-to-date data recording arise in the production area which necessitate special hardware (process computers, automatic signals).

The type of functional assignment thereby determines the scope and required currency of the data exchange. Establishing the "natural" interfaces within a planning procedure, to provide the orientation for a hierarchical breakdown of data processing is, therefore, an important task for business economics (see *Scheer, CIM 1990 p. 126 ff.*).

B.II.2.2. Unification of Business Procedures in Associated Enterprises

Networking of EDP systems makes the direct transfer of business data between parent firm and subsidiary within a group possible. These data can then be immediately evaluated for the purposes of liquidity planning, cost comparison and consolidation of accounts. Direct evaluation of data combined from several sources requires a certain level of uniformity in the relevant EDP programs and databases. Even in groups where the subsidiaries constitute largely independent profit centers, the desire for overview evaluations based on networking possibilities therefore results in a trend towards uniform accounting procedures with the demand for correspondingly uniform hardware and software implementations (see *Prüsmann, Standardsoftware 1983*).
Only in this way it is possible to prepare and directly process data in the subsidiary in a uniform manner and on an up-to-date basis. It is thereby also easier for the head office to access the subsidiaries' data records.
The use of uniform EDP systems has the added advantage of involving lower development costs.
Since networking possibilities cause the EDP systems of different firms to move closer together at the informational level, the disadvantages of completely decentralized organizational forms, such as duplication of tasks, multiple development efforts, different standards of applications, diverse hardware and software systems, suddenly become more obvious. Networking, therefore, forces a more uniform hardware and software concept. Many groups, therefore, opt for the general use of some specific standard software.
The tendency towards decentralized data processing to take advantage of microcomputers therefore needs to be extended to take account of the demand for centralization of the development and design of EDP systems. In particular, the structure of the network itself demands a central development concept.

This kind of central responsibility for information processing also needs to be anchored in the organizational structure of the corporation.

Figure 2.B.II.09 presents a suggestion for the organizational embedding of information processing within the group. The holding company should devote at least one staff position to the coordination of basic decisions with respect to hardware and network configuration, database use and links with standard applications software. In each product area a management unit is responsible for the information systems. This unit has responsibility for all factories and branches within the product area, and is subdivided into "applications" and "systems" departments. The "systems" department makes all decisions relating to the structure of the network between factories and headquarters, hardware and system-related software. This is in accordance with the importance of this department derived above, and ensures that the subsequent organizational units fulfil the standardization requirements needed for the network structure.

Centralized applications development is also supported, whereby groups are formed to handle the individual specialist areas.

The programmers form a pool, and can be assigned to different projects as required.

The organization department supports and monitors the implementation of planned rationalizations, especially in the case of inter-departmental applications (process chains).

The user advice department is becoming increasingly important as a result of the growing number of individual computer users (personal computing); it also decides whether tasks should be handled centrally or decentrally in the specialist departments.

The computer center is located hierarchically one level below the applications and systems department.

The administration area carries out (central) purchasing and allocates EDP costs to the users in accordance with their utilization of benefits.

The organizational form developed emphasizes the importance of central applications and systems development. This provides support for the standardization of business procedures and reporting. Of course, EDP departments may be established in physically distant firms, but these are technically subordinate to the information systems area.

As far as business procedures are concerned, the demand for standardization of these procedures between enterprises means that the business solutions for cost accounting, production planning and control, order handling, etc., must be examined to ascertain the extent to which they are suitable for the size of firm or for particular production

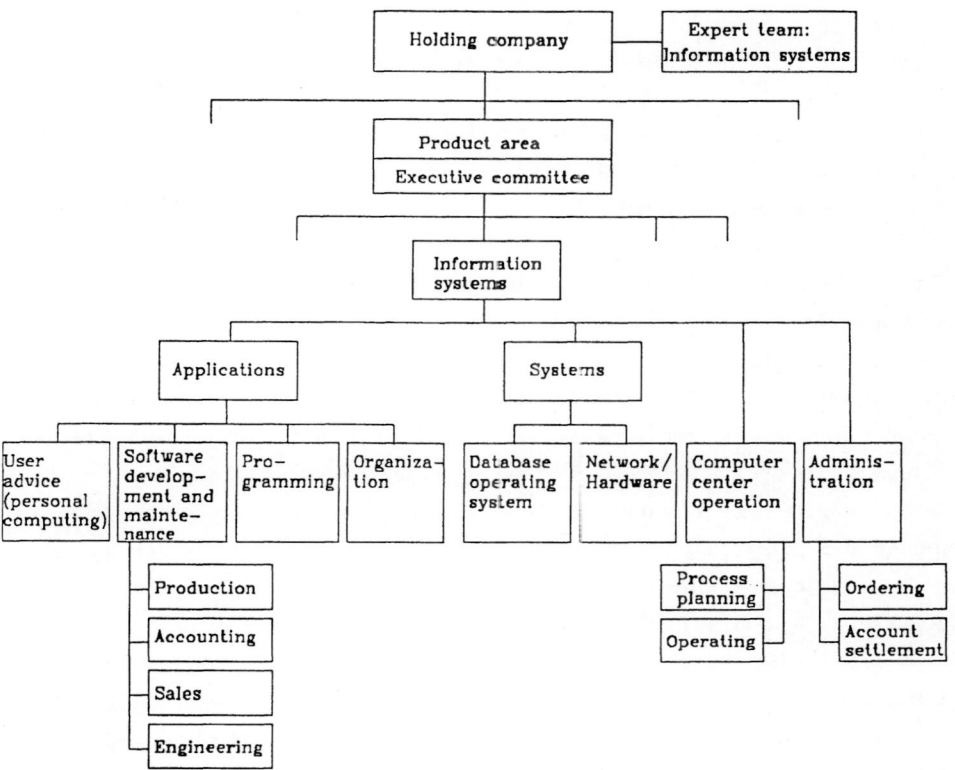

Fig. 2.B.II.09: Organizational breakdown of information processing

structures and sectors. The demand for standardization within a group can simply mean
the standardization of a nucleus of business applications, around which the affiliated
companies can build additional extensions which are tailored to their individual needs.

B.II.2.3. Inter-Company Redistribution of Functions Using Inter-Company Process Chains

Inter-company networking allows the integration of process chains beyond company
boundaries to include customers and suppliers.

This results in process rationalization and considerable redistribution of functions
between the partners. These are based on the same effects as were considered in the case
of internal process chains:

-       Data integration reduces redundant recording and storage procedures and speeds
        up processes by reducing transfer times.

Functional integration consolidates sub-functions into new sets of tasks and assigns them to new locations (in this case partners).

Figure 2.B.II.10 represents the steps in a logistic chain with the functional sequence: purchasing, order processing, production planning and control, dispatching, receipt of goods, invoicing and payment handling. A three level process between consumer, producer and supplier is considered.

A dot indicates which of the partners is primarily responsible for the execution of a processing step.

In the first instance it is assumed that all informational relationships between the business partners are executed on paper. It appears that the process chains between consumer and producer run in parallel, even though the consumer's decision whether to purchase a car (which is represented by the purchase planning process) is certainly different from the more formal procedure of purchase planning within an industrial firm.

Although the information flow is only represented in outline, five pieces of paperwork must be sent from customer to supplier and five from supplier to customer.

The physical dispatch of the products is also indicated.

The link between sales and purchasing logistics for the producer is represented as requirement planning, in which the need for in-house and bought-in parts is established and subsequently processed by purchasing. Using information technology the logistic chain can be considerably streamlined by the comprehensive data flow and the relocation or elimination of functions.

The new process chains are represented in Figure 2.B.II.11. Alterations are indicated by the relocation or elimination of the dots representing processing steps. The consumer's ability to access the manufacturer's data records, using Videotex for example, eliminates the need for postal handling of placing and processing of orders, since these can be carried out directly by the consumer. Ordering can also be handled using a mailbox system. As a result, the consumer assumes the order recording function, since the data are taken over directly by the manufacturer's system as soon as they have been electronically transmitted.

Between manufacturer and supplier a system analogous to the running total concept is assumed. This means that framework contracts have been agreed between manufacturer and supplier which are effected in current call-offs. The call-offs are made electronically.

Ordering and order processing are further integrated in that the customer (the consumer with respect to the manufacturer, or the manufacturer with respect to the supplier) can independently carry out availability checks and hence quantity and deadline planning. Since the orderer enters his order into the system himself, he can also generate

101

		Process	Retail customer	Manufacturer	Supplier

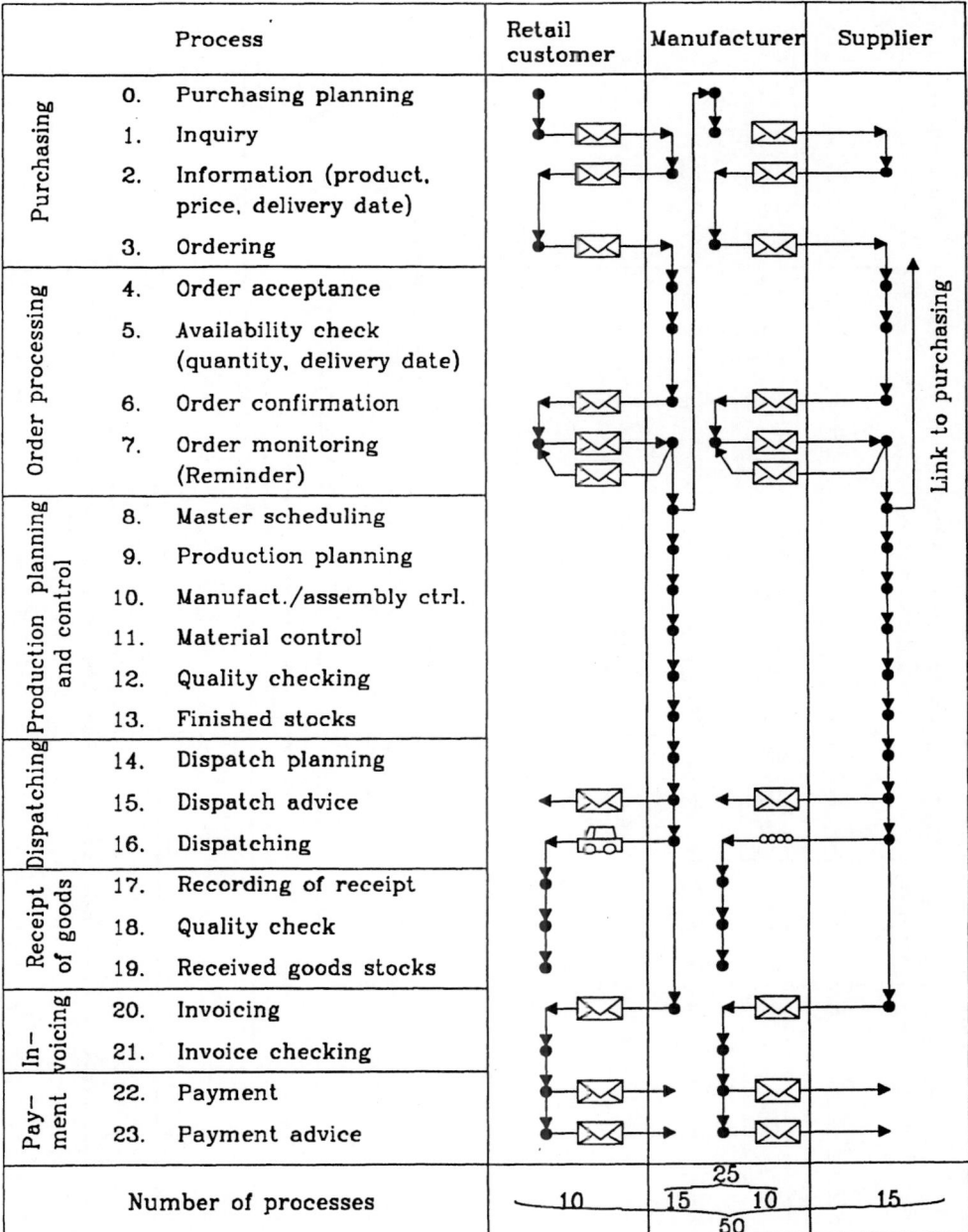

Fig. 2.B.II.10: Traditional execution of a process chain

102

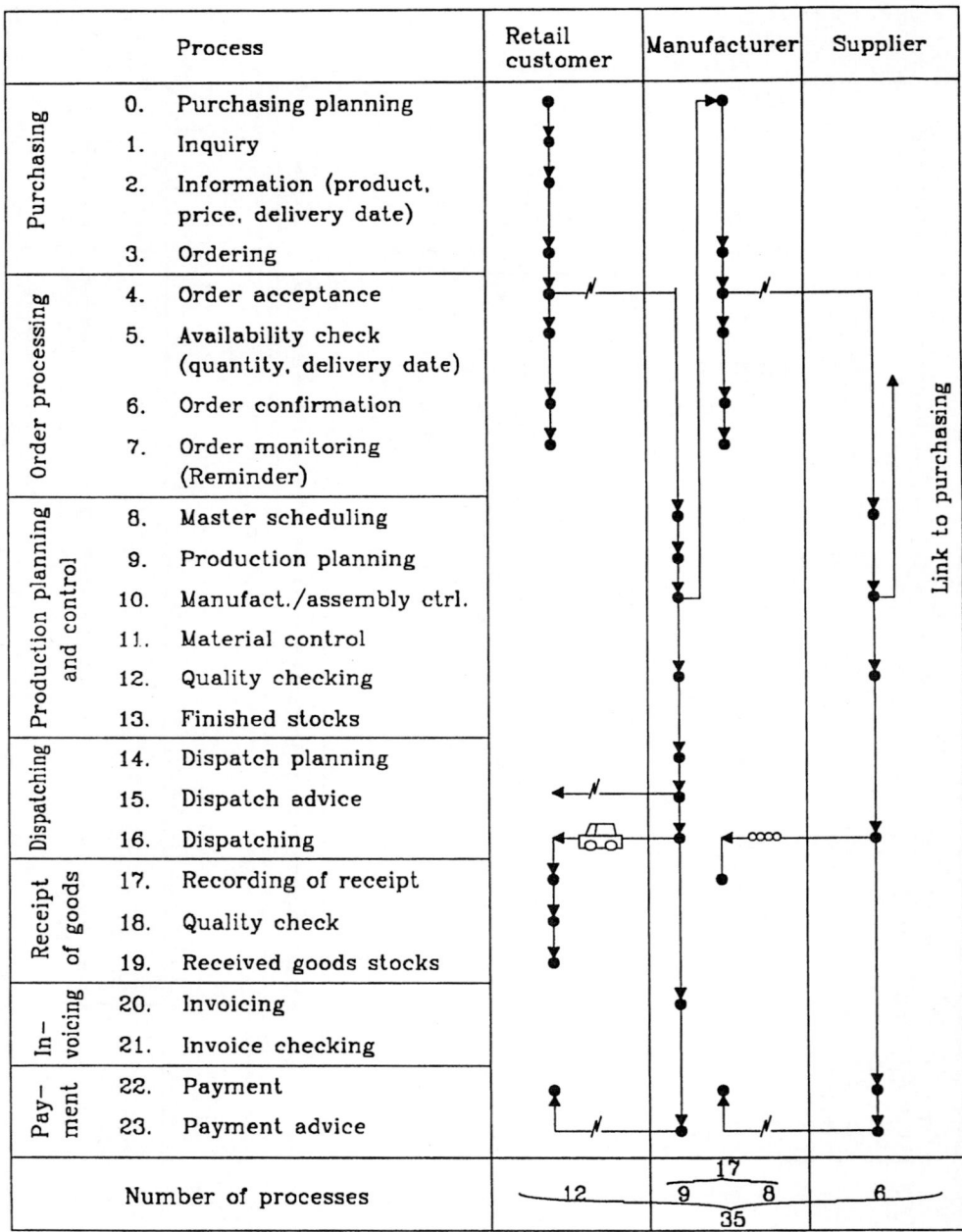

	Process	Retail customer	Manufacturer	Supplier
Purchasing	0. Purchasing planning			
	1. Inquiry			
	2. Information (product, price, delivery date)			
	3. Ordering			
Order processing	4. Order acceptance			
	5. Availability check (quantity, delivery date)			
	6. Order confirmation			
	7. Order monitoring (Reminder)			
Production planning and control	8. Master scheduling			
	9. Production planning			
	10. Manufact./assembly ctrl.			
	11. Material control			
	12. Quality checking			
	13. Finished stocks			
Dispatching	14. Dispatch planning			
	15. Dispatch advice			
	16. Dispatching			
Receipt of goods	17. Recording of receipt			
	18. Quality check			
	19. Received goods stocks			
In-voicing	20. Invoicing			
	21. Invoice checking			
Pay-ment	22. Payment			
	23. Payment advice			
Number of processes		12	9 8 (17 / 35)	6

Fig. 2.B.II.11: Reduction in data exchange and relocation of functions between partners

confirmation in accordance with his scheduling. Order monitoring can also be carried out by the purchaser right up to dispatch advice by accessing the production and dispatch planning data through specific queries.

The invoice no longer needs to be sent to the customer, instead he can effect payment himself by direct debiting via electronic clearing points linked to the banking sector.

In the logistic chain between manufacturer and supplier the links between purchasing and order processing also become closer. Here, too, the manufacturer can independently carry out availability checks and order monitoring by accessing the supplier's material planning programs.

In general, with increased information-technological interdependence, there is a tendency for functions which were previously carried out by the seller in the order processing context to be taken over by the buyer in the order planning context. This applies both between consumer and manufacturer and between manufacturer and supplier. In contrast functions in the receipt of goods area are taken over by the seller (for example: quality checks on receipt of goods are eliminated for the customer; to compensate the supplier's final inspection must be carried out more strictly.

To summarize the general effects of the increased interdependence:

- Information transfers on paper between the logistic partners are drastically reduced.
- As a result of the closer temporal linkages between the operative functions of production, assembly, ordering and delivery, planning functions between the sub-steps are eliminated.
- Reduced data entry reduces the need for monitoring procedures.
- Functions are relocated between the partners.

These effects are illustrated in the examples by the number of procedures to be handled: The number of procedures is reduced from 50 in Figure 2.B.II.10 to 35 in Figure 2.B.II.11.

Systems with a similar problem structure have in the meantime also begun to appear in the trading and service sectors. An example of an inter-company system that has already been implemented in practice is the computerized information and sales system AMADEUS (see *AMADEUS-Produktinformation 1988; Ischebeck, Betriebsübergreifende Informationssysteme 1989*), which is presented briefly below.

The aim of AMADEUS is to meet the growing demands of travellers, airlines and other suppliers of tourist services by providing impartial information. As is shown in Figure 2.B.II.12 the direct access technique makes it possible to access not only the most

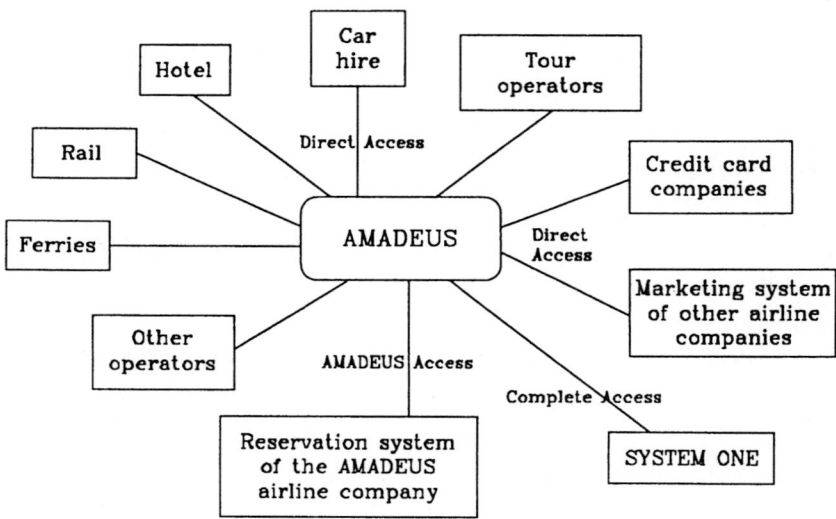

Fig. 2.B.II.12: AMADEUS access possibilities

important airline companies, but also hotels, car hire firms and tour operators. Queries to the supplier concerning current availability figures and other up-to-date information can be made directly from the system. Complete access is the method generated by direct computer links between AMADEUS and the American partner SYSTEM ONE. AMADEUS access offers the user intelligible access to the systems of the AMADEUS airline companies. This access mechanism makes it possible to obtain availability figures indicating the number of free seats on a given flight direct from the airline inventory system. As support and extension to the central AMADEUS services the decentralized information and sales system TAMS (Travel Agency Management System) is available to individual travel agencies. So-called "user-friendly functions" support both on-line procedures for reservation and sales operations (Front Office System = FOS) and, using individually implementable software tailored to the individual travel agency, the administrative tasks of the agency (Back Office System = BOS). The FOS functions consist primarily of customer profiles and order data recording with user-friendly entry formats. The BOS functions cover financial accounting for the travel agency, management and information systems for recording and monitoring budgets, the handling of mailing campaigns and the generation of financial and marketing statistics. With the help of the Travel Expense Management System (TEMS) each travel agency can carry out for its customers the production of travel expense accounts, monitoring of travel advances and budgets and the recording of direct and indirect travel costs.

The integration of inter-company process chains leads to new forms of cooperation. If functions are to be more strongly interdependent this requires closer partnership between customers and suppliers. This means that the negotiation of contracts concentrates more on the long term structure of the handling system than on individual business transactions, which are instead largely pre-defined by the framework contract. Given the costs involved this can lead to a pronounced concentration on a few business partners.

B.II.3. Business Structuring of EDP System Networks

B.II.3.1. Standardization of Business Applications Supporting Data Exchange

Data exchange between different partners presumes agreement on the syntax of the data transferred, such that they can be understood by the partners.

Even a simple business transaction, such as the reservation of a flight, or the handling of a trading operation, as represented in Figure 2.B.II.13, involves diverse partners such as industrial firms, trading companies, haulage contractors, public authorities, banks, insurance firms, transport companies, etc. This implies the exchange of a large number of diverse documents, such as offers, purchase orders, delivery notes, freight bills, bills of lading, customs declarations, etc. The heterogeneity is further increased by the fact that different partners can use different formats for the same document. For example, each firm has its own invoice or purchase order format.

The kinds of business transactions are multifarious and dependent on the industrial sector, for instance. In business transactions between banks, for example, monetary payments are predominant, whereas in trading firms it is the exchange of goods, and in industrial firms it is the handling of orders and the transfer of product information (CAD data) that need to be processed.

In transferring data the protocols of various networks need to be heeded. Here, too, there is great diversity resulting from the heterogeneity of different manufacturers' hardware and the network systems they offer.

Since this heterogeneity places strong limitations on data exchange, efforts are being made at all levels to ensure the standardization necessary for easier communication. This process calls upon business economics to analyse its concerns with respect to the necessary data requirements in order to provide a basis for a comprehensive standardization. This is possible for many operative procedures and their associated

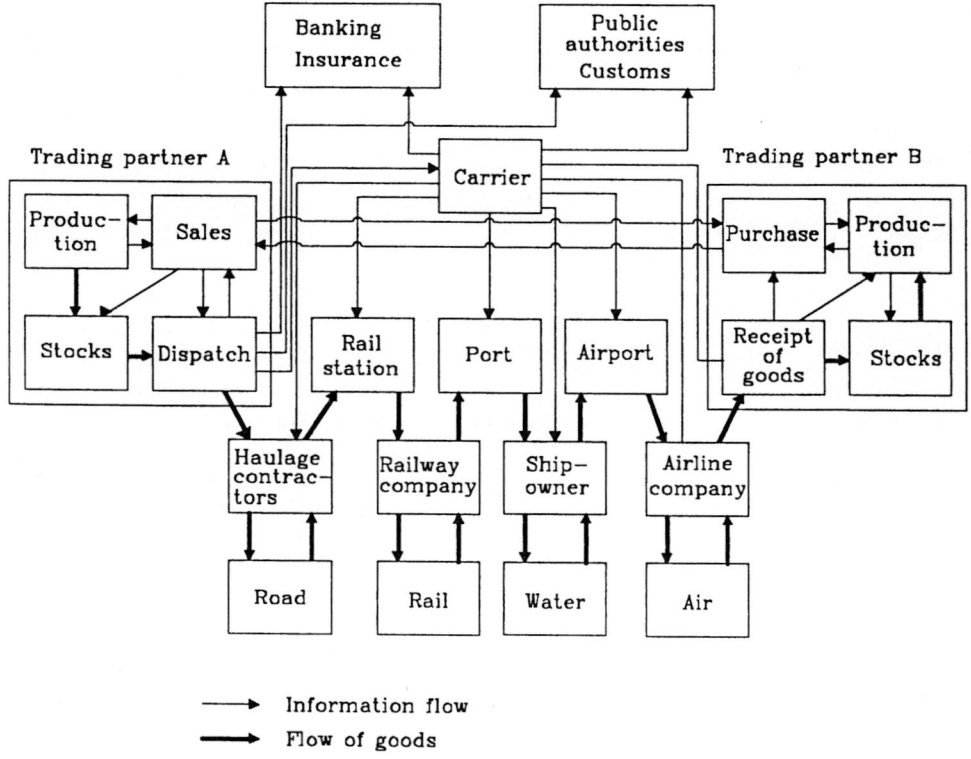

Fig. 2.B.II.13: Handling of a trading operation

(from *Buchmann, EDIFACT 1988, p. 2-20*)

documents. There are also considerable standardization possibilities for typical evaluative business tasks, such as financial accounting, given the legal or procedural rules. For example, financial accounting is clearly structured by the concepts of accounts, entry records and account assignment rules. It is actually surprising that, in spite of this, there exists a large number of EDP systems with differing data structures for this inherently standardizable function. From the data transfer viewpoint, therefore, the demand arises that the sender need only enter the processing location, the type of task and the business data required, without having to know anything about the EDP components hardware, operating system, application program, database system or the kind of transfer network. For an entry in the financial accounting system this means that it is only necessary to specify the entry location and the business data needed directly for the entry procedure, such as account, contra account, amount, date, and entry text.

Current standardization efforts are concerned on the one hand with the more technical issues of data transfer, but on the other with the standardization of content-bearing documents. Here, a trend can be observed from the initial sector-specific, national standardizations towards multi-sector, international agreements. Although in the development of standards for content-bearing documents typical business procedures such as order processing are being considered, the influence of university departments of business economics is still minimal. Instead, they are being developed by international standardization organizations with strong practical support (see *DIN, Schnittstellen 1989*).

For technical data transfer the **ISO/OSI Reference Model** constitutes a basis for the development of so-called open networks, in which diverse hardware and systems software can be linked together. This is effected via a system of protocols, to be adopted by hardware and software manufacturers.

The ISO/OSI Reference Model (see Figure 2.B.II.14) consists of seven layers. Both the sending and the receiving side of a link require these seven layers, and the same layers of the sending and receiving side communicate with each other. The sending station carries the data from top to bottom through the layers providing them with control information

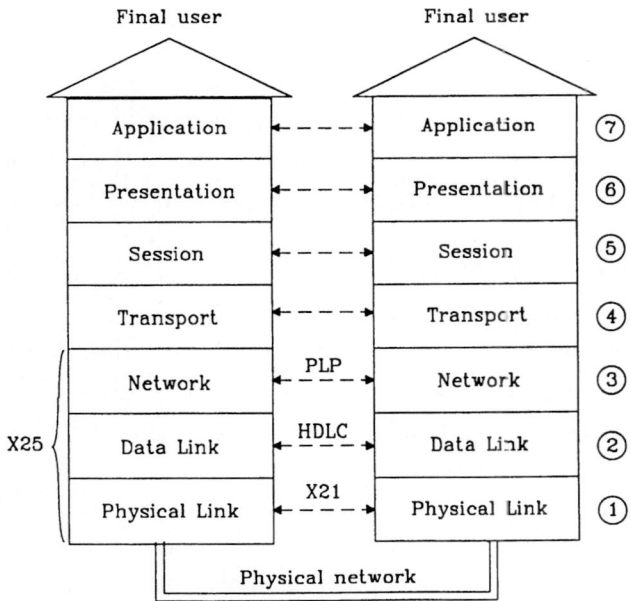

ISO   International Standards Organization
OSI   Open Systems Interconnection
PLP   Packet Level Protocol
HDLC Higher Level Data Link Control
X21 ⎫
X25 ⎭ Protocol references from CCITT

Fig. 2.B.II.14: The ISO/OSI Reference Model

and then proceed on the receiving side from bottom to top where the corresponding control information is removed. The communication between the layers is controlled by **protocols**. The bottom three layers are concerned with pure data transport, whereas the top four layers can also take over application-related tasks. In particular, the seventh layer is responsible for generating communication between applications.

Although the EDP manufacturers have their own network concepts (e.g. IBM with SNA or DEC with DECNET) there is a tendency to adopt the architecture of the ISO/OSI Model or to make it compatible with their own network concept.

Protocols have to be defined for each individual layer of the ISO/OSI Model. To this end suggestions are made by various international organizations (e.g. IEEE or CCITT). This means that diverse implementation characteristics arise even where the ISO/OSI Model is adopted. Examples of concrete ISO/OSI Model implementations are the Bildschirmtext system from the Deutsche Bundespost, the **MAP** protocol (Manufacturing Automation Protocol) developed for manufacturing industry, or the **TOP** protocol (Technical Office Protocol) developed for office applications. The individual implementations pay particular attention to developing protocols for the upper layers, which are determined by their special application requirements. For data transport at the lower levels the already existing protocols can generally be adopted.

For example, at the application level within MAP the language MMS/RS 511 has been developed for the control of production facilities. The language is independent of the particular facility, i.e. it provides commands that can be applied equally to both machine tools and robots, for example.

For office applications the X.400 standard for exchanging documents within the electronic mail context should be mentioned.

From the business economics viewpoint the applications to be defined at the seventh layer of the ISO/OSI Model are still to be regarded as "EDP-technical", however. For example, file transfers are regulated by a standard (FTAM). The necessary content for any business economics task is established over and above the ISO/OSI Model.

The functioning of an application-oriented standard will therefore be demonstrated using the already well-developed data format **EDIFACT** (Electronic Data Interchange for Administration Commerce and Transport). The EDIFACT standard was agreed by the ISO in 1987 as an international norm. International organizations, particularly the United Nations Economic Commission for Europe (UN/ECE) were involved in its development. The norms have been adopted in Germany by the Deutsches Institut für Normung e.V. as DIN 16556.

The syntax regulations for the message type "invoice" are first being considered under EDIFACT, further regulations for documents such as purchase orders, dispatch notes, etc., will follow.

Whereas EDIFACT regulates the representation of data, the ISO/OSI Model establishes the transfer of these data. EDIFACT aims at creating close links with the ISO/OSI Model services, for example, by using the file transfer (FTAM) or electronic mail (X.400) functions so that by means of this combination open data exchange can be implemented.

To demonstrate the significance of EDIFACT the current data exchange situation is represented in Figure 2.B.II.15a. At present there exist several sector-specific standards, for example that of the Verband der Deutschen Automobilindustire (VDA) (the German automobile industry association), the wholesale and retail standard SEDAS, or the individual standards of large industrial firms, such as BAV from Siemens.

An enterprise that receives electronically transmitted invoices from several suppliers must be in a position to convert the diverse formats within their handling programs (e.g. for invoice checking). Conversely, when their customers require invoices in diverse formats the invoices from their invoice creation program must be converted into these different formats.

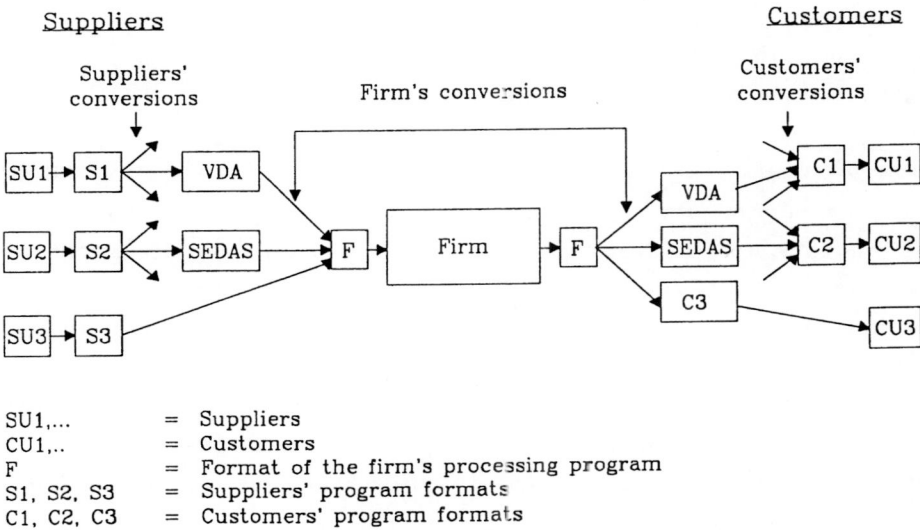

SU1,...   = Suppliers
CU1,..   = Customers
F   = Format of the firm's processing program
S1, S2, S3 = Suppliers' program formats
C1, C2, C3 = Customers' program formats

Fig. 2.B.II.15a: Conversion of multiple data formats

Given the existence of a common standard, however, EDIFACT translates the output of each partner from his individual format into the standard format, and the input from the standard format into his individual format. In contrast with the first case, where the

110

enterprise needed to undertake three conversions on both the receiving and sending sides (in total six), this is now reduced to only two. This assumes additionally that the handling programs are not set up to deal with the standard, but retain their individual structure (in the first instance). Of course, the effects on the enterprise shown in Figure 2.B.II.15b also arise for the customers and suppliers concerned if they work together with several partners.

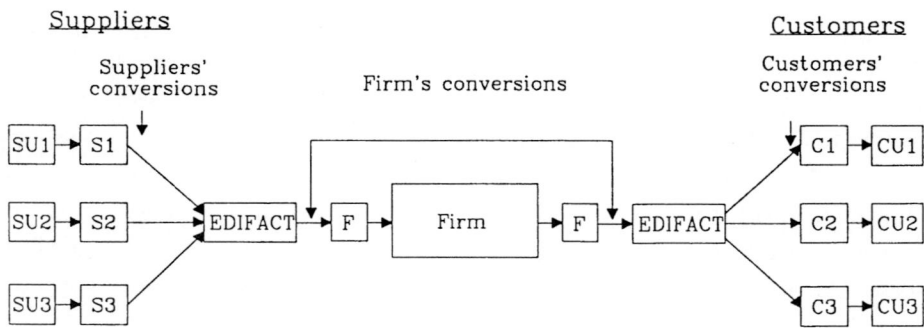

Fig. 2.B.II.15b: Conversions by the standardized use of EDIFACT

In detail, the EDIFACT regulations determine the **punctuation, vocabulary** and **syntax,** as in any language. Figure 2.B.II.15b indicates the structure of a transfer file. The individual data transfer files are embedded in a link connection. A transfer file consists of several message groups, which in turn consist of messages, etc.

A **data element** describes the individual attribute to be transferred, such as article number, order number, price, etc. Data elements are always placed within a segment in a particular order so that they can be identified by their position. **Data element groups** consist of pieces of information that belong together in terms of their content.

Data elements are of variable length to allow economy of transfer. If an element does not exist only a hyphen needs to be placed between the elements.

The same structuring principle is reapplied at the next level of consolidation. Data elements or data element groups that logically belong together are combined into **segments** (e.g. bank code, account number and bank into the banking connection segment). Non-existent segments are also replaced simply by a hyphen.

A **message** is the combination of all segments needed to represent a business transaction such as an invoice or an order.

The individual structural elements are always separated from each other by **header** and **end segments**.

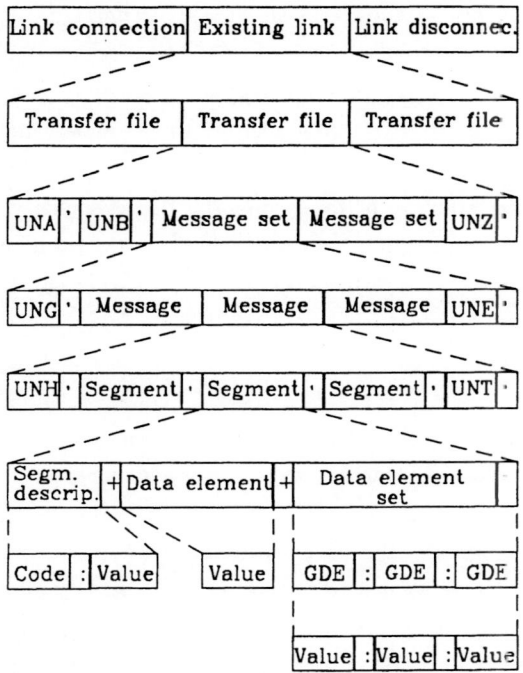

Link connection	Existing link	Link disconnec.

Transfer file	Transfer file	Transfer file

| UNA | ' | UNB | ' | Message set | Message set | UNZ | ' |

| UNG | ' | Message | Message | Message | UNE | ' |

| UNH | ' | Segment | ' | Segment | ' | Segment | ' | UNT | ' |

| Segm. descrip. | + | Data element | + | Data element set |

| Code | : | Value | | Value | | GDE | : | GDE | : | GDE |

| Value | : | Value | : | Value |

UNA   : Field separator specification
UNB   : Effective data header segment
UNZ   : Effective data end segment

UNG   : Message set header segment
UNE   : Message set end segment

UNH   : Message header segment
UNT   : Message end segment

GDE   : Data element set

Fig. 2.B.II.16: Transfer file structure

(from *Hermes, Syntax-Regeln für den Datenaustausch 1988, p. 9*)

An extended application arises when the data exchange does not occur directly between the business partners, but when so-called **clearing points** are interposed. Here, data can be accumulated and then forwarded to the recipient as closed items. In this way further efficiency improvements in the operation can be achieved.

The EDIFACT standard has also been recognized by a series of other organizations, e.g. by the Computer Integrated Manufacturing Commission in DIN, which develops norms for data exchange within industrial firms. EDIFACT is included as part of the basis for order processing.

As well as the standardization of data formats that are relevant to data exchange, the standardization of application functions can also be analysed. This is of particular significance in connection with the relocation of functions between partners. For example, if plausibility checks are relocated from the customer to the supplier, the contents of these checks must also be agreed. For these reasons the standardization of data is merely a first, simple step in the support of inter-company process chains. Business economics theory, which has contributed little thus far to the definition of data standards, could provide considerable assistance in the development of standards for processing functions.

At the technical transmission level, the **ISDN** (Integrated Services Digital Network) standard has been introduced. This makes it possible using a quasi "plughole" concept to effect diverse services such as telephone, telefax, video, television, data transfer, etc., using a single telephone number. This technical integration of diverse services makes it easy to provide them at the individual workplace. This is of particular significance for office workplaces. The integration of technical services also supports functional and data integration, since it facilitates a mixture of different information sources and the access to diverse application functions (see *Bullinger, Fröschle, ISDN und Unternehmensorganisation 1989*).

B.II.3.2. Optimization Methods for Structuring EDP System Networks

Aspects of the business economics structuring of EDP system networks for an enterprise are: establishing the degree of centralization/decentralization of applications, assigning functions to the hierarchical levels of the enterprise, and specifying the data exchange with business partners, including functional relocations. Business economics can develop modelling approaches for the optimization of this system. Possible approaches are provided by model formulations from transport theory, production planning, location planning or investment planning, for example.

In currently available approaches to cost-optimal structuring of computer networks it is the EDP costs and effects that are in the foreground. The effects on business economics factors, however, are no less significant (see *Helber, Gestaltung optimaler EDV-Systeme 1981*).

A model for the optimal structuring of a distributed data processing system based on line capacities and the assignment of data to nodes was developed by Mahmoud and Riordan as early as 1976. This can be used as a basis for an extended business economics optimization approach.

In **Mahmoud and Riordan's model** a given network topology is assumed, whereby several copies of a file are permissible which are then placed in secondary stores at various nodes (see *Mahmoud, Riordan, Distributed Information Networks 1976*). Since the data flow between nodes is independent of the file allocation, this approach simultaneously determines the capacity of the given links. The object is to determine a cost-optimal system. Side conditions are a maximum permissible delay in the execution of user wishes and a minimum availability (reliability) of the files needed. The **delay time** consists of waiting times at the nodes and transfer times on the lines. The **data traffic** between the nodes consists of file queries and the responses they generate, and data traffic for updating files and the responses this generates. Two extreme solutions for file allocation are conceivable. If each file is stored only once in the computer network the storage costs are minimal. But with such a configuration the query-related data traffic is maximized, since there is only a small probability that the node generating the query is also the node where the required file is stored. The other extreme is where a copy of each file is stored at each node of the network. The solution displays maximal storage costs. The data traffic arising from queries, however, is minimal, whereas the data traffic associated with updates is again considerable.

The following terms are used to formulate the model (further terms will be introduced in the course of the discussion):

Indices:

i   link (communication in one direction only)

j   capacity level of a link

k   location (node)

l   file

Variables and Data:

K = total costs of the system (\$/month)

K_S = total storage costs (\$/month)

K_T = total communication costs (\$/month)

T_{av} = average delay (sec)

$\bar{T}$ = prescribed average maximum delay (sec)

Z_l = average availability (reliability) of file l

$\bar{Z}_l$ = prescribed average minimum availability of file l

Disregarding integer and non-negativity conditions, the problem can be defined in abbreviated notation as follows:

<1> K = K_S + K_T $\rightarrow$ min

     total costs   total storage costs   total communication costs

<2> T_{av} $\leq$ $\bar{T}$

     average delay   maximum delay

<3> Z_1 $\geq$ $\bar{Z}_1$ $\forall 1$

     average availability   maximum availability

The following treatment examines how the individual terms combine with and affect each other.

The **total communication costs** K_T can be calculated as

<4> $$K_T = \sum_{ij} d_{ij} \cdot y_{ij}$$

Where

d_{ij} = costs (\$/month) for link i at capacity level j

y_{ij} = $\begin{cases} 1, \text{ if link i has capacity level j} \\ 0, \text{ otherwise} \end{cases}$

This represents, therefore, the sum of the communication costs for a given period. (Explicit specification of the limits of the summation is not given.)

The side condition

<5> $\sum_{j} y_{ij} = 1$ $\forall i$

ensures that each link is allocated only one capacity.

The **total storage costs** K_S are given by

<6> $$K_S = \sum_{kl} b_{kl} \cdot x_{kl}$$

where

b_{kl} = costs of storing file l at node k

x_{kl} = $\begin{cases} 1, \text{ if file l is stored at node k} \\ 0, \text{ otherwise} \end{cases}$

Next, the delay time conditions are analysed more closely.

The **delay** of a message is dependent on the length of the message, the capacity of the link, and the amount of data traffic per unit of time. **Data traffic** (in messages/sec) at node k which is linked with file l in another node k' consists of four components:

u_{kl} = query traffic from node k to file l

v_{kl} = update traffic from node k to file l

$\bar{u}_{kl}$ = return traffic resulting from query traffic u_{kl}

$\bar{v}_{kl}$ = update traffic resulting from update traffic v_{kl}

The first two variables relate to messages being sent out by node k, the last two to messages being received by node k.

The number of copies of file l in the system is defined as

$$q_l = \sum_k x_{kl}$$

and it is assumed that the data traffic from node k to a copy of file l is evenly distributed over all copies.

The total data traffic $\gamma_{kk'}$ from a node k to a node k' is then:

<7> $\gamma_{kk'} = \sum_l \{ [u_{kl}/q_l] [1-x_{kl}] \cdot x_{k'l}$

Query from node k to node k'
[to one of q_l files]
$1-x_{kl} = 0$, if file l is at node k

$+ v_{kl} \cdot x_{k'l}$

Update from node k to node k'
[to all q_l files]

$+ [\bar{u}_{k'l}/q_l] [1-x_{k'l}] \cdot x_{kl}$

Responses from node k to node k' to
queries from node k' to node k
[from one of q_l files]

$+ \bar{v}_{k'l} \cdot x_{kl} \}$

Responses from node k to node k' to
updates from node k' to node k
[from all q_l files]

This generates the total data traffic γ for the network

<8> $$\gamma \quad = \sum_{k} \sum_{k'} \gamma_{kk'}$$

$$= \sum_{k} \sum_{l} [(u_{kl} + \bar{u}_{kl}) (1 - x_{kl})$$

$$\underline{\hspace{6cm}}$$

query-related traffic

$$+ (v_{kl} + \bar{v}_{kl}) (q_l - x_{kl})]$$

$$\underline{\hspace{6cm}}$$

update-related traffic.

S_i indicates the set of sender nodes whose data are being communicated via link i to a node $S_{i'}$ belonging to a non-intersecting set. If a deterministic routing algorithm is assumed, i.e. if the route that a message takes from a sending to a receiving node is known, the data traffic on link i is given by

<9> $$\lambda_i \quad = \sum_{\substack{k \in S_i \\ k' \in S_{i'}}} \gamma_{kk'}$$

With the help of the results of analytic queueing theory (see *Mahmoud, Riordan, Distributed Information Networks 1976*) the average delay of a message can be determined from these values (see *Kleinrock, Queueing Systems 1976*):

<10> $$T_{av} = \frac{1}{\gamma} \cdot \sum_{i} \frac{\lambda_i}{\mu(c_i - \lambda_i/\mu)} = \frac{1}{\gamma} \cdot \sum_{i} \frac{\lambda_i}{\mu c_i - \lambda_i}$$

Where

$1/\mu$ = average message length in bits

c_i = transfer capacity of the link.

All the variables of the side condition <2> are thereby known.

The **availability** (reliability) of a file is expressed by the probability that the file can be accessed when a user wishes. The availability of a file within a computer network is determined by the probability of the failure of the link i and the node k on the route from sender to recipient. Since there exist several copies of a file and the links to them are not independent of each other (parts of the route can be identical) analytic determination of the probabilities is difficult, or possible only in special cases, e.g. for a star network.

Mahmoud and Riordan, therefore, make the simplifying assumption that the probabilities of failure of the routes are independent of each other. The probability that file l can be accessed from node k, i.e. that at least one copy can be reached via an intact route, is given by

<11> $\qquad z_{kl} = 1 - \prod_{k'} (1 - r_{kk'} \cdot x_{k'l})$

$r_{kk'} = \qquad$ the given reliability of the route from k to k'

If W_{kl} designates the entire data traffic between node k and a file l, then

<12> $\qquad W_{kl} = u_{kl} + \bar{u}_{kl} + v_{kl} + \bar{v}_{kl}$

So the reliability Z_l of a file l weighted by the data traffic is determined by

<13> $$Z_l = \frac{\sum_k z_{kl}\, W_{kl}}{\sum_k W_{kl}}$$

Consequently, the reliability side conditions for a file l are given by

<14> $\qquad Z_l \geq \bar{Z}_l$

This optimization model is an integer, non-linear model.
Its solution presents considerable difficulties, so that for large-scale problems heuristic procedures must be used. However, the model demonstrates that it is in principle possible to find cost-optimal solutions for structuring problems of EDP system networks.

C. Applications Software

Business procedures and problem-solving are increasingly being influenced by the conceptualizations contained in applications software. To the extent that business economics regards its main task as the structuring of reality, it must attempt to ensure that its theoretical results are incorporated in applications software. The various "techniques" for creating applications software and their characteristics are, therefore, of particular importance. This applies especially to standard software, since it is becoming increasingly widespread and also serves as a model for many in-house developments. In addition to software engineering, therefore, standard software will be considered in detail. Many methods used in business economics require the use of electronic data processing for their solution. This applies, for example, to data- and computationally-intensive optimization models that have been developed within operations research. In this context EDP makes it possible to apply theoretically developed modelling of solutions, and thereby generates new impetus for further developments. Method banks make software available to appropriate applications, and thus form the third area of emphasis within applications software.

With expert systems, a new form of applications software is being developed, which not only represents an alteration of applications software architecture, but also an alteration of the understanding of problem-solving within business economics.

C.I. Computer Aided Software Engineering (CASE)

In comparison with the other techniques under consideration, software engineering constitutes a kind of "meta-technique", since it describes procedures for determining a desirable combination of EDP techniques for the solution of a specific problem. Although the term CASE relates explicitly to software, the design process covers the entire information system consisting of user interface, database, applications philosophy and process control. However, since the costs of software development and maintenance are always increasing in comparison with hardware costs, the methods concentrate primarily on these areas.

The aim of computer aided software engineering is to produce software systems on an industrial basis (see *Balzert, Software Systeme 1982, p. 3 ff.*). This means that software systems need no longer be produced as an "individually handicrafted product", but within a rationally functioning manufacturing format, such as serial production (see *Bauer, Software Engineering 1977, p. 530*).

An obstacle to this, of course, is that a software system is by nature always a unique product. Even for standard software systems, which have multiple applications, the emphasis is on the development of the first system. The subsequent reproduction by duplication is trivial in comparison.

If the object of the applications software are problem issues from business economics then the techniques for defining the problem and translating it into a system design have a particularly close relationship with business economics' handling of its subject matter.

C.I.1. Description of Software Engineering

C.I.1.1. Principles, Methods, Tools

Since software engineering has been subject to a great deal of theoretical and practical coverage (see e.g. the references in *Stetter, Softwaretechnologie 1983; Hering, Software-Engineering 1989; Balzert, Software-Systeme 1982; Österle, Informationssysteme 1981*) a multiplicity of methods have been developed, which often differ from each other in only trivial respects. Nevertheless, certain standards and development trends can be recognized.

The general aim of all the development methods is to reduce the complexity of software development. **Complexity** refers to the difficulty with which a software system can be understood by human users (see Österle, *Informationssysteme 1981, p. 58*). As design support it is possible to distinguish between **principles, methods** and **tools** (see *Balzert, Software-Systeme 1982, p. 22 ff.*). **Principles** are general rules that must be adhered to in software development. Examples are the hierarchy principle, i.e. the breakdown of a problem into sub-problems, or the locality principle, i.e. the concentration of logically integrated information at one location,

A **method** gives substance to a principle in the form of a valid procedural method. The hierarchy principle, for example, is converted into a concrete method by way of a prescription for breaking down a problem into sub-problems, such that a tree structure emerges.

Tools are then the concrete EDP-supported aids to implementation of the method.

C.I.1.2. Phase Concepts

The **System Development Life Cycle (SDLC)** is used to structure the software development process. A typical breakdown of the development phases is (see *Balzert, Software-Systeme 1982, p. 17*):

1. planning,
2. definition,
3. design,
4. implementation,
5. delivery and introduction,
6. maintenance and operation.

In the **planning phase** the basic aims and requirements for the new system are determined. In particular, these need to be reconciled with the general strategic planning of the enterprise.

In the **definition phase** the demands on the system arising from user requirements are defined, a planned system is developed and, by comparing this with the actual situation, an economic feasibility study is conducted.

The result of the definition phase is a system specification, which provides the starting point for the **design phase**. Here, individual methods for meeting the requirements specified in the definition phase are determined. In particular, the system modules are defined and the data structures described.

Implementation consists of programming and system testing.

In the context of **delivery and introduction** the user is made familiar with the system.

The **maintenance and operation** of the system consists of functional extensions and the integration with neighbouring, new or amended systems. At the same time the system must be continuously adapted to new technical developments in the environment (e.g. change of operating system, network links).

It is now well-accepted that the largest portion of the costs of a software system arise after its completion, that is in the maintenance and operation area. It is also recognized that errors in the development of a software system are more serious the earlier they are made and the later they are discovered. For this reason, after initial emphasis on the implementation area, software development support increasingly concentrates on the early phases, particularly the definition and design phases.

The phase concept represents at first sight a sequential process characterized by increasing provision of detail. In practice, however, this process cannot generally be maintained in this idealized form, instead, feedback loops result from amendments to user requirements or lack of clarity in their definition. In order to avoid too long an interval between the definition of user requirements and their fulfilment in a running system, whereby the user starts to feel as if nothing is happening, so-called prototyping is recommended.

In **prototyping** a running computer system is developed out of the initial user requirements as quickly as possible. This system can be demonstrated to the users and compared with their requirements.

This enables the user to appreciate the consequences of his requirements, so that he can modify them or make them more precise. Prototyping can, on the one hand, be implemented as part of the system definition phase, serving as a method of determining user requirements, and providing an extension to user questioning or data analysis. However, it can also be considered as an alternative approach to the phase concept, whereby the prototype is the starting point for the ultimate system and is subject to continuous further development via feedback loops with the future users. This latter approach is particularly recommended for the development of expert systems, that is, for the solution of unstructured or badly structured problems (see *Kurbel, Pietsch, Expertensystem-Projekte 1989*).

C.I.1.3. Analysis and Design Methods

It is the aim of CASE to accompany the entire life cycle of applications systems with a combination of methods. In this way the uniformity of the defined requirements with respect to functions and data should be ensured throughout all phases. The tools to be applied are combined into Software Production Environments (SPE).

The methods developed in the CASE context can be applied in diverse phases. The following discussion briefly introduces some methods which are particularly applicable in the phases of system definition and system design which are important in business economics terms.

It has already been established that
1.   the support of process chains, and
2.   structuring of the enterprise resource data
occupy the foreground in the development of modern information systems.
The CASE methods can also be distinguished on the basis of whether they place more emphasis on the functional or on the data approach. Functions here refer to the operational structure perspective of process chains.

Data- and **functionally-oriented procedures** are, of course, closely related. Data are described by indicating from which functions they are generated and by which functions they are needed (see *Österle, Informationssysteme 1981, p. 84*); functions are described by the transformation of input data into output data. Each view extends and necessitates the other. Nevertheless, the methods can be distinguished on the basis of their orientational emphasis.
A **data-oriented** approach describes the static, logical data structures, i.e. entity types, relationship types and attribute types, and represents the data flow between the functions (i.e. all the data that are inputs to, and outputs of, a function). In the system design and implementation the data are defined down to the level of the physical record structure.
A **function-oriented** approach describes the content of the transformation of an input into an output, breaks a function down into a hierarchy of sub-functions, and establishes the functional sequence within a procedural logic (see *Richter, ADVIS-Methodenpackage 1981, p. 01.08.0 ff.*).

Data-Oriented Description

The logical design of data structures has already been handled extensively (see Chapter 2, Section A.I.). It should be noted, however, that many software engineering tools have up to now paid insufficient attention to the design of data structures.

The representation of the data flow provides a desirable extension to a static analysis of data structure. The **data flowchart** and **bubble diagram technique** are introduced as clear, simple representational methods, whereby the bubble diagram technique is the more effective. They both establish the link between data structures and functions (process chains). The process description (e.g. in the form of a process chain diagram) provides the individual sub-functions and the data model the file names.

Data flowcharts represent the data needed by the specific functions and the data stocks resulting from the processing. They make clear the sequence in which tasks are processed and represent the interdependence between data and program functions within a process chain. Norms have been established for the symbols representing the various data media and processing forms (see Figure 2.C.I.01).

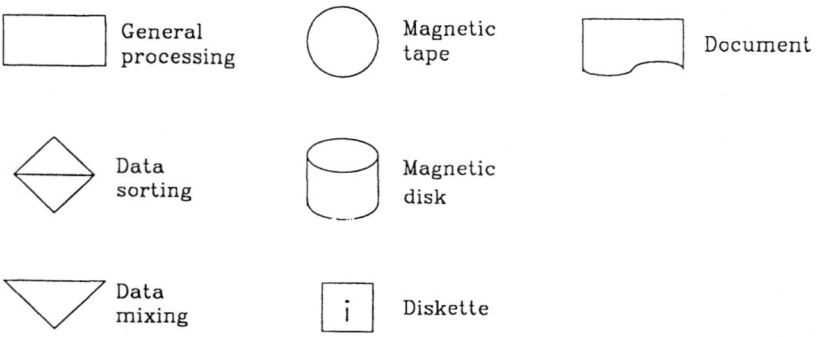

Fig. 2.C.I.01: Data flowchart symbols (in accordance with DIN 66001)

The data flow from the process chain for order processing in batch operation is represented in rough form in Figure 2.C.I.02.

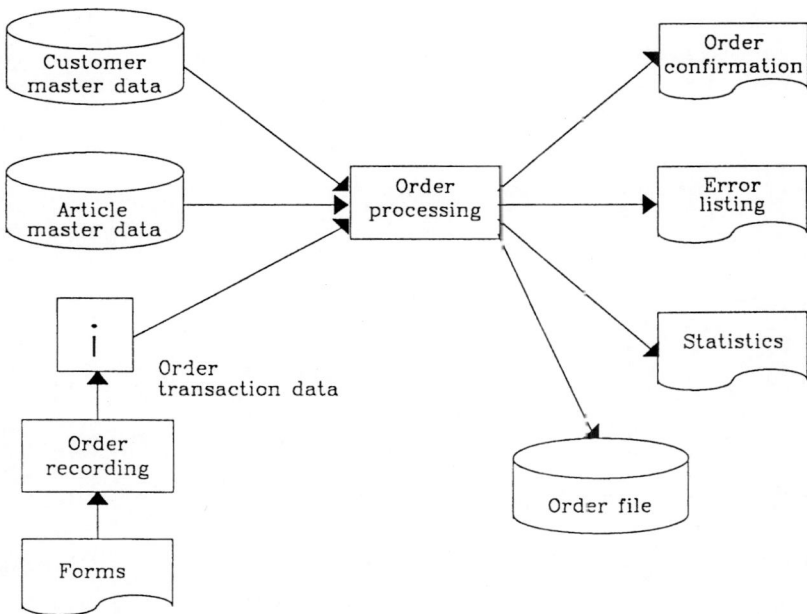

Fig. 2.C.I.02: Data flowchart for order processing in batch operation

The order data are written to diskettes at data recording points and then transferred to order processing. The processing also requires customer and article master data. The plausibility check first establishes the validity of the article and customer numbers and then reserves the order quantities from stocks on hand. Then the order confirmation, error messages and order receipt statistics are printed. The order data, supplemented with additional information from the master files and an accepted delivery date, are then stored in the order file.

The use of data flowcharts is widespread, and described in many introductory EDP texts.

Using **bubble diagrams** (see *De Marco, Structured Analysis 1979*) data interfaces between individual program functions can be represented in greater detail and with greater flexibility (see *Richter, ADVIS-Methodenpackage 1981, p. 03.040*). However, no indications of the storage medium (disk, diskette, etc.) are given.

The more important symbols in bubble diagram technique are given in Figure 2.C.I.03:

124

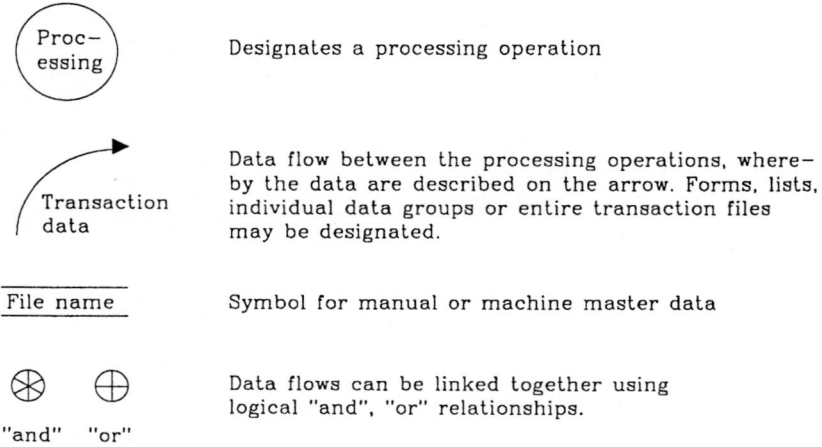

Proc-essing   Designates a processing operation

Transaction data   Data flow between the processing operations, where-by the data are described on the arrow. Forms, lists, individual data groups or entire transaction files may be designated.

File name   Symbol for manual or machine master data

⊗   ⊕   Data flows can be linked together using logical "and", "or" relationships.
"and" "or"

Fig. 2.C.I.03: Symbols used in the bubble diagram technique

The self-explanatory example of order processing given in Figure 2.C.I.04 indicates the greater representational potential as compared with the data flowchart.

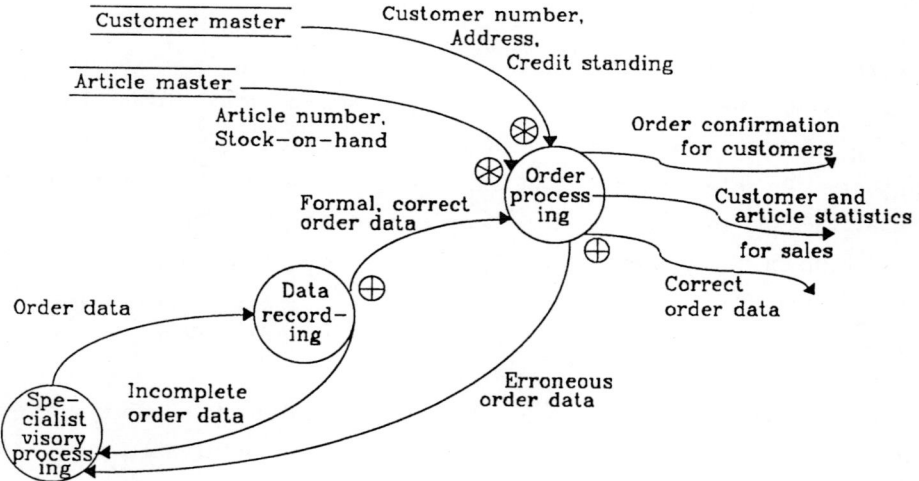

Fig.2.C.I.04: Bubble diagram: order processing

The bubble diagram technique can be employed both at the rough planning level and for more detailed design, and thereby supports uniformity within the phase concept.

Since bubble diagrams are largely unformatted and can be interpreted almost without explanations, they are a very suitable means of communication between business economics and EDP.

The link with static descriptions of data structures is generated with reference to file names and attribute names. These terms are introduced for the design of data structures and then adopted for the data flowcharts.

The processing represented by the bubbles are sub-processes/work steps within a process description, e.g., in conformity with a process chain diagram (see Figure 2.A.III.01). Bubble diagrams, therefore, represent the linking of static data descriptions and process descriptions into a procedural model (see Figure 2.C.I.05).

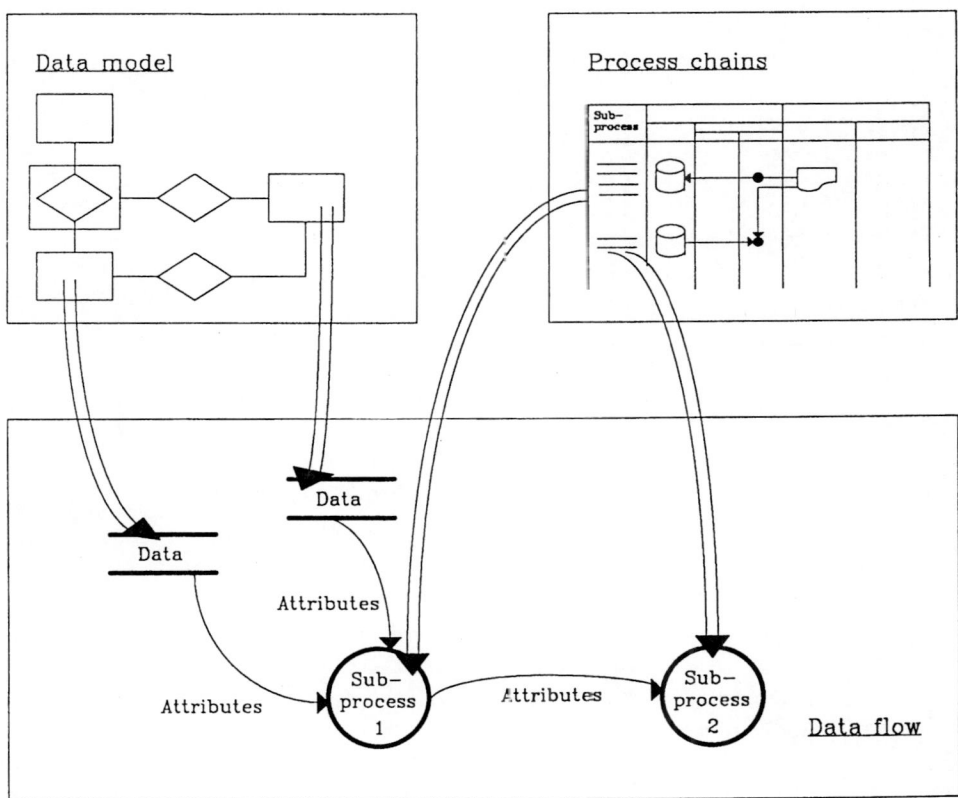

Fig. 2.C.I.05: Links between data and process models

Function-Oriented Description

In representing functions the **hierarchy** principle should first be mentioned as a way of reducing the complexity of process chains. For representational purposes HIPO hierarchy diagrams (HIPO = Hierarchy plus Input-Process-Output) are suitable. **Hierarchy diagrams** are also applied in many other software development methods. To describe the functions themselves, i.e. the transformation rules from input to output, HIPO or Nassi/Shneiderman function diagrams are suitable (see *Nassi, Shneiderman, Flowchart Techniques 1973, p. 12 ff.*)

Hierarchy diagrams are self-explanatory, as is demonstrated by Figure 2.C.I.06 for the example of order handling. They can be prepared for various hierarchy levels, as is indicated in the figure for the reservation sub-function.

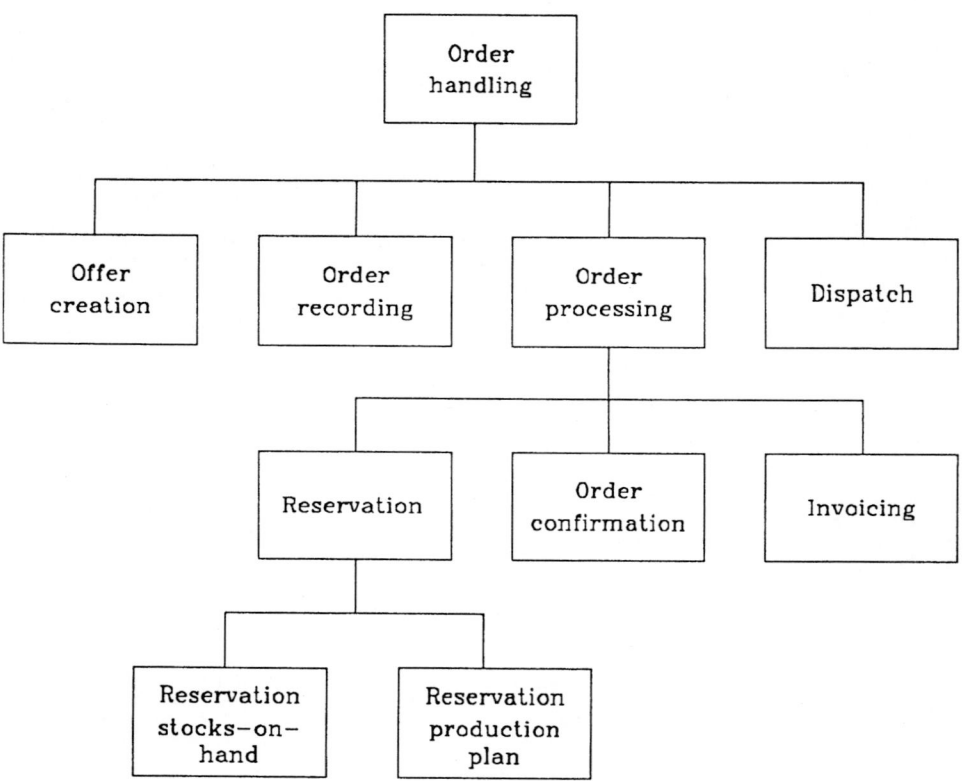

Fig. 2.C.I.06: HIPO diagram: order processing

To describe a function and the temporal sequence of execution of functions **program flowcharts** frequently used to be used. However, they have the disadvantage that they are unclear for complicated structures with many branchings, and they do not support structured programming. In particular, repetition of program parts are difficult to recognize.

HIPO function diagrams show the flow between input, processing and output. **Structured programming** uses only the three **control structures** sequence, branch and repeat. As a result, the jumps that give rise to unclear, and hence error-prone, programs are avoided. At the same time structured programming breaks down functions into modules (structural blocks). A **module** is a functional entity with a defined entry and exit.

Figure 2.C.I.07 presents the symbols for the control structures, and Figure 2.C.I.08 describes an excerpt from order handling using these representational tools.

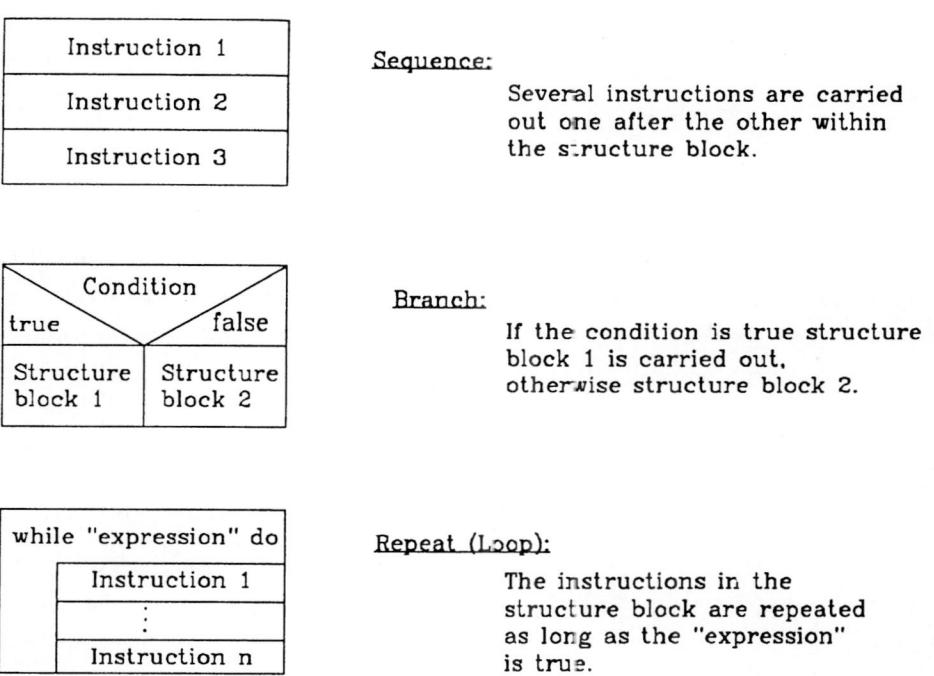

Sequence:
    Several instructions are carried out one after the other within the structure block.

Branch:
    If the condition is true structure block 1 is carried out, otherwise structure block 2.

Repeat (Loop):
    The instructions in the structure block are repeated as long as the "expression" is true.

Fig. 2.C.I.07: Control structures for structured programming

Structograms are appropriate not only for the description of global relationships but also for detailed processes and programming projects. As a result, they are also very suitable for the differentiated representation of economic decision rules.

To describe the interaction between human and computer in interactive processing **interaction diagrams** were introduced in Chapter 2, Section B.I.3. as a further description language. As an extension to this, **structure charts** for module building and transaction definition should be mentioned (see *Awad, Management Information Systems 1988, p. 460 f.*)

128

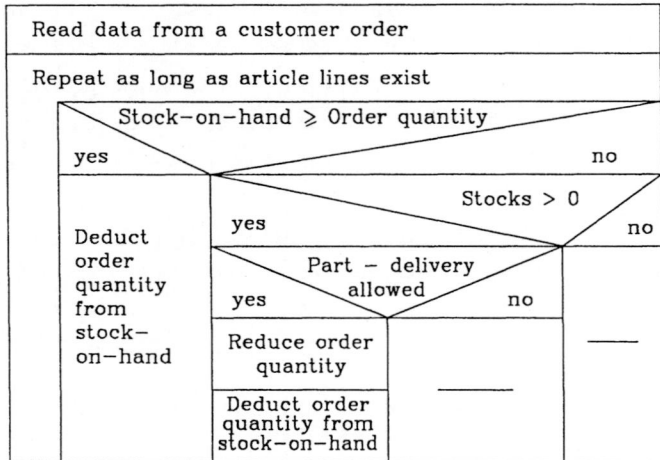

Fig. 2.C.I.08: Structogram for order processing

The methods mentioned are supported in EDP terms by **software production environments**. Examples are PREDICT CASE, IEW, PROMOD, STRATOS and Excelerator. The Excelerator system allows the construction and administration of graphics for system development, and supports data description (data dictionary), documentation and analysis. For example, the bubble diagrams and entity relationship data model that have been discussed are given graphical support (see *Index Technology, Excelerator 1988*).

The transition from the conceptual design and its transformation using a CASE tool is represented in Figures 2.C.I.09a to 2.C.I.09c. Figure 2.C.I.09a shows how the suitable computer graphics for the entity relationship model of Figure 2.A.I.08 can be created with the help of the system IEW.

Entity types are represented by boxes, as in Figure 2.A.I.08. Relationship types can also possess attributes and consequently are not represented merely by arrows, but by a rhombus within a box. These relationship types can themselves enter into relationships and are then reinterpreted.

The two symbols at the points of the arrows indicate the number of instances of the relationship concerned. The symbol nearest to the object indicates the maximum number of instances of the relationship, the next one the minimum. A tripod indicates "many" instances, a line "one"instance, and a circle "no" instances.

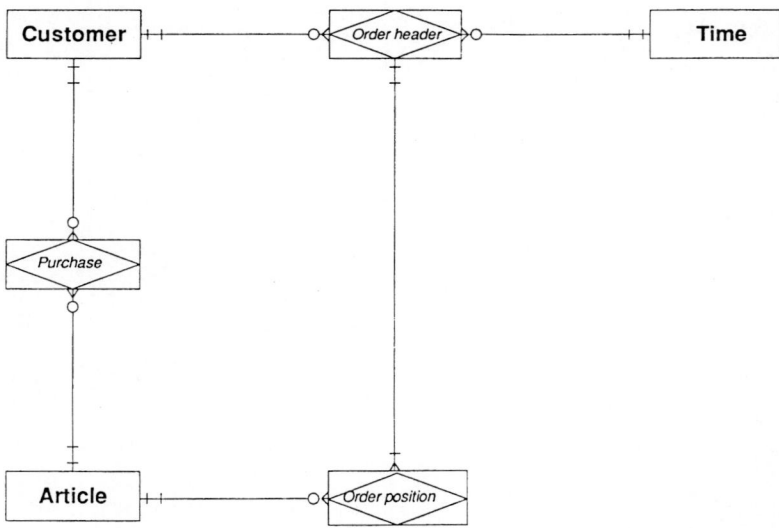

Fig. 2.C.I.09a: Constructing an ERM using the CASE tool IEW

Thus, an article enters into at least "no" and at most "many" order positions. An order position, in turn, consists of at least "one" and at most "one" article, that is of "exactly" one.

The specification of the lower limits is of interest with respect to the integrity conditions.

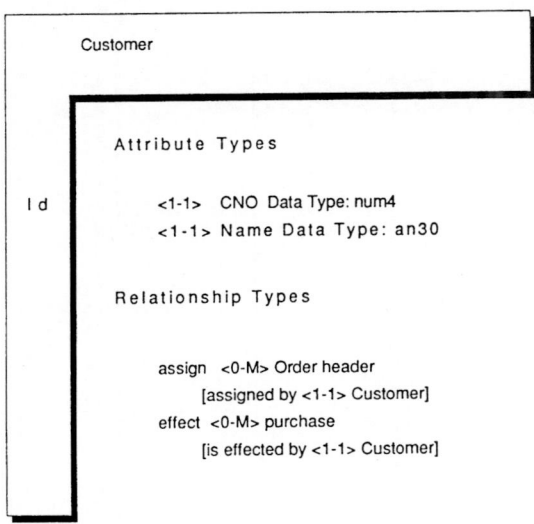

Fig. 2.C.I.09b: Defining a relationship using the CASE tool IEW

```
CREATE TABLE Customer
   (CNO                    INTEGER                NOT NULL,
    Name                   CHAR(30)               NOT NULL);

CREATE UNIQUE INDEX ?index_name
   ON Customer
     (CNO);

CREATE TABLE Time
   (Date                   DATE                   NOT NULL);

CREATE UNIQUE INDEX ?index_name
   ON Time
     (Date);

CREATE TABLE Order header
   (CNO                    INTEGER                NOT NULL,
    Date                   DATE                   NOT NULL,
    Handled by             CHAR(30)               NOT NULL);

CREATE UNIQUE INDEX ?index_name
   ON Order header
     (CNO,
      Date);

CREATE TABLE Article
   (ANO                    INTEGER                NOT NULL,
    Description            CHAR(30)               NOT NULL);

CREATE UNIQUE INDEX ?index_name
   ON Article
     (ANO);

CREATE TABLE Purchase
   (CNO                    INTEGER                NOT NULL,
    ANO                    INTEGER                NOT NULL,
    Quantity               INTEGER                NOT NULL);

CREATE UNIQUE INDEX ?index_name
   ON Purchase
     (CNO,
      ANO);

CREATE TABLE Order position
   (ANO                    INTEGER                NOT NULL,
    CNO                    INTEGER                NOT NULL,
    Date                   DATE                   NOT NULL,
    Quantity               INTEGER                NOT NULL,
    Price                  INTEGER                NOT NULL);

CREATE UNIQUE INDEX ?index_name
   ON Order position
     (ANO,
      CNO,
      Date);
```

Fig. 2.C.I.09c: Data description for the database system DB/2

The next step specifies the attributes for each entity and relationship type in tabular form, and the formats of the attributes. In addition, the maximum and minimum number of instances of attributes can also be indicated in a table. An example of this is given for the CUSTOMER entity type in Figure 2.C.I.09b.

The relational data model is created from these descriptions. Additional manipulations of primary and secondary keys can be undertaken here, and further indices agreed. For reasons of space these tables are not presented here. In the next step the relational data model of the database schema for a concrete database system is automatically created. This is presented for the example in Figure 2.C.I.09c.

At the present stage of development of the tool, however, it may be advisable to process the code generated once more. Further developments should eliminate existing weaknesses in the code generation, however.

C.I.2. Business Economics Implementation of Software Engineering

It is already clear from the description of the methods that there is considerable relevance to the business economics implementation. This provides an effective opportunity for economic theory to present its problem-solving models in EDP-suited form. This will not only ensure greater EDP relevance, the structured approach will also enrich the business economics perspective.

In decision-oriented business economics the following procedural sequence has often been recommended:

1. establishing objectives,
2. model building,
3. decision-making.

However, the objectives have generally been taken as given, and the decision-making stage simply equated with the solution of the model.

The incorporation of the decision problem in the larger context of data provision, organizational integration with associated applications, etc., however, has not been considered.

The software development process, therefore, covers a wider problem area. The inclusion of decision models would occur in the course of software design. The simplicity and clarity of the graphically-oriented procedures that have been discussed make it possible for business economics to offer an EDP-suited representation of its problem-solving approaches without great additional learning costs. In this way the language barrier between business economics specialists and EDP specialists can be substantially reduced. Quite independent of their EDP-relevance, these descriptive methods present an efficient and clear extension to the verbal and mathematical problem-solving approaches which are typical of business economics.

C.I.3. Business Economics Structuring of Software Engineering

Business economics can have effects on the development of software engineering in three fields:

1.   Provision of economic methods for project control.
2.   Further development of the software engineering concept.
3.   Support of individual phases using economic methods.

Software development tasks conform to the definition of **projects**: they are time-taking activities with a definite start and finish, and they consist of a series of interconnected sub-processes. For this reason, business economics tools for project planning and control could be effectively applied to software development projects. Examples are time planning for the use of network planning techniques and the associated procedures for cost and capacity planning (see *Hansel, Lomnitz, Projektleiter-Praxis 1987; Kuba, Projektorganisation 1987*).

Given the proximity of the first three phases of the software development cycle with the business economics problem formulation, the entire concept of the development process can be discussed in terms of its business economics aspects. For example, the linear phase concept can be weighed against the prototyping concept of interlocking feedback loops.

Even within individual sub-steps there are close links with business economics issues. Determining the economic feasibility of the planned project is a part of phase 2: system definition or the feasibility study. In this context alternative ways of achieving the objective need to be generated and evaluated. Procedures for assessing the economic feasibility of EDP projects have been being developed within business economics for a considerable time. Of course, there are considerable divergences from material investment projects: in addition to monetary variables, a wide range of qualitative cost and benefit factors are also included in the calculation. The integration effects resulting from the formation of process chains and data integration described above increase the difficulty of calculating cost and benefit factors for individual projects. For this reason integration methods, such as have been developed in business economics for investment planning, could, in extended form, provide new approaches to the economic structuring of information systems.

C.II. Standard Applications Software

C.II.1. Description of Standard Software

Standard applications software are program systems for solving applications problems developed by software houses and hardware manufacturers for an anonymous market. Figure 2.C.II.01 indicates the position of standard applications software and instances thereof within the total software environment.

Although in the early years of using EDP, applications software was created by the user, more recently the use of standard software has become increasingly predominant.

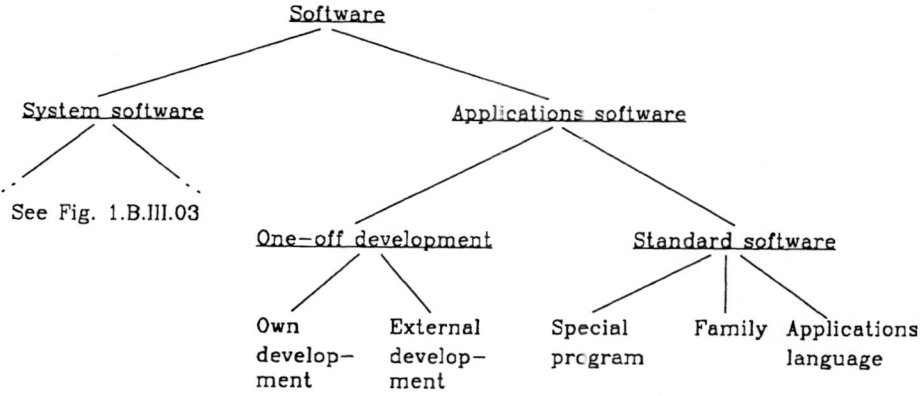

Fig. 2.C.II.01: Software classification

In the half-yearly ISIS report (see *Nomina. ISIS-Software Report 1989*) suppliers of standard software present their products along with the number of implementations. Of course, the relatively low implementation figures in the ISIS report are indicative of the large number of products, which is at odds with the definition of standard software given above. Many systems are developed individually for specific users, but are then offered to other users as a means of covering the development costs.

The reasons for the increased use of standard software are the improvements in the business economics and EDP-technical quality, cost advantages and time-saving in comparison with in-house developments. Figure 2.C.II.02 presents the proportion of the various costs of an in-house developed application system throughout its life cycle, based

134

on several empirical investigations (see *Österle, Informationssysteme 1981, p. 20 ff.*). It appears that only a quarter of the costs are incurred during development, whereas three-quarters arise after installation, i.e. during the maintenance phase.

If the individual development phases are examined to determine whether the use of standard software would bring cost advantages, diverse results emerge.

By using standard software, the implementation costs (including programming) and the testing costs in the **development phase** are reduced, since the standard system is available already programmed and tested. This advantage is diminished, however, if adjustments to individual user requirements require substantial program amendments.

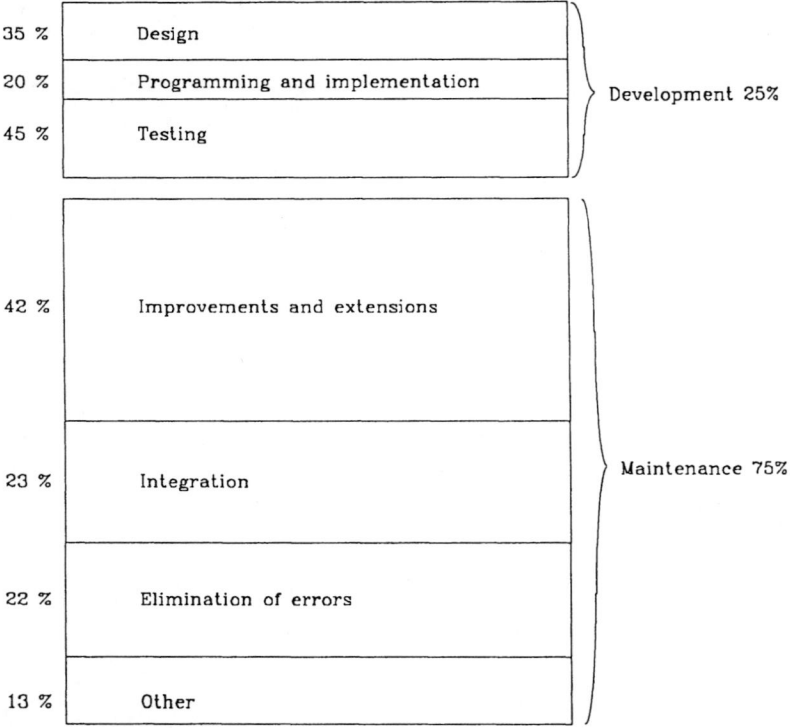

35 %	Design	
20 %	Programming and implementation	Development 25%
45 %	Testing	

42 %	Improvements and extensions	
23 %	Integration	Maintenance 75%
22 %	Elimination of errors	
13 %	Other	

Fig. 2.C.II.02: Software cost relationships for in-house developments

In developing the **planned system**, however, scarcely any cost reduction is achieved, since a comprehensive planned system particularly needs to be developed for the use of standard software. From this a program specification is derived for the choice of a suitable package. On the other hand, information should also be taken from software suppliers during the course of developing a planned system for in-house development, since this can often provide interesting and advanced business economics solutions.

In the **maintenance** area the costs of eliminating errors, making extensions and integrations are lower for standard software than for in-house developments. Since standard software is implemented by many users it is in general relatively error-free, even if the user is a so-called pilot user. Standard software is continuously updated by the manufacturer to meet present EDP-technical standards in order to improve its marketability. At the same time user demands for extensions and improvements are continuously being taken into account, so that each user benefits from the suggestions of other users. The relocation of responsibility for maintenance to the manufacturer is in itself a substantial advantage of using standard software.

Since the development costs for standard software can be spread over many users the acquisition price for the individual user is correspondingly lower. As a general rule it can be said that the price of a standard software package is only about 5% to 20% of the cost of an in-house development. It should be noted here, however, that the costs of any adaptions or extensions needed to the standard system must be added to the purchase price. Nevertheless, there usually remains a considerable cost advantage.

Since the costs applied in Figure 2.C.II.02 can largely be equated with personnel costs, this indicates a high capacity tie-up within the EDP department for maintenance tasks. This has given rise to a situation where in many EDP areas there is scarcely any capacity free for development; in this context there is talk of the crisis of applications software and applications backlog. In order to alleviate this, procedures are being developed in the software engineering context for the more rational creation of software systems. Care is needed in assessing their time-saving properties, however. At the moment, therefore, the use of standard software is the most effective means of speeding up the introduction of applications systems.

In standard software it is possible to distinguish between language-oriented systems, special programs and software families (see Figure 2.C.II.01). In **language-oriented systems** functional "building blocks" are provided for specific application areas, out of which the user can build a system for his special needs. Examples of this kind of system are the MIMS system (Mitrol Industrial Management System) from General Electric Information Services (see *General Electric, MIMS 1981*) for the production planning and control area, PROKOS from mbp for cost accounting, or INFPLAN from Siemens AG for cost accounting and planning. More recently, IBM's Application Enabler concept for developing CIM systems is worthy of mention. Their advantage lies in their considerable flexibility, but they have the disadvantage that the user must develop the solution model in business economics terms largely on his own.

Special programs are used for precisely specified tasks, for example, fixed asset accounting, dispatch control or maintenance planning. Their advantages arise from the high standard of business economics and EDP techniques employed, but they have the disadvantage that they are difficult to link up with neighbouring systems.

Applications software families are integrated systems for a larger area of business applications (entire departmental areas, or even inter-departmental).

In this context integration implies that the programs are built on each other. Data are autonomously transferred from one program to another (e.g. also by the use of a common database system), and there exists a unified concept for the user interface (e.g. screen forms, interactive control) and for data protection.

Business functions coverage	ADV/ORGA (L.S)	COMMAND (FRIDA)	IBM (COPICS)	IBM MAPICS II	NIXDORF (COMET)	PANSOPHIC (PR/MS)	PLAUT (M120)	SAP (R.)	SIEMENS (Sitline-IS)	STEEB (S...)
Sales										
– Order processing	x		x	x	x	x	x	x	x	x
– Dispatch	x	x	x	–	x	x	x	x	x	x
– Statistics	–	x	x	x	x	x	x	x	x	x
Financial accounting										
– Accounts receivable	x	x	–	x	x	x	x	x	x	x
– Accounts payable	x	x	–	x	x	x	x	x	x	x
– Investments	x	x	–	x	x	–	x	x	x	x
– Assets	x	x	–	x	x	x	x	x	x	x
– Material (value)	x	x	–	x	x	x	x	x	x	x
Personnel										
– Wages and salaries	x	x	–	x	x	–	–	x	x	x
– Personnel information	x	x	–	–	x	–	–	x	x	x
Cost accounting										
– Cost types	x	x	x	–	x	x	x	x	x	x
– Cost centers	x	x	x	–	x	x	x	x	x	x
– Cost unit period	x	–	–	x	x	–	x	x	x	x
– Cost unit	x	–	–	x	x	–	x	x	x	x
Production planning and control										
– Master data	x	x	x	x	x	x	x	x	x	x
– Require. breakdown	x	x	x	x	x	x	x	x	x	x
– Capacity scheduling	–	x	x	x	x	x	x	x	–	–
– Job–shop control	x	x	x	x	x	x	x	x	x	–
– Opera. data collection	–	x	x	x	x	–	–	x	x	–
Material management										
– Inventory management	x	x	x	x	x	x	x	x	x	x
– Stock control	x	x	x	x	x	x	x	x	x	x
– Purchasing	x	x	x	x	x	x	x	x	x	x

State at December 1989

Fig. 2.C.II.03: Functional coverage of standard software families

The R. family from the software house SAP constitutes an integrated concept for the areas of order processing, financial accounting, cost accounting, material management and production control. The family M110 from Plaut Software AG is an integrated system for business accounting. The software house ADV/ORGA offers a software family for the payroll, cost accounting and financial accounting areas. The Integrated Software (IS) from Siemens AG also adopts this approach. In general, the trend towards the development and application of program families can be observed. The functional scope in business economics terms of some well-known standard software families is shown in Figure 2.C.II.03.

The advantage of using a program family is that it is already completely integrated by the manufacturer. The complete implementation of a program family is impeded, however, if the user has already installed in-house developed or other purchased systems for some of the functions. Only in those cases where the user

- is subject to a considerable backlog, or
- has existing systems which are outdated in EDP-technical or business terms, and must in any case be reworked,

can an entire software family be installed immediately. The implementation costs associated with this, however, should not be underestimated.

C.II.2. Business Economics Implementation of Standard Software

The question as to which business functions display the standardizability or uniformity needed to allow the widespread use of standard software, leads to the question of which factors influence standardization.
Figure 2.C.II.04 represents several factors which either support or hinder the standardization of problem-solving approaches in business economics.

Legal prescriptions concerning the form that the business problem-solution may take are a significant motive for uniformity of problem handling. This applies in financial accounting, for example, in the form of the rules of commercial law, the principles of adequate and orderly accounting, and fiscal law. The same applies to the calculation of gross and net wages and salaries, where income tax and social insurance regulations are relevant. For this reason, standard software systems for these areas are especially widely used.
If an established business model exists for an application area this also has a standardizing effect. An example of this is the production planning and control model for serial manufacturing which has been widely accepted. For cost accounting, however,

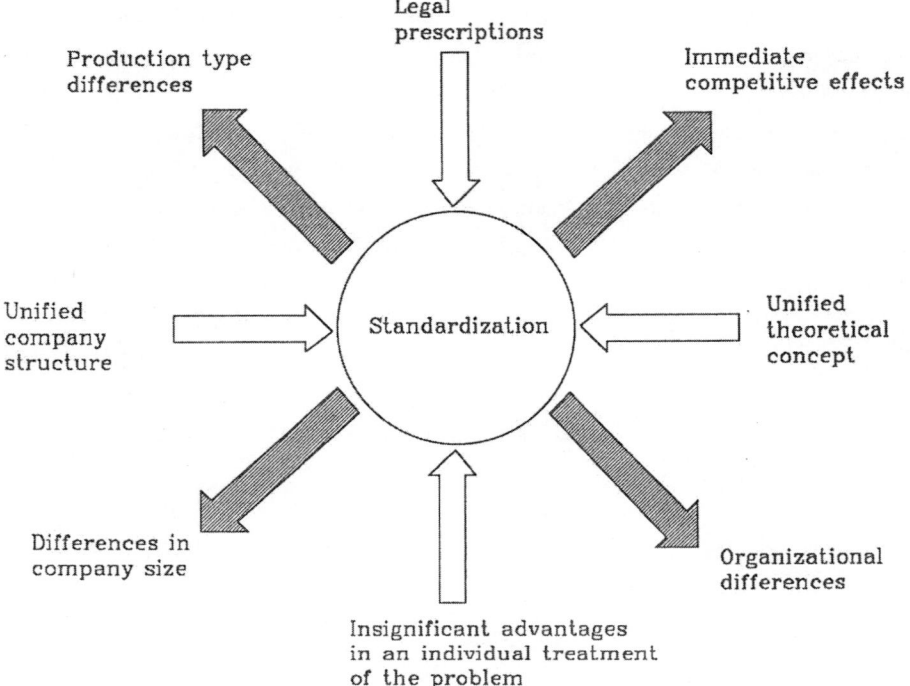

Fig. 2.C.II.04: Factors for and against the standardization of problem-solving approaches in business economics

there are a number of diverse proposals, e.g. full costing or marginal costing, standard costing or planned costing, either flexible or fixed. This could be one reason why supply of standard software for cost accounting has only recently started to show signs of growth, since powerful programming systems have become available which offer a wide range of procedures that can be implemented in a modular fashion.

There is also still no fully structured business economics system available for enterprise planning, so the standard software on offer here in the form of planning languages merely provides tools for individual solutions.

Even when factory-specific solutions have only minor advantages over the adaption of a standard solution, this is in itself a motivating factor towards standardization.

If there are uniform operating structures depending on size, organizational form, and manufacturing production type, then uniform solutions can be developed on a wider basis.

Factors displaying the reverse of these characteristics motivate against standardization. Solutions which provide advantages over competitors are a particularly strong reason for individualized developments. This applies, for example, to software for a particularly friendly service and customer-oriented order handling.

In the production area diversity of organizational form and production type mainly affect capacity management, whereas master data management and material management are largely standardizable. The size of the operation affects, on the one hand, the degree of complexity of the solutions, but also the willingness to accept standard solutions. Smaller enterprises often have access to neither the expert skills, nor the capacity or the financial means to develop individual solutions, and for this reason, they are more willing to adapt themselves to existing standard software than are larger enterprises.

A compromise between individualized software and uniformity is provided by standard software aimed at particular clusters of operating types.

Analysis of the standard software available shows that the same criteria are used to form the application clusters as are typically used to provide structure within the discipline of business economics. Global software covering all areas is impossible, since it is only conceivable as "general business economics" at a high level of abstraction. Thus, standard software oriented at **business functional areas** is available for production, purchasing, sales, personnel and accounting, which is not at first sight oriented towards any specific sector. It transpires, however, that these systems are usually aimed at certain dominant operating types, often at applications in large industrial firms. However, the same observation also applies to the functionally-specific business theories, which are also typically oriented towards the industrial firm as the most comprehensive and complex operating type.

In addition to functionally-oriented software, software also exists for different **sectors**. This already constitutes about one third of the entire business applications software.

Sector-specific differences primarily affect the output creation and order handling areas. Thus, standard software is available for the overall sectors of industry, trading, banking, and insurance, but also within these sectors according to further criteria such as special industrial branches or certain organizational forms. For example, programs exist for haulage, the building trade, the graphics industry, automobile trading, etc.

A systematic business economics analysis of the applicability of standard software based on operating type and functional possibilities for unification has not yet been undertaken, although its significance has been emphasized in publications on the market for standard software (see *Horvath, Petsch, Weihe, Standard-Anwendungssoftware 1986; Hansen, Amsüss, Frömmer, Standardsoftware 1983; Pressmar, Hansmann, Standardsoftwaresysteme 1978*).

Even large manufacturers do not adopt a systematic approach to software creation. Instead, one often gets the impression that standard software is created by chance. This is indicated, for example, by the fact that several different solutions exist for the same application whereas important application areas are not covered within a program family. Because software development is becoming increasingly expensive, however, and at the same time more crucial to overall market success, a strategic change in the direction of a more systematic approach is appearing. This means that intensive market studies need to be undertaken to determine application possibilities and hence existing operating structures. This offers business economics the opportunity to contribute its understanding of operating forms.

At present industrial economics is largely concerned with the operating form of the mechanical engineering firm, whereas questions relating to the chemical industry with its batch production, or the consumer goods industry receive only subordinate treatment (see also the criticism of the one-sidedness of industrial economics in *Schäfer, Industriebetrieb 1978, p. 10 f.*). The same effect is also apparent in the range of standard software available. It has already been mentioned in the discussion of EDP systems for production planning and control that serial manufacturing within the organizational form of job-shop production is dominant. These systems, however, are scarcely adequate for assembly line and batch production. In such cases the firm must either develop its own systems or use systems from smaller software houses which have specialized in the areas neglected by the larger manufacturers.

The more standard software is specialized towards the peculiarities of particular operating types, the smaller by definition will be its market. Differing approaches are adopted, therefore, to make the standard software as variable as possible to cope with diverse application forms. One such approach is that of **modularization**, that is the subdivision of a software system into self-contained sub-systems, which can be linked together via precisely defined interfaces. With a high degree of modularization the user can choose those sub-areas that are adequate for his problem.

By defining so-called **user exits** individual algorithms can be incorporated using standard programs. A user exit is a precisely defined program or file status which allows the user to program his individual order quantity formula into a purchasing package, for example.

A particularly flexible kind of adaptation is provided by the use of program generators. Here, the user can indicate on a checklist the functions that he requires. Figure 2.C.II.05 gives an example of this from the financial accounting area for the Nixdorf COMET system (see *Nixdorf, COMET 1978*).

The entries are checked by computer to ensure that they are logically consistent in business economics terms, and to determine whether all the preceding functions required for a desired function have also been selected. Using these entries a special program ((the customizer) generates a program containing only these functions.

Such possibilities for adapting standard software to individual user requirements are collectively referred to under the term **CUSTOMIZING** (see *Stahlknecht, Customizen 1983*).

```
          Data processing system  8870/1          Page CH
          COMET 3.2                                22.11.89

General checklist 010000
       2 . 6


00275     Working with foreign currencies?

:**
          Yes  = Automatic conversion to domestic currency possible
          No   = No foreign currency desired
://
:no
: _ _ _ _ _ _ _ _ _ _ _ _ _ _ _ _ _ _ _ _ _ _ _ _ _ _ _ _ _


00276     First possible foreign currency code for debitors?

:**
          The first foreign currency code from which the various currencies
          are assigned to the individual accounts receivable should be
          entered.
          If the system includes foreign currency 1 account receivable is
          needed for each currency (max. 19).
          If there are no foreign currencies in the system then a max. of
          20 accounts receivable (in the domestic currency) can be set up.
://
:10
: _ _ _ _ _ _ _ _ _ _ _ _ _ _ _ _ _ _ _ _ _ _ _ _ _ _ _ _ _


00278     Are several foreign currencies required per personal account?


          Yes  = The foreign currency code 20 allows the entry of various
                 foreign currencies
          No   = A personal account can only have the specified foreign
                 currency
://
:no
: _ _ _ _ _ _ _ _ _ _ _ _ _ _ _ _ _ _ _ _ _ _ _ _ _ _ _ _
```

Fig. 2.C.II.05: Checklist for COMET

Figure 2.C.II.06 classifies application areas on the basis of their degree of standardizability, and indicates the kind of support provided by prefabricated software.

Standardizability	Applications	Kinds of support using "pre-fabri-cated" applications software
high	Net wage calculation Financial accounting Master data management PPC Material management	Branch-independent standard software
moderate	Cost type, cost center accounting Operational data collection Purchasing	Modular programs Parameter-controlled programs Program generators
little	Order processing Capacity planning Gross wage calculation Cost accounting	Branch-specific or other "special" standard software Applications languages In-house developments
none	Enterprise planning Market research	Planning languages Report generators In-house developments

Fig. 2.C.II.06: Standardizability of business applications and possible forms of EDP support

In addition to the use of rigid standard software **or** flexible evaluation systems, a combination of structured applications software and flexible evaluation extensions can be used. To do this each business area can be broken down into generally valid core functions and specialized functions (see Figure 2.C.II.07).

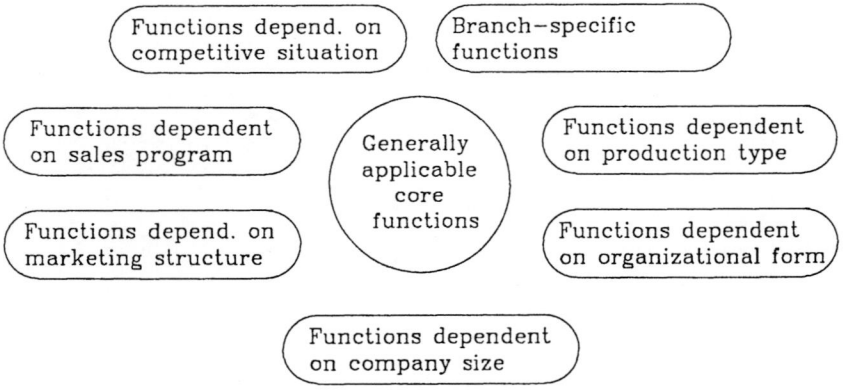

Fig. 2.C.II.07: Breakdown into core functions and specialized functions

Working out these kinds of functions and their dependencies, and establishing both their qualitative changes and their quantitative dimensions is an important prerequisite for the development of standard software that is of high quality in business economics terms. Here, too, the typologies provided by business economics can provide a starting point.

The boundary between standard and ad-hoc evaluations within a business accounting area concerns, on the one hand, the question of the organizational framework required, and, on the other, the flexibility needed.

In **integrated information systems** the areas involved build upon each other. This requires considerable discipline in the orderly development of those functions that provide data for other areas. They must, therefore, be incorporated into a clear organizational model. This also presupposes an established, comprehensive business economics model.

For example, for the internal accounting system, covering the accounting levels: cost type accounting, cost center accounting, cost estimation and contribution costing, this kind of self-contained model exists, which can be implemented in a comprehensive programming system. This concept has the advantage that it is logically self-contained. On the other hand, it has the disadvantage that it is often insufficiently flexible to handle case-specific queries. In addition, the results are often presented in the form of lists, whose structure is a compromise between various user requirements. As a result, their acceptability to each **individual** user is correspondingly low. For this reason, it makes sense to offer within the self-contained system only those evaluation functions which are absolutely essential for the process, or which are regularly required by all users.

These basic functions can then be extended by a flexible evaluation system. The user-oriented query languages of database systems, report generators, planning languages, or microcomputer spreadsheet programs can be employed in this context. A prerequisite is that these instruments can access the data generated by the accounting programs.

Basis-program systems, therefore, have the task of ensuring the uniformity of the data flow between the sub-functions of an integrated system, and providing a database for flexible and specialized evaluations on the basis of its established conceptual schema. Figure 2.C.II.08 presents this model of a user-oriented information system.

The use of microcomputers (personal computers) in a large enterprise, therefore, requires that these be in a network with the central EDP system. To perform their individual evaluations the specialist departments can then transfer excerpts from the central database to their microcomputers and evaluate them decentrally with user-friendly spreadsheet programs. The central EDP system manages the data stocks, however. As a result, the data protection functions can be handled centrally so that the specialist departments can concentrate entirely on their evaluations.

144

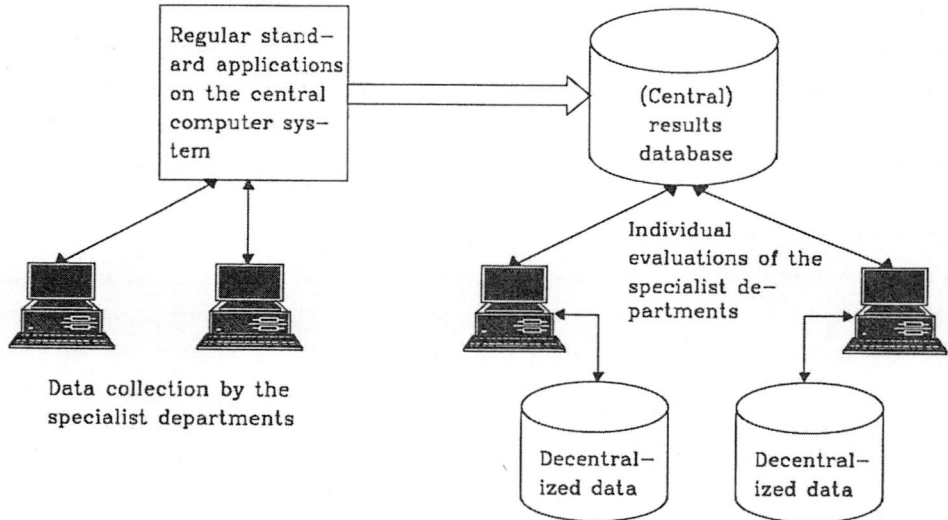

Fig. 2.C.II.08: Model of a user-oriented information system

It should be noted that in this kind of system the use of evaluation tools eliminates these business functions from the central programming system, allowing them to be carried out independently by user. This means that the clarity and uniformity of the business concept offered by comprehensive software systems could be compromised. The use of flexible software tools would then imply an improvement in the software techniques, but a disimprovement in the business economics standard achieved.

It is, therefore, important that business economics define clear concepts for the separation of standard functions and ad-hoc functions in the personal computing context.

Another equally important area for business economics is the development of expert systems (see Chapter 2, Section C.IV.). This offers the possibility of incorporating knowledge based on practical experience into a formal decision support system.

The progressive use of EDP also has an effect on methods of testing business accounting systems. In the context of external and internal testing, checks are made "around the computer". Here, only input data are provided and compared with the EDP results produced. This form of testing is, however, no longer adequate for increasingly complex information systems.

For this reason, the data checks must be supplemented by logical program checks. This requires that the tester be provided with suitable tools both for carrying out the audit and for determining the validity of the test. In the course of the EPSOS project (see *Ahlers et al., Prüfungsgerechtheit 1982*) criteria for test validity were developed, and using the interactive system EPSOS-D concrete COBOL programs can be evaluated in accordance with these criteria to provide information concerning testability and testing costs. In addition, the system supports the risk-oriented testing of software systems.

A consideration of the issue of testing software systems in theory and research is an important demand on EDP-oriented business testing theory.

C.II.3. Business Economics Structuring of Standard Software

The essential significance of standard software for business economics lies in its powerful structuring of reality. This is clear from the fact that all the major EDP manufacturers are being urged by their customers to provide standard software. They have in the meantime become the most significant suppliers, although this was never their intention. It can be explained, however, by the fact that customers prefer "solutions from a single source", and that standard software developments in parallel with manufacturers' operating system developments seem the most secure.

If business economics is interested in translating its results into practice quickly and extensively its contribution to standard software systems can be very effective.

Two sets of issues arise relating to how business economics can affect the development of standard software:

1. What is the standard of currently available standard software systems in business economics terms, and how might it be improved?

2. How to recognize in good time the apparent development trends in standard software and develop the appropriate business economic concepts?

The quality of business economics modelling approaches in standard software is diverse. It extends from simple "programming" of manual solutions through to novel concepts using the full range of EDP possibilites, e.g. in retail information and control systems.

The differentiation of many standard software approaches bears witness to the standard of business economics research, e.g., software for areas of operational accounting are already very well developed.

In principle, though, it is still the case that simple business accounting functions predominate in the standard software, and that, apart from simple lot-sizing formulae or forecasting techniques, planning and decision models scarcely exist.

146

A significant business aspect of standard software at present is the integration concept of software families. An assessment of this is, therefore, an important task for business economics.

The quality of standard software is determined not only by the calibre of the business economics content, but also by the exploitation of EDP potential. For instance, the possibilities of the consistent use of interactive processing have not yet been fully exploited, instead existing batch processing programs are often "made interactive" by the addition of interactive components for master data management.

The application of database systems has also not yet been fully utilized. It is true that hardware manufacturers offer their standard software systems which can be supported by their own database systems, so as to achieve joint product effects on sales. But this is not the case for software houses. For them, linking a standard software system to a specific database system essentially limits their market to the users of that database system. The standardization of database interfaces, such as SQL for relational database systems, will be of help here, however.

Other software houses attempt to delay using database systems as far as possible and implement quite complex data management functions using traditional data processing forms. It is to be expected, however, that the user's desire to use flexible database languages and to exploit the protection methods that database systems offer, means that this approach cannot be successful in the long run.

Another possibility is to employ a slimmed-down database system as a "black box" in each applications system. This is not entirely free of problems for the user, however, since he then has to employ several database systems in parallel with the associated system overhead.

C.III. Method Banks

C.III.1. Description of Method Banks

Standard applications software has a large multiplier effect on how widely the business economics models it contains are used. In the same way standard software for mathematical optimization procedures in the form of method banks encourages the use of these planning techniques. The interdependence here is so close that the use of complex optimization techniques for realistic problems is dependent on the use of the computational and storage capabilities of EDP installations.

Just as in the case of standard applications software, EDP has influenced further developments in EDP-suited solution procedures. For example, EDP programs for solving large linear programming models contain special procedures and algorithms for efficient storage use and avoiding rounding errors. By doing this well-known programming systems, such as MPSX from IBM, APEX III from CDC, MPSI from Siemens, MACSYMA from Symbolics, or the IBM applications system (AS) are in a position to solve LP models with several thousand variables or side conditions in a few minutes. By specifying a good starting solution computational times of only a few seconds are needed, so that even the solution of larger LP models can be handled interactively.

The use of programming systems for solving LP problems has led to a standardization of entry data in the so-called **MPS (Mathematical Programming System) format**. The coefficients of the LP matrix can thereby be generated independent of the specific program system to be used. This is of considerable help in using matrix generators, to be considered below.

The MPS format can be explained using a simple example. First, an LP model for production planning is represented in the usual notation (see Figure 2.C.III.01).

The first index (preceding the production variable name x) indicates the period, the second index (following the variable name) indicates the product. There are two capacity types (production levels) A and B, which both products must pass through.

$$
\text{Goal} = 5 \cdot {}_1x_1 + 3 \cdot {}_1x_2 + 2 \cdot {}_2x_1 + 6 \cdot {}_2x_2 \implies \text{Max !}
$$

Side conditions for capacities:

$2 \,{}_1x_1 + 3 \,{}_1x_2 \leq 120$	Capacity type A	⎱	1. Period (January)
$1 \,{}_1x_1 + 4 \,{}_1x_2 \leq 140$	Capacity type B	⎰	
$2 \,{}_2x_1 + 3 \,{}_2x_2 \leq 130$	Capacity type A	⎱	2. Period (February)
$1 \,{}_2x_1 + 4 \,{}_2x_2 \leq 150$	Capacity type B	⎰	

$$
{}_1x_1 > 0, \quad {}_1x_2 > 0, \quad {}_2x_1 > 0, \quad {}_2x_2 > 0
$$

Fig. 2.C.III.01: Optimization problem

In the MPS format the following data entry structure is adhered to (see *Schmitz, Schönlein, Optimierungsmodelle 1978, p. 58*):

1. Name of the problem.

2. Assignment of names for objective functions and side conditions (ROWS section).

148

3. Entry of the coefficient matrix (COLUMNS section); the matrix is read in columns and each coefficient is described by entering the column name, row name and value. If several coefficients are listed in one row the (identical) column name is not repeated.
4. The values for the right hand side are read into the RHS section by entering RS, line name, and value, where RS is the name of the right hand side.

	JANX1	JANX2	FEBX1	FEBX2	Type	RS
GOAL	5	3	2	6	Max	
JANCAPA	2	3			$\leq$ (L)	120
JANCAPB	1	4			$\leq$ (L)	140
FEBCAPA			2	3	$\leq$ (L)	130
FEBCAPB			1	4	$\leq$ (L)	150

Fig. 2.C.III.02: MPS representation of the problem in tableau form

For the transition to the MPS format it is useful to represent the problem in tableau form. Here, the period indices are replaced by abbreviated names of the months, and the indices are written on the same level as the letter to which they belong.

EDP support for planning techniques is also shown in simulation techniques, especially the Monte Carlo method. This method is based on the numerical solution of similar cases and is thereby well suited to EDP handling. It is scarcely conceivable that this method could have achieved its current significance if powerful computers had not been available. With the help of special programming languages (simulation languages) such as GPSS (General Purpose System Simulator), SIMULA and SIMSCRIPT it is possible using macro commands for even untutored EDP users to program the essential elements of simulation systems, such as the production of random numbers, queue management, and the handling of priority rules and output routines.

The example would then read in MPS notation:

```
NAME                PLANNING            (self-selected name)
ROWS                                    N = Nonrestricted
    N   GOAL                            L = LESS (less than or equal to
    L   JANCAPA                                      condition)
    L   JANCAPB
    L   FEBCAPA
    L   FEBCAPB
COLUMNS
        JANX1       GOAL        5
        JANX1       JANCAPA     2
        JANX1       JANCAPB     1
        JANX2       GOAL        3
        JANX2       JANCAPA     3
        JANX2       JANCAPB     4
        FEBX1       GOAL        2
        FEBX1       FEBCAPA     2
        FEBX1       FEBCAPB     1
        FEBX2       GOAL        6
        FRBX2       FEBCAPA     3
        FEBX2       FEBCAPB     4
RHS
        RS          JANCAPA     120
        RS          JANCAPB     140
        RS          FEBCAPA     130
        RS          FEBCAPB     150
ENDATA
```

Fig. 2.C.III.03: MPS notation

In general the aim is to ensure that the user of mathematical planning and optimization techniques is principally in possession of specialist knowledge. Knowledge of the mathematical methods used and the EDP handling is of secondary importance, as is indicated in the user profile in Figure 2.C.III.04.

This is supported by method bank and model bank systems, in that a user can, via the uniform user interface of a control system, communicate using data from a database, methods from a method bank and models from a model bank (see Figure 2.C.III.05). A uniform user interface is understood to mean that the user can communicate with all components using the same commands, screen forms and entry formats.

The **database** contains all the data needed for the application as well as the linkages between them.

The terms **method bank** and **model bank** are not used consistently. A method refers to a procedure for solving a particular class of problems, and a model to the representation of

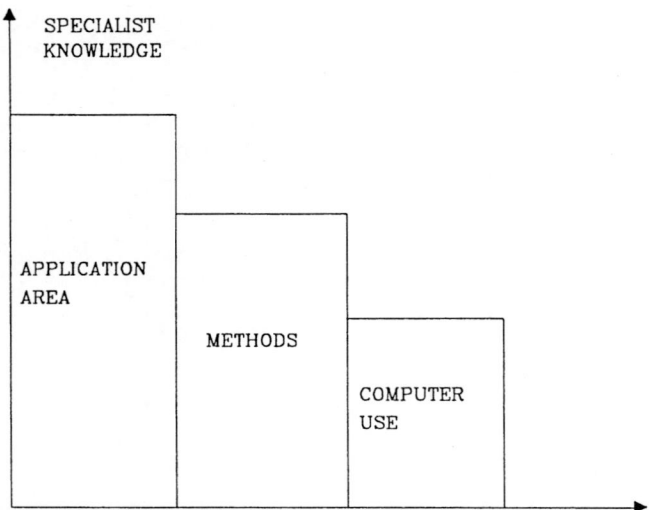

Fig. 2.C.III.04: Profile of a method bank user
(from *Bodendorf, SAMBA 1981*)

a real system (see *Alpar, Methodenauswahl 1980, p. 40*). Adopting this definition, a method bank contains, for example, statistical or mathematical algorithms for solving well-structured problems, whereas a model bank contains the structure of real problems. With reference to an economic model this means, for example, that the kind of time series

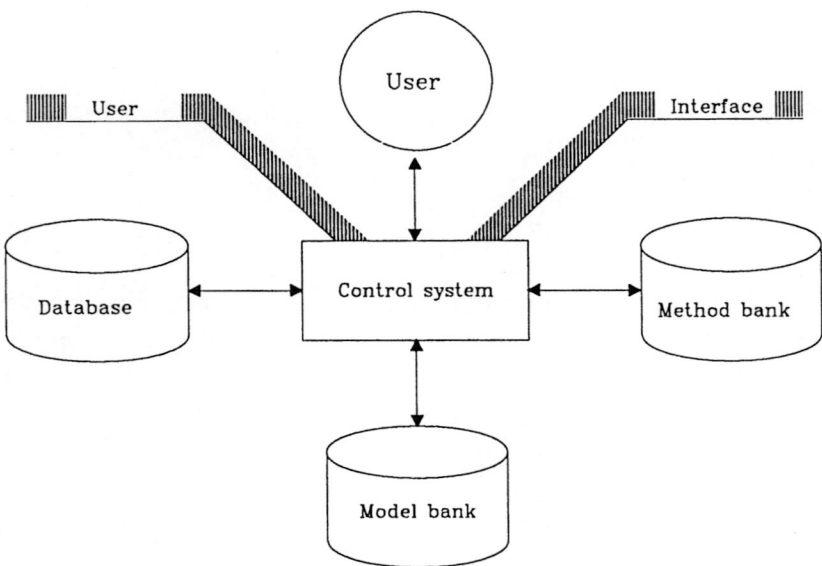

Fig. 2.C.III.05: Incorporation of the method bank within an information system

data involved, their relationship to each other, and the individual sets of equations are stored as a model in the model bank, whereas the regression analysis procedure used to solve the model are stored in the method bank.

However, since modern method banks are not only a collection of programmed methods, but also contain support for providing data for, and determining the parameters of, the method, they are increasingly taking over functions which, in terms of the definitions, are actually assigned to model banks. For this reason, the divisions shown in Figure 2.C.III.05 may be useful for conceptual distinctions, but are no longer strictly adhered to in real systems.

The **control system** provides the user with comfortable user guidance, efficient entry formats and help formats.

The uniformity of the user interface is also indicated by the fact that system responses to specific queries are in a particular form. This also applies to the form of error messages, for example.

Within the user interface a **lay mode** is provided for untutored users, whereas experienced users can use an **expert mode** to obtain the information they need in only a few interactive steps.

Using **help functions** the user can, in the course of solving a problem, be directed to parts of the documentation or error handling possibilities.

C.III.2. Business Economics Implementation of Method Banks

The practical application potential of optimization models is often offset by the data provision difficulties. Here, direct links between databases and linear optimization method programs via matrix generators provides effective support. Two steps need to be followed: In the first step interface programs extract data from the numerous files in operative EDP applications and place them in a transfer file. Standardized matrix generators can then fill the LP matrix with data from this file. Matrix generators not only provide tools for the entry of coefficients, but at the same time support the preparation of the model, i.e. the definition of the rows and columns of the LP matrix.

The use of data transfer programs from the operative applications is supported by increasing standardization of data structures. So, in EDP systems for production planning and control, the databases for bills of materials, work schedules, and equipment have largely the same structure (see the database structure in Figure

3.B.I.05). This effect is exploited by the PROMOS system (see *Kneip, Scheer, Wittemann, PROMOS 1981*) (see Figure 2.C.III.06).

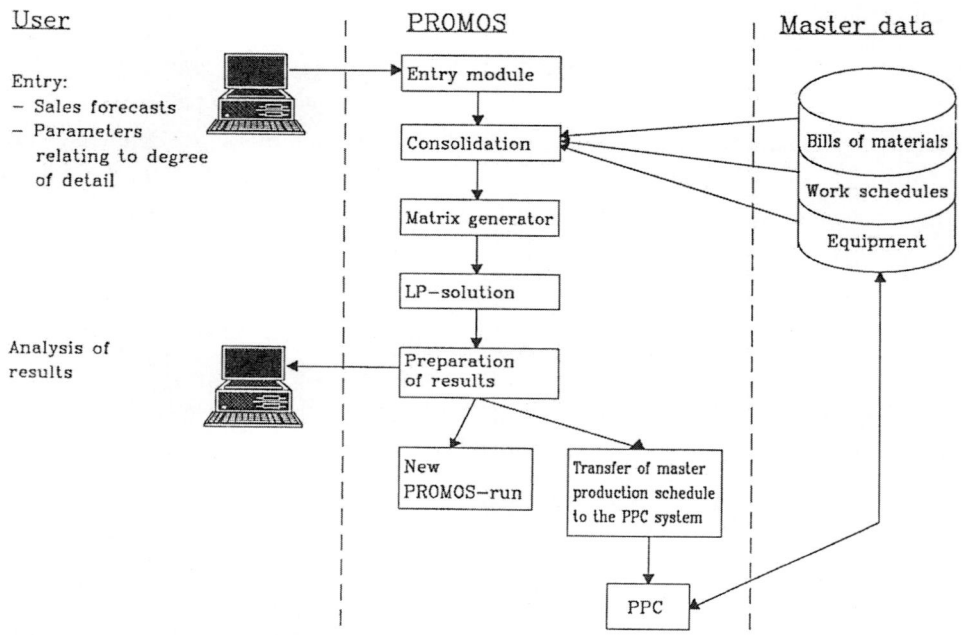

Fig. 2.C.III.06: The PROMOS system

The PROMOS system generates an LP model for production and sales planning from the database for the production area on the basis of end products or end product groups. Side conditions for sales, purchases, stores and capacity are automatically generated from the database. The breakdown of the bill of materials relationships to end products generates the variables for the assemblies to be incorporated and the bought-in parts to be purchased. The capacities required for in-house produced parts are determined from the relationship between work schedules and equipment groups, and the relevant capacity side conditions are entered automatically.

The result of the optimization is a production plan which is consistent with capacity conditions and purchasing policy. This production plan can then serve as the master production schedule for a classical production planning and control system.

The user can interactively specify sales forecasts for the end products and product groups to be included, and also determine the level of detail for the aggregation of products to product groups.

At the same time he can also enter parameters relating to period length and the number of periods to be considered. A data consolidation program creates a transfer file from these entry data and the master data for bills of materials, work schedules, and equipment. The matrix generator prepares this file for transfer to the LP solution program. The preparation of results can also be controlled interactively. As soon as the result is acceptable to the user it can be passed on to the production planning and control system as the master production schedule.

PROMOS is a matrix generator with a built-in model structure. Special languages (matrix generator languages) exist for the easy creation of matrix generators, with whose help a model can be "programmed". The matrix generator program thus produced is then executed, and creates the LP matrix in MPS format.

An example of a widely-used matrix generator language is the system OMNI (see *Haverly Systems, OMNI 1981*). The functional method is demonstrated using the LP model for production planning introduced above (see Figure 2.C.III.01).

Three tables for capacity requirements, right hand side and objective function coefficients are given as transfer files, from which the MPS notation is created.

Since the coefficients for the capacity requirement is independent of the period the CAP table in the LP matrix is simply duplicated for each period (see the tableau in Figure 2.C.III.02). The capabilities of matrix generators prove themselves in the automatic duplication of these basic data.

Table CAP

Lines \ Columns	1	2	3
1		A	B
2	x_1	2	1
3	x_2	3	4

Table RHS

Lines \ Columns	1	2	3
1		JAN	FEB
2	A	120	130
3	B	140	150

Table Goal T

Lines \ Columns	1	2	3
1		JAN	FEB
2	x_1	5	2
3	x_2	3	6

Fig. 2.C.III.07: Tables as transfer files

The ROW section, that is the definition of the row names, is then generated by the following instruction:

```
FORM       ROW
     GOAL = OBJ (The objective function is given the name Goal)
     (PER) CAP (C) = MAX FOR PER = TABLE RHS (1, )
                         FOR C   = TABLE CAP (1, )
```

Fig. 2.C.III.08: Generation of the ROW section

The expression MAX describes the type of side condition, in this case a "less than or equal to" equation (L).

The bracketed parts of the expression (PER) CAP (C) describe variable parts which are generated from the tables with the help of the subsequent run commands. The relationship furthest to the right varies most quickly. In brackets after the table names (row number, column number) are specified. If no values are given all the defined index values are processed. Thus RHS (1,) and CAP (1,) mean that all values in the first line should be processed. The result is:

```
N   GOAL
L   JANCAPA
L   JANCAPB
L   FEBCAPA
L   FEBCAPB
```

Fig. 2.C.III.09: Result of Fig. 2.C.III.08

The COLUMNS section is generated by an analogous expression:

```
FORM   VECTOR (PER) (VAR)   FOR PER = TABLE RHS (1, )
                            FOR VAR = TABLE CAP (1, )

   GOAL = TABLE GOAL T ((VAR), (PER))

   (PER) CAP (C) = TABLE CAP ((VAR), (K)) FOR C = TABLE CAP (1, )
                   WHEN (TABLE CAP ((VAR), (C)) .GT.0)
```

Fig. 2.C.III.10: Generation of the COLUMNS section

The condition in the last line ensures that a triple is only established if the relevant element in the capacity matrix is larger than (.GT.) 0.

The output of the results is given in Figure 2.C.III.11. This was done with the LP5000 program from Siemens. It consists of the result data for the side conditions (section 1) and the variables (section 2). The activity column in section 1 indicates capacity that has been taken up, the slack activity column indicates the proportion of total capacity that is not assigned. The dual activity column contains the values of the dual variables. For example, a value of 2.5 in the capacity condition JANCAPA indicates that increasing capacity A by one unit under otherwise identical conditions would generate an additional contribution of 2.5 units.

The activity column in section 2 gives the result values for the variables. Input cost contains the objective function coefficients of the initial matrix. The value 4.5 in the reduced costs column implies that a one unit increase in the variable value of JANX2 (initially zero) reduces the value of the objective function by 4.5. This is a consequence of substitution effects, since a weak contribution variable is replacing a strong contribution variable in the solution.

```
2 NOV 1989      *** PLANNING PROBLEM – OPTIMIZATION ***        SIEMENS LP5000 V5.0


IDENTIFIER SECTION
        PROBLEM...   NAME..    PLANUNG
                     MODE..    LP
                     CLASS.    LP
                     STATUS    OPTIMAL*
        FUNCTIONAL   NAME..    GOAL
                     OBJECT    MAXIMIZE
                     VALUE.        532.00000
        RESTRAINT.   NAME..    RS
        ITERATION.   COUNT.         3


SECTION 1 – ROWS                   PRIMAL–DUAL OUTPUT
```

NUMBER	..LABEL.	AT	... ACTIVITY...	SLACK ACTIVITY	..LOWER LIMIT.	..UPPER LIMIT.	. DUAL ACTIVITY
1	GOAL	FR	532.00000	−532.00000	NONE	NONE	−1.00000
2	JANCAPA	UL	120.00000	.	NONE	120.00000	2.50000
3	JANCAPB	BS	60.00000	80.00000	NONE	140.00000	.
4	FEBCAPA	UL	130.00000	.	NONE	130.00000	0.40000
5	FEBCAPB	UL	150.00000	.	NONE	150.00000	1.20000

```
SECTION 2 – COLUMNS                PRIMAL–DUAL OUTPUT
```

NUMBER	..LABEL.	AT	... ACTIVITY...	..INPUT COST..	..LOWER LIMIT.	..UPPER LIMIT.	.REDUCED COST.
6	JANX1	BS	60.00000	5.00000	.	NONE	.
7	JANX2	LL		3.00000	.	NONE	4.50000
8	FEBX1	BS	14.00000	2.00000	.	NONE	.
9	FEBX2	BS	34.00000	6.00000	.	NONE	.

Fig. 2.C.III.11: Output of the LP results

Matrix generator languages for linear programming models are offered in accordance with standards by hardware manufacturers and software houses. They are principally used for solving large optimization models.

The use of LP models is concentrated chiefly on the mineral oil and chemical industries. The strict application of the possibilities of matrix generators and the exploitation of the potential of standardized data structures in formulating models can provide effective support for the application of linear programming models in the context of EDP-oriented business economics.

C.III.3. Business Economics Structuring of Method Banks

Method bank systems manage collections of statistical and mathematical solutions for well-structured problems. In recent years diverse criteria for their user-friendliness have been developed. In addition to criteria based on software technology (see *Rickert, Konzeption von Methodenbanken 1982, p. 169 ff.*) special mention should be made here of the user-oriented criteria (see *Mertens, Bodendorf, Methodenbanken 1979, p. 533 ff.*).

These are:
- the richness of the collection of methods,
- documentation of the methods,
- data security and protection,
- selection assistance,
- interpretation assistance.

The **richness** of a collection of methods is indicated by the number of methods contained providing descriptive statistics, time series analysis, correlation calculation, linear and non-linear optimization, simulation procedures, etc.
Comprehensive method collections are offered, for example, by the well-known systems SPSS, BMD, and METHAPLAN. As well as providing programs for algorithmic solutions, a user-friendly method bank also offers programs for the graphical presentation of results as part of its standard contents.

Since the description of a method is not automatically self-explanatory of its entire content, precise **method documentation** of the procedural method is required. This should be available interactively to the user. The documentation of the METHAPLAN system (Siemens), for example, contains documentation at three different levels: an overall directory, a method class directory and the documentation of the individual methods. In the documentation of the individual methods a description of the theory is given, the EDP application part is presented, and the functioning of the method is described with the aid of an example.

As in database systems, method bank systems must take precautions against the unintentional destruction of programs and data. Furthermore, it may be necessary to ensure that access to certain methods is limited to a restricted group of users. This can be important if, by the skillful combination of methods, it would be possible to circumvent the anonymity of person-specific data records.

A frequently observed obstacle to the **acceptance** of method collections is that they offer a large number of diverse methods which are largely unfamiliar to the user. This generates uncertainty on the part of the user. In the course of a carefully conducted application he must first familiarize himself with a large number of method descriptions, until he encounters a suitable procedure for his application. In order to simplify this selection process, systems providing **user guidance** have been developed. Since the lengthy guidance of the user to a suitable evaluation method can be cumbersome, however, experts can also by-pass these support functions.

In the METHAPLAN system a menu is simply used to offer hierarchical steerage through the multiplicity of methods. The individual procedures are sub-divided into thirteen classes. Further problem-specific support in making a selection is not offered to the user (see *Rickert, Konzeption von Methodenbanken 1982, p. 175*). In contrast, the MADAS system (see *Mertens, Bodendorf, Methodenbanken 1979*) offers data-oriented selection assistance. Each piece of data is described by its scale. Depending on the problem to be solved, the number of data elements to be included, and their statistical properties, the user is guided by decision tables to suitable statistical procedures in the method bank. Figure 2.C.III.12 (see *Mertens, Bodendorf, Methodenbanken 1979, p. 536*) shows a **decision table** for the problem of the bivariate structural analysis of two time series.

In the conditions part of the decision table questions are posed concerning the scale of the input variables. Depending on these input values, the fourteen rules presented in the condition indicator part assign the statistical procedure in the action indicator part. For example, in the case where both input variables are measured on a nominal scale the calculation of the contingency coefficient is suggested. If details of the scale of the data are already stored in the master records, the user can be directed to a suitable method by the program system, which automatically applies the stored decision tables once the input variables to be compared have been specified.

Choice of methods for bivariate structural analysis	Rules													
	1	2	3	4	5	6	7	8	9	10	11	12	13	14
1 Dichotomous	1	1	0	0	0	1	1	0	1	0	0	0	0	0
1 Normally distrib.	–	–	–	–	1	–	–	0	–	1	0	–	–	1
1 Nominal	–	–	1	1	0	–	–	0	–	0	1	0	0	0
1 Ordinal	–	–	0	0	1	–	–	–	–	0	0	–	–	0
1 Metric	–	–	0	0	0	–	–	–	–	1	0	–	–	1
2 Dichotomous	1	0	1	0	1	0	0	1	0	1	0	0	0	0
2 Normally distrib.	–	–	–	–	–	1	0	–	1	–	–	0	–	1
2 Nominal	–	1	–	1	–	0	0	–	0	–	0	1	0	0
2 Ordinal	–	0	–	0	–	1	–	–	0	–	–	0	–	0
2 Metric	–	0	–	0	–	0	–	–	1	–	–	0	–	1
Phi	x													
Kontingenz		x	x	x										
Spearman/Tie					x	x								
Kendall/Tie							x	x						
Punkt–Biseral									x	x				
Wilcox/Freeman											x	x		
Kendall/Tab													x	
Produkt–Moment														x

Conditions part — Condition indicator part (top block); Action part — Action indicator part (bottom block)

Fig. 2.C.III.12: Decision table for the choice of methods in bivariate structural analysis

The well-known method bank system SIBYL/RUNNER (see *Makridakis, Wheelwright, Forecasting 1978*) for forecasting techniques also offers help in the choice of method. Here, queries are made concerning both the data properties and the problem characteristics. These are: the planning period, the data pattern, the model type, the permissible forecasting costs, the desired degree of accuracy, the permissible complexity of the procedure and the availability of past data (see *Makridakis, Wheelwright, Forecasting 1978, p. 4*). These points are, of course, only loosely related to the interactive framework of the SIBYL/RUNNER system. In particular, it is not impossible for a user, acting independently, to choose an unsuitable procedure for his problem. However, a good method bank system should contain not only selection mechanisms but also prohibition mechanisms against the use of unsuitable methods.

The DEMI system offers an interactive framework for forecasting problems, which follows the logical structure of a decision tree (see *Brombacher, Marketing-Informationssystem 1981; Scheer, Absatzprognosen 1983, p. 46 f.*).

Figure 2.C.III.13 shows an excerpt from an interactive tree, and Figure 2.C.III.14 the associated excerpt from the computer interaction. It shows how a user is directed to the use of the Winters model as the suitable forecasting technique given his forecasting task and the available database.

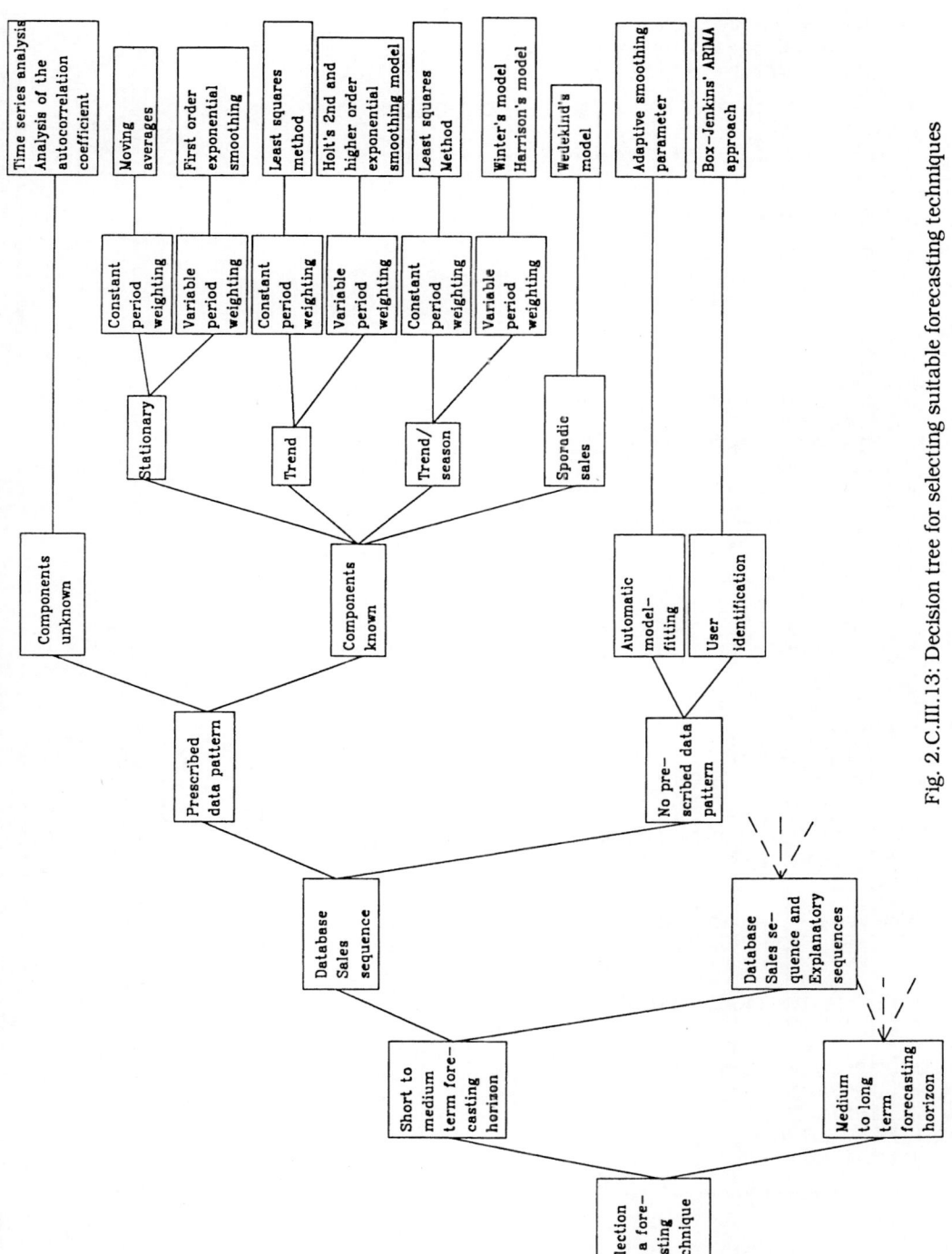

Fig. 2.C.III.13: Decision tree for selecting suitable forecasting techniques

THE "FORECAST INTERACTION" PROGRAM GUIDES YOU TO AN ADEQUATE
FORECASTING PROCEDURE FOR YOUR PROBLEM AND SUPPORTS YOU IN YOUR
CHOICE OF MODEL.

ARE THE DATA NEEDED FOR YOUR FORECAST ALREADY STORED ON
DISKETTE?
IF YES ENTER Y IF NO ENTER N
Y

FOR WHAT FORECASTING HORIZON SHOULD THE FORECAST BE
PRODUCED?
A) SHORT TO MEDIUM TERM (I. E. UP TO ONE YEAR)
B) MEDIUM TO LONG TERM (I. E. MORE THAN ONE YEAR)
PLEASE ENTER A OR B
A

WHICH DATA SHOULD BE USED IN GENERATING THE
FORECAST?
A) ONLY PAST VALUES OF THE TIME SERIES TO BE
   FORECAST
B) OR ADDITIONAL EXPLANATORY VARIABLES ?
PLEASE ENTER A OR B
A

IS THE DATA PATTERN OF THE TIME SERIES KNOWN?
IF YES ENTER Y IF NO ENTER N
Y

SHOULD THE FORECAST BE CHOSEN
A) ON THE BASIS OF THE KNOWN DATA PATTERN
B) OR SHOULD A SELF-FITTING PROCEDURE BE
   CHOSEN?
PLEASE ENTER A OR B
A

DOES THE TIME SERIES DISPLAY A TREND?
IF YES ENTER Y IF NO ENTER N
N

DOES THE TIME SERIES DISPLAY REGULAR SEASONAL FLUCTUATIONS?
IF YES ENTER Y IF NO ENTER N
Y

HOW MANY PAST DATA ARE AVAILABLE?
(PLEASE ENTER NUMBER)
36

APPROPRIATE FORECASTING PROCEDURE:
WINTERS MODEL

A) EXECUTION OF THE CHOSEN PROCEDURE
B) REPEAT THE INTERACTIVE SEARCH OR
C) TERMINATE THE INTERACTION?
PLEASE ENTER A, B OR C
A

```
PROCEDURE FORECAST
BY EXECUTING THE WINTERS MODEL
```

Fig. 2.C.III.14: Computer interaction for selecting suitable forecasting techniques

Recent proposals suggest that a user should merely describe his problem verbally. This input is then processed by a text analysis system and a suitable method is selected using identified descriptors.

Just as important as the support of the method selection process is support in the interpretation of results. In this context the user must be warned against impermissible interpretations, for example, the use of spurious correlation. Here, it is useful to provide the user with textual information familiarizing him with the significance limits for his specific result, or to provide him with the inferences of specific significance levels, such as are given in statistics textbooks (see *Bodendorf, SAMBA 1981*).

C.IV. Expert Systems

C.IV.1. Description of Expert Systems

C.IV.1.1. Definition of Expert Systems

Whereas with decision support systems the emphasis is on the "support" and the decisions themselves are made by the user, expert systems are more closely involved in the problem-solving process, i.e. they make decisions in a quasi-independent fashion. According to Feigenbaum's definition (see *Harmon, King, Expertensysteme 1989, p. 3*), an expert system is an intelligent computer program which uses knowledge and inferential processes to solve problems which are difficult enough to require considerable human specialist knowledge (expert knowledge) for their solution. In order to reduce unrealistically high expectations of expert systems, the more modest term **knowledge based systems** is also increasingly being used.

Expert systems constitute a sub-area of **artificial intelligence**. Accordingly, the aim is to represent the problem-solving behaviour of a human expert. Human experts possess a large amount of knowledge of a specific area and, as well as applying logical, representable methods, they also use rules of thumb (heuristics) and intuition to solve exceptional cases.

In classical programs all possible cases within a problem are "programmed out". But this can only be applied to well-structured problems (see Figure 2.C.IV.01). The apparently simple task of "going to the cinema this evening" is, however, badly structured and cannot be represented by a classical program with a well-structured model (see case (b) in Figure 2.C.IV.01). The task is badly structured because the goal is not explicitly defined (which cinema and which film are intended), the means of reaching the cinema are not unequivocally specified (e.g. by car, foot, taxi, bus, ...) and the problem space is unlimited (there is no restriction to cinemas in a certain part of town, location, etc.) (see *Harmon, King, Expertensysteme 1989, p. 34*).

Expert systems attempt to solve this kind of problem by describing the knowledge of the factual contents and a procedure for linking this knowledge with the objective (**inferential mechanism**). For example, a human solves the above problem of a cinema visit, in that he has knowledge which can provide him with information relating to the cinema program (e.g. newspaper advertisements, program information services). By using bus timetables and town plans he has access to further information. By combining knowledge of distance and speed, temporal restrictions can be established which limit the number of relevant alternatives. By combining general knowledge (timetables, cinema programs) with temporal restrictions for the current situation, the complexity of the problem can be reduced and a solution is finally attainable.

Expert systems thus attempt to provide the best possible approximations for badly structured problems (case (c) in Figure 2.C.IV.01).

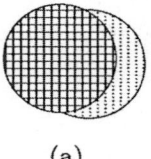   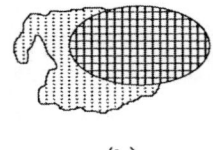   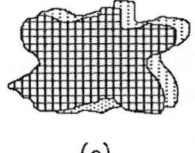

(a)   (b)   (c)

Data processing: real problem and its representation are largely congruous

Badly–structured problem, well–structured model

Expert systems: approximation to the badly–structured problem

▦ Real problem

▦ Representation of the problem and the model

Fig. 2.C.IV.01: Degree of structuring of the problem and the model
(from *Kurbel, Pietsch, Expertensystem-Projekte 1989, p. 134*)

Expert systems also occupy a central position in the development of "fifth generation computer systems".

The term "fifth generation computers" was coined in a Japanese program for developing a new generation of computers which was presented in 1981. Scientists and technicians from eight Japanese firms and two national research laboratories are working on this project which was instigated by the Ministry of International Trade and Industry (MITI). The aim of this program is to develop computers which are capable of learning, making

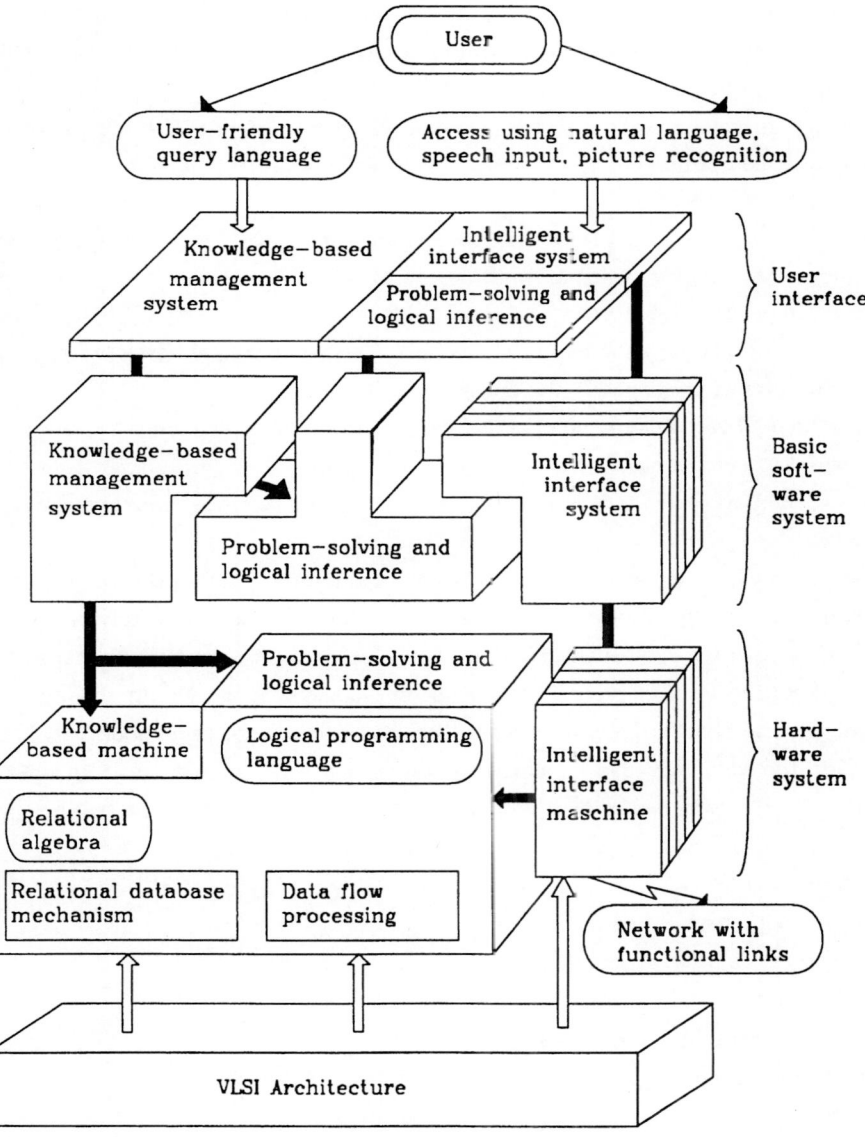

Fig. 2.C.IV.02: Fifth generation computer system

associations, making decisions, and behaving in many ways which have up to now been the exclusive preserve of human rationality. Knowledge Information Processing Systems (KIPS) will be central. The computer should be small, robust, and inexpensive. Figure 2.C.IV.02 represents the schematic structure of a fifth generation computer with its interfaces.

The entire program is broken down into three phases. In the first three year plan a prototype of an expert machine based on the PROLOG language will be developed. This should be capable of handling several thousand rules.

In the following four year plan this system will be developed further, and in the last three year plan a super computer is to be produced which can process ten thousand knowledge rules.

The machine should be capable of understanding spoken and written words and graphical input. The linking of verbal input and written output should also be achieved using a text processing system. Later parts of the research project are to be developed using the results achieved in the earlier stages, e.g., further technical development with the CAD/CAM systems developed in the first phase.

A significant effect of the 200 million dollar program is the publicity which it has aroused in the entire EDP community in the last few years, and in the formidable degree of integration needed to unify the diverse hardware, system software and applications developments.

Doubts have been expressed as to whether the aims and the timescale of the program are achievable, but the effects on future informatics research are already unmistakable.

In particular, the call for inexpensive yet powerful computers for user support leads one to suppose that this kind of computer will assume a significance within the human sphere equivalent to that of the written word (see *McCorduck, Fifth Generation 1983*). In the meantime the idea has also generated imitative activities, such as the European program ESPRIT (European Strategic Program for Research in Information Technology) brought into being by the EC, with research emphasis on

-       advanced microelectronics,
-       software technology,
-       advanced information processing,
-       office systems,
-       computer integrated manufacturing,
-       infrastructure projects.

Special programming languages, such as PROLOG, LISP or C++ are available for EDP-technical implementations of expert systems. They allow the flexible development of expert systems, albeit at considerable cost. In order to limit the creation costs so-called shells have been developed. **Shells** are expert systems without a knowledge base. For instance, "MYCIN", the expert system for medical applications, is available without the medical knowledge base as a shell for other applications. Other well-known shells that can be implemented on workstations or microcomputers are: KEE, NEXPERT, S1 or PERSONAL CONSULTANT. Other large computer systems, which are primarily available for commercial applications are ESE (IBM), TWAICE (Nixdorf) and BABYLON (GMD).

C.IV.1.2. Structure of Expert Systems

The basic structure of an expert system is presented in Figure 2.C.IV.03. The knowledge of facts and rules within an expert system is stored in the knowledge base. This knowledge is brought together via a **problem solving component** (inferential mechanism) to generate an appropriate procedure for a given objective. The **explanatory component** provides the user with elucidation of the solution process. With the help of the **knowledge acquisition component** knowledge derived from the experience of human experts is incorporated in the knowledge base.

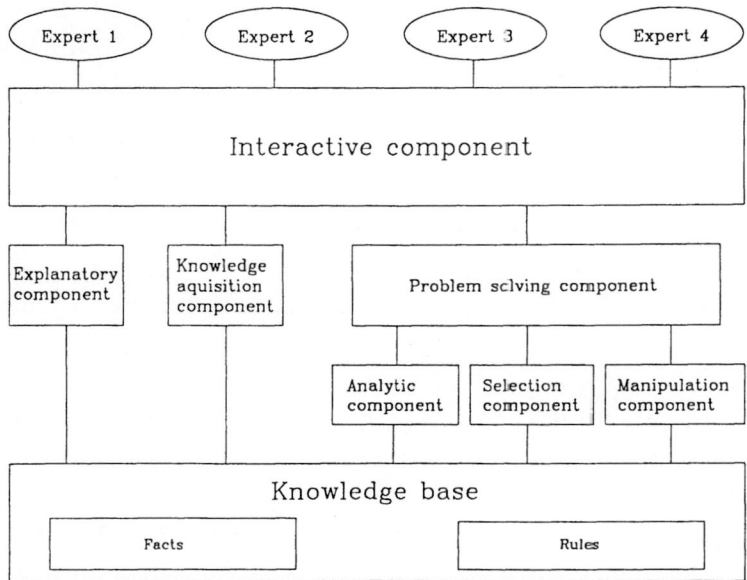

Fig. 2.C.IV.03: Structure of an expert system

The **interactive component** establishes links with the user by way of a user-friendly interface (e.g. using natural language).

The knowledge base, problem solving, explanatory and knowledge acquisition components will be discussed briefly below.

C.IV.1.2.1 Knowledge Base

The knowledge base is at the heart of an expert system. For the human expert, too, the extent of his knowledge is of primary importance. Human memory networks are described using so-called **chunks**. These consist of a symbol (see Figure 2.C.IV.04) and associated related symbols that are activated whenever the object (in Figure 2.C.IV.04 "dog") is thought of.

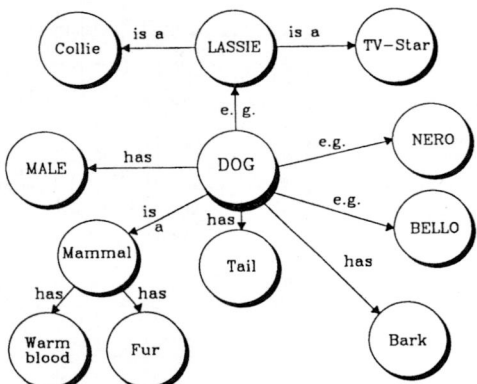

Fig. 2.C.IV.04: Chunk

(from *Harmon, King, Expertensysteme 1989, p. 28*)

An example of greater relevance to business economics is given by Hausknecht and Zündorf for the concept "annual accounts" (see Figure 2.C.IV.05).

Human experts have a large number of such chunks (50,000 - 100,000) at their disposal, which have been stored in the course of a lengthy learning process, but which are then available in the brain for speedy recall.

Expert systems make use of similar forms of knowledge representation. **Semantic networks**, which are similar to chunks, are formed to describe objects and the relationships existing between them (factual knowledge).

The factual content of an instructive and widely quoted example of a scene from Sherlock Holmes is shown in Figure 2.C.IV.06 in semantic network form.

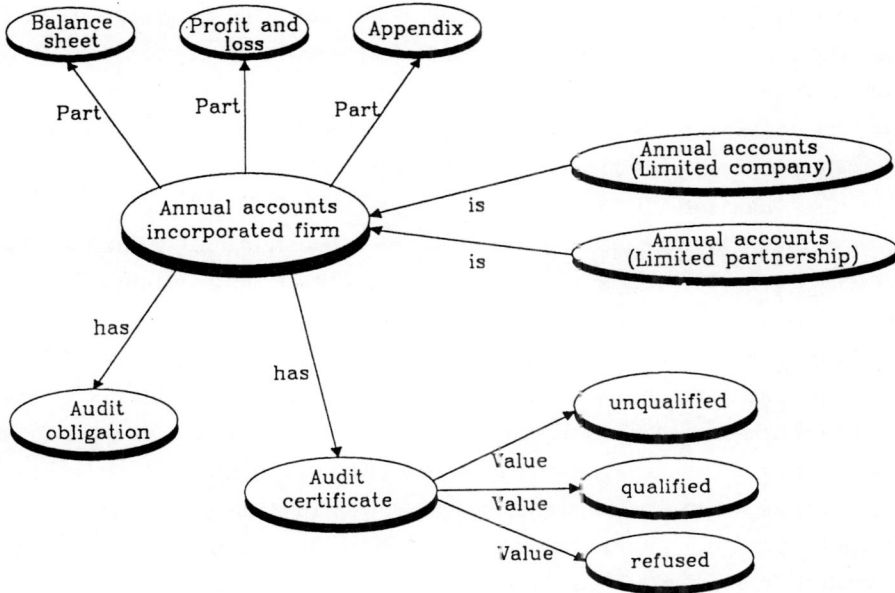

Fig. 2.C.IV.05: Semantic network for the annual accounts of an incorporated firm

(from *Hausknecht, Zündorf, Finanz- und Rechnungswesen 1989, p. 22*)

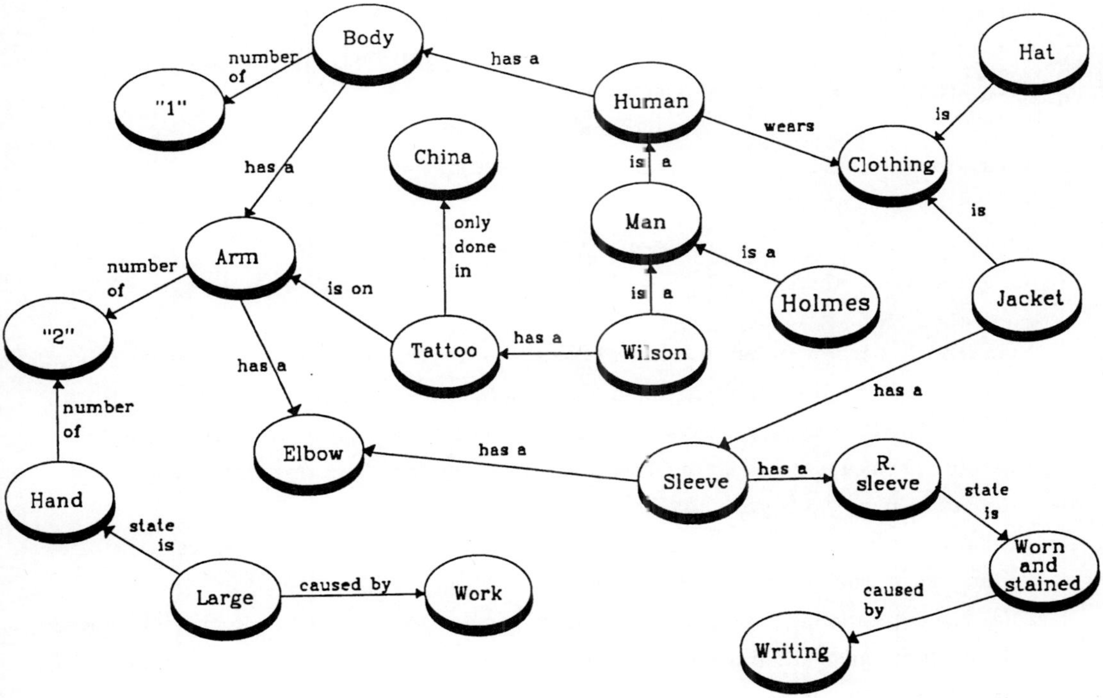

Fig. 2.C.IV.06: A detective's knowledge base

(from *Harmon, King, Expertensysteme 1989, p. 42*)

Semantic networks consist of **objects** (nodes) and **edges** which represent links between the nodes. Objects can be physical or conceptual constructs which are connected using links such as "is a", "has a", or "consists of". The larger the number of links the more confused the diagram becomes. For this reason, operations such as generalization, individualization, and aggregation are employed to simplify the representation (see *Trost, Wissensrepräsentation 1984, p. 55*).

Another way of representing knowledge is the **"object-attribute-value"** declaration. For example, the excerpt "Wilson is a man" from Figure 2.C.IV.06 can be expressed by the triple: object = man, attribute = name, value = Wilson.

In so-called **frames** an object is described by all the associated information. Each attribute of an object is represented by a "slot" containing the current value of this attribute. Procedures can also be assigned to the slots. To this extent slots represent a link between declarative and procedural knowledge. **Procedural knowledge** comprises procedures, methods, heuristics or techniques of applying **declarative knowledge**, that is knowledge of the objects within a specialist area and the relationships existing between them. Procedural knowledge is frequently represented by rules.

A **rule** consists of one or more premises and a conclusion. The knowledge represented in the semantic network of Figure 2.C.IV.06 concerning the origin of the tattoo and the relationship between hand size and physical work can be expressed in the following rules, for example (see *Harmon, King, Expertensysteme 1989, p. 49*):

Premise:	if	the tattoo is a fish and
		the colour of the fish scales is pink,
Conclusion:	then	the tattoo originates from China

| Premise: | if | a person's right hand is larger than the left, |
| Conclusion: | then | he is occupied in manual labour (0.6). |

Since conclusions often have no causal basis, but are based on human experience, they may be subject to uncertainty. This is indicated by the allocation of **confidence factors**, which are defined for the interval (0,1), for example. If the conclusion concerning hand size and physical labour of the individual is merely such an assumption, it can be assigned a factor 0.6, for example.

Semantic networks are not only suitable for declarative knowledge, since they also contain the procedural parts of the rules.

The representational forms using semantic networks, objects, values, attributes, relationships, rules and frames are in part only different perspectives on the same factual content. For example, the rules introduced above can also be expressed in the form of an "object-attribute-value" representation (see Figure 2.C.IV.07):

	Object	Attribute	Value
if	Tattoo	Motif	Fish
	Fish scales	Color	Pink
then	Tattoo	Origin	China

Fig. 2.C.IV.07: Further means of representing rules

In the knowledge base a distinction can be drawn between static and dynamic knowledge. **Static knowledge** represents the general facts and rules of an area of knowledge at the start of the problem solving process. **Dynamic knowledge**, in contrast, relates to the current problem issue and is entered into the system by the user in the course of the interactive process. By incorporating this knowledge the knowledge base can, therefore, be extended.

C.IV.1.2.2. Problem Solving Component

The problem solving component (inferential component) has the task of steering and monitoring the problem-solving process in its use of the stored knowledge (facts and rules). This requires operators and process control. The most important **operator** is a derivation rule which derives new knowledge from the stored knowledge. The simplest derivation rule is the **"modus ponenz"**. This signifies that "if a is known to be true" and the rule "if a, then b" applies, it will be concluded that b is also true.

For instance, if it is known that the right hand of the person Wilson is larger than his left, this current knowledge can be combined with the previously introduced rule concerning the general relationship between hand size and manual work to generate the following conclusion: If Wilson's right hand is larger than his left hand, then he is occupied in manual work. This special knowledge about Wilson can then be newly entered in the knowledge base.

With respect to **process control** it is possible to differentiate on the basis of:
- the scope of the solution search,
- the direction of the solution search,
- the means of resolving conflicts.

The possibilities can be represented graphically as in Figure 2.C.IV.08.

With respect to the **scope** of the solution search a distinction is drawn between depth and breadth searches. In a **depth search** the suitability of one solution alternative is investigated as completely as possible, without fully considering all other possible alternatives. In a **breadth search**, in contrast, at a given stage in the solution process all the relevant alternatives are analysed before the next stage is initiated.

With respect to the **direction** of the solution search a distinction is drawn between backward and forward chaining. In **backward chaining** the starting point is the goal to be achieved and the process is one of a backwards analysis of the prerequisites for its achievement. In **forward chaining**, in contrast, the data available for the particular case are analysed as to possible implications and continuing in this manner a solution is sought. In the first case of backwards chaining, therefore, execution elements are checked for consistency with the goal to be investigated and then their suitability is determined on the basis of an analysis of the prerequisites. With forward chaining, however, the available data are compared with conditional elements, in order to discover suitable rules to be followed subsequently.

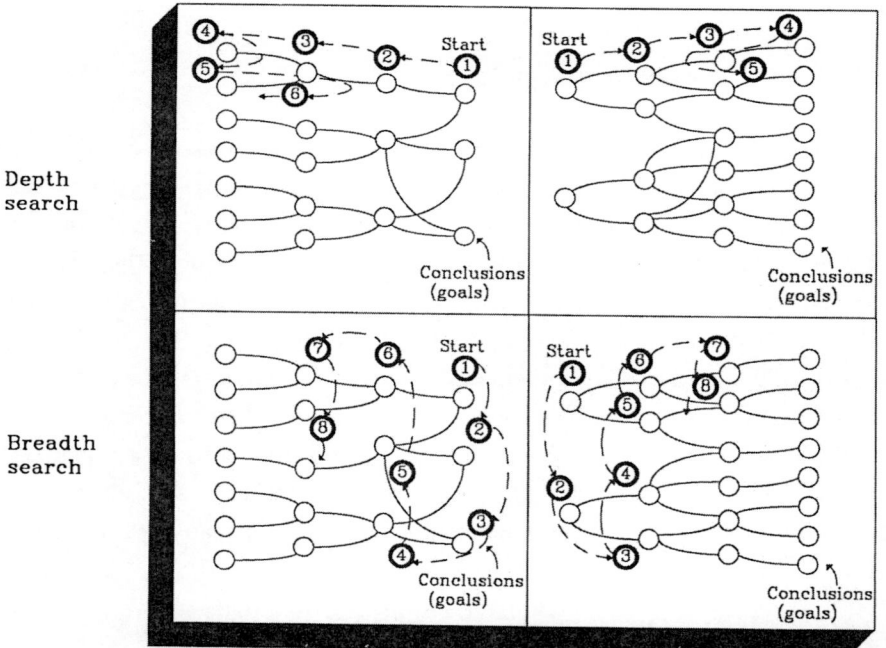

Fig. 2.C.IV.08: The most important search strategies used by inference machines

(from *Harmon, King, Expertensysteme 1989, p. 64*)

Figure 2.C.IV.09 shows a table with rules for the cinema visit considered above.

Using backward chaining can result in the following process: the problem solving goal is always the determination of actions. In rules 4, 5, and 6 the implications of actions are considered: the actions are, therefore, the starting point for the chain. In rule 4 the action "take a taxi" is established. But this means that the premises "drive" and "town center" must be fulfilled. In rule 1 the mode "drive" is generated. This depends on the numerical value of the distance. The distance can be determined by a query. If the user's reply is "2 km" then rule 1 is not valid. Rule 2 also generates the mode "drive". It is analysed next. In addition to the distance, the time available is also queried. If the answer is 10 minutes, for example, the specification of 2 km and 10 minutes fulfil the premises of rule 2. In a breadth search rule 3 would also be analysed at this point (in fact, given the details, it does not apply), whereas a depth search would return immediately to rule 4. In rule 4 the first part is now fulfilled and the location of the cinema must be analysed. For simplicity it is assumed that the answer to the query is "town center", so that rule 4 is fulfilled. The remaining rules 5 to 7 are now analysed, but they do not apply in this case.

Rule	IF: (Premise)		THEN: (Conclusion)
1	Distance > 5 km	⟶	Mode is "drive"
2	Distance > 1 km and time < 15 min.	⟶	Mode is "drive"
3	Distance > 1 km and time > 15 min.	⟶	Mode is "walk"
4	Mode is "drive" and location is "town center"	⟶	Action is "take a taxi"
5	Mode is "drive" and location is not "town center"	⟶	Action is "use car"
6	Mode is "walk" and weather is "bad"	⟶	Action is "take overcoat and walk"
7	Mode is "walk" and weather is "good"	⟶	Action is "walk"

Fig. 2.C.IV.09: Rules for a visit to the cinema

(from *Harmon, King, Expertensysteme 1989, p. 61*)

Backwards chaining has proved itself efficient in many working expert systems. However, good expert systems make use of both approaches.

Conflict solving mechanisms determine which rules are to be applied if several rules are available. For example, rules generated by experienced experts might be applied with higher priority than rules placed in the knowledge base by less experienced experts.

C.IV.1.2.3. Explanatory Component

The user of an expert system should always be able to comprehend the system's processes and conclusions. The explanatory component should provide assistance here in response to "what", "how" and "why" queries (see *Bendig, et aL, Betriebswirtschaftliche Problemstellungen 1987, p. 57*).

Examples of such queries for the case of the cinema visit considered above might be: What is a mode of transport? Answer: "drive", "walk".

In the case of a "why" query, a part of the inferential chain is presented and explained to the user. On output of the action "take a taxi" the user could ask: "Why should I take a taxi?" and would then receive the explanation of the distance and time connections. With "how" queries user assistance can be requested. For example: "How can I manage to be in time to see a film?"

Although the explanatory component is presented as a special characteristic of expert systems, it is poorly developed in most implemented systems. Often it is limited to the mere provision of records of the chain of implications for the rules analysed. Furthermore, this is often presented to the user in a form that is not easily understandable (especially in the case of shell-based systems).

For this reason much expense and research is being directed at this system component at present.

C.IV.1.2.4. Knowledge Acquisition Component

The acquisition of knowledge for the knowledge base is also a frequently claimed and emphasized property of expert systems. It is often eclipsed by the other components, however, because of its complexity. The sources of the knowledge in the knowledge base are not only the documentary knowledge from specialist literature, databases, etc., but above all the knowledge of the human expert. The transfer of knowledge into an expert system requires its adjustment to the representational possibilities of the system. In transferring human knowledge the **knowledge engineer** is engaged as an intermediary between the expert and the expert system. By way of discussions with the expert the knowledge engineer must be able to identify the specialist knowledge and prepare it in suitable form. The long term aim is to enable experts to enter their knowledge into the knowledge base themselves either using intelligent interfaces or by giving the appropriate training.

The knowledge acquisition component is not only used to acquire knowledge, however, it also checks the knowledge introduced for completeness and freedom from contradiction with the already existing knowledge.

C.IV.2. Business Economics Implementation of Expert Systems

The problem areas within business economics offer a wide field of application for expert systems. This was recognized at an early stage in the course of the informatics-oriented development, since some of the first expert system prototypes were concerned with issues from business economics and related areas, such as order configuration and investment counselling. In addition, initial experience in their use has been available for some years for economic application areas. This makes it all the more surprising that economic theory and research only discovered the potential and implications of expert systems for business economics at a relatively late stage. Furthermore, the first presentations at scientific conferences and in scientific publications were made by representatives of business informatics. Specialists from business economics and the operations research discipline, which is particularly closely related to the expert systems area, only then reacted to these stimuli.

C.IV.2.1. Competing Approaches

In developing expert systems the core of informatics, which at least in Germany is oriented both in theory and research primarily at theoretical constructs and basic principles, has succeeded in penetrating applied disciplines with an independent problem-solving method.

In business economics thus far the development of models for well-structured problems has predominated. This is particularly clear in the area of operations research, which, in Germany in the 1960s, was strongly influenced by business economics. The relatively low application standing of such models is an indication that many approaches do not conform with the reality that the models represent, but rather describe case (c) in Figure 2.C.IV.01 where a badly-structured decision situation is represented by a well-structured model and thereby accounts for only part of the reality. More recent developments in operations research, particularly in connection with the discussion of multiple objectives or the fuzzy set theory have already abandoned the naive approach of well-structured decision problems. With the development of expert systems even more pliable forms of problem-solving, such as dominate in practice, can be handled by scientific means. This applies, for example, to the use of rules of thumb, knowledge based on experience, and the handling of partially true information.

The significant interactive component of expert systems also emphasizes strongly case-specific problem-solving as opposed to the period-oriented approach that is predominant in many classical business economics models.

This not only makes it possible to handle this kind of heuristic decision-making, but also to document it. In the real world this means that experience is no longer lost, but can be transferred to other decision-makers or made available to them for evaluation by way of expert systems.

However, the euphoria generated by every new development should not hide the fact that expert systems also have their weak points.

Applications up to now have been restricted to relatively small problem areas, which are explicitly defined as suitable for the use of expert systems. The alarmingly small proportion of expert systems at the so-called "running" stage indicates the numerous obstacles to their development, implementation, and application (see *Mertens, Expertensysteme in Funktionsbereichen 1988*).

For well-structured decision problems such as transport problems or mixing problems in the mineral oil industry, where mathematical modelling methods have already been developed with considerable success and much experience, expert systems certainly offer no better alternative. Their relatively simple structure (knowledge base and simple inference strategies) is seen as inadequate for decisions in complex organizations (see *Jarke, Wissensbasierte Unterstützung verteilter Entscheidungen 1989*). Even within expert systems the naive supposition remains that the entire decision situation can be represented by a model (the expert system itself). Potential interactive processes are quasi-anticipated in this model, too. The user is primarily treated as the provider of data. The multi-facetted general knowledge which is available to the human problem-solver, which can also be used, possibly in non-causal form, to solve exceptional cases, is not available to the expert system.

Despite these limitations expert systems open up new possibilities for research and applied business economics. Areas with considerable practical relevance that have been neglected up to now can be broached. This is demonstrated by existing developments (see the reports of expert system developments in *Scheer, Betriebliche Expertensysteme I 1988 and II 1989*). The development of an expert system for design stage cost estimation, for example, has opened up an area of cost accounting which, despite its enormous practical relevance, has not been considered by business economics approaches. Cost estimation methods in business economics generally assume the existence of data concerning bills of materials, work schedules and cost center rates. In the early stages of product development, however, only fragments of these data are known. It is therefore necessary to incorporate novel approaches such as rules of thumb or the relationship between the already known geometric or weight properties of the product and the expected costs

C.IV.2.2. Application Areas

There already exists a wide range of business economics applications for expert systems, in marketing, purchasing, quality assurance, production planning and finance (see the extensive compilation in *Mertens, Borkowski, Geis, Expertensystem-Anwendungen 1988*). The following overview gives an impression of the possibilities and groups of expert systems (see *Scheer, Steinmann, Themenbereich Expertensysteme 1988, p. 15 ff.; Mertens, Allgeyer, Däs, Betriebliche Expertensysteme 1986, p. 6. ff.*):

-   Analysis and diagnosis systems
    evaluation of the PPC database,
    causes of equipment failure,
    analysis of equipment use,
    diagnosis of the causes of missed deadlines,
    --   customer order-related,
    --   production order-related,
    analysis of throughput times and diagnosis of defects,
    --   machine-related,
    --   order-related,
    analysis of quality data,
    cost analysis,
    --   relative distribution of production costs,
    --   cost comparisons between products,
    --   calculation of alternatives (e.g. production technology).

-   Selection systems
    data management and search systems,
    --   bills of materials,
    --   work schedules,
    --   supplier data etc.,
    data evaluation and consolidation systems.

-   Intelligent checklists
    meeting of customer order deadlines,
    curative and preventative maintenance,
    order handling support,
    --   temporal processing,
    --   factual processing of content.

- Advice systems

  decisions concerning customer order acceptance,

  assignment of production orders to equipment,

  release of production orders according to equipment load,

  capacity adjustment (medium and long term),

  relocation possibilities.

- Configuration systems

  equipment layout,

  composition of a product from components (variants),

  work schedule creation from standard work schedules,

  layout of production installations (FPS, islands, ...).

- Planning systems

  master production scheduling,

  material requirement planning,

  capacity requirement planning,

  material flow planning.

- Access systems

  choice of methods,

  -- master production scheduling,

  -- material requirement planning,

  -- capacity requirement planning,

  intelligent data dictionary,

  jurisdiction rules.

- Help systems

  effective use of the PPC system,

  -- EDP techniques,

  -- PPC functions,

  -- PPC processes,

  effects and causes of errors, error recognition.

- Instruction and training systems

  training,

  -- PPC processes,

  -- hardware/software.

- Decision systems
  external purchases or in-house production,
  material requirement calculation.

- Monitoring systems
  meeting of deadlines,
  -- customer orders,
  -- production orders,
  -- material availability,
  quality evaluations,
  machine use.

Of course, the points listed above, which derive from the PPC area, merely represent catchwords relating to a very complex decision space. The concurrence of several of these points generate, on checking the process logic of the concurrence and the prerequisites, the application area for an expert system.

C.IV.3. Business Economics Structuring of Expert Systems

The business economics task in developing expert systems consists in:
1. finding appropriate problem areas,
2. transforming the knowledge available within business economics into a suitable representational form for expert systems,
3. providing human experts for the acquisition of experiential knowledge,
4. developing procedures for the creation of expert systems.

The choice of suitable problem areas has up to now been a matter of chance, and more the result of the interests of individual researchers than the importance or suitability of the application area. With greater pervasion of knowledge about expert systems it is to be expected that a trend towards more content-based choice will develop.

In transferring business economics knowledge to the knowledge base of expert systems it has often become clear that the knowledge recorded in textbooks is incomplete. To this extent, there is pressure towards more complete, and more exact recording of business economic facts.

In a similar fashion to the principle of **decision support systems**, which combine exact procedures for well-structured aspects of a decision problem with the human problem-solving capacity, this can also apply to expert systems (Expert Support Systems = ESS). In expert systems both exact modelling approaches and heuristic solution strategies are combined. In this way researchers can create a smooth transition from their traditionally "exact" fields of activity.

The development of expert systems for real problems is dependent on cooperation with human experts for the transfer of experience-based knowledge. Business economics as a science can, therefore, make only a small contribution to these special problems.
Of course, procedures for acquiring business economics knowledge can be developed.

Since the development of expert systems, like that of software products, is associated with considerable temporal and financial costs, it is appropriate to develop procedural approaches to their construction and to the control of the process. This generates scope for research areas concerned with the advantages or disadvantages of phase-oriented or prototype-oriented system development, and the provision of suitable instruments for project control (see *Kurbel, Pietsch, Expertensystem-Projekte 1989*).

The development of "fifth generation" computers has significance for business economics in that the use of EDP capabilities within the enterprise will become increasingly taken for granted, as is the use of telephones at present. In the process, EDP systems will no longer be used only for pre-formulated and structured tasks, or to provide responses to the user's ad hoc queries, but also within certain limits to undertake creative tasks by the application of artificial intelligence.

Chapter 3: EDP-Oriented Business Economics Solutions

In Chapter 2 the significance of individual EDP techniques for business economics was discussed, in considering the components of an information system. In the course of this discussion it has already become clear that the information techniques are interconnected and mutually interdependent. For this reason, the following chapter presents EDP applications in which the instruments for computer-supported business economics systems are integrated. Some of these diverge considerably from the classical business economics approach. This contrast makes the character of the EDP influence on business economics issues immediately obvious.

Strict utilization of EDP applications is increasingly altering the competitive position of the enterprise. In Part A, therefore, approaches to establishing the strategic significance of EDP applications are considered, and procedures for developing an information strategy are presented.

In Part B sector-specific EDP applications for industry, trading, banking, and insurance are discussed, and in Part C general applications in accounting, marketing, personnel management, enterprise planning, and administration (office automation).

A. Strategic Significance of EDP-Oriented Solutions

The use of information technology is of strategic significance in two respects. Decisions concerning the use of special technology, such as database systems or network concepts are binding over a long period, and determine the enterprise's information processing possibilities for a considerable time. On the other hand the skilful use of information technology can influence the enterprise's strategic orientation.

Strategic planning is understood as a procedure whereby the long term goals of the enterprise are established, along with the basic means of achieving these goals.

By adapting existing approaches to general strategic planning, methods of elucidating the strategic effects of information technology have been developed. Before briefly presenting these methods, an example of the concrete effects on competitive policy of using information technology is presented. Then, in the third section procedures for developing an information strategy are outlined.

A.I. Example

A widely quoted practical example showing the competitive effects of the thorough application of information technology is the seat booking system of the US airline company American Airlines (AA). The SABRE system (Semi Automative Business Research) stores the most important international flight timetables. American Airlines has sold this system to over 12,000 travel agencies, thereby also making the company an important supplier of applications software. Information technology has, therefore, opened up a new product area for the company. At the same time the system has influenced the company's competitive position within its own market. The system is created in such a way that American Airline flights are given preference over those of other airlines, in that where several suppliers can offer a suitable flight, American Airlines' offer always appears on the screen first.

The significance of the system has already become obvious not only in that the "distortion" in the presentation of offers has had to be removed under pressure from the American antitrust agencies, but also in that other airlines have developed similar systems in order to at least check American Airlines' advantage.

This example also makes it obvious that the competitive effect cannot be viewed statically: The first supplier to create closer links with the customer generates thereby an initial advantage. With the more extensive information possibilities provided to the customer by similar systems the relative market position of the customer is strengthened, since there is now greater market transparency also with respect to other suppliers (see *Mertens, Plautfaut, Informationstechnik 1986, p. 10 ff.*).

A.II. Methods of Determining Strategic Effects

The strategic significance of information techniques is indicated primarily by a change in the enterprise's market position. Individual effects that have been discussed in the literature are:

- changes in competitive factors (see *Eidenmüller, Wettbewerbsfaktor 1989*),
- effects on the value creation chain (see *Porter, Millar, Wettbewersvorteile 1986*),
- the concept of critical success factors (see *Rockart, Critical Success Factors 1982*),
- portfolio analysis (Boston Consulting Group).

The **competitive situation** in a particular sector is determined by five factors (see Figure 3.A.II.01):

- the market strength of the consumer (purchaser),
- the height of the barriers to entry in the market (for new competitors),
- the degree of substitutability for a product by new products,
- the market strength of the seller (supplier),
- the intensity of competition between the existing competitors.

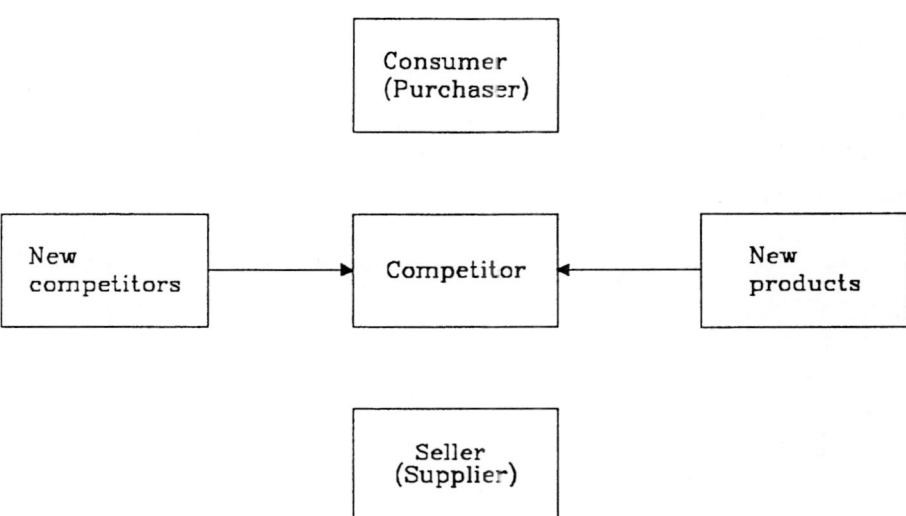

Fig. 3.A.II.01: Competitive powers within a market

EDP-oriented applications concepts can affect each of these individual factors. Greater use of information technology allows the purchaser to discover more easily the current terms for a larger range of suppliers. This strengthens the **market position of the purchaser.** The same applies to the use of inter-company information networks. In the first stage a supplier can indeed achieve a competitive advantage by providing his customer with greater information possibilities concerning his products, e.g. via links with his own EDP system; at the next stage, however. when other suppliers do the same, the purchaser can more easily make selections from diverse sources and thereby strengthens his position. This was clear in the American Airlines example presented above.

The **barriers to market entry** are raised if information technology is employed intensively, since setting up a complete infrastructure (network, database system, or development of complex expert systems) requires a high level of investment. On the other hand. the skilful use of information technology can also facilitate market entry, e.g. by

182

generating the scope for offering EDP-supported service functions and leaving the capital-intensive production to the existing enterprises. Examples of this are the use of CAD systems in the electronic engineering field (where only design is undertaken), or the takeover of engineering and project control functions in the plant construction field.

The **substitutability** of products can be improved by using CAD in conjunction with flexible manufacturing techniques, since this allows variants with new performance characteristics to be created easily from a basic product.

The **market power of the supplier** is increased if he can offer computerized services, e.g. "round-the-clock" ordering using Videotex.

The **competitive intensity** between existing competitors is generally increased, since the use of information technology allows greater differentiation in product development, pricing policy and production costs.

According to Porter, an enterprise can affect its **competitive position** by the choice of three fundamental strategies (see *Porter, Wettbewerbsstrategie 1988, p. 62 ff.*):

1. Striving for **cost leadership**:
   In this case information technology is used primarily to support operative systems.
2. **Product differentiation**:
   Here, information technology can increase the individuality of the product by using CAD, CAE, or expert systems for customer-oriented configuration.
3. Establishing **market niches** (market specialization):
   Here, a combination of the two previous strategies is adopted.

Each enterprise is embedded in the **value creation chain** between suppliers and purchasers (see Figure 3.A.II.02):

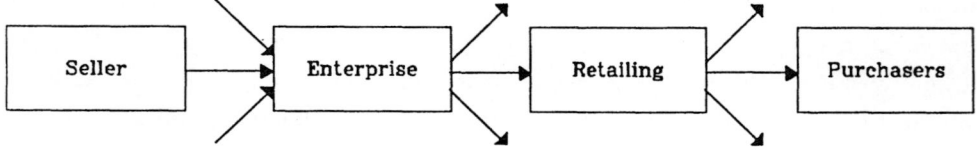

Fig. 3.A.II.02: Total value creation (value chain)

By using information technology the enterprise can increase the amount that customers are prepared to pay for the increased value of the product, and reduce the costs that need to be incurred in achieving its value creation. Here, Porter and Millar distinguish between **primary activities** at the operative level (see Figure 3.A.II.03) (*Porter, Millar, Wettbewerbsvorteile 1986, p. 27*):

- internal logistics,
- production,
- external logistics,
- marketing and sales,
- customer service,

and the **secondary support activities** which accompany them:

- infrastructure of the firm,
- personnel,
- technical development,
- purchasing.

Since in all of these components there is increasing investment in the use of EDP, as is shown by the systems presented in Figure 3.A.II.03, information technology is effective in both directions, that is, in increasing value creation and in reducing incurred costs.

According to Rockart, **critical success factors** (CSF) are those factors which are primarily responsible for the success of the enterprise and which, therefore, must be paid particular attention. Rockart assumes that the number of these success factors for a particular enterprise is limited (on average between 4 and 6), and satisfactory results on these factors is sufficient to ensure the enterprise success (see *Rockart, Critical Success Factors 1982*). Although the success factors differ depending on the enterprise situation and sector, typical factors are: quality for the automobile industry, or cash flow for an enterprise in financial difficulties.

Secondary activities

Infrastructure	Office automation				
Personnel	Personnel information system				
Technical development	CAD, CAE				
Purchasing	Requirement planning and ordering system				
	Driverless transport system	PPC, CAM	Dispatch control	Marketing information system	Spare parts planning
	Internal logistics	Produc-tion	External logistics	Sales/ Marketing	Costumer service

Value creation

Primary activities

Fig. 3.A.II.03: Enterprise value creation

184

The analysis and determination of critical success factors can be used to form the basis for the orientation of information processing. Applications systems, which can have a particularly positive influence on the critical success factors of a firm, are thereby assigned a high development priority, for example.

Information technology not only supports the means of output creation and exploitation, but increasingly affects the product itself. This is indicated in Figure 3.A.II.04 in which the informational content of the product is contrasted with the importance of information techniques in value creation in a **portfolio** diagram.

INFORMATION INTENSITY OF THE VALUE CREATION CHAIN	H I G H	OIL REFINERY MECHANICAL ENGINEERING	BANKING INSURANCE AIRLINES
			⟶ Trend
	L O W	CEMENT INDUSTRY MINING	↑ T r e n d PRINTING
		LOW	HIGH
	INFORMATION CONTENT OF THE PRODUCTS		

Fig. 3.A.II.04: Information intensity of processes and products

The introductory example of American Airlines illustrates the position of airline companies, for whom the product (service, transport) is increasingly being extended by information services (reservations, information, bookings).
In general there are trends towards increasing significance of information techniques in both value creation and product development.

A.III. Procedure for Developing an Information Strategy

The approaches discussed for elucidating the strategic content of comprehensive EDP applications systems can constitute the starting point for development of an information strategy. This generates a close integration of the planning of information processing and strategic enterprise planning. Planning an **information strategy** can be undertaken in four stages (see *Awad, Management Information Systems 1988, p. 399*):

1. The starting point is the strategic enterprise plan,

   if the enterprise does not have such a plan, the strategic goals and fundamental approaches of top management need to be established.

2. Transformation of the strategic enterprise goals into information processing goals.

3. Development of alternative information system proposals.

4. Discussion of the alternatives with the management.

IBM presented a structured procedure for strategic planning of information processing at an early stage in its **BSP (Business Systems Planning)** method. It is based on a four stage process (see *IBM, Business Systems Planning 1984*):

1. Definition of enterprise goals.

2. Definition of the firm's most important business processes.

3. Definition of the firm's data structures.

4. Definition of the information system architecture.

Within this procedure points 2 and 3 emphasize the importance of the consideration of process chains and of data as an enterprise resource which have been considered in this book. It is claimed that the BSP method has been used by over 1,000 American firms to instigate the planning of their information processing. It consists of a sequence of processing steps, which are carried out in a top-down process with the enterprise management.

Another approach to determining a model for integrated data processing in industrial enterprises has been developed by the author and has now been tested in numerous enterprises. Central also to this approach is the determination of the enterprise-specific process chains, their data structure support, and the embedding of the information strategy in the general enterprise strategy. The **Y-CIM Strategy** is developed in eight stages (see *Scheer, CIM 1990 p. 69ff.*):

1. Determination of enterprise goals with respect to the use of information technology.

2. Process chain analysis.

   A project team establishes the most important process chains by interviews in the specialist departments.

3. Critical success factors.

   In order to give the enterprise management the possibility of checking the information system with respect to the goals to be pursued, critical success factors are defined. For example, the goal of increasing manufacturing flexibility can be expressed in concrete, and also measurable, terms as a reduction in set-up times and order throughput times.

4. Formation of functional levels.

    The individual links in the process chains investigated are assigned to functional levels of the enterprise, so that the links with the organizational structure can be created.

5. Data structures.

    The design of data structures receives particular attention, since it is a prerequisite for process integration.

6. Applications software.

    Requirement profiles for the applications software to be employed are developed for the process chains that have been developed.

7. EDP-technical model.

    The EDP-technical model is developed from the goals to be pursued, the critical points in the operational structures of the value creation chains that are derived therefrom, the assignment of functions to functional levels, the data structures needed, and the applications software to be employed.

8. Introduction strategy.

    Given its complexity, implementation of the overall model is broken down into sub-projects and effected with the help of a project organization.

B. Sector-Specific EDP Systems

B.I. Industry

EDP applications in the industrial firm are given special attention, since they possess the longest tradition and have played a pacemaking role for other sectors.

Industrial firms are characterized by two large computerized information systems: the production planning and control system which primarily accompanies the order flow, shown in the left fork of the Y-CIM model in Figure 3.B.I.01, and the information system in the right fork of the Y-CIM model, which relates to the more technical EDP systems covering product description and control of production units.

The production planning and control (PPC) systems, which are determined by the order flow, handle issues which are also of central significance in the industrial branch of business economics (see *Hackstein, Produktionsplanung und -steuerung 1989*). However, the PPC systems that have been developed from the EDP perspective display a different planning philosophy and different emphasis from the business economic approaches.

Although the systems shown on the right hand side of the Y are referred to as technical systems, they are nevertheless of considerable business economics significance. The integration concept **Computer Integrated Manufacturing (CIM)** aims at a holistic consideration of all the functions of the industrial firm. To this end a complete information system for business and technically-oriented tasks is developed. CIM also relates to fundamental business economics issues and will alter processes in industrial firms considerably. This presents a challenge to business economics to participate in this development process.

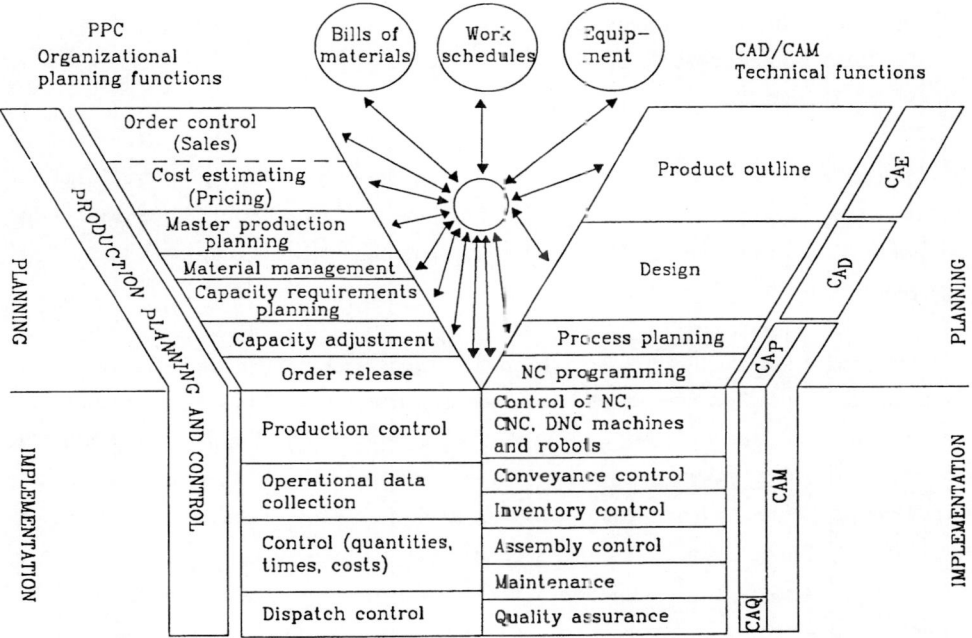

Fig. 3.B.I.01: Y-CIM model of the information systems for an industrial firm

B.I.1. Production Planning and Control (PPC)

B.I.1.1. Description of PPC

A planning concept for computerized production planning and control has developed both for standard software and for many in-house developments in industrial firms, which is characterized especially by the use of the EDP techniques of database systems, a high degree of interaction, and the networking of diverse hardware.

Examples of widely used standard software systems for production planning and control are:

- CAS from CAS (Computer Anwendungs-Systeme),
- MAPICS II from IBM,
- COPICS from IBM,
- CIMOS from ISG,
- ISI from Siemens,
- RM-PPS from SAP AG,
- PM/3000, MM 300 from Hewlett Packard,
- PSsystem from SCS Systemtechnik,
- FORMAT from Markwart Polzer,
- PIUSS-O from PSI.

PPC systems are distinguished by the fact that they not only support planning functions but also the necessary master data for bills of materials, work schedules (operations) and equipment. Given the considerable quantity and complexity of the data structures, **data management** is of particular importance.

Bills of materials (or formulae in chemical processes) record the structural and quantitative composition of end products from intermediate products and raw materials (see the product tree for two end products P1 and P2 in Figure 3.B.I.02a). The **production coefficients** are entered on the edges. They indicate how many units of a lower level part enter into one unit of a higher level part. If materials or assemblies enter into several higher level parts - as is very common in manufacturing industry - storage of the complete product trees would give rise to considerable data redundancy. In the example eleven pieces of parts information and nine pieces of structural information (production coefficients) would have to be stored. For this reason, the product trees are consolidated into network structures corresponding to Figure 3.B.I.02b. This representation is equivalent to the familiar gozintograph from business economics.

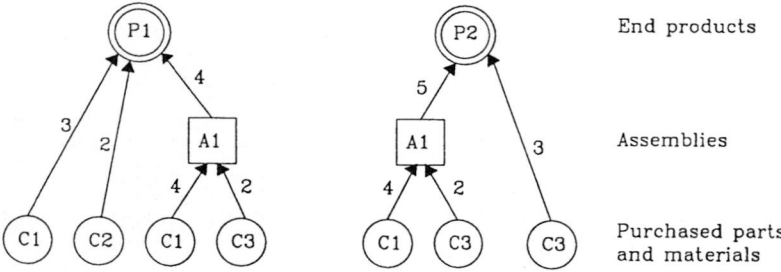

Fig. 3.B.I.02a: Product trees for two end products

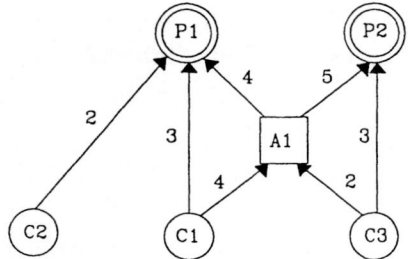

Fig. 3.B.I.02b: Gozintograph for Fig. 3.B.I.02a

A **gozintograph** presents each part and each structural relationship only once, so that only six pieces of parts information and seven pieces of structural information occur. Since a part can enter into several higher level parts and a part can be composed of several lower level parts the data structure forms a m:n relationship within the entity type PARTS. This is presented in Figure 3.B.I.03 as an ERM. The entity type PARTS is represented by a rectangle, the relationship STRUCTURE by a rhombus, whereby the relationship is of type "m:n".

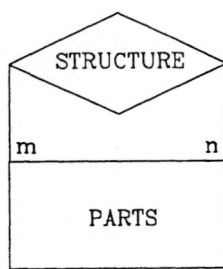

Fig. 3.B.I.03: ERM representing product structure

The entire parts structure of Figure 3.B.I.02b is presented in tabular form in Figure 3.B.I.04. Both the entity type PARTS and the relationship type STRUCTURE are elucidated as tables. The keys which uniquely identify a row are always underlined. This representation follows the relational model and is self-explanatory.

PARTS

Parts no.	Description	Stocks on hand	...
P1	End product 1	5	
P2	End product 2	10	
A1	Assembly 1	100	
C1	Material 1	50	
C2	Material 2	40	
C3	Material 3	8	

STRUCTURE

Higher lev. part no.	Lower lev. part no.	Production coefficient	...
P1	C2	2	
P1	C1	3	
P1	A1	4	
A1	C1	4	
A1	C3	2	
P2	A1	5	
P2	C3	3	

Fig. 3.B.I.04: Tabular representation of the parts structure in Fig. 3.B.I.02b

The EDP-technical implementation of this structure in a database system must ensure that a part can be broken down into its constituent components (bill of materials), and that for any part there is an indication of the higher level parts in which it is incorporated (parts utilization).

The data structure of a bill of materials cannot be stored in simple file-oriented storage forms without redundancy. For this reason, special data management systems for the storage of bills of materials were developed at an early stage, from which general database systems were later developed. One of the first systems of this kind was the BOMP (Bill of Material Processor) system from the firm IBM.

Figure 3.B.I.05 shows the structure of the master data for production planning and control as an ERM. In addition to bill of materials information, work schedule information is also given. A part can have several **work schedules**, if alternative production possibilities exist (in different plants or using different technological

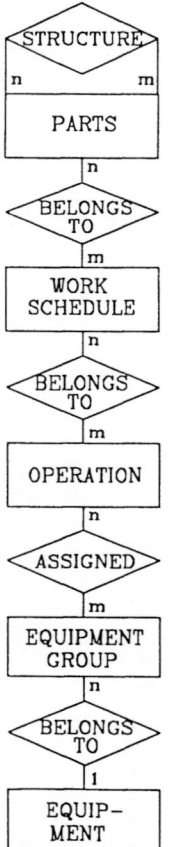

Fig. 3.B.I.05: ERM for PPC master data management

processes). Conversely, parts which are similar in production-technical terms can also be produced using the same standard work schedule (n:m relationship).

A work schedule generally consists of between five and seven operations, which describe the sequence of individual steps to be carried out in processing a part. An **operation** can be assigned to diverse work schedules as a standard operation (n:m relationship).

An **equipment group** consists of several pieces of equipment that can be treated in planning terms as equivalent.

If an operation can be carried out on several different equipment groups, and one equipment group can carry out several operations then, a n:m relationship exists between the entity types OPERATION and EQUIPMENT GROUP. The relationship describes those properties relating both to a specific operation and to a specific equipment group, e.g. set-up times, standard times, spoilage rates.

The data structure in Figure 3.B.I.05 displays the complex interdependences within the master data of the production area. This ensures the flexibility needed for evaluation purposes. For example, if a piece of equipment fails it is possible to determine which operations and ultimately which internally-produced parts will be affected.

For a moderately sized manufacturing firm the following orders of magnitude for the number of entities are realistic (see *Scheer, Produktionsplanung 1976, p. 19*):

- 40,000 parts entities (including 100 end products and 10,000 internally-produced parts),
- 280,000 structural entities,
- 20,000 work schedule entities (with 2 work schedules per internally-produced part),
- 100,000 operation entities (with 5 operations per work schedule),
- 200,000 equipment assignments (with 2 assignments per operation),
- 150 equipment groups,
- 750 pieces of equipment (with 5 pieces of equipment per group).

In larger firms the management of several hundred thousand parts records, millions of structural records and operation records can be necessary.

Such large volumes of data not only determine the complexity of the master data management, but also affect the planning philosophy.

The planning levels of the EDP-oriented successive planning model are:

1. master production scheduling,
2. requirement breakdown,

192

3.   process scheduling,
4.   load leveling,
5.   job shop control,
6.   operational data collection.

In the course of **master production scheduling** the production program for the coming planning period (e.g. 6 months or 1 year) is determined in type and quantity terms. This planning step is given EDP support by the provision of sales forecasting procedures and the transfer of customer order management data. Many PPC systems, however, assume that a master production schedule is provided by the sales department.

In the course of the **requirement breakdown** the need for intermediate products through to raw materials is calculated from the production program by breakdown of the bills of materials. Gross/net calculations deduct existing stocks from the gross requirements to generate the resulting net requirement for intermediate products and materials to be produced or purchased. These net requirements are consolidated as production or purchase orders in accordance with lot-sizing. The orders are then simultaneously subject to rough scheduling, taking throughput times into account.
To determine lot sizes heuristic procedures, such as the part period method or flexible economic lot-sizing, are used, which also allow for variations in requirements over time. (see *Scheer, Produktionsplanung 1976, p. 104 ff.*).
Since the requirement breakdown requires only the bills of materials and the inventory accounts, these steps are often carried out first.
The subsequent capacity management requires that work schedule, operation and equipment information are also subject to computerized management.

In the course of **process scheduling** part-specific orders of the production program are broken down into operations using operation and equipment information and are subject to differentiated scheduling. The assignment of operations to equipment groups allows the aggregate capacity load on the groups to be determined for the individual periods. The results are presented graphically for each equipment group (possibly in colour) and highlight excess or lack of capacity. The overview given in Figure 3.B.I.06 distinguishes between the capacity load arising from orders already in production, orders released for production, and planned orders (see also *IBM, COPICS (SL & R) 1983, p. 19*).

In order to generate a production program that is both permissible and balanced, capacity excesses and shortfalls are balanced out in the course of **load leveling**. The procedures used by standard software allow for the use of overtime, escape equipment, and increased production intensity. These measures leave the temporal processing of the operations essentially unchanged. If this is inadequate, an attempt can be made to reschedule operations on bottleneck equipment to periods with a lower capacity load. In order not to disrupt the temporal flow of operations for a specific order, all operations (including those that are assigned to equipment with free capacity) are rescheduled. To do this some highly developed procedures use priority rules to choose the orders to be rescheduled, for example, CAPOSS-E in the COPICS system from IBM (see *IBM, CAPOSS-E 1983*).

Load profile: Capacity point (Equipment group) Drilling machine NC 5/28

Period (week)	% of plan. capacity	% of actu- al capa.	Percentage load
1	100	105	
2	100	107	
3	90	95	
4	90	80	
5	110	100	
6	110	120	
7	100	80	
8	100	70	

Percentage load scale: 0 10 20 30 40 50 60 70 80 90 100 110 120

- Load from orders in process
- Load from released orders
- Load from planned orders
- – – Planned capacity

Fig. 3.B.I.06: Capacity load overview for an equipment group

Job shop control transforms the results of the planning stages completed thus far into their practical implementation. The planning period considered is correspondingly shorter. In the first step production orders with planned starting dates within the coming planning period (e.g. 2 weeks) are checked to determine whether the components and tools required are available. If they are, the orders are released for production.

194

This order release has the same significance for implementation as the master plan has for requirement and capacity planning (see Figure 3.B.I.08). Released orders are assigned to queues for the equipment groups and are scheduled in accordance with capacity restrictions and the production flow. This detailed scheduling is also controlled using complex priority rules. The outcome is that production sequences and start and end deadlines are established for the stock of orders. The resulting data generated at considerable computational cost are very sensitive to alteration. Figure 3.B.I.07 shows a frequently used representation of this state of affairs. It shows how a plan created at the weekend for the following week is so strongly affected by events such as equipment failure, acceptance of rush orders, employee absences, delays, etc., that by Friday only 10% to 20% of the relevant planned values for that day are still valid.

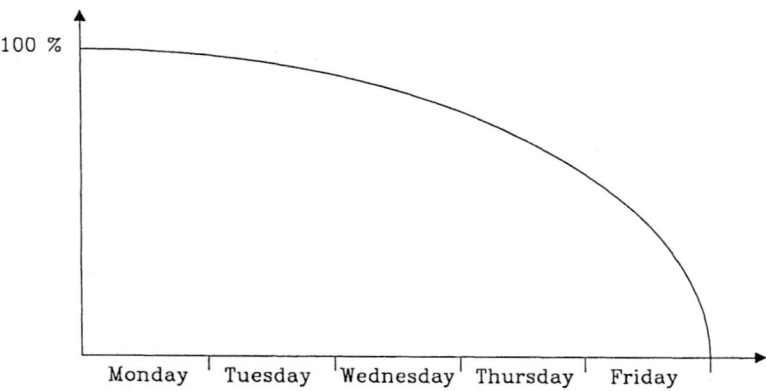

Fig. 3.B.I.07: Validity of the relevant planned values over time

In the course of **operational data collection** the realized quantity and time values for orders and employees, equipment stoppages and downtime, and the use of materials and tools in the planning and control process are reported. Up-to-date job shop control, in particular, requires continuous information about the actual status of the production process.

Production facilities often employ special hardware systems for operational data collection, such as terminals which are not susceptible to breakdown, or automatic annunciators, which sometimes also require process computers. As a result, data collection systems generally give rise to networking of several computer systems.

The individual planning stages of the PPC system adopt differing planning periods, which get shorter from top to bottom. Whereas master production scheduling may cover a period of six months or more, in job shop control a planning horizon of one week or even one day may be desirable.

B.I.1.2 Business Economics Evaluation of PPC

The important points of intervention are the determination of the master production schedule and order release (see Figure 3.B.I.08) since these planning steps have a strong determining influence on the following stages.

Business economics deficiencies in the planning concept exist above all in an inadequate support for the determination of the master production schedule. The input of the sales program is, therefore, based on many roughly estimated values. A possible explanation of the lack of emphasis on this first planning step is that it requires close coordination between production and sales. In organizational terms this is often associated with considerable frictional costs.

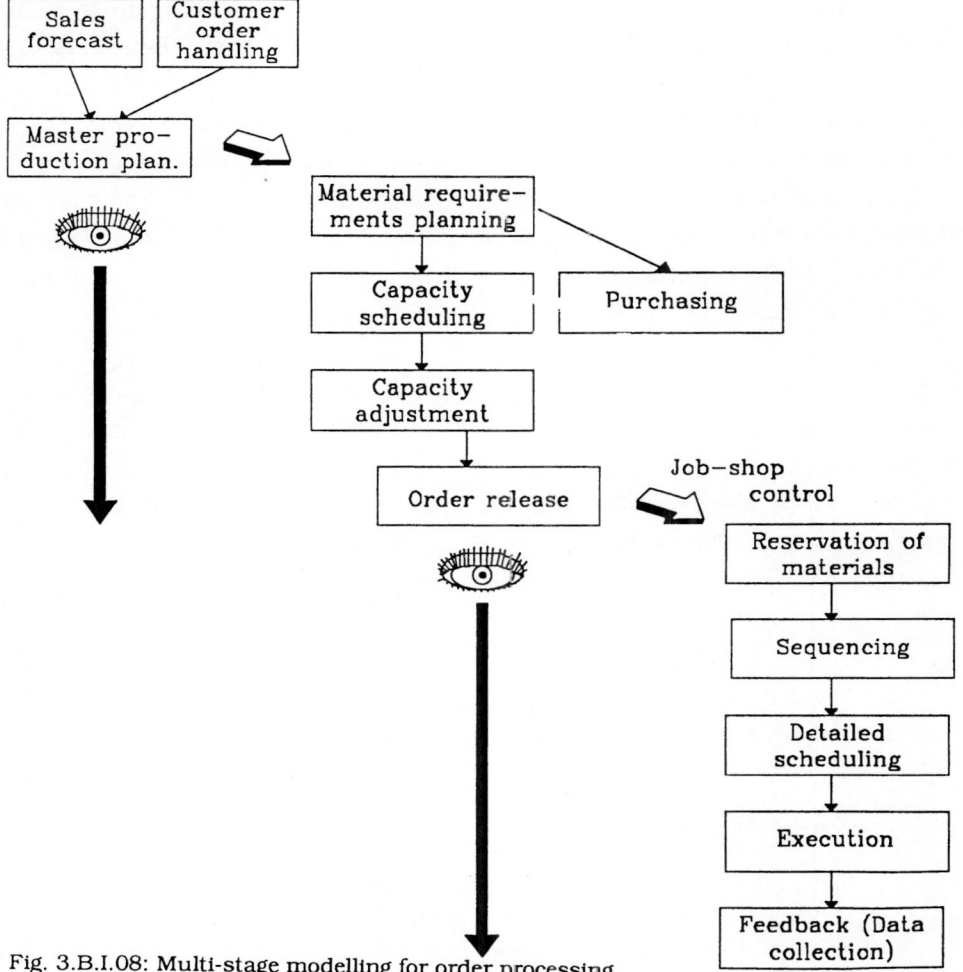

Fig. 3.B.I.08: Multi-stage modelling for order processing

Since the input values determine the subsequent planning stages, however, their quality is of considerable significance which also establishes the form of the subsequent planning results. Rough planning methods should, therefore, enable greater coordination between sales and the production area in establishing the production program. Of course, the quantitative details of the planning elements to be handled must be taken into account. Aggregative simultaneous models based on end products or end product groups could be useful here (see *Wittemann, Produktionsplanung mit verdichteten Daten 1985*).

The planning techniques used in PPC systems for lot formation, load leveling, and sequencing are heuristic, and their effects are sometimes not very transparent to the user. These procedures have been ignored for a long time by the traditional business economics literature. Here, effective methods are available for business economics research which take realistic quantity conditions and the incorporation in an adequate EDP framework into account. The Wagner Whitin algorithm already provides a desirable improvement (see *Wagner, Whitin, Economic Lot Size Model 1958*). In the capacity planning context, PPC systems use procedures based on priority rules. However, given the temporal interdependence between operations from one order and between orders this is a planning situation which demands a simultaneous approach. The planning complexity is further increased by the considerable quantitative range of the activities to be scheduled. For this reason, adjustment procedures often lead to uncontrollably high computational times.

Given the relatively unsatisfactory experience with batch-oriented heuristic approaches to load leveling and sequencing, the use of a man-machine dialog appears more promising. On the screen the capacity situation of the equipment groups is displayed to the planner. At the same time the queue of orders at a machine group is shown along with indications of buffer times, etc. (see Figure 3.B.I.09a/b). The planner can then interactively reschedule individual operations and carry out simulations for various alternatives until he finds a satisfactory result.

The interactive decision process can be rendered even more efficient, however, by the provision of sensible decision suggestions by the EDP system, since the user alone is overburdened by the complexity of the planning situation. This also provides grounds for the use of expert systems (see *Steinmann, Wissensbasierte Anwendungen 1989*).

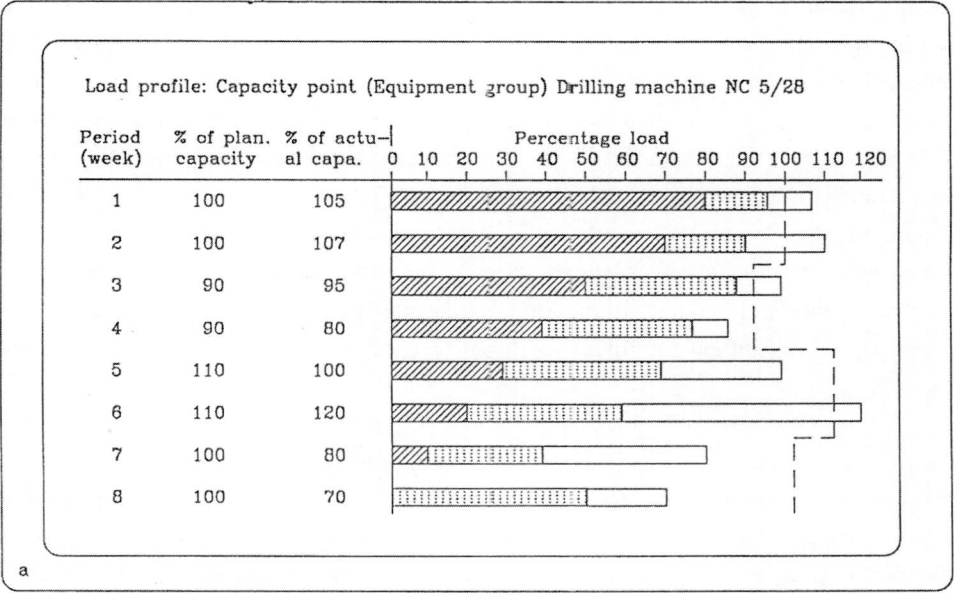

Fig. 3.B.I.09a: Capacity load profile (graphical)

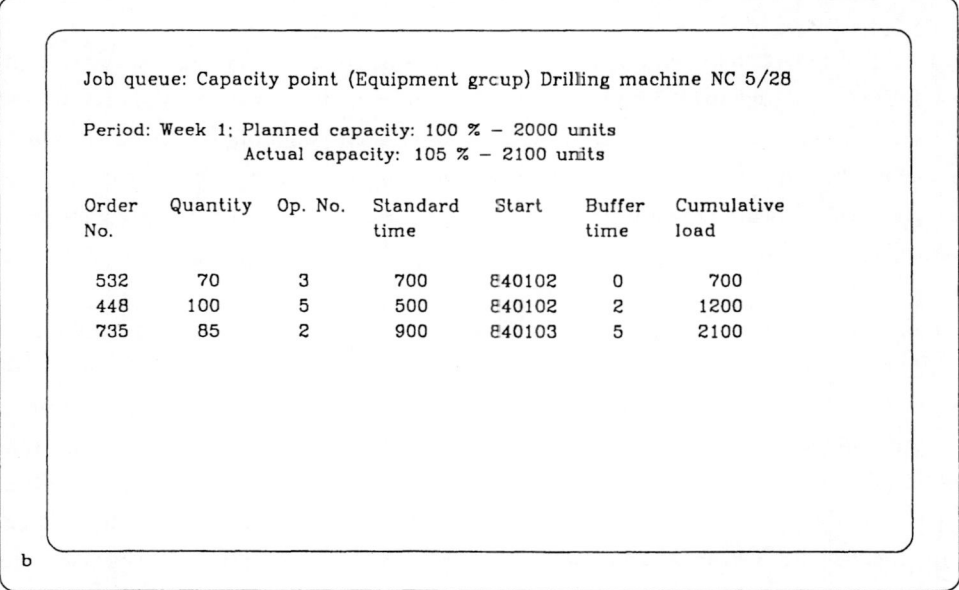

Fig. 3.B.I.09b: Capacity load profile (tabular)

The use of PPC systems has increased considerably in recent years. The planning philosophy presented here is suitable primarily for operations using serial manufacturing organized according to the principle of job-shop production. Manufacturing which is strongly oriented towards customer orders, especially one-off production, demands that the relationship of the production orders to the customer can be maintained by carrying the customer order number throughout. For batch production, this is offered by only a few systems, and is associated with considerable data management problems.

In addition, the systems are aimed at manufacturing structures with considerable processing intensity. Here, numerous purchased materials and components are combined through many intermediate stages to produce a few extremely complex end products.

However, it is typical of the consumer goods industry that a multiplicity of diverse end products are manufactured from relatively few raw materials in only a few production stages. They are often manufactured in mass production and vary only in terms of differences in packaging. Issues relating to the temporal integration of the individual production lines are therefore dominant. The PPC systems also present implementational problems for chemical processes where the production process is characterized by technologically-related cycles.

Despite the limitations mentioned, the successful implementation of PPC systems is an example of how independent planning philosophies derived in conjunction with the development of EDP systems can provide more effective solutions to the problems of managing large quantities of data and the complexity of the planning process by using database techniques, interactive functions and hardware networks, than the optimization models for production and process planning offered by business economics theories.

In contrast to successive planning, business economics models for production planning use simultaneous approaches, usually based on linear programming (see *e.g. Kilger, Optimale Produktions- und Absatzplanung 1973*). A rough estimate of the number of variables and side conditions to be included, however, makes it immediately obvious that the creation of detailed LP programs for manufacturing industry would fail as a result of the extremely high volume. (see *Scheer, Produktionsplanung 1976*). This is a direct consequence of the lack of attention that business economics approaches pay to data provision in comparison with the logical formulation of the model.

Some of the differences between the business economics approaches and those of PPC systems are presented in Figure 3.B.I.10.

	EDP systems for production planning and control	Production planning models from business administration theory
Planning concept	Step—wise planning	Simultaneous planning
Decision rules	Heuristic	Optimizations
Tools	Simple rules	Mathematical models
Emphasis	Operative completeness	Decision optimality
Provision of data	Comprehensive data management concept for bills of materials, work schedules, equipment	Scarcely handled
Integration with neighboring applications	Data links with bookkeeping, cost accounting, sales	Only decision interdependences in the context of complex global models
Level of knowlegde within academic institutions	Low	High
State of application in practice	High	Low

Fig. 3.B.I.10: Comparison of the differences between business economics and EDP system approaches to production planning and control

In contrast to PPC systems, which explicitly distinguish between the differing timescales of long term rough planning (master production scheduling), medium term material and capacity planning and short term production control, many business economics optimization approaches emphasize the simultaneous planning of process and production programs (see *e.g. Adam, Sortenfertigung 1971*).

The business economics models place individual decision problems in the foreground, whereas PPC systems emphasize above all the comprehensive support of the entire order process.

In PPC systems the database also provides support for neighbouring application areas. For example, the material management system can provide the entries for accounts payable bookkeeping, or the sales system incorporated in the PPC system can provide entries for accounts receivable. Bills of materials and work schedules form the basis for cost estimation, and the results of operational data collection are passed on to both payroll accounting and continuous costing. Such data interdependences are not provided for by business economics planning models.

The concept of EDP-supported PPC systems has only recently been acknowledged in industrial economics textbooks. The research contribution of business economics is correspondingly slight. However, it is to be expected and hoped, that, given the increasing use of PPC systems and their considerable structural influence as the backbone of the information supply for the industrial firm, this situation will change (see *Scheer, EDV und OR 1980; Glaser, PPS-Systeme 1989*).

B.I.2. Computer Integrated Manufacturing (CIM)

B.I.2.1. Description of CIM

The term CIM can be traced back to Harrington's book "Computer Integrated Manufacturing" which appeared in 1973, where the basic treatment relates to the shop floor level (CAM) (see *Harrington, Computer Integrated Manufacturing 1973*). Here, however, the term CIM is interpreted much more widely to refer to the integrated information processing of an industrial firm in the sense of the "computer steered industrial firm" (see Scheer, CIM 1990). Thus, CIM comprises the primary business-related systems of production planning and control (PPC), as well as the more technically-oriented systems referred to using the terms Computer Aided Design (CAD), computerized monitoring and control of production (Computer Aided Manufacturing = CAM), Computer Aided Planning (CAP) computerized engineering activities, particularly in product design (Computer Aided Engineering = CAE) and Computer Aided Quality Assurance (CAQ). Within the CAM context new manufacturing techniques such as computerized machine tools, robots, storage and transport systems are also supported.

The upper part of the Y-CIM model in Figure 3.B.I.01 specifies the planning and design phases that precede the production process. The link between the technical and business functions is generated via the common use of primary data for bills of materials, work schedules and equipment. However, the systems are assigned to organizationally distinct areas.

The PPC system is utilized by logistics, material management, purchasing and process planning, whereas CAE and CAD are employed in design.

In the lower part, which relates to the production process, both systems are also organizationally more closely linked. The shop floor control functions are closely linked via CAM with temporal and spatial order control and with operational data collection. Control of machine tools and order scheduling can be carried out using the same production computer (process computer). Automatically controlled production machines can report start and end information or monitoring results automatically to the operational data collection system. Since the levels of the production planning and control system have already been treated, the more technically-oriented functions will now be considered, so that the business implications can then be discussed.

Just as the levels of the PPC system constitute a continuous process, the EDP-supported technical functions in the right fork of the Y in Figure 3.B.I.01 are also interconnected, although this has not always been as clearly appreciated as the implementation of the CIM concept requires.

In the **Computer Aided Design (CAD)** context the designer is provided with support for design and drawing creation. In the process he can call up drawings of already existing parts from a database and amend them or combine them with other drawings to create a new drawing. The call-up and further processing of previously stored drawings secures a considerable rationalization effect.

According to the geometric representation possibilities, it is possible to distinguish between two-dimensional and three-dimensional CAD systems. Two-dimensional systems can only represent surfaces. Systems working in three dimensions can store forms as wire models, surface models or volume models.

Of these, volume models offer the clearest representation. A program for creating a volume model is presented in Figure 3.B.I.11. A new part is designed by combining basic volume models. The process makes particular use of PLUS and MINUS operations. The program instructions presented are largely self-explanatory given the expressions provided for the parts and the axes (see *Beier, CAM-System 1982, p. 5*).

With the help of CAD systems the geometric forms represented on the graphics display can be rotated, enlarged or reduced. Special terminals allow particularly high resolution and thereby exact geometric reproduction and also support the use of colours. By accessing existing basic geometric structures, such as circles, rectangles, trapezoids, etc., the creation of a new design is facilitated.

In addition to automated drawing creation, calculations are also supported. Particularly well-known is the Finite Element Method (FEM), with whose help the distortion of a form resulting from given forces can be calculated; for example, the deformation of the bodywork of a car on crossing a curbstone (see *Warnecke, Bullinger, Lienert, Produktionsbereich 1980, p. 60*).

It is also part of the scope of CAD to store finished drawings in a database in easily accessible form, and to handle the technical documentation.

Since the technical drawing contains all the parts of a component, the bill of materials can automatically be derived from it without it having to be re-entered into the EDP

```
PARTNO/EXAMPLE 11
DY=12
```

```
V1=PRIREC/60,DY,-90

V2=PROFIL/ZAX,-65
   CONTUR/CLOSED

P1=POINT/60,80
   BEGIN/60,0,YLARGE,YPAR,60
   RGT/(CIRCLE/P1,(80-DY))
   RGT/(LINE/P1,ATANGL,150)
   RGT/(CIRCLE/P1,80)
   TERMCO
```

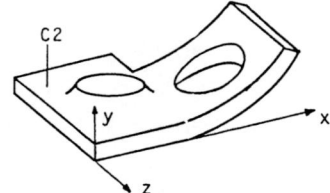

```
   TRANSF/30,DY,-50
V3=CYL/YAX,10,36

C1=SOLID/V1,PLUS,V2,V3,ROUND,5

   TRANSF/REF,90,-10,-32.5
V4=CYL/YAX,60,40
```

```
C2=PENTR/C1,MINUS,V4
```

```
FINI
```

Fig. 3.B.I.11: Drawing creation with the help of a CAD program

system. The production coefficients can thereby also be automatically determined by using programs to "search" the drawing for identical parts. It follows that important production planning data are generated within the CAD context. Thus, a particularly close relationship is created between CAD and the PPC system.

CAD software is primarily developed by specialist software houses, which often enter into partnership with manufacturers of minicomputers who do not offer any standard software of their own for production planning and control. Consequently, the danger of isolated solutions arises. This demands the creation of a clear concept for linking the database for planning functions and the computerized design system.

This has been recognized by several manufacturers of PPC systems and efforts are being made to link their PPC and CAD systems which were initially conceived as isolated systems. This link might be created, for example, by transferring the bills of materials generated via file transfer to the database in the PPC system. This kind of link does not, however, achieve the use of a **common** database (see the various degrees of integration in *Scheer, CIM 1990, p. 163*).

The requirement that the CAD and PPC databases be integrated applies not only to the system manufacturers, but also to the system users. Since CAD systems are frequently selected by the design department alone, the functional range dominates their evaluation, and not questions of hardware or software links with the planning area. These linkage possibilities, however, are in the long term more important than the availability of special functions.

Many systems are only at a very early stage of development and are being continuously extended. However, if diverse hardware and database systems are already installed effective integration is permanently excluded. For this reason, the principle of integration should have priority in system design.

In the **Computer Aided Engineering (CAE)** context additional functions supporting engineering tasks are offered. In addition to graphical CAD capabilities, the possibility of developing prototypes within the computer can largely replace the creation of real prototypes. With the help of simulation studies which also allow the movement of parts on the screen, statements about the technical characteristics of a new product can be made although the product does not physically exist. These kinds of investigations extend to simulated crash tests for newly developed automobiles.

By controlled investigation of many alternatives the cost of the product can be cut, weight reduced, security and precision improved, disturbances such as vibration and noise eliminated, and energy-saving effects achieved.

Computer Aided Manufacturing (CAM) relates primarily to the control of machine tools. NC (numerical control) machines are controlled using paper tape as the data medium. The workpiece and the necessary tool (e.g. a drill) are loaded on the machine (e.g. drilling machine); the machine independently drills holes in the predetermined locations, the workpiece being moved appropriately. The information needed to process the workpiece concerning cutting speed and feeding are recorded on the data medium in digital form.

Special programs such as EXAPT and APT can be used to create the NC code. With the help of such languages machine-independent NC programs are first created, which are then translated into a special program tailored to the properties of the machine tool to be used.

The primary requirement for the creation of NC programs is the geometry data for the workpieces.

Since these have already been established and stored during the design process, NC programming access to the stored design data can considerably reduce, or in the case of automatic programming even eliminate, the programming costs. The use of CAD will, therefore, lead to greater integration of the technical functions, since the software systems for drawing creation will automatically generate the design bills of materials and the NC program. The tendency towards the creation of process chains that was already recognized above as a general consequence of the strict use of databases and interactive processing is, therefore, also apparent here.

More recently computers are increasingly being used to control NC machines directly, i.e., the use of paper tapes is eliminated. In CNC (computerized numerical control) machines all machine control functions are taken over by a computer linked to the machine. This gives rise to increased flexibility in the ability to repeat an operation, for example, since the program stored in the computer does not have to be reloaded (see *Warnecke, Bullinger, Lienert, Produktionsbereich 1980, p. 67*).

In DNC (direct numerical control and also distributed numerical control) systems several CNC controlled machines are linked together via a minicomputer. This is in a position to provide the entire facility centrally with programs and control instructions.

In **Computer Aided Planning (CAP)** the work scheduler interactively uses time rates for job operations and set-up processes, performance data, and equipment cost rates to establish operation standards and equipment assignments (see *Beier, CAM-System 1982*). The traditional methods of establishing work schedule and operation data are considerably more costly. In addition, information derived from planned-actual deviations and the process planning experience based on this information is of greater significance. Given ever shorter product lives this source of information is increasingly drying up, so that there is a tendency for the quality of work schedule and operation data to deteriorate. For this reason, CAP methods are of considerable importance not only in terms of their rationalization effects, but also in improving the quality of planning data.

Computerized storage systems combine chaotic stockkeeping with an automated transport system. Articles are automatically placed in empty storage spaces and then removed in accordance with certain priority rules (especially in racking control systems).

Electronically controlled **supply systems** use driverless transport vehicles to transport goods through production halls on "roads" formed from induction loops. The computer can select optimal routes and monitor the transport process.

The control of **industrial robots** is also an important EDP application area. Robot movements are freely programmable in several axes and they are thereby capable of taking over flexible tasks in the handling, welding, painting and assembly areas (see *Lünzmann, Roboter, 1982*).

In the context of **flexible manufacturing systems** (see Figure 3.B.I.12) several of the EDP techniques mentioned are combined (see *Gunn, Fertigung 1982, p. 95*). In a flexible manufacturing system several programmable machines are combined and linked together using a computer controlled transport system. A DNC minicomputer controls the processing sequence, indicated in Figure 3.B.I.12 by the numbered sequence of operations.

The NC program to be carried out is transferred from the minicomputer to the microcomputer of the currently active CNC machine. At the same time the tool needed is specified and then autonomously selected from the available tools and loaded by the machine. The reloading of a new tool is, therefore, integrated in the production process and no longer constitutes relevant changeover time. In the case of machine breakdown an alternative machine is automatically activated without interruption of the production process.

Flexible manufacturing systems are, therefore, capable of producing differing, if similar, parts through several shifts without interruption and without human involvement. They represent a departure from the job shop (activity) principle replacing it with the flow (object) principle. They have the advantages of speeding up throughput times and reducing production stocks, which are obtained at the cost of greater capital tie-up in the stock of equipment.

The types of computers used for the tasks mentioned are generally process computers. They must be capable of realtime processing, since the production machines linked to them need to be temporally synchronized with the computer control. In realtime processing incoming signals have absolute priority and are immediately processed by the computer. In contrast, the time-sharing operating systems typical of commercial computers assign sequential delays to users so that queues result and response times are unpredictable. This means that immediate processing cannot be guaranteed.

Figure 3.B.I.13, which is based on an exposition by General Electric Information Services, shows the integration of production planning and control, design and product planning, production and storage control which are linked together by way of unified data management and network control. (An alternative graphical representation of the integrated factory of the future is given in the fold-out in *IEEE, Automation 1983*.)

206

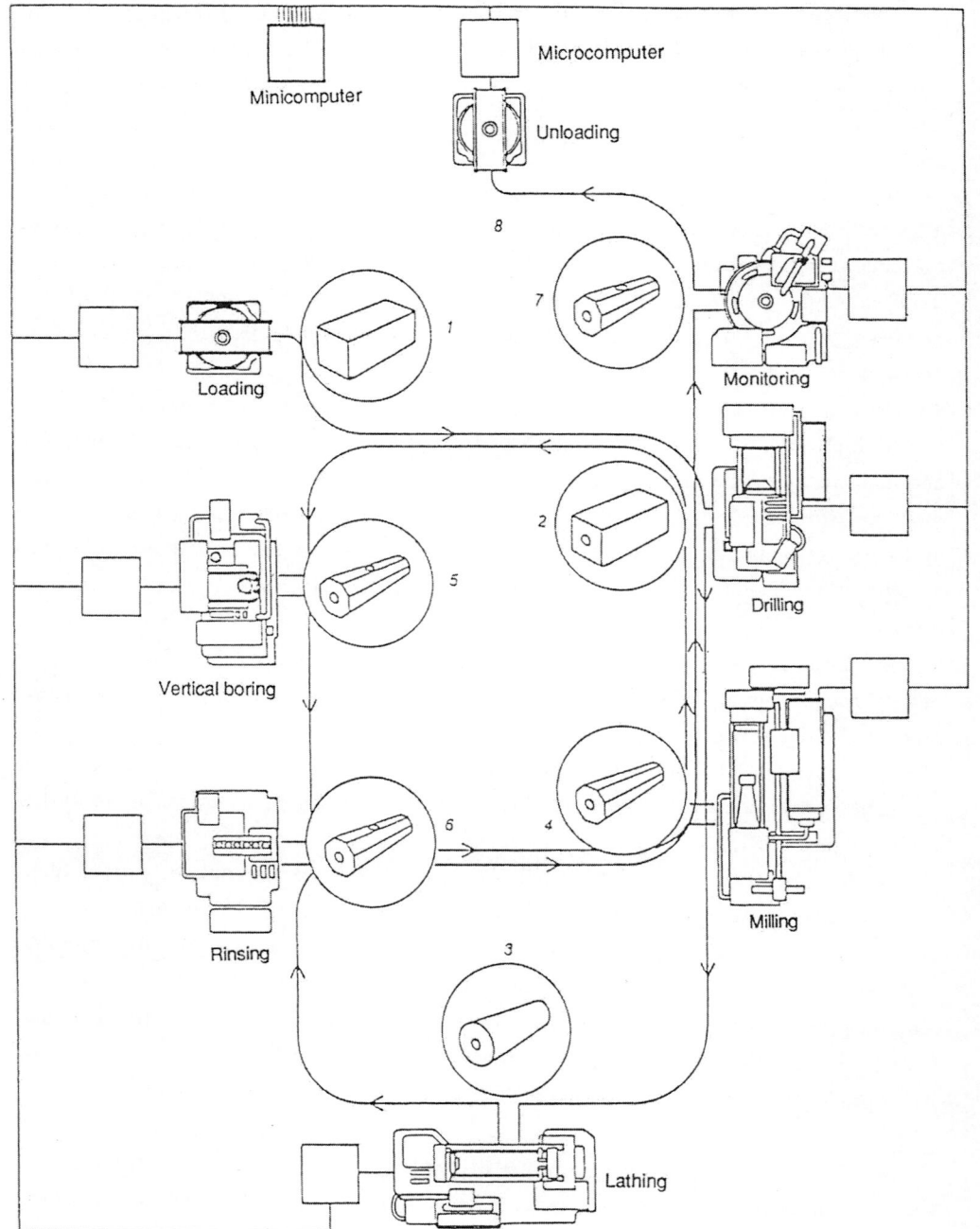

Minicomputer

Microcomputer

Unloading

8

7

Monitoring

Loading

1

2

Drilling

5

Vertical boring

6

4

Milling

Rinsing

3

Lathing

Fig. 3.B.I.12: Components of a flexible manufacturing system

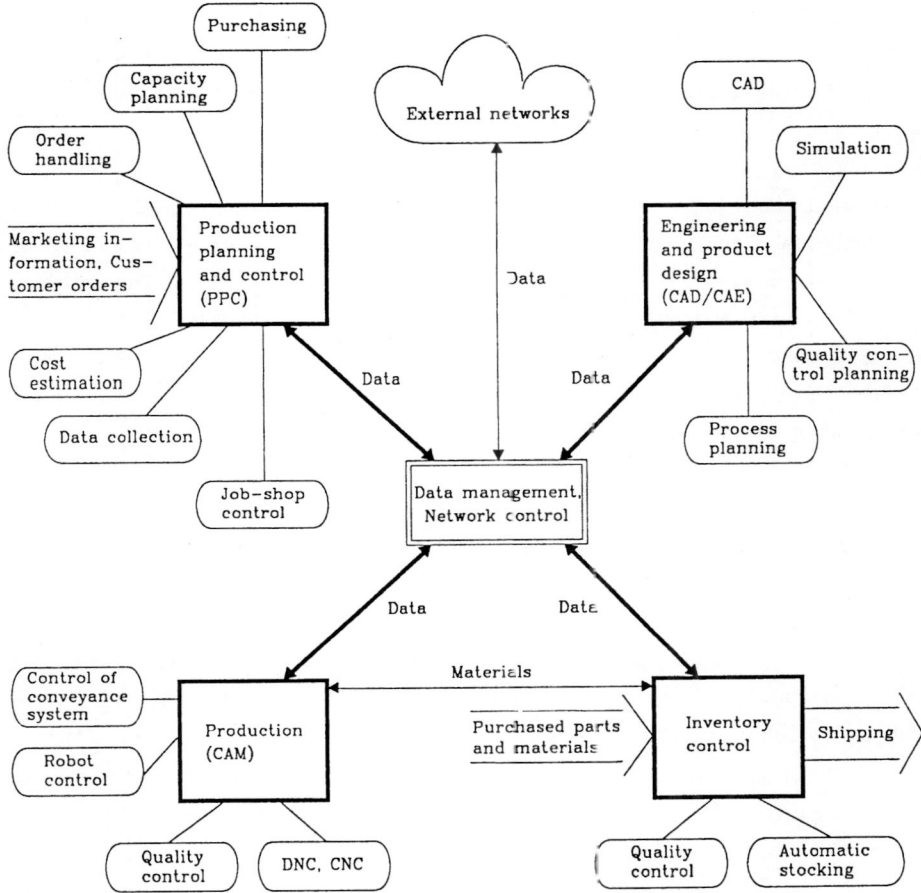

Fig. 3.B.I.13: Functional integration in the factory of the future
(after *General Electric*)

The four sub-areas indicate once more the range of future EDP applications in the production area. As well as informational links within the industrial firm, external relationships are also indicated. These relate firstly to the sales market via market information and customer orders which are processed by the order management system within production planning and control. Purchased parts and materials, which are recorded and managed by storage control, indicate the links with the purchasing market. Storage control also handles the dispatch of finished end products. Figure 3.B.I.13 also represents the relationship with external networks via central network control. Via this link highly specialized applications software from external service firms can be used by the individual functions, and communication functions with suppliers and customers handled. It is to be expected that the relationship between suppliers and large manufacturers, e.g. in the automobile industry, will become so close that alterations to the manufacturer's production program will be passed on automatically to the databases of the supply firms' planning programs. Such apporaches are already apparent at present.

This kind of integrated concept can only be developed and introduced gradually. However, this makes it all the more important to pay attention to the overall concept in creating partial solutions, so as to ensure that isolated one-off solutions do not arise. This danger is at present considerable, since highly specialized hardware and software systems are available for individual application areas, whereas thus far no computer manufacturer offers an immediately implementable, comprehensive, overall concept. Nevertheless, the implementation of CIM will prevail, especially as successful practical examples become more widely known.

B.I.2.2. Business Economics Evaluation of CIM

The detailed consideration of the business economics implications of CIM is justified by the fact that the arguments are also relevant to other sectors. This is also indicated by the use of concepts like CIB = "Computer Integrated Banking", which apply the basic principles of CIM to other sectors (see *Zapp, Computer Integrated Banking 1989, p. 121*).

A concrete CIM implementation will first be introduced to facilitate the derivation of business economics implications (see *Scheer, Planungs- und Steuerungsfunktionen 1988*).

The Californian glass manufacturer Guardian Industries has made personal computers available to its most important customers free of charge. The computers are used to provide the customers with data relating to Guardian Industries' production program, in particular as regards article numbers, descriptions, production dimensions, possible colours and prices. These data are kept up to date for the customer by the firm via a data network. Customers inform the firm of orders by accessing the stored data and checking the plausibility of being able to deliver the desired colours, dimensions, etc. In this way the orders that the firm receives already contain the correct order data. This means that for Guardian Industries the usual reconciliation procedures involved in order recording are eliminated.

The incoming orders are aggregated and distributed on the sheets of raw glass using a layout optimization program, so as to minimize wastage. Once the orders have been distributed to the sheets of raw glass the geometry for the subsequent cutting operations is established so that NC programs can be generated automatically. Thus, the order assignment automatically generates the cutting programs for the cutting robots.

The production process is monitored continuously. Production errors lead to the creation of re-orders, so that at the end of the production run complete customer orders have always been produced. The job of managing part orders is therefore unnecessary.

From the readily available order data supplier orders are automatically communicated via remote data processing to the supplier. On the basis of these data the supplier can produce customized packaging materials (boxes).

The interdependence of order recording, production planning, NC programming, material management, quality assurance and dispatch makes it possible for Guardian Industries to guarantee a delivery time of less than one day: in concrete terms this means that all orders that the firm receives before 4pm can be dispatched by 8am the following morning.

This example demonstrates the philosophy of CIM: the entire order flow from the customers through production to the suppliers is regarded as a unified task. In contrast, in an organization with functional specialization, which remains the dominant form, the sales system, production planning and control system and material management are each regarded as independent tasks, which are merely linked via interfaces where necessary. This is the consequence of an organizational structure based on functional breakdown.

The written CIM strategy of Guardian Industries is also notable. It specifies the following fundamentals:

- Guardian is to be market cost leader.
- As a result of the 24-hour operation of the computer system orders can be accepted around the clock.
- There are no stocks of semi-finished or finished goods.
- Important customers are bound to the firm by the order acceptance service. Important customers are responsible for the accuracy of order data.
- Only complete customer orders are delivered.
- Orders which are received by the firm before 4pm are dispatched by 8am the following day.

Each of these factors makes economic sense, and they give rise to the demands on the computing system as regards:

- reliability of the EDP components in maintaining 24-hour operation,
- the use of a relational database system to support data integration,
- realtime operation of process control,
- the use of communication networks to link the sub-systems.

The current discussion of CIM often tends to be couched more in terms of the second set of considerations, that is in instrumental terms, while the fundamental possibilities of the strategic implications of a consistent exploitation of CIM technology remain neglected. **However, this discussion makes the following clear: CIM is an eminent business economics problem and enables the transition from a functionally specialized to a process organization.**

As the example shows, the design and implementation of a unified CIM system is extremely complicated and requires comprehensive business economics, organizational, computer-technical and production-technical knowledge. Once the system is established, however, the routine planning and business control functions become largely trivial. The organizational streamlining of the process eliminates the management of stocks of semi-finished goods, the management and planning of part deliveries, etc. **The greater the organizational unification of process chains the lower the coordination costs within the chain.** This is the consequence of reduced specialization, in which the efficient coordination of temporally independent links in the chain occupies the foreground.

Shifting the weight of routine planning and control onto the correct business economics CIM configuration can also be illustrated using other examples. In the creation of IBM's highly automated plant for producing electronic typewriters in Lexington, the initial requirement was that the automation of the factory should reduce production costs to one third of their original level. The entire plant was constructed on the basis of this economic requirement. However, intervention in the current production process can scarcely alter the costs arising from the investment decisions.

It is well known in the automobile industry that nearly all cost-effective decisions concerning the materials to be used, the level of in-house production as opposed to external purchasing, the production methods to be used, and so on, are determined during the five year development period. The costs of the current process can be influenced to only a minor degree by planning functions as compared with these basic choices.

Empirical investigations have shown that whereas design amounts to only 10% of the cost of a product, it determines over 70% of the costs (see also *Warnecke, Bullinger, Lienert, Produktionsbereich 1980, p. 59*), since it establishes materials and production methods. For this reason, it is necessary to employ cost information during the design process. Figure 3.B.I.14 indicates the interactive process for a customer-oriented variant design, where cost estimation is embedded in the design process.

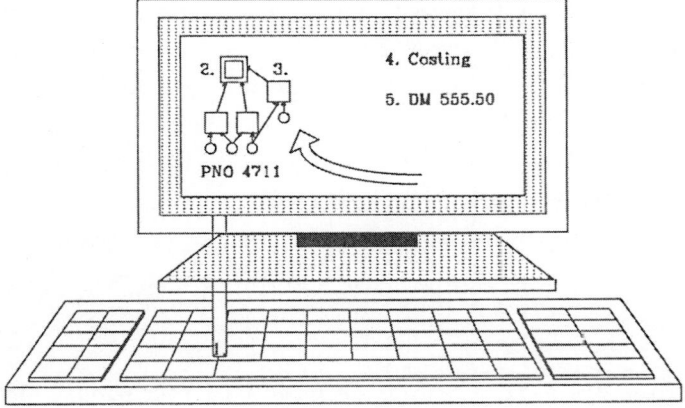

1. Enter PNO of an initial part
2. Output bill of materials for initial part
3. Incorporate amendment
4. Product costing
5. Costing result
6. Decision whether the design is satisfactory

Fig. 3.B.I.14: Cost estimation for variant design

At the same time results from material management (availability of certain materials, delivery times and data concerning suppliers) can be accessed by design. For parts which are temporally critical orders can be generated interactively by the designer. Once again this implies a close link between business and technical functions. This requires that technicians employed in design and product planning are familiar with the basic framework of economic terminology. It also means that economic optimization and decision-making techniques can be more extensively implemented than has been the case up to now. For example, cutting optimization can already be carried out at the design stage.

At the Institut für Wirtschaftsinformatik (IWi) in Saarbrücken an expert system has been developed in which the entire process of designing a product is carried out in a cost-oriented manner (see *Scheer, Bock, Konstruktionsbegleitende Kalkulation 1988*). Similar approaches have been taken at the Lehrstuhl für Konstruktion im Maschinenenbau (mechanical engineering department) at the Technische Universität in Munich (see *Ehrlenspiel, Kostengünstig Konstruieren 1985*).

Business economics can provide methods to support the creation of highly automated systems for both cost accounting and investment planning. The classical methods of investment assessment based on the simple processing of pre-specified payment streams are inadequate. The dynamic information technology environment requires the inclusion of qualitative and risk factors. Benefit analysis may provide a starting point for qualitative investment analysis, but complex simulation models show greater promise in the long term.

Cost accounting, which at present is aimed primarily at cost control of current processes, needs to involve itself more in issues of cost creation. A design stage cost estimation framework is needed to inform the designer about the cost implications of his decisions regarding material specifications, tolerances, etc., and to provide him with suggestions for cheaper alternatives.

In the development of CIM there is a trend towards **object-related decentralization** within production. The activity principle, which is manifest in the job shop principle, results in orders having to be transported from one job shop to the next after every processing step. This has given rise to high throughput times. In contrast, with an object-oriented organization a certain spectrum of parts is manufactured in its entirety, in that several operations are integrated in one single machine, or alternatively several machines are arranged in accordance with the production flow and linked by a transport system for the flow of materials. This development is characterized by the use of terms such as processing centers, production islands and flexible manufacturing systems.

With respect to production planning and control this kind of decentralization implies that independent control systems for detailed planning need to be installed for the organizational units. The detailed control is thereby separated off from the classical production planning and control system, conceived as a central computer function, and individually designed for the particular decentralized production units. The higher level planning system then works merely with basic key deadlines, whereas detailed scheduling at the operation level is left to the decentralized units.

Such developments are currently being implemented using EDP-supported control centers (Leitstand).

In the joint project "Manufacturing of parts families", supported by the Forschungsministerium (Ministry for Research), both organizational and EDP-technical solutions for these manufacturing forms are being developed by software houses, users, and research institutes.

The decentralization of PPC functions is not an isolated process, however. Data arise during production which are also used for simultaneous cost estimation and for recording gross wages. For this reason, the decentralization of production control also needs the support of an accompanying model for cost accounting and wage recording.

The integration principle for streamlining process chains does not stop at the boundary of the firm. Logistic chains with customers and suppliers can also be handled with EDP support. Inter-company data exchange requires not only the technical compatibility of the EDP systems, but also the ability to understand the content of the data exchanged. Consequently, this necessitates not only standardization of the technical data transfer, but also standardization of the documents to be exchanged.

Data exchange in CIM is particularly relevant to the more technical information: geometric data from a CAD system or control programs for NC machines. Increasingly, however, order data are also being exchanged, particularly in the context of just-in-time production. This means that the entire order processing documentation must be provided, from queries, through price agreements, delivery notes, invoices, payment orders, etc. At the same time the information content of these documents, and hence the need for them at all, becomes questionable.

With an agreed skeleton contract, prices and other delivery conditions are already established. If the manufacturer himself then calls off supplies at short notice from the supplier a subsequent invoice prepared by the supplier contains scarcely any information, since the recipient already knows all the data relating to quantities and prices, because he has either agreed the content in the long term, or has himself generated the content in the course of the call-off (see *Wildemann, Just-In-Time 1987*). It now suffices for the payee to check that the payment is correct, whereas in the traditional process invoice checking is carried out by the manufacturer and the supplier must also check the receipt of payment.

The significance of inter-company data exchange lies not only in the relocation of functions within the chain, but also especially in the entire economic rationalization which arises for all links in the chain. Speedy groundwork in establishing CIM standards, such as the efforts being made by DIN (Deutsches Institut für Normung) or better still at the European or worldwide level, is an important economic challenge.

The creation of CIM process chains integrates the functions of the firm at the operative levels. However, the accompanying evaluative processes of accounting are built upon these operative processes. They extend from controlling through to decision and planning support systems for the management of the firm. If the basic processes are changed the overlying EDP systems must be adjusted accordingly. For instance, if the control of a CNC system is taken over by an intelligent machine control which simultaneously records process data for analysis purposes, these must also be made available to the order feedback system, to cost accounting and to the performance-linked pay-roll accounting system. This demands considerable coordination in the planning of business and technical information systems.

As a result of the increased integration of testing procedures within the production flow, there is a tendency towards total monitoring of production. This applies, for example, to non-destructive automatic weighing devices in the area of controlled measuring instruments. This tendency towards total monitoring reduces the need to apply sampling procedures, for which a multiplicity of methods have been developed in the quality control area of business economics.

With an integrated approach to CAD and NC programming the explicit definition of work schedules and operations can in technical terms be eliminated; they are now implicitly contained in the NC programs. Operation information is still needed, however, for capacity planning and statistical cost accounting, so that they still have to be held for these business economics purposes.

At present operational master data are assigned multiply to the individual functions, and managed there in functionally-specific information systems. For example, bills of materials, work schedules, and equipment data are managed by the EDP system for production planning and control. These data are not accessed only by the PPC system, however, but are at the same time needed as a basis for cost estimation or as design support. This means that these master data need to be considered as independent organizational objects and organized independently of the individual functions. Rather they provide perspectives for the diverse application areas. Only in this way it is possible to maintain the same currency and availability in all functions. This is obvious to the economists in the firm when they attempt to introduce on-line cost estimation, but find that the master data are held in the PPC system and the cost accounting system possesses a different database.

Since the management of product description data within CIM constitutes a focal issue as a result of the close interdependence of PPC and CAD systems, business economics is also affected here to a considerable degree.

At present the medium term planning horizon dominates business economics EDP systems. Many planning systems are aimed at planning periods of around six months, e.g. requirement planning within material management, production planning or cost planning. Long term strategic processes, in contrast, receive little support, as do short term control processes, which sometimes relate only to a matter of days. As has been shown, the emphasis within CIM is on the long term structure of systems on the one hand, and, on the other, short term processing, as expressed by the just-in-time principle, for example. This necessarily implies that the medium term planning functions are accorded less importance - one need only think of lot size optimization which received so much attention in the past, which now, with the demand for a lot size of 1, is almost obsolete.

The current organizational and operational structure of the enterprise is strongly oriented towards the advantages of functional specialization. A general trend towards more object- and process-oriented organization is becoming apparent, however. This is evident in the structuring of the entire enterprise into divisions formed on a product group basis, or within production by functional units based on object criteria, such as processing centers or production islands. The organization of CIM process chains is a further element within this set of arguments.

Enterprises are already beginning to apply this principle in that the production island is given responsibility for order handling, process planning and production control functions.

Despite the tendency towards more process-oriented operational and organizational structure, an existing error should not be replaced by a new one. Whereas at present the introduction of CIM is impeded by the functional organizational structure, a new information system should not in turn support a single narrow organizational structure. Rather the requirement should be that an enterprise-wide information system, and especially the underlying database, should provide an array of information that is suitable for diverse organizational structures. Only in this way it is also possible to support dynamic enterprise alterations resulting from affiliations, breakdown into sub-divisions, etc., without major restrictions.

Many modern EDP trends are being exploited by the newly developed CIM systems rather than by the more traditional business economics EDP applications. This applies, for example, to the use of high-definition workstations, the use of relational databases, the use of high quality graphics systems or the introduction of networks. One need only compare the difference between a centrally-oriented evaluation system, which at best offers primitive graphics in the form of points and lines, with the quality of the 3-D graphics and simulations offered by a CAD/CAE system.

Given the close interdependence of the technical and business processes and of the operative processes and the evaluative, planning and decision systems that build upon them, however, uniformity in the quality of information processing is essential.

The aspects of CIM that are significant for business economics are summarized in the following nine points:

1. CIM is an enterprise strategic model.
2. The creation of CIM systems demands considerable specialist competence and new methods of investment analysis.
3. CIM demands decentralized business control methods.
4. CIM boosts the inter-company exchange of data and requires standards for business data.

216

5. CIM demands close links between the process and evaluative levels.

6. CIM leads to the independent (application-neutral) management of master data.

7. CIM alters the time scale of planning processes.

8. CIM requires a process- or object-oriented organizational structure.

9. CIM boosts the use of EDP in business economics functions.

B.II. Trading

Computerized **Retail Information and Control Systems** (RICS) refer to the article-specific quantitative and evaluative monitoring of goods through receipt of goods, storage, withdrawal of goods and material planning/ordering used in trading firms (see Figure 3.B.II.01).

In addition, this circular flow provides data for financial accounting, inventory support and management information.

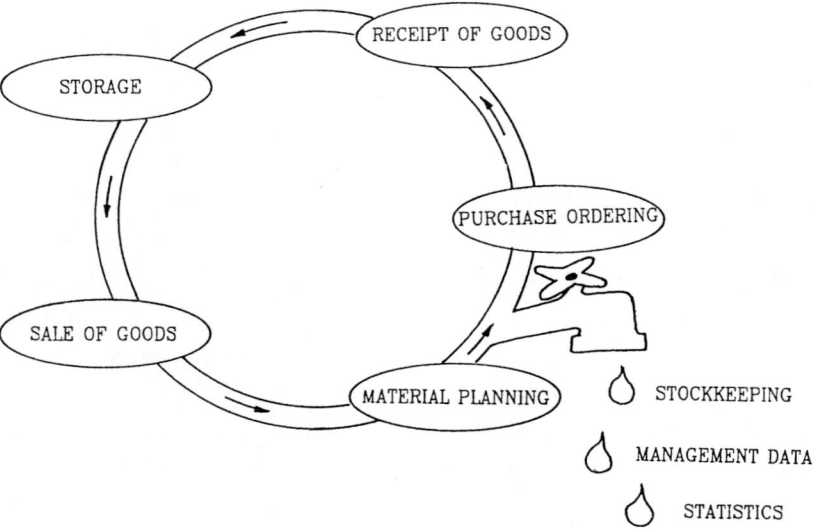

Fig. 3.B.II.01: Monitoring of goods in a retail information and control system

Retail information and control systems are actually employed at both the retail and the wholesale trading levels. At the **wholesale level** order handling and invoicing dominate with the management of customer and accounts receivable files. At the **retail level**, however, customer files with the associated open item bookkeeping is the exception, since cash sales over the counter are the norm.

The important EDP characteristics of retail information and control systems are the exploitation of up-to-date data resulting from the interactive recording of movement of goods and payment transactions, the exploitation of the storage possibilities of EDP systems allowing article-specific identification of stocks and movement of goods, and the networking of data terminals (tills) with central EDP systems, and of branches with their headquarters. At the same time special hardware systems (scanners) are installed for data entry at the till, to link up scales for variable weights of fresh products, and to establish inventory levels using mobile data recording devices in the storage area.

Typical functions of a retail information and control system at the retail level are presented in Figure 3.B.II.02.

The article number of the good is automatically recorded by the till for each sale. OCR characters, magnetic strips and bar codes can be used for this purpose. The labels on the goods are passed over special reading devices (scanners) which can automatically read the article number and other information, e.g. the price, from the label.

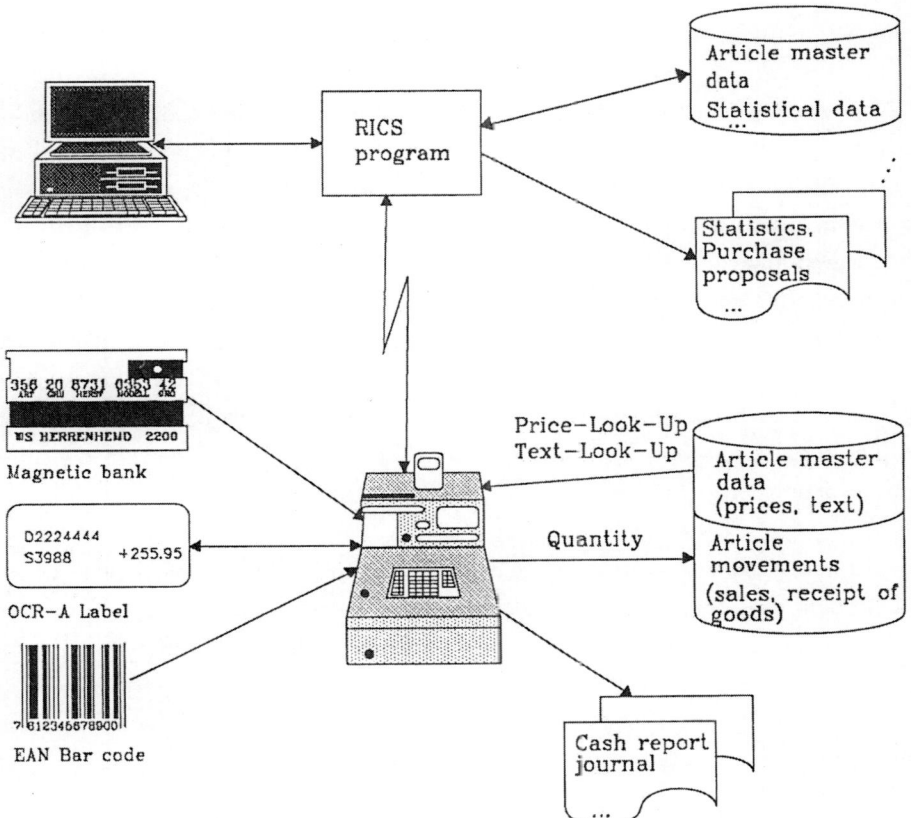

Fig. 3.B.II.02: Retail information and control system at the retail level

An international norm, **EAN**, has been created to provide standards for the numbering of articles. The EAN system was originally developed to provide article numbering for Europe, but has meanwhile been adopted by the International Article Numbering Association, to which over 32 member organizations belong (see *Zentes, EDV-gestütztes Marketing 1987, p. 29 ff.*). The EAN, or international article number, consists of 13 positions, whose structure is shown in Figure 3.B.II.03.

Cuntry code		Federal company number					Producer's individual article number					Test number
4	0	1	2	3	4	5	0	0	3	1	5	4
Centrale für Coorganisation für die BRD		FRANZ SCHUSTER KG Travestr. 20 2400 Lübeck					Lübecker gift—packed marzipan 100 g					99 % Security

Fig. 3.B.II.03: Structure of an international article number (EAN)
(from *Zentes, EDV-gestütztes Marketing 1987, p. 30*)

The EAN is generally labelled by the manufacturer in the form of a bar code. The extent of labelling is highest in the case of foodstuffs, where well over 90% of goods are labelled. Goods which are not labelled by the manufacturer can also be encoded by the trading company in accordance with the EAN structure.

The American/Canadian UPC system (Universal Pradac Code) has a similar structure to the EAN numbering and is compatible with it.

With increasing use of the European article number (EAN), which is attached to the goods by the manufacturer, there is no longer any need for individual company-specific article numbers to be used. By using price-look-up and text-look-up the system can access the stored prices and text on the basis of the article number, so that the price does not need to be affixed to the article.

In a **master-slave system** several tills are connected to an intelligent master till in which the article data are stored. Where intelligent tills with their own storage capacity are used, however, an abbreviated set of articles are held on diskette or hard disk in the till itself.

On the basis of the till transactions a cash report can be created at the end of a day, in which total turnover is broken down according to article group, for example.

In the case of affiliated retail companies the actual retail information and control computer is often in the physically distant headquarters. The retail information and control computer then calls up the transaction records from the decentralized files in the evening, whereby the dial line between the retail information and control computer and the intelligent tills can be set up from either the central or the decentralized location.

Given the Deutsche Bundespost's lower data transmission tariff for Datex-P, continuous data transfer throughout the day can also be considered. This allows increased system security, since breakdown does not endanger the entire day's data, but only those of a few transactions which can be repeated more easily once the system is up again. On the basis of the transaction data transferred the retail information and control computer can generate evaluations of so-called "runners" and "shelf warmers". First, stocks of each article are updated for each branch by booking additions and withdrawals, and information concerning bottlenecks is passed back to the tills. Price changes can also be read to the article files at the branches.

One important task of the retail information and control system is to undertake better material planning. Comprehensive information is made available for this purpose (see Figure 3.B.II.04).

P L A N N I N G   L I S T   DATE: 11–24–89   PAGE 1–001

DESCRIPTION	PACK.		ANO	PURCHASE PRO- POSAL	STOCKS	AVERAGE WEEKLY TURNOVER	TURNOVER IN THE LAST 4 WEEKS				ORDER	
							W1	W2	W3	W4	Q.	DATE
MEIER KG, 2000 HAMBURG												
COOKIES 24 OZ.	24 BOX	1	*07001		1017	13	22	10	24	16	25	10–28
CRACKERS 60 OZ.	60 BOX	1	*07007		27	0,2				1		
CRACKERS 24 OZ.	30 BOX	1	*07008	16	253	0,7	10			17		
GETRÄNKE GMBH, 2000 HAMBURG												
JUICE 32 FL. OZ.	12 BOT	1	*28252	4	66,8	1,4	1	3		2		
BAUER KG; 4000 DÜSSELDORF												
SOUR CREAM	6 BOX	1	*22653		797	4,8	13	3		6	50	11–2
SCHREIBER GMBH, 5000 KÖLN												
SOAP 10 OZ.	6 BOX	51	*29116	51	544	14	18	23	7	8	20	11–2
											5	11–2

Fig. 3.B.II.04: Retail information and control system planning list

The articles are listed according to supplier with details of average usage, forecast values, stocks in transit, etc. By combining articles from the same supplier bulk order possibilities are indicated.

The currently available standard software systems as well as in-house developments leave room for improved planning support by incorporating forecasting techniques and order quantity optimization.

At present the management and monitoring of massive quantities of data is predominant. However, for these purposes alone the use of retail information and control systems is worthwhile.

On receipt of goods not only up-to-date movements at branch level are recorded and passed on to headquarters with the usual call-off, but at the same time support for invoice checking and article labelling is also given. For example, labels (also in bar code) can be printed by an attached printer.

Business economics problems arise in affiliated enterprises in delimiting the functions between the branch and headquarters. This applies particularly to material planning. The branch commonly views autonomous planning and purchasing as an elementary trading function. However, improved information at the headquarters level means that there are

Order process

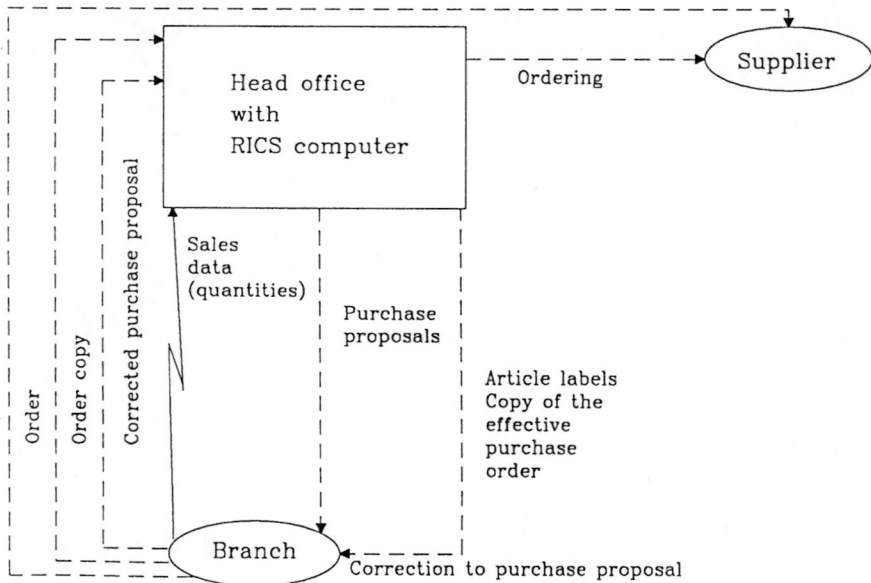

Fig. 3.B.II.05: Information flow within a retail information and control system for a purchase order

substantial advantages to centralized planning (see Chapter 2, Section B.II.2.1). Figure 3.B.II.05, therefore, presents a suggestion for handling purchasing which is based on the principle of providing the branch with a centrally created list of suggestions for material planning, but continuing to allow the branch to carry out its own purchases decentrally. This principle can be variably structured according to article group, such that the headquarters can also undertake purchases.

The foregoing description of till functions referred only to article-specific data. However, in addition to article-specific data such as price and supplier, it is also possible to enter vendor number and customer number. If magnetic code is used it is possible to provide sales personnel and customers with ID cards which store identification data on a magnetic strip so that this data can be automatically recorded. Customers can be induced to accept customer ID cards by setting up a discount system, which can also be effected automatically.

Trading firms can also give out credit cards, which can be used to establish customer accounts for payment handling. On presentation of the credit card the information on the magnetic strip, which is also needed to identify and authenticate the customer, can be used to allocate purchase information to the customer.

A further possibility for recording simple customer information is by direct entry of customer characteristics by the vendor. The 7-Eleven group in Japan uses a special entry key at the checkout to record the sex and age of the customer simply from appearance (see *Zentes, EDV-gestütztes Marketing 1987, p. 174*). This means that at every sale the four information systems: customer, article, supplier and vendor, are served (see Figure 3.B.II.06).

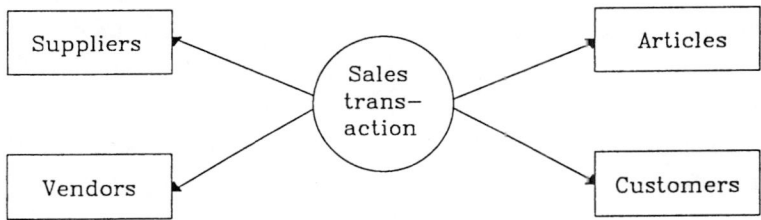

Fig. 3.B.II.06: Effects of a sales transaction

This information is available for performance-related wage calculation for sales personnel, order planning, granting of customer rebates, and choice of supplier, and provides the basis for a wide range of managerial evaluations. The information possibilities of a retail information and control system can only be fully exploited if management is also provided with up-to-date support in its decision-making (see *Zentes,*

Warenwirtschaftssysteme 1982, p. 23). For example, precise article and time information can be used in determining pricing policy or to control short term sales campaigns.

EDP-supported retail information and control systems have a considerable influence on processes within trading firms and also affect the organizational structure. The removal of information barriers with headquarters, resulting from up-to-date data transfer from the branch systems, increases the tendency towards centralization, since material planning advantages can thereby be exploited. At the same time differentiation of the accrued data allows the use of forecasting and planning techniques formulated by business economics (see *Scheer, Warenwirtschaftssysteme 1982*).

The closed retail information and control system represented is increasingly being extended by electronic data exchange links with external partners. In this context Zentes speaks of an integrated retail information and control system (see *Zentes, EDV-gestütztes Marketing 1987, p. 48*). Important potential partners here are: market research institutes, industrial firms, other trading firms and employees.

The considerable currency and detail of sales data are increasingly being exploited by market research institutes via direct access to the trade associations. An **association** is a defined survey group of consumers or trading firms, which regularly collects purchase or sales information.

The best known trade association is that established by the firm A. C. Nielson. By direct transfer of till information to the market research institute up-to-date evaluations of sales campaigns and other short term sales promotion measures can be carried out.

The **SEDAS** system (Standardregelung für ein einheitliches Datenträgeraustauschsystem - standard regulations for a unified data medium exchange system) which has been developed by CCG (Centrale für Coorganisation) has created a norm for the exchange of invoice data between manufacturers (industry) and trading firms (see also Chapter 2, Section B.II.3.1). By creating a clearing house between industrial and trading firms the number of relationships, and hence the administrative costs, can be reduced considerably (instead of n:m data relationships there are only n+m) (see *Zentes, EDV-gestütztes Marketing 1987, p. 40*).

Networks between retail and wholesale firms are already well-developed in some sectors such as pharmaceutical supplies. Here, orders from the retail level can be entered into a data collection system which is then called up by the wholesale firms and transferred to their material planning system (see *Petri, Externe Integration 1990*).

In the context of **POS (point of sale)** applications, on recording of the sales transaction at the check-out terminal of the retail information and control system a data link to the banking system is established for payments by credit or check card.

In the **teleshopping** context customers can communicate directly with the retail information and control system, via a Videotex link, for example.

The possibility of employees at remote workplaces handling invoicing and planning functions also applies in the trading sphere.

The integration of retail information and control systems into inter-company networks extends the rationalization effects of using EDP in trading, but also emphasizes the strategic, i.e. competitive, policy significance of the use of EDP. The networking of wholesale to retail is therefore used as a textbook example of the strategic significance of information and communication technology (see *Petre, Customers 1985*).

B.III. Banking

Typical banking operations such as payment transactions arise in large numbers and are essentially equivalent. It is therefore obvious to automate them in order to reduce costs. This rationalization objective dominated the use of EDP in banking up to around 1980.

Increasingly, however, EDP is being recognized as a strategic marketing tool for achieving competitive advantages by being able to offer more extensive customer services. This electronic customer service is referred to as "**Electronic Banking**" **(EB)**. The central aspect is the inclusion of the customer as a user of the bank's EDP system. At a later stage the customer's EDP system will be linked with that of the bank, so that data from one system can immediately be further processed by the other system. At the same time the banks offer the use of user-friendly information and program systems.

Whereas at present this EDP support has only been achieved in sub-areas, and, therefore, is better referred to as "Computer Aided Banking", the comprehensive networking of the systems gives rise to **Computer Integrated Banking (CIB)** (see *Zapp, Computer Integrated Banking 1989*). This represents a similar development to that in industry where the linking of the various CAx-technologies gives rise to CIM.

The significance of EDP for banking firms is also indicated by the fact that here, and in insurance, the first board of management members responsible for information processing have been appointed.

B.III.1. EDP Support for Individual Banking Transactions

Traditional EDP applications in banking relate to payment transactions, counter services, the accounting of transactions and support for foreign exchange transactions.

Recently the introduction of customer self-service in obtaining cash and making payments has been of increasing importance (see *Cordewener, Kundenbediente Datenstationen 1982; Czech, et al., Mikroelektronik 1983, p. 26 ff.*).

In the context of **cheque transactions** the use of accompanying documentation is largely eliminated. This means that the data from a cheque are stored electronically at the redeeming bank and only these data are passed on to the issuing bank, possibly via several clearing houses. The cheque itself remains at the bank where it was presented. For data recording purposes automatic document readers can be used which are capable of reading not only the details such as the account number which are recorded in OCR characters on the cheque, but also the payee, the amount to be paid and other details in various machine typefaces and in handwriting (see *Kreuzer, Datenverarbeitung 1983, p. 12*).

In making out **mass payment orders**, such as the payment of wages and salaries, firms typically rely on the exchange of data medium. The payment instructions are stored on magnetic tape or diskette and handed over to the house bank, which then passes them on to clearing banks which execute the transfers to the recipients' banks.

In the **electronic banking** context the direct transfer of data via networks is possible. For data transfer within banking organizations comprehensive computer networks are used. Within the banking organization this relates to the transfer of data between branch and headquarters. However, these internal networks also have access to inter-institutional networks on up to international communication networks such as S.W.I.F.T. (Society for Worldwide Interbank Financial Telecommunication) which is capable of handling payment transactions over national boundaries.

The links with inter-institutional and international network systems demand a high level of standardization of network protocols and database accesses in order that diverse hardware and database systems can be linked up (see *Roemer, Gemeinsame EDV 1981*). For this reason, the banking applications are pathfinding in the creation of open networks. The S.W.I.F.T. network, for instance, is regarded as one of the most important private worldwide networks (see *Dube, Eisele, Massenzahlungen 1982, p. 45*). In Germany the cooperative banks use the so-called GENO network for handling payments within cooperative credit institutions. This network is based on DATEX-P which, as an open network, allows links with diverse user hardware systems.

For **counter transactions** terminals are well-established (see Figure 3.B.III.01). These record receipts and payments for Giro and saving transactions, which are then processed by the central host computer. At the same time access to the master data in the central host computer allow comprehensive customer information concerning account balance, etc., to be provided and printed decentrally. The master data also serve to provide plausibility checks for data entry. Microcomputers (PCs) are increasingly being used as counter terminals, which, in the case of breakdown of the central system or the network, are still capable of making decentralized evaluations, and recording and partially processing transactions.

Computerized customer service has led to the reintegration of activities at the bank employee's workplace, which had previously been broken down into sub-functions for batch processing, and thereby into workplaces with different responsibilities for Giro transactions, savings, customer information, etc. This reintegration leads to improvements in customer service, since the customer can receive information about different services and his various accounts at a single counter without time-wasting visits to, and queueing at, different counters.

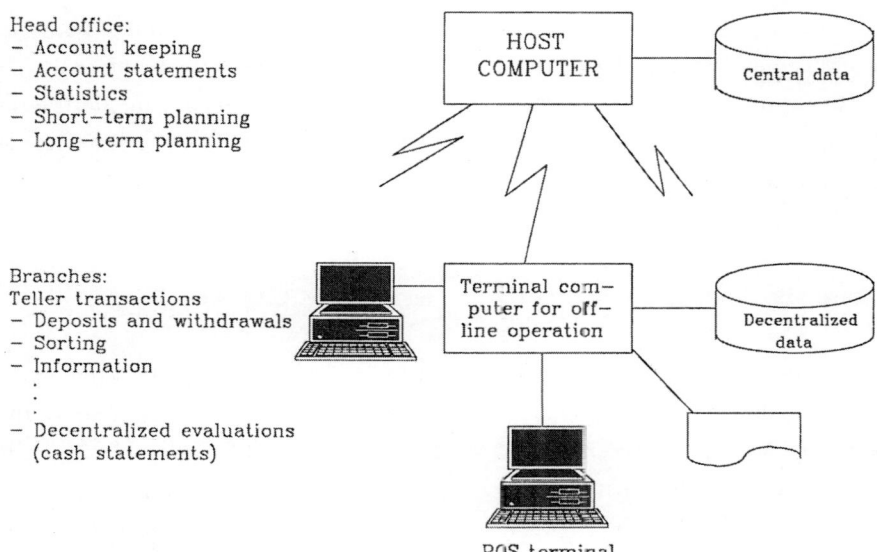

Fig. 3.B.III.01: EDP applications in banking

In the context of the computerized **processing of banking transactions** at headquarters integrated interactive systems are increasingly being used. They process the business transactions recorded in the context of current account bookkeeping, deposit account bookkeeping, foreign exchange transactions through to the handling of loans and bills. Continuous processing allows the daily creation of current balances and economic evaluations.

Foreign exchange transactions depend on the use of up-to-date information. By accessing service systems providing current exchange rate information (Reuter monitor system), permanent telephone links to the most important bank places and foreign exchange dealers, as well as access to their own EDP facilities, a multiplicity of information is collectively available at the foreign exchange dealer's workplace. Online systems support the decisions to be made, in that exchange calculations can be carried out within seconds and the positions reached can be continuously stored (see *Bingemann, Devisenhandel 1982*). The documentation function of automatic storage thereby acquires special significance.

The multifarious use of EDP in the banking sector has not only generated rationalization effects, it has also improved **customer service**. By freeing employees from routine tasks customer advice can be accorded more weight. At the same time the degree of interactive processing and networking within this economic sector has caused an exceptional increase in the currency of the information flow and payment transactions. This is an important prerequisite for monitoring risk, which is particularly relevant to international banking transactions. At the same time the database can be used for short term planning. This creates the preconditions for developing and applying modelling approaches to forecast the stream of payments and optimizing investment decisions.

B.III.2. Electronic Banking/Computer Integrated Banking (CIB)

Electronic banking draws the bank customer more closely into the EDP handling of classical and new banking transactions. The term is used here, therefore, to refer to the electronic customer link. Sometimes the term is broken down into internal electronic banking and external electronic banking in order to differentiate between internal electronic banking and customer-oriented EDP support (see *Maciejewski, Electronic Banking 1989, p. 23 f.*).

As regards the inclusion of **private customers**, the central issue is to make bank services available as far as possible in "self-service" form, so that the bank employees' time thereby saved can be offered in the form of other services (particularly in providing advice). In the support for **business customers**, however, new services offering **customer links**, and new areas of business are being opened up.

The banks have not discovered EDP as a marketing tool in spontaneous isolation, but rather to hinder the penetration of "non-banking" enterprises, such as credit card organizations, large trading firms, filling station networks and insurance firms, into typical banking business.

Five services are offered for private customers:

1. electronic cash dispensers and bank statement printers,
2. plastic cards as means of payment,
3. home banking using Videotex,
4. POS links,
5. information and "non-banking" services.

Electronic cash dispensers are already widespread. Using identification (cheque card) the customer can withdraw cash sums within a certain limit outside bank opening hours. The ID card has a magnetic strip, from which the machine "reads" the card number and asks for a personal identification number (PIN) in order to authenticate the user as legitimate. For this purpose a link has to be established with a database containing the authorization data. If the service is being heavily used this can involve waiting times. There has, therefore, been discussion and testing of a chip card, for which a microprocessor can take over the authentication "offline". With the help of a **chip card** other functions can also be carried out, such as debiting of the cash withdrawn from the account balance stored in the chip. For data security purposes the chip can hold the PIN, account balance, and other data in coded form by using so-called cryptographic codes (see *Limmer, Chipkarte 1988*).

Bank statement printers allow the bank customer to call up statements of his account, once again after he has identified and authenticated himself.

The aim is to develop multi-functional terminals or workstations which will allow not only cash withdrawals and statement printouts but also other bank services to be provided in self-service form.

Depending on the terminal's capabilities the following services can be provided:

- cash deposits,
- cheque deposits,
- issue of travellers cheques,
- money transfers from current account to cash account,
- payment of bills to third parties either by cash or transfer,
- indication of account balance.

The terminal is provided with a card reader to identify the customer, a keyboard for choosing services, a numerical keyboard for entering the PIN, account number and amount, a luminous display, a screen and a printer.

In general such services meet with substantial user acceptance.

Given special credit card services, and since trading organizations have also introduced **credit cards** as a means of payment, this form has also been adopted by banks. In comparison with America and also other European countries, the use of this means of payment is still relatively low in Germany. Here, the use of Eurocheques has been established as an effective means of payment. With increasing international interdependence (the single European market 1992, foreign travel), however, the credit card can be expected to gain increasing prevalence as a means of payment here, too. On presentation of a credit card an online link with a database is again used to authenticate the user and check his credit limit. By introducing chip cards these functions can also be supported offline.

In the context of Videotex-supported **home banking** the customer can call up information about his account balance, enter transfers and standing orders, and make interactive queries to advice services. Although in principle this offers great possibilities through to the use of expert systems for individual advice, the generally low acceptance of Videotex by private customers has dampened expectations.

POS systems refer to the link between intelligent tills in the trading sector with the EDP system of the banking sector. A customer can pay in a POS-affiliated trading firm using his cheque card, whereby an online link is created to handle identification and authentication checks and to debit the amount to be paid from the customer's account. Since the rationalization effects for traders have not been estimated as very high, this service is not yet very well-developed, despite successful trial runs in Berlin and Munich.

Information systems can be established to **provide** intermediary services in the sale of houses and land, whereby interested private customers can receive suggestions of suitable property from a database in accordance with his requirements, which can be presented visually using a linked slide system. A linked financing program establishes a suitable financing plan for the customer given his individual possibilities. The use of EDP thus extends the banking business to cover intermediary services. In the same way insurance services can also be intermediated or offered.

In the case of electronic banking for business customers banks are increasingly developing from institutions that deal in money, into institutions that deal in information **about** money.

Depending on the customer's EDP capabilities and the degree of networking, diverse areas of application are opened up. For example, if the business customer has no EDP facilities of his own the banking institution can take over EDP services such as pay-roll accounting. For this purpose, employee master data are stored and monthly performance data are recorded by the bank. The wage payment is then effected electronically to the employee's account.

To support transfers and direct debits for customers without EDP customer and supplier data can be stored as master data. This means that the addresses and account numbers are recorded in the bank's EDP system. The customer then only needs to provide the bank with an abbreviated list of customer and supplier numbers and the amounts to be paid or received.

If the customer is linked with the bank system via a terminal information services can be used. Banks provide links with national and international information services concerning money matters (e.g. stock market information) and also general economic data.

Cash management systems are offered for the control of cash stocks. This makes it possible to consolidate the balances in various accounts with the credit institute concerned, or even with other institutes up to worldwide links. In addition to pure information functions, automatic overdrawal and consolidation are also offered.

To handle the comprehensive data links the bank system uses international networks such as S.W.I.F.T., or private networks such as the MARK III information service system offered by General Electric Information Service.

Given access to the customer's computer a new dimension in cooperation between bank and firm is opened up. It is not only possible to call up information, but this can be further processed immediately in the firm's computer and the results passed back to the bank's computer. For example, in the context of a cash management system the current stock of money can be ascertained and stored in the customer's computer. By using another bank service attractive investment possibilities can be identified and the amount to be invested determined with the help of a customer-specific optimization program. The result is sent back to the bank in the form of an investment order.

Here, enterprise-specific financial and liquidity planning interact with the banking system's information services and individual evaluation programs or with the use of banks' investment optimization programs.

The number of systems offered by the individual banks (e.g. the systems WORLD CASH ACMS, CORBITEX, COBIS, COINFO, COSTAMM, etc., from the Commerzbank, or dredis, drekon, drehaus from the Dresdner Bank, or db-data from the Deutschen Bank) indicate that at present a multiplicity of isolated EDP support is available. The link between the bank's computer system and the customer-specific system is usually created of necessity by using PC industrial standards. The data links here are faced with the same limitations from the lack of network standards as are other inter-company functions (see *Commerzbank, Handbuch Electronic Banking 1988*).

Nevertheless, already existing applications indicate the extent to which the character of banking will be altered by the use of EDP.

B.IV. Insurance

Insurance firms employ EDP above all to support employees in their work, for investment planning, and for field service control.

The use of interactive systems is extremely high in this service sector. In the more advanced insurance companies one terminal is already shared by less than two employees (see *Boysen, EDV-gestütztes Rechnungswesen 1983*).

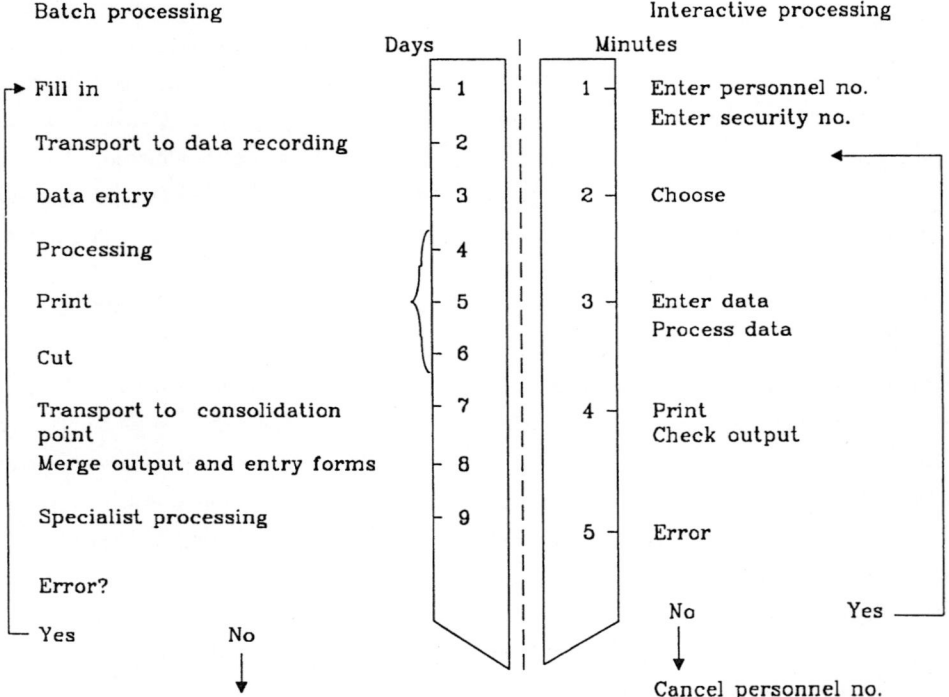

Fig. 3.B.IV.01: Reducing processing time by introducing interactive processing

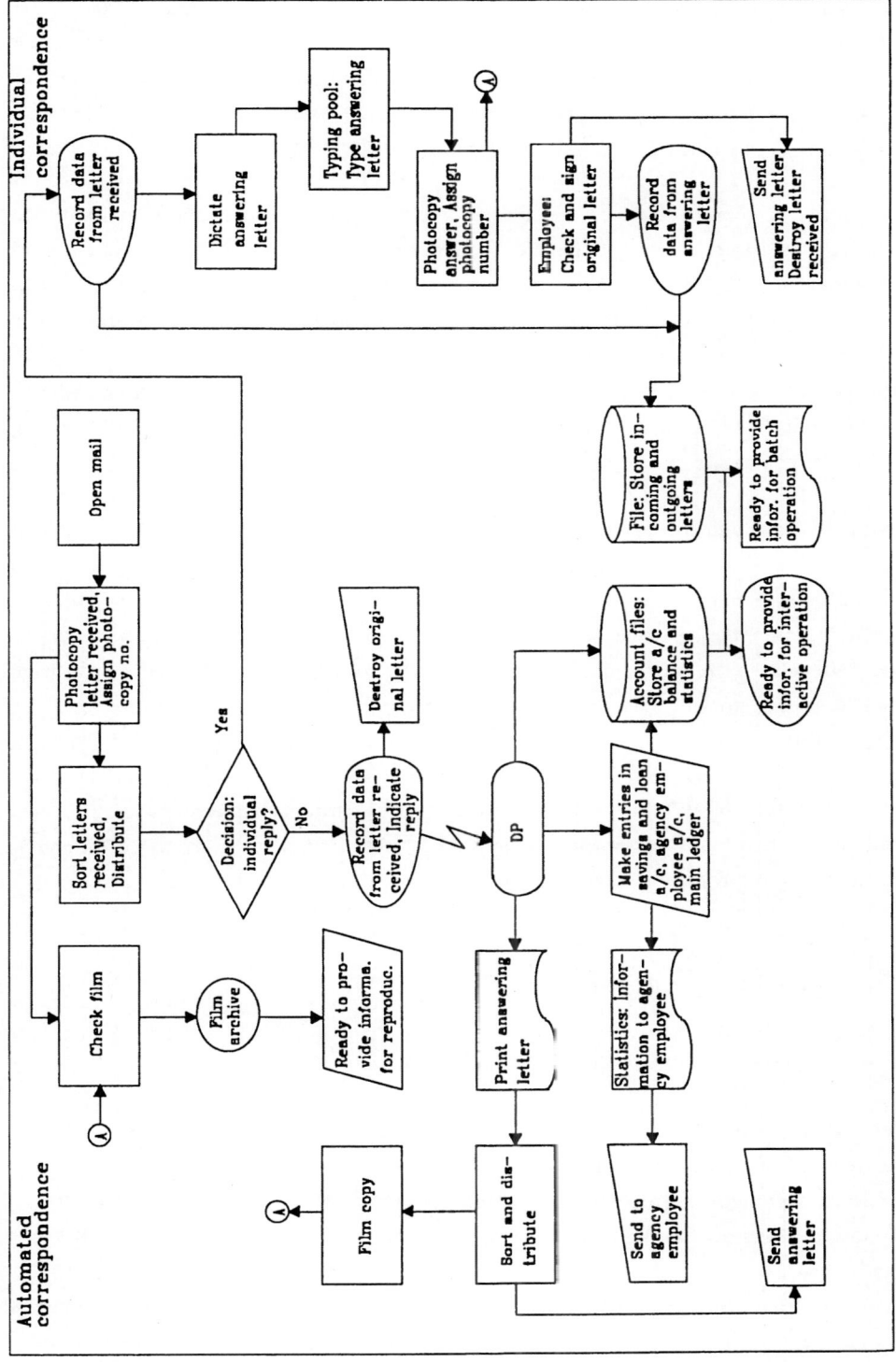

Fig. 3.B.IV.02: Largely file-free processing

As a result it is possible to provide customers with up-to-date information about the status of their insurance policies. Figure 3.B.IV.01 uses an example from the Bundesversicherungsanstalt für Angestellte (BfA) to show how the introduction of interactive programming was capable of reducing the processing time for an operation from nine days to a few minutes (see *Rohrlach, BfA 1981, p. 12*).

The support for **correspondence** and **text processing** is also very advanced in insurance companies, to the extent of file-free processing and at least partly automated correspondence. Figure 3.B.IV.02 presents the procedure of largely file-free processing in a building society, which is very similar to correspondence processing in insurance (see *Barth, Rohleder, Aktenlose Sachbearbeitung 1983, p. 19*).
Once incoming letters have been sorted it is decided whether individual correspondence is necessary or whether a standardized answer consisting of letter modules incorporating customer-specific data can be composed.

Online investment management for mortgages, promissory notes, fixed interest securities, stocks, houses and land can be supported effectively using an integrated information system (see *Lieske, Vermögen verwaltet 1981*).
Insurance companies use decentralized recording systems or online terminal links to enter data relating to new customers, claims, etc. from field agents. To create links from the field agents to the local headquarters extensive networks are set up, as in the banking sector.

The introduction of Videotex will also enable the insurance business to develop new forms of cooperation between customers and insurance headquarters in providing information and advice and in closing deals.

C. Non-Sector-Specific EDP Systems

C.I. Accounting

Accounting is traditionally an intensive application area for electronic data processing. One reason for this is the large number of business transactions to be processed, for which the storage and computational capabilities of EDP can be used particularly effectively. Nevertheless, the use of EDP has not led to any fundamentally new business approaches as compared with manual processing, such as have been highlighted for production planning and control, for example. This is scarcely surprising for financial accounting, which is primarily structured in accordance with the legal prescriptions of commercial and fiscal law. Cost accounting and the accounting of results, on the other hand, do offer the possibility of developing new EDP-oriented business economics approaches, given the multiple purposes they serve and the diversity of business economics forms they take.

C.I.1. Financial Accounting

It is the task of financial accounting to portray the enterprise's relationships with the external world and to represent its business transactions in their entirety. It is subdivided into **general ledger accounting** and **subsidiary accounting** for organizationally independent sub-areas. Figure 3.C.I.01 presents these areas.

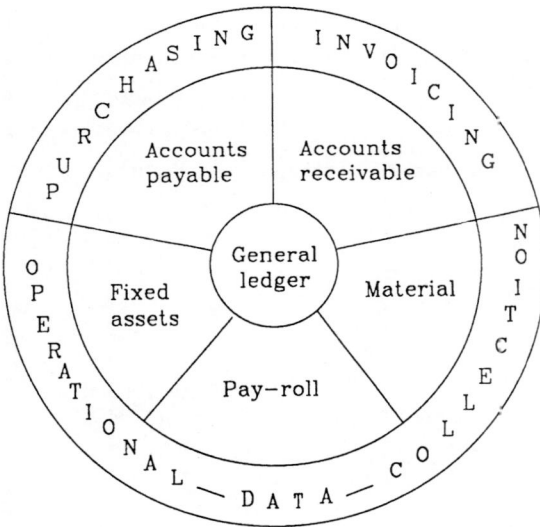

Fig. 3.C.I.01: Financial accounting and prior areas

Subsidiary accounting processes the individual cases and stores them in detail. Consolidated compound entries are then passed on to general ledger accounting.

Accounts receivable and payable, particularly in the form of open item bookkeeping, are handled separately on account of the quantity of transactions, and are referred to as personal accounts.

The other areas of subsidiary accounting fulfil other functions as well as providing data for general ledger accounting.

234

Asset accounting also determines the calculated depreciation for cost accounting. In addition, there are close links with the maintenance planning and the production planning and control systems.

In **pay-roll accounting** the accounting of wages and salaries is carried out as an essentially independent task.

In **material accounting** the value of materials used is determined for cost accounting, and there are close links with material planning.

Since the subsidiary accounts are the most important providers of data for the general ledger accounts, there is a considerable tendency towards data integration, in that data generated by subsidiary accounting are automatically passed on to general ledger accounting. This tendency towards integration has a simultaneous effect on other prior systems, which in turn provide data for subsidiary accounting (see Figure 3.C.I.01).

For example, the invoicing system automatically generates entries for accounts receivable when producing invoices.

In the course of **invoice checking** data from material management or purchasing, such as purchase order, receipt of goods and supplier data, are accessed interactively, such that, after the invoice check itself, the entry record for the open item in accounts payable and, where appropriate, payment instruction can be generated (see Figure 3.C.I.02). These data can largely be taken from previously stored processes without the need for manual entry.

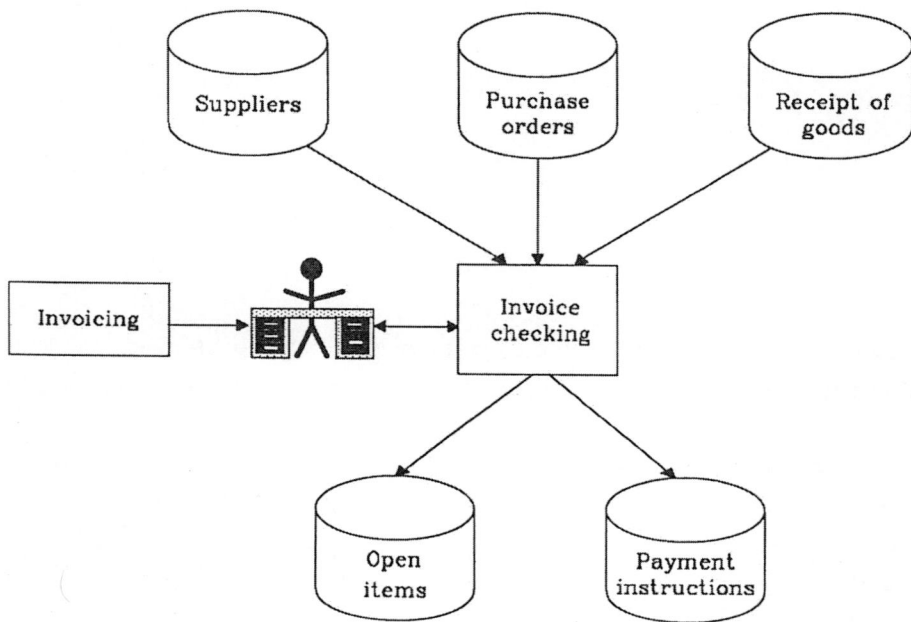

Fig. 3.C:I.02: Invoice checking

It should be noted that invoice checking is frequently incorporated in EDP systems for material management because of the close data relationships, whereas organizationally it is part of accounts payable bookkeeping. Lack of integration between the EDP systems for material management and accounts payable forces the bookkeeper to work with two different EDP systems (see *Krcmar, Schnittstellen 1983, p. 341*). Just as online cost estimation has been incorporated into production planning and control systems because of the proximity of bills of materials and work schedule data, although in terms of content it is part of financial accounting, invoice checking is relocated in material management because of the greater proximity of order and receipt of goods data, although it is closer to financial accounting in terms of its content.

In the context of **operational data collection** current data concerning machine running times, employee performance data, and material usage are recorded. These data thereby form the basis for asset accounting, gross wage accounting and the quantitative material usage for material accounting (see Figure 3.C.I.01).
The general tendency existing in financial accounting for general ledger accounting to be broken down into individual business transactions within the subsidiary accounts, is thus taken further in the prior EDP systems.

Interactive processing has become widely prevalent for bookkeeping. In the ISIS catalog of standard software systems for financial accounting the vast majority are offered in an interactive version. In addition to the fusion of data entry and bookkeeping activities, which give rise to reduced processing costs, this ensures that data records are up-to-date. This is not necessary for all types of accounts, of course, but ensures that the required current data records for processing reminders and payments are available. Whereas batch processing broke down entry procedures between various departments (financial accounting, data entry, and computer center), interactive processing ensures that the bookkeeper is once more responsible for handling the entire processing (see Figure 2.B.I.05).
In creating suggested payment lists in the accounts payable context, or notification of payments received in the accounts receivable context, assignment and decision problems can be supported interactively. In the case of collective payments, the amounts can either be assigned in accordance with predetermined rules, or assigned manually to the open items indicated on the terminal (see Figure 3.C.I.03).

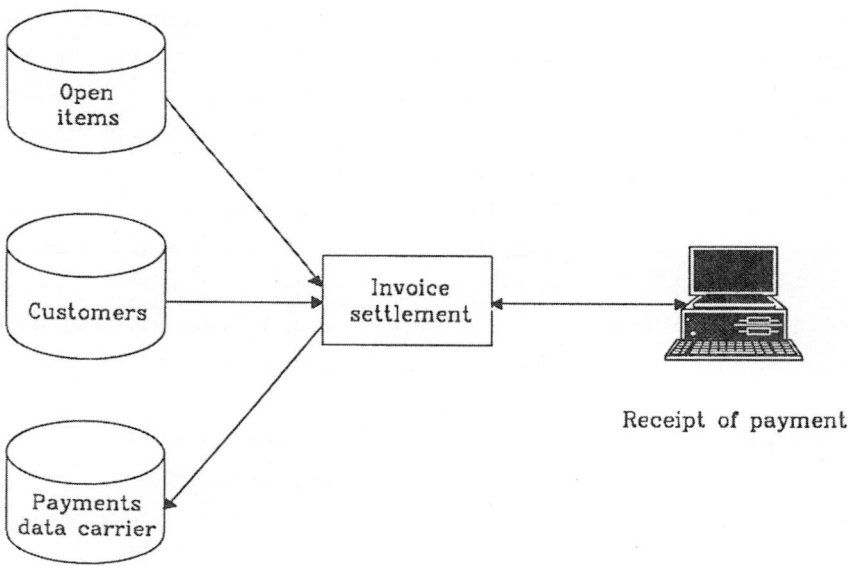

Fig. 3.C.I.03: Invoice settlement

Strictly interactive bookkeeping would mean that a business transaction from invoicing is passed on immediately to accounts receivable and then from there, as part of a compound entry, to the general ledger accounts. If errors arise they can only be eliminated by cancelling the relevant transactions. For this reason, a weaker form of interactive processing is used. The transactions are first stored in intermediate files as so-called pseudo-entries, and the final entries are only made at greater intervals (e.g. daily) once they have been released by the bookkeeper. In the meantime, however, the pseudo-entries are linked to the relevant accounts, so that they are available for the provision of up-to-date information.

An intermediate position is one where in the course of data entry merely formal checks are carried out which do not require access to the master files, but the actual entries are effected in batch runs. However, this form, which does not exploit the significant advantages of a direct and comprehensive plausibility check, is becoming less important. User-friendly EDP accounting systems allow the management of various clients, so that a single system can handle legally independent firms within a group. This allows standardization of reporting, and up-to-date inter-group information and comparison. The use of consolidation techniques, which can handle foreign currencies and bilateral supplies between group companies, allow group-level management information to be produced at short notice (see *Müller, KONSYS 1983*).

Up-to-date databases within financial accounting also make current business economics evaluations possible. At the same time the data can be made available for enterprise planning e.g. for profitability and investment analyses. Effective areas of development and application of the relevant planning models are thereby opened up within EDP-oriented business economics.

C.I.2. Cost and Results Accounting

Cost and results accounting covers the areas of cost type accounting, cost center accounting, cost unit accounting (cost estimation) and cost unit period accounting (operating statement).

Cost accounting is a subsequent function, since it scarcely produces data of its own, apart from the planning data resulting from planned cost estimation, but rather is dependent on the prior EDP systems (see Figure 3.C.I.04).

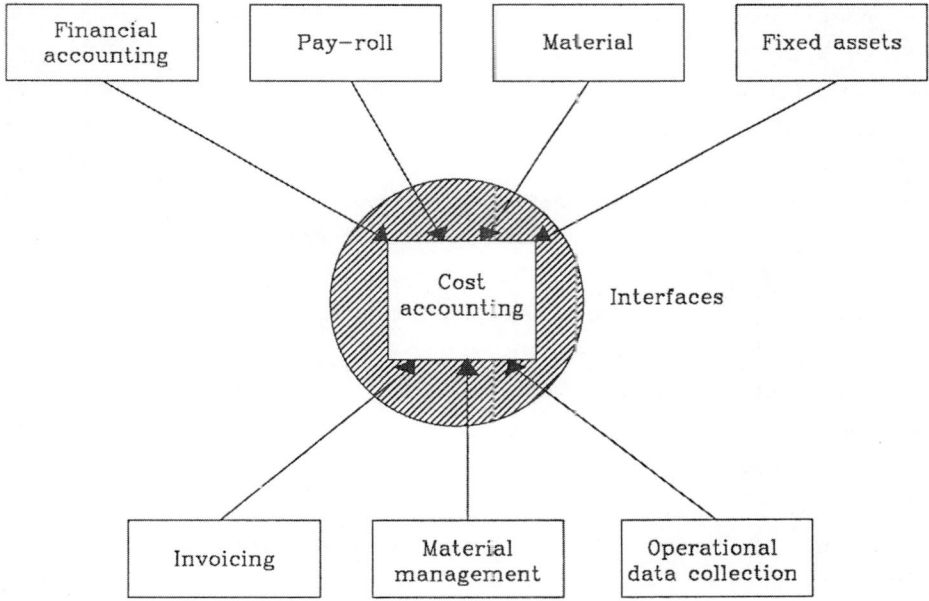

Fig. 3.C.I.04: Data provision for cost accounting

Important suppliers of data are financial accounting, pay-roll accounting, material accounting, and asset accounting. As already observed in financial accounting, there is also a tendency here to record data directly from original documents and to make preliminary entries for cost accounting. This means that invoicing, material management and operational data collection all directly provide data for cost accounting. If preliminary entries, i.e. establishing of cost types, cost centers and, where appropriate, cost units, are already undertaken by these systems, this demands a high degree of integration at the data and program level. To carry out plausibility checks for the preliminary entries master data from the various business application areas must be available.

Various alternatives arise for making preliminary entries depending on the stage at which it is undertaken. For example, in the case of external deliveries and services (see *Krcmar, Schnittstellen 1983, p. 340*) the entries can already be made when orders are placed, or at invoice checking in the material management or financial accounting context, or by the cost accounting department in the course of cost type accounting.

In the case of **cost type accounting** making preliminary entries at an earlier stage means that the data recording function of this activity is largely eliminated. The essential task of cost type accounting then consists of the reconciliation of cost accounting data with the other areas, and the revaluation of financial accounting processes using cost estimation cost unit rates.

With a high degree of integration cost accounting can directly access the stored original documents; if the systems are separate, however, the data are accessed by cost accounting via data interfaces and are consequently subject to redundancy.

Within **cost center accounting** cost types are distributed in accordance with their incurrence. Of particular importance here is the apportioning of internal outputs. Heuristic procedures, such as the step ladder method, are used to handle mutually interdependent outputs. A system of exact equations involves considerable calculation costs. It is in precisely such cases that EDP techniques can usefully be employed. It is surprising, therefore, that up to now this approach is to be encountered only in isolated cases and in individually created systems.

In the course of **cost estimation** the direct costs of the products are determined. There are a multitude of possible calculation procedures, corresponding to the different production structures and cost accounting methods. This extreme variability has impeded EDP support. A further problem arises from the already mentioned links with the production area data, particularly bills of materials, work schedules and equipment data. If cost estimation is only carried out in an annual batch run for the entire production program then the data from the production area can be taken over for this comprehensive processing run via data interfaces. However, if interactive cost estimation is to be possible these data must be available either online via a direct data link, or they must be subject to permanent parallel storage within cost accounting. Given the enormous quantity of data and the associated maintenance costs, however, this is scarcely practicable.

In the course of **cost unit period accounting** differentiated contribution costing is undertaken using various reference bases. In general, revenue accounting lags behind cost accounting approaches with respect to its degree of differentiation (see *Mertens, Rechnungswesen 1983, p. 24*).

Whereas interactive processing is widely accepted both in theory and in practice in the financial accounting context, this does not apply to the same extent in cost accounting. The existing business economics cost accounting methods (calculation of actual costs, normal costs and the various forms of planned costs associated with various partial costing approaches (fixed, variable, marginal costing)) are predominantly period-based, i.e. the evaluations relate to longer periods, e.g. months. This fact is often used as an argument in favour of batch processing as the only sensible form of evaluation. This does not take into account, however, that periodic evaluation does not necessarily imply batch evaluation. Batch evaluation means, above all, the transfer of control of the computational process to the EDP system. However, it is perfectly possible for periodic evaluations to be initiated at the terminal and executed interactively, even if the response times of the EDP system are somewhat greater.

Furthermore, in the cost accounting context event-related evaluations need to be carried out which require interactive processing either because of the need for currency, or because an interactive decision process is being applied. For example, in the order negotiation context cost estimations for one-off products can be undertaken, decisions relating to lot sizes or the choice of procedures can be supported using ad hoc calculations, and information relating to costs and revenues can be obtained interactively from various departments.

A strictly interactive approach is also favoured on more technical grounds, such as the greater simplicity of the system concept for integrated interdependences (see *Plattner, Kostenstellenrechnung 1983, p. 89 - 91*).

The use of database systems in accounting, and particularly in cost accounting, is increasing. Whereas at a conference held in 1980 only one or two systems for cost accounting showed signs of approaches to the incorporation of database techniques (see *Kilger, Scheer, Plankosten- und Deckungsbeitragsrechnung 1980*), at a conference on the same topic which took place three years later nearly all the standard software systems presented were supported by databases (see *Kilger, Scheer, Rechnungswesen und EDV 1983*). The use of databases supports precisely the data integration with prior areas which is possible here, as well as variable online evaluation possibilities.

Since cost accounting is one of the most important sources of information for the management of the enterprise, it must be capable of responding to many types of query.

This gives rise to the requirement that data should be stored in unconsolidated form as long as possible. Following Schmalenbach's formulation, this unconsolidated database is referred to as **basic accounting** (see *Sinzig, Rechnungswesen 1989, p. 47 ff. and the literature presented there*).

Both periodic evaluations and ad hoc calculations for special evaluations can build upon this basic accounting. The term basic accounting must be considered questionable in this respect, however, since Schmalenbach also subsumed parts of the periodic evaluations under this term. Nevertheless, this idea has been very fruitful in the discussion of EDP-oriented accounting over recent years. The logical basic accounting (see Figure 3.C.I.05) does not need to be identical with a unified physical database, since many of the original data are already stored in various prior systems and are available for special evaluations by using the same database system.

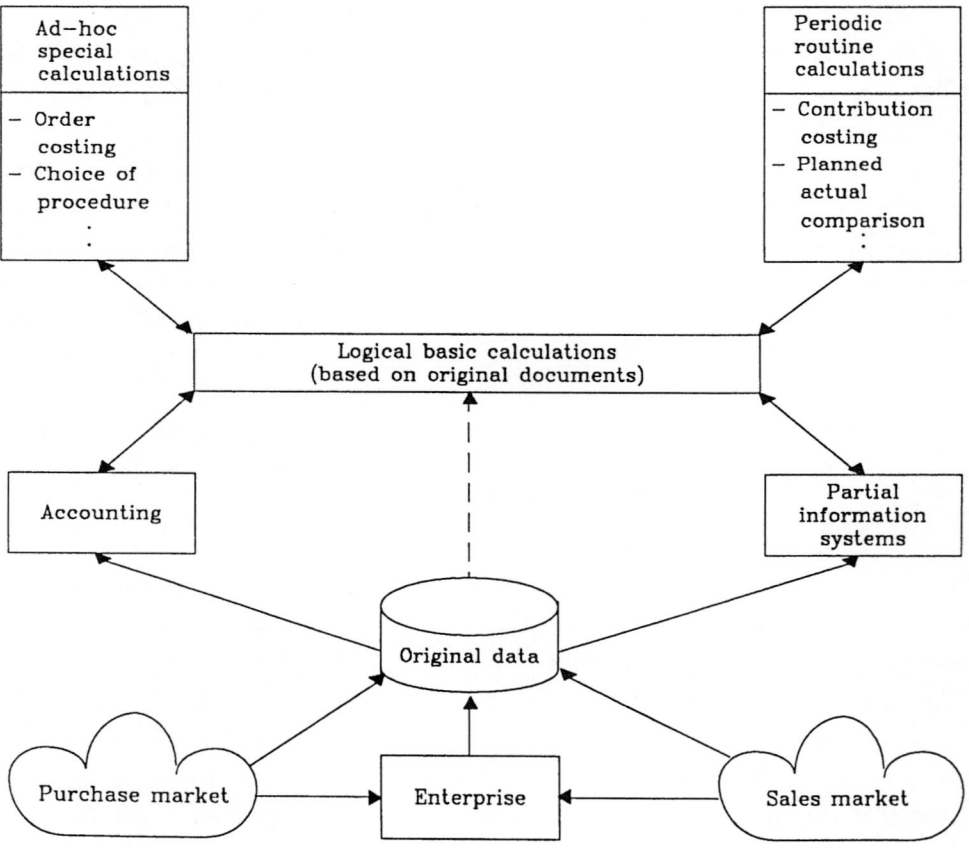

Fig. 3.C.I.05: Incorporation of basic accounting in a cost accounting system

The concept of database-oriented accounting, particularly cost accounting, makes it possible not only to use conceptually clear and articulated cost accounting procedures, e.g. Kilger's system (see *Kilger, Plankostenrechnung 1988*), but also to implement the principle of a flexible cost accounting system based on direct costs (see *Riebel, Deckungsbeitragsrechnung 1985*).

The use of a unified data system for managing the enterprise's master data also allows various departments to access cost accounting information. For example, sales can use contribution margins relating to articles, sales areas and customers for profit optimizing control purposes. It is also worth mentioning the already frequently cited application area for the use of cost information in product development.

These principles are also being increasingly acknowledged by those software systems which up to now have offered self-contained accounting systems (see *Bretschneider, Integriertes Rechnungswesen 1983*). From the various accounting functions a **cost information system (CIS)** is constructed in the form of a database which can be accessed both by cost accounting personnel and also by other departments (see Figure 3.C.I.06). Personal computers which are linked with the central EDP system can also be used here. Since accounting systems already consolidate many data, however, this idea does not fully correspond to the concept of a cost accounting system founded on basic accounting represented in Figure 3.C.I.05.

To provide clear concepts with which to exert influence on the current discussion and on a suitable computerized cost accounting system is an important task for EDP-oriented business economics.

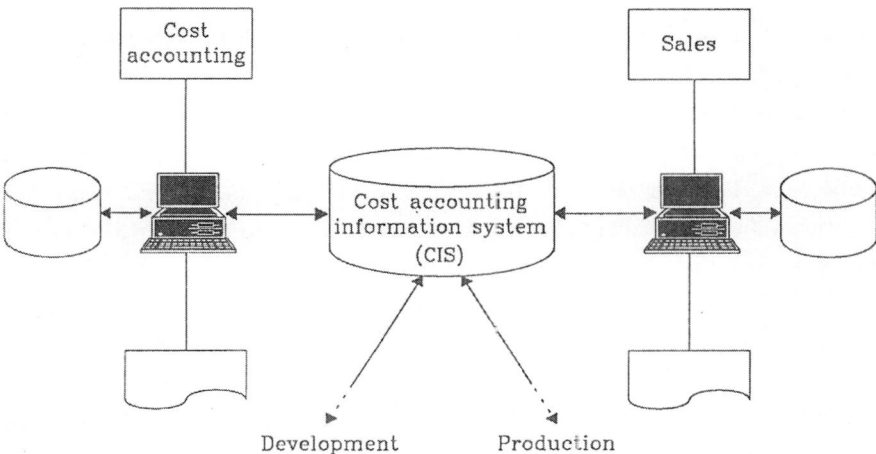

Fig. 3.C:I.06: Cost accounting information system (CIS)

C.II. Marketing

In comparison with other business functions, EDP support for marketing is still underdeveloped. This is all the more surprising given that this area also works with large quantities of data. This applies both to the internal enterprise information concerning receipt of orders, sales, prices, advertising, etc., and also to the regularly acquired external market research data from trade association investigations, etc. User-friendly evaluation systems and presentation possibilities using graphics systems provide a multitude of EDP applications (see *Thorne, Datenverarbeitung in Marketing 1981*). The use of international service networks, such as EURONET, makes it possible to access the databases of international organizations (UNO, EC) or national public institutions such as the Statistische Bundesamt (Office of Statistics).

The considerable currency of data provided within trading firms by the use of retail information and control systems is a good reason for the manufacturers of consumer goods to maintain up-to-date marketing data. In advanced **marketing information systems** within the consumer goods industry, product managers can inform themselves, in advance of a customer visit, of the customer's current turnover, his payment behaviour, his market share, etc. (see *Röske, Gansera, Strategisches Marketing 1981*).

The introduction of electronic panels increases the currency of this external source of information considerably (see *Zentes, EDV-gestütztes Marketing 1987, p. 150 ff.*). The data are not only provided in "paper" form, but can be offered to the user for internal storage via data medium exchange (magnetic tape or diskette), or, in the case of direct EDP links or at least a terminal link, direct access is also possible.

The quality of internal marketing data is being increased as a result of the increasing development of marketing information systems, in which data extracted from the operative sales systems are stored for user-friendly evaluation. Here, further information collected by the firm's sales representatives can be added to the pure sales data with the help of **mobile data recording (MDR)**. This can be effected in especially user-friendly and up-to-date form by using portable PCs, which on the one hand provide support for the sales activities, and on the other provide additional important information for marketing evaluations (see *Zentes, EDV-gestütztes Marketing 1987; Deusch, Freihalter, Mobile Datenerfassung 1989*).

The use of EDP offers considerable advantages in the recording of primary information. **Computerized interviews** can be carried out, which not only offer rationalization benefits, but also reduce the influence of the interviewer (see *Kroeber-Riel, Neibecker,*

Computergestützte Interviewsysteme 1988). At the same time non-verbal investigations for the analysis of consumer behaviour can be carried out with computer support. The consumer's unconscious behaviour can be registered by observation, and then analysed. Attention recording systems, electronic analysis of reaction times and the intensity of expressions of approval or disapproval of video or advertising spots provide basic data for diverse analyses (see *Neibecker, Apparative Marktforschung 1987; Kroeber-Riel, Neibecker, Computergestützte Interviewsysteme 1988).*

Many marketing analyses provide no direct links between sales policy instruments and the economic success factors of profit or turnover, instead indicators are simply established. For example, the success indicator determined for advertisements is the amount of attention or memorability generated; however, these do not generate any automatic link with the economic goals. Connecting up the complex network of indicators, economic variables and experiential knowledge is therefore an effective application area.

The use of expert systems also opens up a wide range of application possibilities in marketing (see *Neibecker, Expertensysteme im Marketing 1989).* Since many marketing decisions, despite being based on a multitude of data analyses, are ultimately made more on the basis of the intuition of the marketing decision-makers, the incorporation of this heuristic knowledge in the knowledge base of expert systems is particularly interesting. Application areas for expert systems, for which prototypes have already been developed, are strategic marketing decisions, market share analysis, sales personnel support, media planning, advertising creation support and the analysis of advertising effects.

C.III. Personnel Management

Calculation of **net wages** is a classic area of EDP application. As a result of the legal prescriptions of tax law and social insurance this area has become largely standardized and is, therefore, particularly suitable for the use of standard software. Since net wage calculation is only carried out before the (monthly) days of payment, it remained a typical batch application for a long time. However, interactive processing is increasingly being used for the **management of master data**. Interactive processing simultaneously provides greater use of the database for ad hoc applications. These might relate, for instance, to queries concerning hiring and firing of personnel, information about the amount of sick leave, absenteeism, presentation of pay-roll accounts and numerous model calculations in the context of wage negotiations and the determination of bonuses.

Gross wage calculation is in many cases still carried out with little EDP support, since here numerous company-specific special cases have to be handled. With the increasing use of operational data collection systems, however, performance data for production employees can be taken over directly and provide the basis for gross wage calculation. With up-to-date operational data collection it is even possible for employees to call up their own accumulated data on their piecework slip records at any time, and thus obtain information about their current wage entitlement.

EDP systems with connected time recording systems also support the introduction of flexible working hours.

Wage payments are effected by the exchange of data media with the banks. This has almost completely eliminated cash payments. At the same time data that has to be submitted in accordance with the Datenübertragungsverordnung (DÜVO - data transfer regulations) can also be supplied from personnel databases by data medium exchange. These data are then passed on to the Statistische Bundesamt (Office of Statistics), medical insurance, pension funds and unemployment insurance and are used there to record employees' entitlements and to make up-to-date statistical analyses. These statistics are then available in turn to the enterprises as information for their own personnel planning.

The use of database systems and interactive processing leads to a situation within personnel management systems where the pure wage calculation function is carried out as a standard function, but increasingly applications for decision support and **personnel planning** are occupying the foreground (see *Heinrich, Pils, Personalinformationssysteme 1983*).

C.IV. Enterprise Planning

Comprehensive optimization models based on linear optimization and simulation have been developed within business economics for enterprise planning (see *Naylor, Corporate Planning 1979; Zwicker, Dynamische Systeme 1981; Mertens, Griese, Industrielle Datenverarbeitung II 1988, p. 18 ff.*).

In addition, user-oriented planning languages have been developed for EDP systems which, although their optimization methods are not as sophisticated, are nevertheless widely used. In contrast with optimization, interactive systems are also provided with support for model creation, for "what if" and "what to do to achieve" applications and Monte Carlo simulations.

The essential features and application potential of these planning languages have already been discussed above for the examples of developing a financial plan and sensitivity analysis (see Chapter 2, Section B.I.2.3).

A risk analysis using the Monte Carlo method is presented in Figure 3.C.IV.01.

RISK ANALYSIS

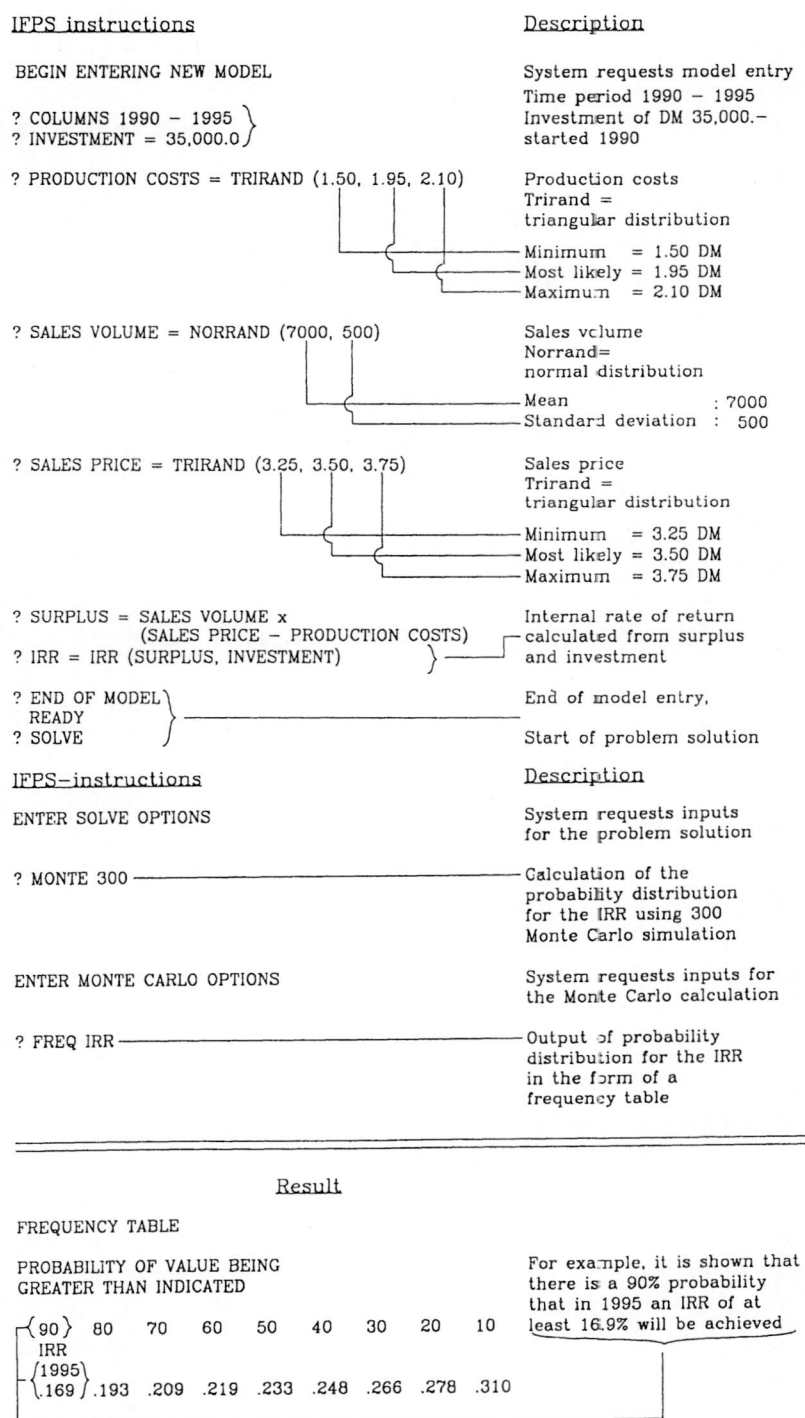

IFPS instructions	Description
BEGIN ENTERING NEW MODEL	System requests model entry
? COLUMNS 1990 – 1995 ? INVESTMENT = 35,000.0	Time period 1990 – 1995 Investment of DM 35,000.– started 1990
? PRODUCTION COSTS = TRIRAND (1.50, 1.95, 2.10)	Production costs Trirand = triangular distribution Minimum = 1.50 DM Most likely = 1.95 DM Maximum = 2.10 DM
? SALES VOLUME = NORRAND (7000, 500)	Sales volume Norrand= normal distribution Mean : 7000 Standard deviation : 500
? SALES PRICE = TRIRAND (3.25, 3.50, 3.75)	Sales price Trirand = triangular distribution Minimum = 3.25 DM Most likely = 3.50 DM Maximum = 3.75 DM
? SURPLUS = SALES VOLUME x (SALES PRICE – PRODUCTION COSTS) ? IRR = IRR (SURPLUS, INVESTMENT)	Internal rate of return calculated from surplus and investment
? END OF MODEL READY ? SOLVE	End of model entry, Start of problem solution

IFPS–instructions	Description
ENTER SOLVE OPTIONS	System requests inputs for the problem solution
? MONTE 300	Calculation of the probability distribution for the IRR using 300 Monte Carlo simulation
ENTER MONTE CARLO OPTIONS	System requests inputs for the Monte Carlo calculation
? FREQ IRR	Output of probability distribution for the IRR in the form of a frequency table

Result

FREQUENCY TABLE

PROBABILITY OF VALUE BEING
GREATER THAN INDICATED

For example, it is shown that
there is a 90% probability
that in 1995 an IRR of at
least 16.9% will be achieved

90	80	70	60	50	40	30	20	10
IRR								
1995								
.169	.193	.209	.219	.233	.248	.266	.278	.310

Fig. 3.C.IV.01: Risk analysis in IFPS

Since this kind of software system was originally made available using so-called time-sharing services which then had to be transferred to dedicated EDP systems, this means that internal enterprise data need to be entered into the system by rather cumbersome routes. Spreadsheet programs, such as VisiCalc, MULTIPLAN, or LOTUS 1-2-3, which are also used for enterprise planning, also have a data provision problem, since they all require a special database.

Since empirical investigations indicate that enterprise management is particularly receptive to visual representations this constitutes a worthwhile application area for business graphics (see the representation of a portfolio analysis conducted using the Boston Consulting Group's model with the help of the EDP system FCS in Figure 3.C.IV.02).

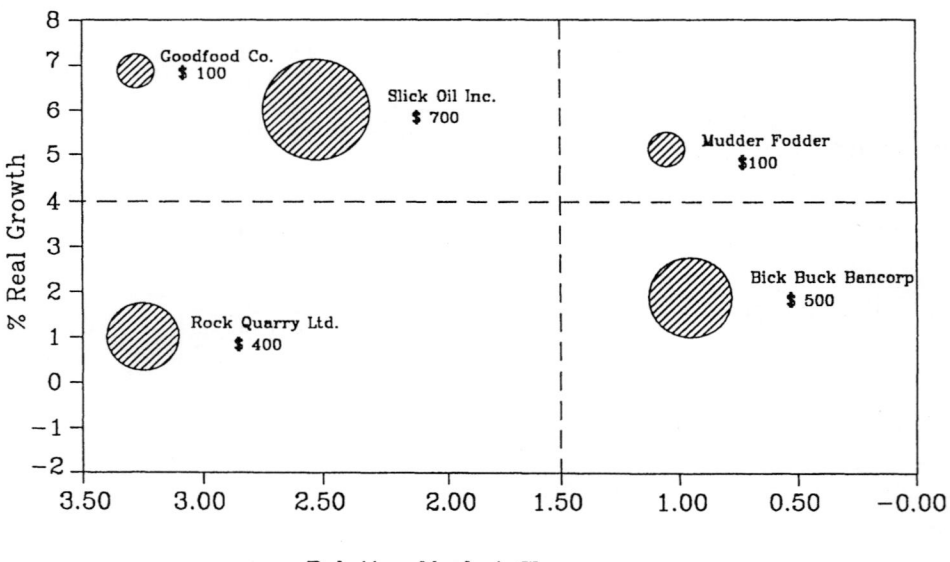

Fig. 3.C.IV.02: Graphical evaluation in the enterprise planning context

It is argued that enterprise planning primarily requires aggregated data which cannot be taken from the operative EDP systems. Time comparisons and forecasting calculations, however, still require many data from the operative systems.

The suggestion here, therefore, is to link microcomputers for enterprise planning with the central EDP system and thus with the central enterprise databases. The possibilities for networking microcomputers ensure that both advantages are combined: terminal emulation or file transfer between central computer and microcomputer mean that data can be extracted from the central EDP system and processed further using user-friendly micro-computer evaluation systems.

The link with time-sharing services may still be worthwhile if they offer particularly highly developed evaluation programs. In addition, links with communication services which make economic statistics data available, for example, are also desirable for enterprise planning.

A comprehensive EDP configuration for enterprise planning is represented in Figure 3.C.IV.03.

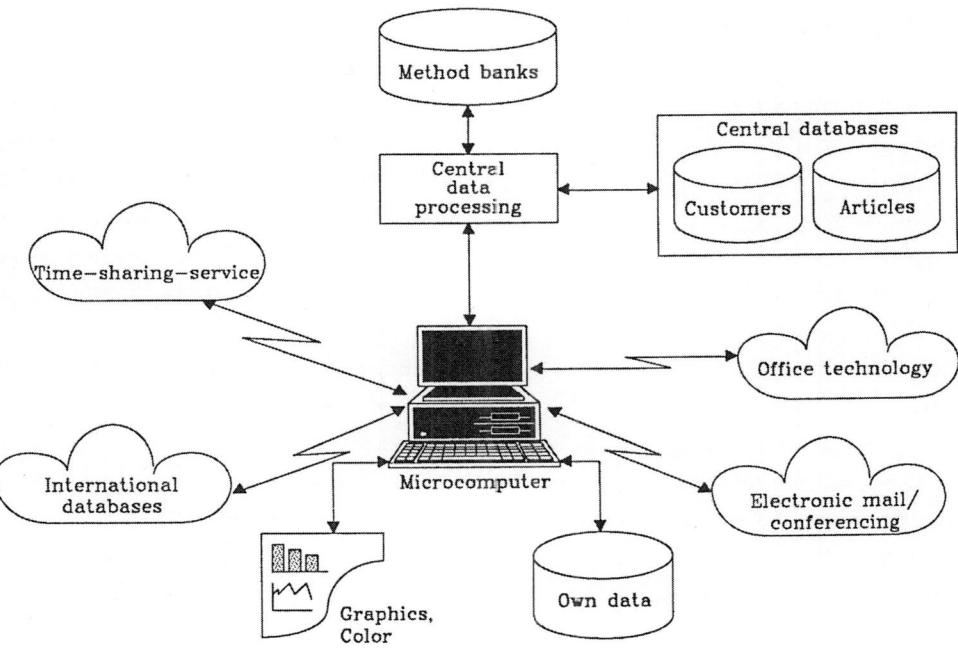

Fig. 3.C.IV.03: EDP configuration for enterprise planning

Since the information requirements of enterprise management are very broad, given the function of coordinating all the operational areas, there is a need here for database query languages. Although these possibilities are technically available at present, they are not widely used, since the use of EDP in the enterprise is dominated by the need to handle the problems of sheer quantity at the administrative and planning levels. Advances in the use of database systems, however, will also open up new applications for enterprise management.

To summarize, the use of diverse data sources, flexible evaluations using graphical support and planning languages for model generation, sensitivity analysis, and Monte Carlo studies offer intensive exploitation of the planning models available in business economics. Furthermore, these instruments can provide the impetus for the further development of enterprise planning methods, since these possibilities still receive too little attention even in recent publications.

C.V. Office Automation

C.V.1. Description of Office Automation

Office automation comprises the integration of diverse EDP techniques. It relates to the processing of data, text, pictures and language, and includes communication services such as electronic mail and electronic conferencing. The problem of linking new systems with already existing systems, particularly classical EDP systems, exists here, too. The aim is to provide the user with a uniform "interface" with these systems. This means the ability to work with uniform commands, screen forms, error messages, data formats, etc., for all applications.

The approaches certainly relate **also** to the support of secretarial functions, but principally cover the functions of qualified specialist staff (see *Schönweitz, Bürokommunikation 1989, p. 44 f.*). The EDP support should be provided not only for repetitive (serial) processes, but also for isolated cases. In these instances similar procedures are sought from electronic "files" and provided to the processor as a basis for interactive alterations. This represents an analogous approach to that in previous situations, such as in the design of customer demand-oriented variants in the manufacturing area, for example.

In Figure 3.C.V.01 office applications are listed and the various EDP instruments for their support are evaluated (see *Scheer et al., Personal Computing 1984*).

Information management covers filing, storage, alteration and retrieval of information. The processing of tasks carried out at the workplace generates data which are stored in the EDP system for further use, or for transfer to other workplaces.

In **problem-solving** it is possible to distinguish between:
-      queries to existing data stocks,
-      simple evaluations by creating tables,
-      calculation of decision alternatives (simulation),

- method-intensive applications using statistical programs or optimization techniques,
- data-intensive problem-solving by linking different files and combining spatially distinct data records, and output-intensive evaluations using graphics systems or mass printing.

In the **text processing** context creation, alteration and archiving of text is supported.

Instruments / Applications	Internal			External					
	Micro-computer	Dedicated computers	Central data processing	Btx	Telefax	Teletex	Mailbox	Time-sharing service	International databases
Information management	M	M	H					M	
Problem solving									
Queries	1	M	H	M				M	H
Simple evaluations	H	M	H					H	
Simulation	M	H	M					M	
Method-intensive	M	H	H					H	
Data-intensive	1	H	H					1	
Output-intensive	H	M	M					1	
Text processing	H	H	1			M			
Desktop publishing	M	H	M						
Communication									
Electronic mail			M	M	1	M	H	1	
Electronic conferencing			M	1				1	1
Remote office work	M	1	1	M	1	1			
Management of personal resources	M	M	1	1			1		

H = high suitability   M = moderate suitability   1 = low suitability   blank = unsuitable

Fig. 3.C.V.01: Suitability of EDP instruments for office applications

Desktop publishing (DTP) refers to the creation of documents containing text, tables and pictures. Here, the variety of typefaces, forms, layouts and quality approaches the standards possible in the printing industry (see *Braun, Zierer, Desktop Publishing 1988, p. 50*).

Specialist office tasks are carried out to a large extent as team work. This demands an intensive information flow between the workplaces concerned in any piece of processing. The **communication** with internal partners, but also with external partners such as customers, suppliers, and field workers, is thus an important work component.

With the help of **electronic mail** (see Figure 3.C.V.02) information can be sent from an entry system at one workplace via a data transfer system to the EDP system at another workplace. Information can be sent to one or more adressees. The recipient is automatically informed of the arrival of new messages, and can order them, call them up, process them, or store them in accordance with his priorities.

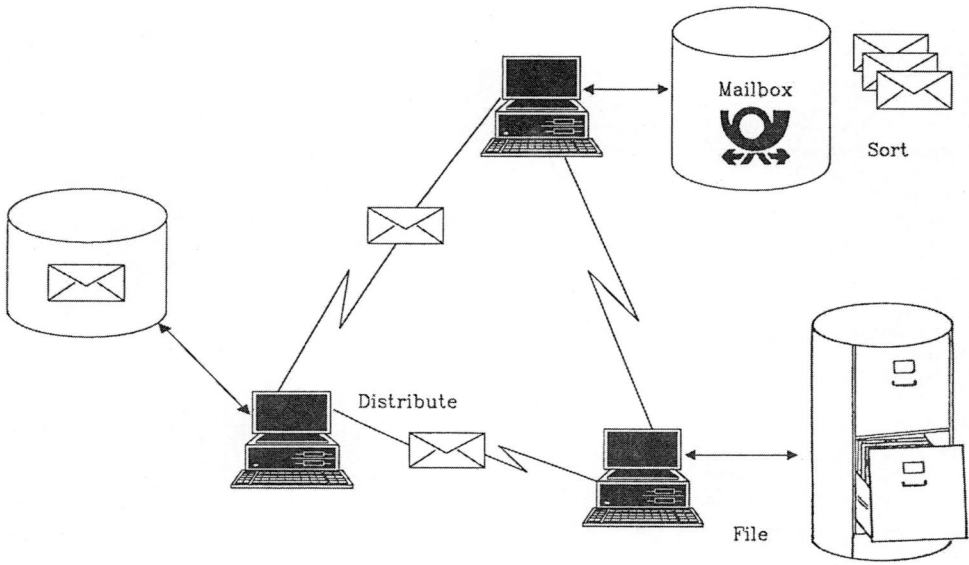

Fig. 3.C.V.02. Electronic mail

In the context of **electronic conferencing** (see Figure 3.C.V.03) the communication network is used not only for the exchange of information, but also for simultaneous processing. The working results of a spatially and temporally distant working team are stored in a central conference file which can be accessed by all the users. In this way, each user is informed of the status of the work of the others (see *Szyperski, Aspekte 1982; Eicker, Telekonferenz 1988*).

Data transfer possibilities mean that it is no longer absolutely essential that employees be physically present at their workplace. Employees can also access the necessary data via terminal from other locations. As a result it is possible to locate employees at offices near to their home or even for them to work from their own home in the context of **remote office work**.

In addition to information concerning the processes he has to handle, the employee can also get the EDP system to manage **data relating to his own work management**, e.g. his appointments diary. The EDP system can then inform him of certain appointments,

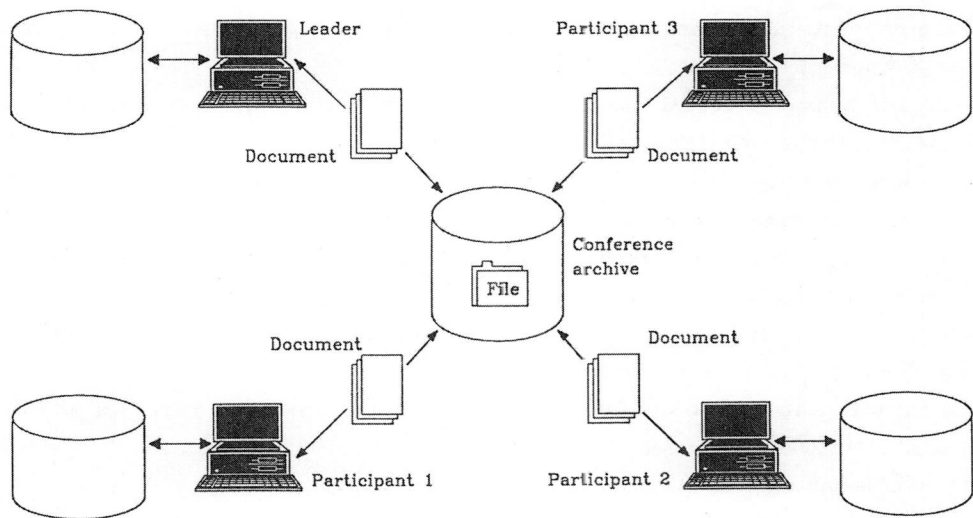

Fig. 3.C.V.03: Electronic conferencing

and remind him of when he needs to start handling a particular work process. The collective management of the appointments of several users allows suitable appointments for conferences to be set up automatically.

Within office automation it is possible to distinguish between internal and external **instruments**, whereby the transfer and origin of information is the deciding factor.

Internal instruments consist of **microcomputers**, which are particularly suitable for simple evaluations using spreadsheet programs and for the output of graphics using linked plotter systems.

Dedicated computers, principally workstations, are suitable for text processing and graphical processing (DTP).

Central data processing can also provide support for specialist activities. Database query languages, which have already been mentioned, particularly those based on relational database systems, make it possible for the employee to manage his own data in the central EDP system and to use them for evaluations. Many of the desired evaluations are anyway aimed at data that are already stored centrally, such as orders, revenues, costs, etc. Comprehensive planning languages support method-intensive evaluations and simulations, e.g., risk analysis using the Monte Carlo technique (see Chapter 2, Section B.I.2.3).

External instruments are Videotex, Telefax, Teletex, mailbox systems, time-sharing services and international databases.

With the help of **Videotex** communication functions within an enterprise, but also between different enterprises, can be effected.

The **postal services** Telefax and Teletex also support communication applications. Of course, the standards expected from a fully developed electronic mail or electronic conferencing system cannot be fully realized. With the help of Telefax pictures can be transferred using a facsimile process. The Teletex system can transfer text to the recipient in original content and format, and thereby possesses the editing functions of word processors and the transmission functions of the Telex system.

In order to communicate via **mailbox systems** each participant receives a kind of electronic mailbox which permits the deposition and receipt of information. By using passwords only authorized recipients can access the information stored in the mailbox.

In addition to the Telebox system from the Deutsche Bundespost, there is a large number of private suppliers (see *Telebox 1989*).

Service companies offer **time-sharing services** which make it possible to use special software, computer capabilities, computer networks and applications advice.

By accessing **international databases** research can be carried out in diverse areas of knowledge (see *Schulte-Hillen, Arbeitsmittel 1988*).

The essence of office automation is to present the user with diverse application and implementation possibilities via a uniform user interface (see *Babcock, Integrated Office System 1983, p. 61; Liebermann, Selig, Walsh, Office Automation 1982, p. 12*). For this reason, the use of the instruments presented in Figure 3.C.V.01 as separate services is inappropriate.

An initial integration of the various services can be realized by extending the functional scope of microcomputers. Microcomputers can not only be used as stand-alone systems, but can be used as terminals by means of terminal emulator programs to create links with time-sharing services and with the central EDP system. In this way file transfer from the central data records to the microcomputer is possible, so that the user can exploit both the central data and the advantages of the microcomputer's user-oriented spreadsheet programs. Many microcomputers can also handle Videotex or be linked up with the postal services Telex and Teletex.

This integration applies to the technical level, but does not in itself create a uniform system interface for the user.

However, these possibilities are offered by special office systems. They cover the integration of text processing, graphics processing, access to electronic archives, data processing and electronic mail. At the same time they allow access to other communication services and to the central EDP system. A uniform software system handles all the functions, so that the user is provided with uniform terminal guidance. Within this approach the aim is to create processing islands within departments which can be linked via networks with other departments, with the central EDP system, and with external communication services (see Figure 3.C.V.04) (see *Schwetz, Bürotätigkeiten 1983 p. 16*).

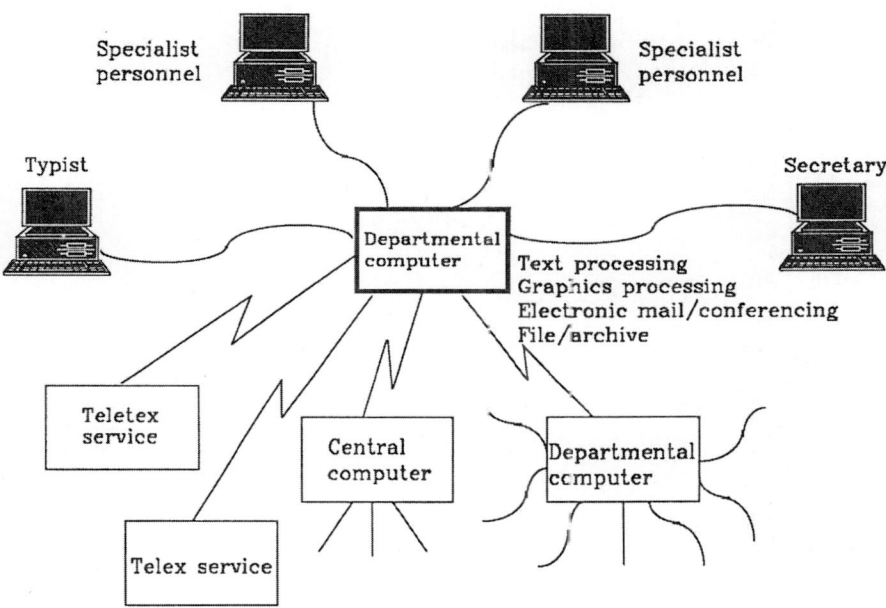

Fig. 3.C.V.04: Functional scope of office systems

The creation of integrated application islands in the office area appears sensible. According to empirical investigations, about 80% of the informational relationships occur within the department, only 20% occur with respect to other departments or external locations. The majority of the communication relationships would be handled via the electronic mail and electronic conferencing functions of the departmental computer.

In the **Office by Example** approach (IBM) the integration of text processing, database access, graphics processing, and electronic mail is also effected via a uniform user interface, i. e. a uniform office language (see Figure 3.C.V.05). The system exists as a pilot version at IBM's Thomas Watson Research Center in Yorktown Heights, and uses the relational database system Query by Example. This system provides the user with pre-formatted tables in which he can enter his query needs in simple form. Access to other databases (IMS) is also provided with the same graphical support.

254

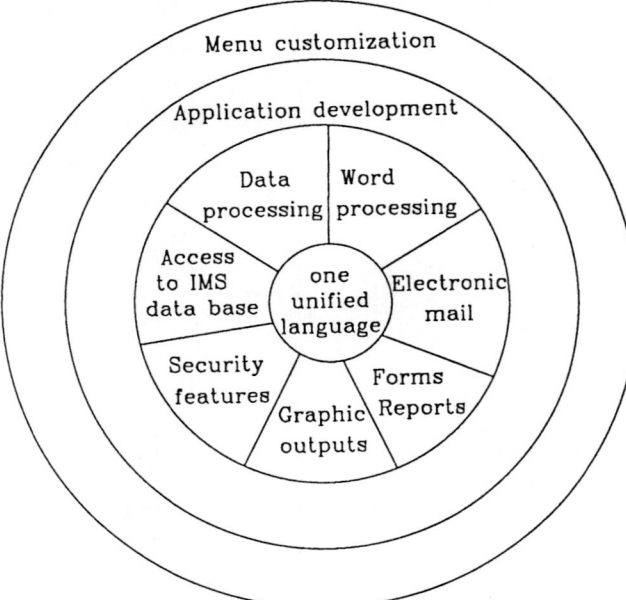

Fig. 3.C.V.05: Office by Example

(from *Zloof, Office by Example 1982, p. 274*)

C.V.2. Business Economics Evaluation of Office Automation

Office automation will have far-reaching consequences for workplaces and processing structures in the administrative area of the enterprise. This also applies to technically-oriented administration of process planning, design, etc., for the application areas. The techniques not only provide support for secretarial and clerical staff, but especially for qualified personnel and middle management.

The integration of processes using database and interactive techniques which was discussed above, is particularly effective here. Comprehensive process chains will be implemented via data integration and electronic mail functions, and currently separate functions will be reintegrated at the workplace. This applies to the linking of text processing and specialist activities, for example. In future, an employee who has to produce a report will be able to copy a text from an existing report on a similar theme at the terminal, extend it, add figures from the files, and bring it up to date.

The distinction between the creation of a report, the preparation of the text in the typing office, and the preparation of diagrams by assistants will thereby be eliminated.

At the same time the employee will have access to powerful tools for applying optimization techniques, database access and simulation techniques. Expert systems are also being developed for specialist activities. This presents EDP-oriented business economics with the task of developing suitable organization and planning concepts for these possibilities.

The dramatic increase in communication possibilities via electronic mail, which is not affected by the limitations on telephone communication that the recipient of the information be present, will alter the organizational structure of the enterprise. For instance, it is to be expected that hierarchical structures will become flatter (see *Jarke, Wissensbasierte Unterstützung verteilter Entscheidungen 1989, p. 33*).

Office activities are, in contrast to the operative applications, unstructured and hence less suitable for prescriptive software formulation. For this reason, office automation is not a concrete application concept, but rather a provision of tools for supporting office activities. The highly communicative office processes are, however, of fundamental significance, if a new research approach is to be followed in which human society is described in general terms as a network of conversations (see *Jarke, Wissensbasierte Unterstützung verteilter Entscheidungen 1989, p. 32 and the literature presented there*).

The provision of tools and data makes it possible to plan office activities more than is currently the case. This means that business economics planning and monitoring procedures, such as are common in the production area, will be increasingly applicable to the office area.

Chapter 4: The EDP-Oriented Business Economics Information Model

The subject matter of this book has been the mutual influence between business economics and information and communication techniques (referred to as EDP techniques, for short) (see Figure 4.01).

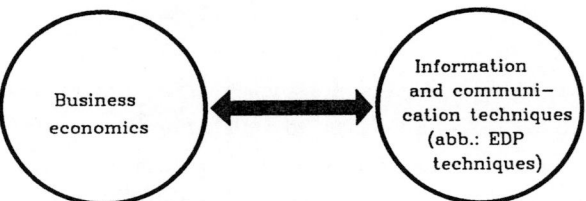

Fig. 4.01: Mutual influence between business economics and EDP techniques

The essential message is that the possibilities of information and communication techniques alter the content of business economics. Data and function integration resulting from the use of database systems allow more independent processing of business procedures such as order processing or purchasing. At the same time closer links between technical and business functions are supported, e.g. in product development.

The use of interactive techniques generates greater event-orientation of planning and decision processes, which shifts the weight from periodic optimization concepts to current control functions.

Expert systems allow the formal processing of heuristic and vague knowledge, which supports the tendency from the processing of structured decisions towards the processing of badly structured decisions.

The possibilities for networking EDP systems give rise to the redistribution of task assignments and decision-making responsibility within organizations.

These results, which were considered in detail in the second chapter, indicate the influence of EDP on business economics issues. Conversely, however, business economics can also have a constructive influence by elaborating the requirements on EDP techniques and incorporating its own optimization tools into the application of EDP techniques. For example, optimization models can be used for assigning resources within computer networks, or economic theories can provide the basis for the design of enterprise data models.

Since the individual EDP techniques for specific business economics applications are interwoven, the third chapter presented concrete business economics EDP solutions, which show the special significance of information and communication techniques. In addition to sector-specific applications for industry, trading, banking and insurance, non-sector-specific EDP systems for accounting, marketing, personnel, enterprise planning and office automation areas were discussed.

In the investigation of individual EDP techniques in Chapter 2 the model of an information system developed in Figure 1.E.III.01, which is presented once more in Figure 4.02, was followed. The user accesses the database and the various functions via process control.

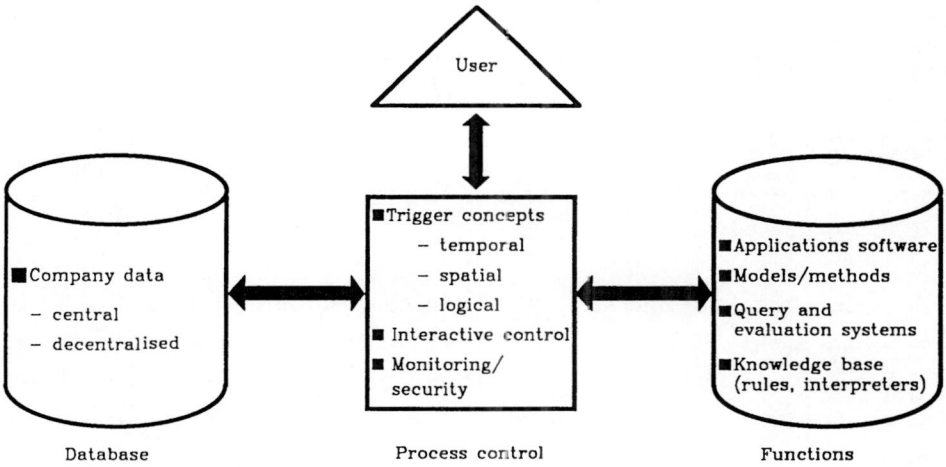

Fig. 4.02: Computerized information system

It became clear that a satisfactory use of EDP techniques also demands new descriptions of business economics relationships. This description of business economics relationships must occur at a higher logical level than is needed for the description of EDP-technical relationships.

Figure 4.03 therefore presents three levels of description for the components of the information system.

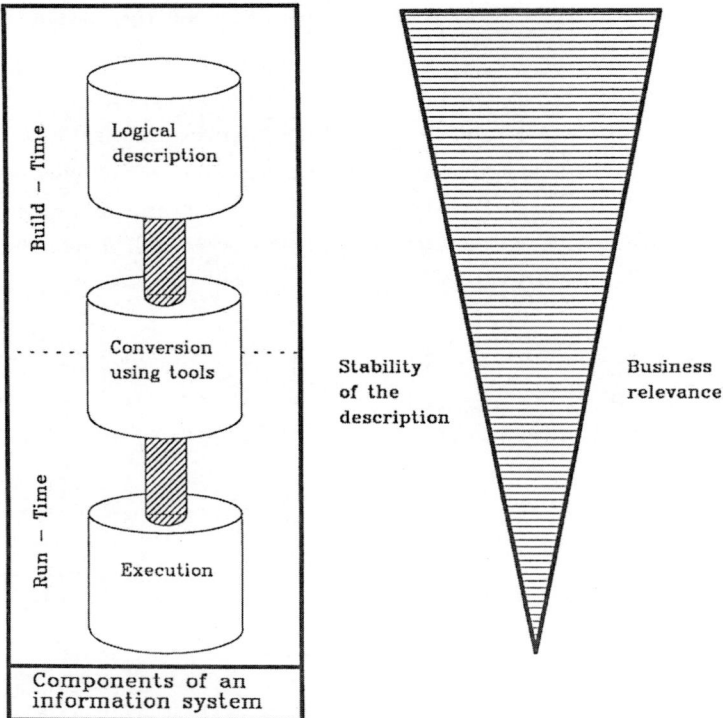

Fig. 4.03: Descriptive levels

At the upper (logical) descriptive level the business economics factors need to be represented at a level of formality suitable for further processing with EDP support. This level, therefore, represents the interface between the specialist business economics knowledge and the formality requirements of the information and communication techniques.

The tools level ensures that the descriptions are transformed into concrete EDP techniques. It is, therefore, intermediary between the logical level and the actual technical execution of the EDP process.

Given the speed of development of EDP techniques the stability of the factual descriptions diminishes with its proximity to the execution level. In concrete terms this means, for example, that changing devices, operating systems, etc., can alter considerably the execution of an EDP process, without the higher level of application of tools such as network management or data dictionaries necessarily being particularly affected (perhaps only a few parameters will need to be changed), while the description of the logical business economics relationships can even remain completely unaffected.

The weighting shown on the right-hand side of Figure 4.03 therefore diminishes through the levels with respect to both the stability of the description and also the business economics relevance.

EDP-oriented business economics should therefore concentrate on the description of the logical facts of the components of an information system. Of course, the relationships with the EDP techniques which have been elaborated in the course of this book also need to be incorporated. Business economics should not consider the tools, hardware, and system level as an **isolated** descriptive object, however.

The description of the logical facts of the components of an information system can be referred to as a **business economics information model**. In order to include the importance of the EDP techniques, however, the term **EDP-oriented business economics information model** is used here. Given the high stability of the design of the logical relationships its construction is also referred to as a "build-time" model. The "build-time" version is relevant over a longer period. In any concrete execution of an EDP process the control accesses the description of the logical relationships (build-time version) from the execution level (run-time version).
This structure makes it possible to assign the results of this book to a model.

Figure 4.04 first considers the **user** as part of the information system. As regards the logical level issues of user ergonomics, presentation techniques (e.g. use of graphics, window techniques) and user guidance requirements in the interactive environment which are of significance for business economics are of primary interest. These issues have been considered in the treatment of interactive techniques and the structure of method and model banks.
Establishing data display and data authorization were also handled in the discussion of interactive techniques.
The consolidation of work steps into larger work units which is made possible by functional integration can be held as a workplace description within an organizational model.
The link between these logical business economics factors (for each of which the existing business economics means of description must be investigated as regards the necessary formalization requirements) and the other components of the information system is generated by the tool level.
Important tools for supporting the presentational possibilities are created using the technical user interface (e.g. X-WINDOWS or MOTIF). Passwords are means of effecting user authorization, and electronic mailboxes can be used to control the workplace-specific stock of orders.

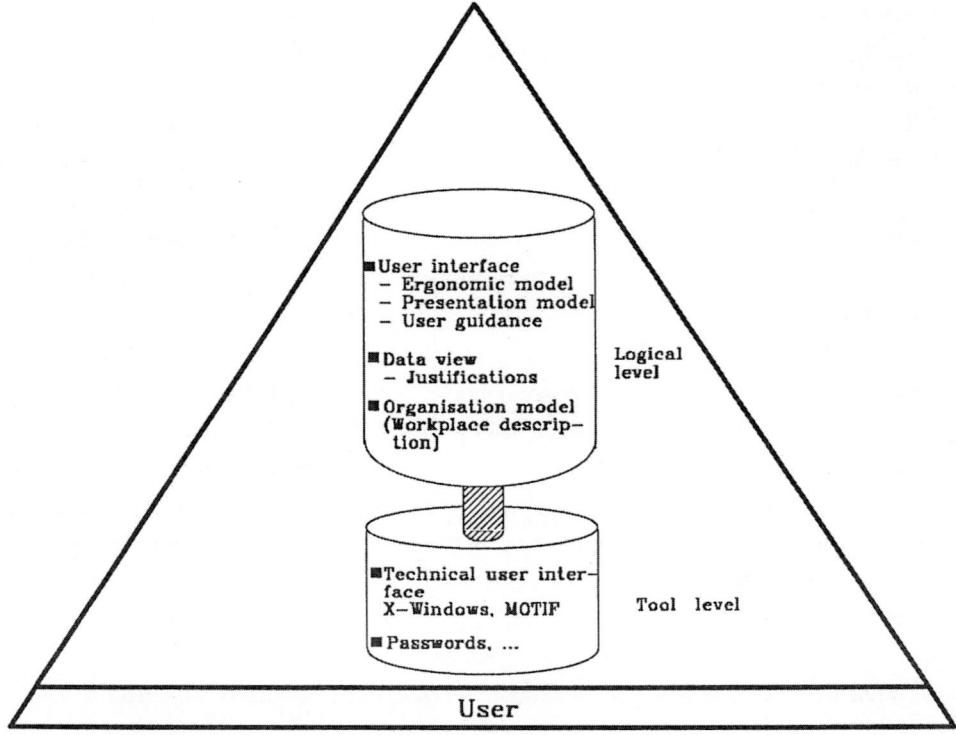

Fig. 4.04: The user as a part of the information system

In Figure 4.05 the three levels are given for the **database** component. At the logical level the data structures are constructed in the form of a **data model**. Area data models can be created for excerpts of the enterprise data model, or process data models for individual enterprise processes. Certain logical views of the data model are also filed.

In Chapter 2, Section A, in the description of the database special emphasis was placed on the design of the logical data structures, since this is increasingly being recognized as the most important component of an information system.

The data structures are managed by tools such as the data dictionary or database description languages for a specific database system (DBS). Query languages, e.g. using the SQL interface, allow data access.

The physical data themselves are assigned to the execution level. They can be assigned both centrally and also decentrally as user-specific data to certain users.

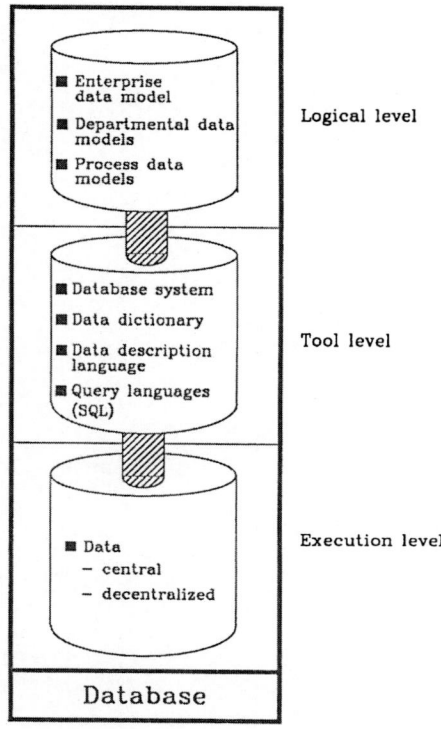

Fig. 4.05: The database as a part of the information system

In Figure 4.06 the **functions** are also broken down according to the levels model. An essential result of Chapter 2 was the greater emphasis on process connections which information technology makes possible, and which are expressed in the concept of process chains. Such chains, e.g. for order processing or product development, can be described using process chain diagrams.

Decision and planning models can be described using decision tables, the rules of an expert system, or in MPS notation, in order to fulfil the formal requirements of information technology.

The **transformation of the business economics content** occurs at the tool level by links with method banks through to computer languages. Computer languages are also understood to cover tools such as fourth generation computer languages or application enablers. Application enablers are quasi-macroprogram modules, which can be employed in various application environments (see *IBM, Das CIM-Unternehmen 1989, p. 55 ff.*).

262

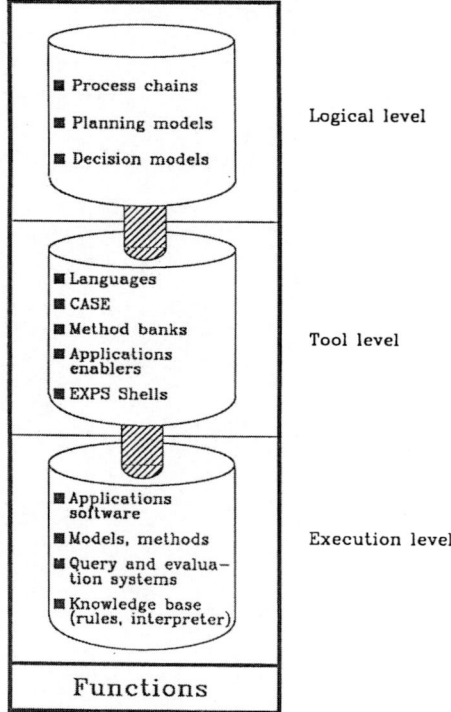

■ Process chains	Logical level
■ Planning models	
■ Decision models	
■ Languages	Tool level
■ CASE	
■ Method banks	
■ Applications enablers	
■ EXPS Shells	
■ Applications software	Execution level
■ Models, methods	
■ Query and evaluation systems	
■ Knowledge base (rules, interpreter)	

Functions

Fig. 4.06: The functions as a part of the information system

The execution level for the business economics functions is then taken over by concrete applications software (including standard software), concrete model and method bank software, query and evaluation systems through to expert systems.

For **process control** the three levels are represented in Figure 4.07. The important element of the business economics description of process control is the assignment of enterprise functions to the individual enterprise levels such as company headquarters, product area, factory, factory area, machine group, down to the individual process. Examples of this description have been presented both for the industrial firm and also for the retail information and control system in Chapter 2 and 3. This is a prerequisite for the description of communication relationships between areas, and between individual workplaces within the areas.

Data flow models, such as can be represented using the De Marco diagram technique, generate the connection between the process chain description and the data model.
A status model describes the various stati that a process can adopt in the course of processing. For example, an order can have the following stati: customer query received,

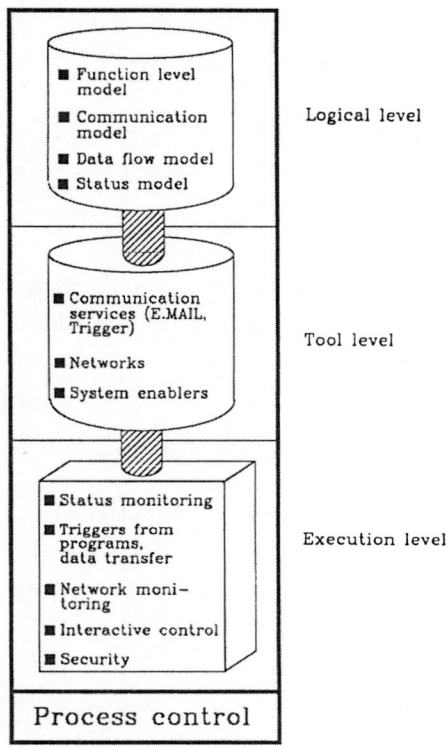

Logical level

Tool level

Execution level

Fig. 4.07: Process control as part of the information system.

successful offer, accepted offer, order in process, order released, order being executed, order completed, and order delivered. The stati, therefore, possess an essential logical function for the process control of process chains. Specific stati can initiate, interrupt or terminate other processes.

EDP techniques (such as the communication services "electronic mail", "trigger" or "network description") again serve as intermediaries between the business economics descriptions and their technical execution. Thus the contents of the status model can be established with the help of the parameters of a trigger system. Tools such as system enablers (see *IBM, Das CIM-Unternehmen 1989*) translate the process descriptions into a form that is independent of the concrete hardware level.

At the **execution level** both the concrete EDP-technical realities and the concrete individual tasks to be carried out must be taken into consideration. It therefore links the applications execution level with the database execution level.

The uniformity of the higher description levels with the lower levels ensures that the current status of the components of the information is available to the execution level at all times.

Figure 4.08 concludes by presenting the relationship between the components of the information system. Alterations at the higher levels are immediately available to the lower levels. At the same time the architecture ensures that alterations at the lower levels have only insignificant effects on the higher levels.

Figure 4.08 therefore represents the concept of an EDP-oriented business economics information model. Although the principal descriptive level of EDP-oriented business economics is the logical view, the lower levels must also be incorporated so that the effects of the information and communication techniques on business economics processes and issues can be recognized and creatively transformed.

The information model that has been developed can also be represented in a detailed and formalized form with the help of the entity relationship model (ERM).

The entity relationship model is used to represent object types (entity types) and the relationships existing between them. With the help of this descriptive language the logical data structures from the application areas can be designed. However, it is also suitable for representing the logical structure of an information system itself, i.e. the elements of the information system are represented as entity types and the relationships between the elements are described using relationship types.

This can be undertaken for all components of the information system, i.e., user, database, functions, and process control for all three levels (logical, tool, and execution levels). **The complete description then constitutes the information model or the meta-information system.**

Since the significance of the database has received particular emphasis here, only the logical **data structures** are represented as an ERM, that is, a meta-data model is created. The logical data structure of an application area was represented with the help of the ERM (real data model). The description of this representational form, that is, the meta-data model, is now also represented as an ERM.

Since both the real model and the meta-model use the same concepts (entity type, relationship type, etc.) the description is difficult. In order to avoid misunderstanding the suffix "real level" is used if the terms relate to the representation of applications within the information system. Additional clarity is achieved by using the term ETYP to refer to entity types from the real level and the term RTYP to refer to relationships from the real level. The suffix "meta-level" is used to handle the description of the components of the information system itself.

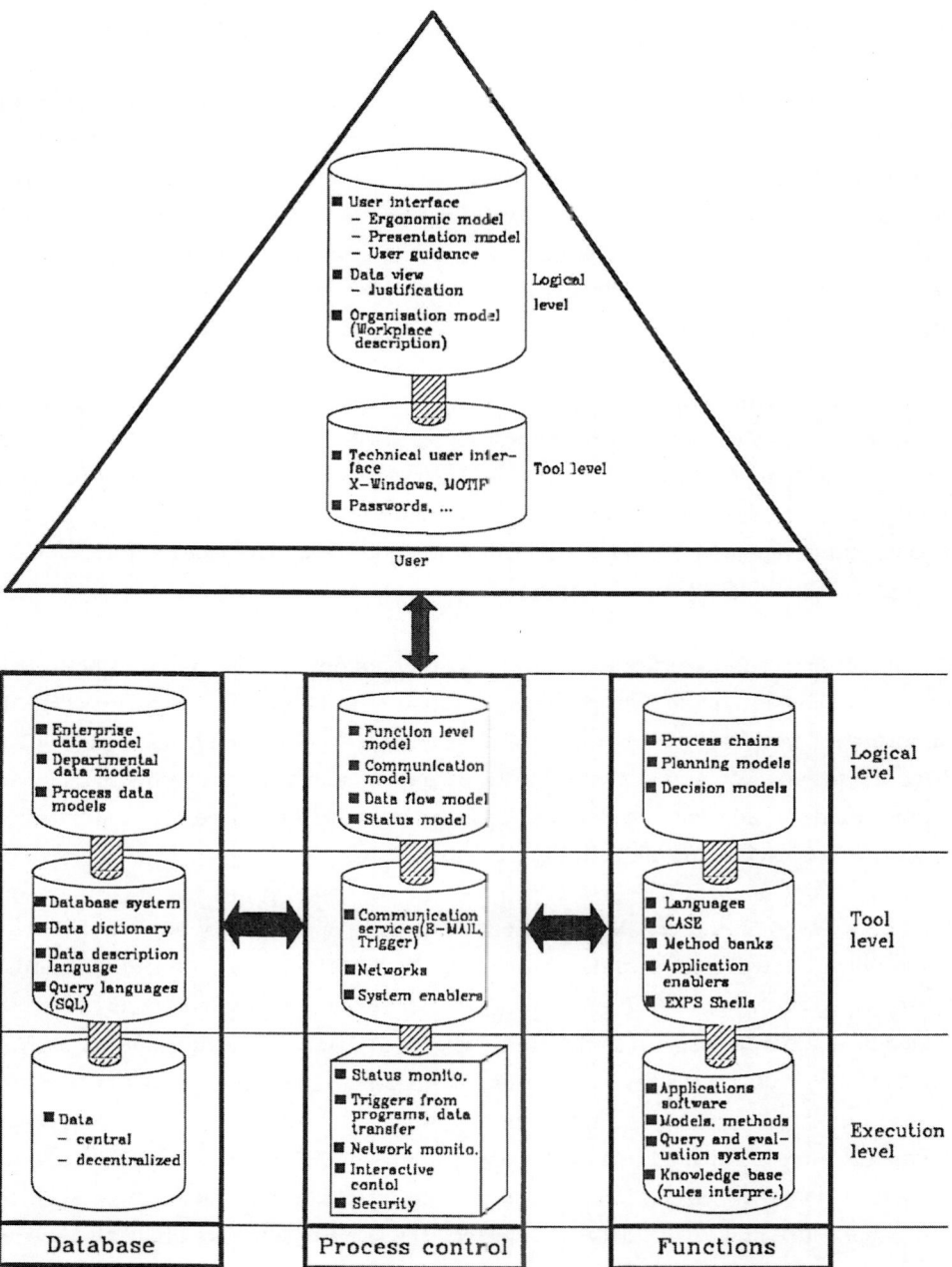

Fig. 4.08: The EDP-oriented business economics information model

The ERM consists of entity and relationship types which are linked together by edges.

In Figure 4.09 the entity types ETYP and RTYP are created for the terms entity type and relationship type at the real level. Their instances are the entity types and relationships types defined for an application area. For the example used in Chapter 2 the entity types CUSTOMER and ARTICLE at the real level constitute instances of the entity type ETYP, and the relationship type PURCHASE at the real level is an instance of the entity type RTYP. The instances of the entity types in Figure 4.09 are each identified by allocating key attributes, ETNO and RTNO.

An edge always represents a link between an entity type and a relationship type at the real level. For this purpose the relationship type EDGE is introduced at the meta-level. Attributes of the entity type EDGE are the maximum or minimum number of permitted instances of this direction of the relationship. Since at the real level several edges lead from an entity type and several edges lead to an entity type there is an n:m relationship between ETYP and RTYP.

At the real level several edges with diverse interpretations exist between an entity type and a relationship type (e.g. in the representation of the bill of materials structure the edges for representing higher and lower level parts). The entity type EDGE ROLE is therefore introduced with the key ERNO, which in such cases allows unambiguous identification of an edge. A specific edge is therefore identified by the attribute combination ETNO, RTNO, and edge role number, ERNO.

Each entity type at the real level is assigned to an identifying key attribute. The key attributes at the real level form the entity type KEY ATTRIBUTE. A 1:1 relationship exists between the entity type ETYP and the entity type KEY ATTRIBUTE. For example, the customer number is assigned to the entity type CUSTOMER as unambiguous identifying key attribute, similarly the key attribute article number to the entity type ARTICLE.

Relationship types are identified by the key attributes of the entity types with which they are linked. For this reason, it is unnecessary to introduce a relationship between the entity type RTYP and KEY ATTRIBUTE. Instead the key attributes are implicitly assigned via the EDGE relationship and the relationship between KEY ATTRIBUTE and ETYP. For ease of understanding, however, a KEY ASSIGNMENT RTYP is introduced as an n:m relationship.

267

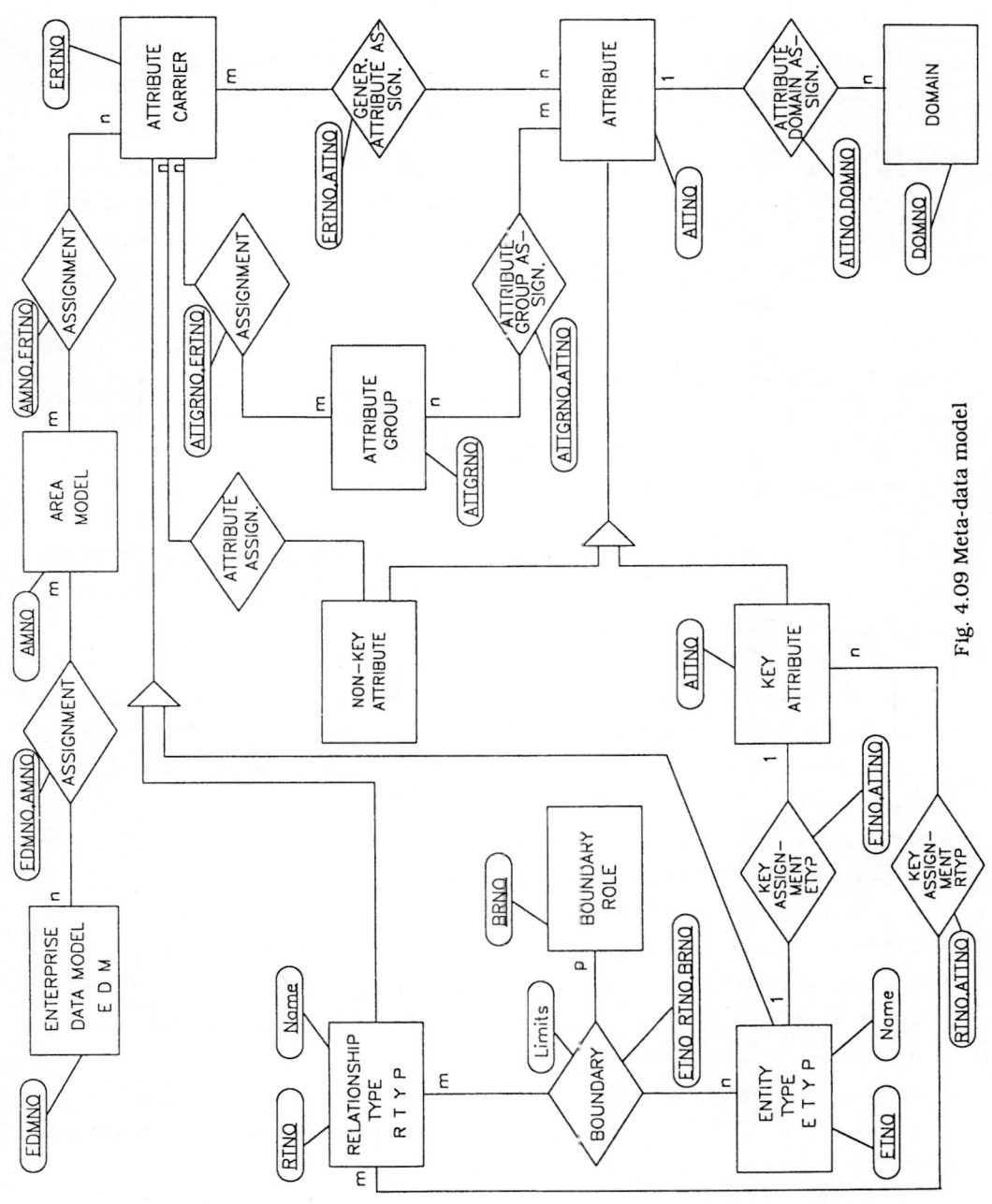

Fig. 4.09 Meta-data model

The entity types ETYP and RTYP are both attribute carriers at the real level, i.e., they are assigned to key and other descriptive attributes at the real level. They are therefore generalized as the entity type ATTRIBUTE CARRIER.

Within an enterprise, data models can be created for certain application areas, such as marketing, production, etc. The attribute carriers belonging to such an area model (entity and relationship types at the real level) are recorded via the entity type AREA MODEL and an n:m relationship to ATTRIBUTE CARRIER. The amalgamation of the area models then generates the enterprise data model (EDM). Since several versions of an enterprise data model may be possible, an n:m relationship between the entity type EDM and the entity type AREA MODEL is set up.

Once the entity and relationship types have been designed with their key attributes, in a second step the non-key attributes are established and assigned.

The entity type KEY ATTRIBUTE is a specialization of the general entity type ATTRIBUTE with the key attribute ATTNO. It is broken down into the entity types KEY ATTRIBUTE and NON-KEY ATTRIBUTE.

The non-key attributes are assigned to the attribute carriers via an n:m relationship. This means that an attribute carrier can possess several key attributes, which is normally also the case. It also means that an attribute can be assigned to several attribute carriers. This applies, for instance, when the attribute "name" is used for both customers and suppliers. The "GENERAL ATTRIBUTE ASSIGNMENT" between ATTRIBUTE and ATTRIBUTE CARRIER consists (with redundancy) of both key and non-key references. It is used for simplification in the further development.

The value set of an attribute is identified by the entity type DOMAIN. Each attribute can be assigned to one domain. In the case of the attribute "name" all existing names can be stored in the domain in the form of a dictionary, and in the case of numerical values the numerical range can be defined.

Attributes which belong together in terms of their content can be combined into groups. For example, the attribute group "address" can consist of the attributes street name, house number, post code and town. It is also possible to form overlapping attribute groups, such that an n:m relationship exists between the entity types ATTRIBUTE and ATTRIBUTE GROUP. Attribute groups can be assigned directly to the attribute carriers, so that a condensed link with the individual attributes is created.

This completes the development of the meta-model for the logical data structuring at the real level. To represent the entire information model it would need to be extended to cover the tool and execution levels, and to include the remaining user, functions, and process control components.

References

Adam, D.: *Sortenfertigung 1971*

    Produktionsplanung bei Sortenfertigung. Wiesbaden 1971.

Ahlers, J. et al.: *Prüfungsgerechtheit 1982*

    Die Messung der Prüfungsgerechtheit von EDV-Buchführungssystemen. Die Wirtschaftsprüfung (WPg), 35 (1982), pp. 529 - 538.

Alpar, P.: *Methodenauswahl 1980*

    Computergestützte interaktive Methodenauswahl. Frankfurt/Main 1980.

AMADEUS-Produktinformationen 1988

    AMADEUS-Produktinformationen. Frankfurt/Main 1988, o. S.

Anselstetter, R.: *Nutzeffekte der Datenverarbeitung 1986*

    Betriebswirtschaftliche Nutzeffekte der Datenverarbeitung. 2nd ed., Heidelberg-Berlin-New York 1986.

Awad, E. M.: *Management Information Systems 1988*

    Management Information Systems (Concepts, Structure and Applications). California 1988.

Babcock, B.: *Integrated Office System 1983*

    Tying it together in the Integrated Office System. Computer Design, 22 (1983) no. 12, pp. 61 - 64.

Balzert, H.: *Software-Systeme 1982*

    Die Entwicklung von Software-Systemen (Prinzipien, Methoden, Sprachen, Werkzeuge). Mannheim-Wien-Zürich 1982.

Barth, U.; Rohleder, H.: *Aktenlose Sachbearbeitung 1983*

    Die aktenlose Sachbearbeitung bei der Bausparkasse Mainz AG. Data report, 18 (1983) no. 1, pp. 18 - 21.

Bauer, F. L.: *Software Engineering 1977*

Software Engineering, An Advanced Course. 2nd ed., Heidelberg-Berlin-New York 1977.

Becker, J.: *EDV-System zur Materialflußsteuerung 1987*

Architektur eines EDV-Systems zur Materialflußsteuerung. Berlin-Heidelberg-New York-London-Paris-Tokyo 1987.

Beier, F.: *CAM-System 1982*

Anforderungen an ein CAM-System. In: CAD/CAM-Anwendungen im Maschinenbau. Ed.: Verein Deutscher Maschinenbau-Anstalten e. V. (VDMA). Frankfurt 1982 (Mit Technologie die Zukunft bewältigen, vol. 1).

Bendig, R. et al.: *Betriebswirtschaftliche Problemstellungen 1987*

Expertensysteme, Systeme zur Lösung betriebswirtschaftlicher Problemstellungen, part 1. Duisburg 1987 (Diskussionsbeiträge des Fachbereichs Wirtschaftswissenschaft, no. 104, ed.: Universität-Gesamthochschule Duisburg).

Berthold, H. J.: *Aktionsdatenbanken 1983*

Aktionsdatenbanken in einem kommunikationsorientierten EDV-System. Informatik-Spektrum, 6 (1983) no. 6, pp. 20 - 26.

Biethahn, J.: *Einführung in die EDV 1989*

Einführung in die EDV für Wirtschaftswissenschaftler. 6th ed., München 1989.

Bingemann, H.: *Devisenhandel 1982*

Kontrolliertes Risiko durch On-line-Information im Devisenhandel. Data report, 17 (1982) no. 2, pp. 17 - 19.

Bleicher, K.: *Organisation 1987*

Organisation. In: Allgemeine Betriebswirtschaftslehre. Eds.: F. X. Bea; E. Dichtl; M. Schweitzer. Vol. 2: Führung. 3rd ed., Stuttgart-New York 1987, pp. 73 - 148.

Bodendorf, F.: *SAMBA 1981*

SAMBA - Ein Methodenbankrahmen um das Statistikpaket SPSS. 2nd ed., Erlangen 1981.

272

Boysen, W.: *EDV-gestütztes Rechnungswesen 1983*

Anforderungen der Geschäftsleitung an ein EDV-gestütztes Rechnungswesen. In: Rechnungswesen und EDV, 4th Saarbrücker Arbeitstagung. Eds.: W. Kilger; A.-W. Scheer. Würzburg-Wien 1983, pp. 11 - 22.

Brandenburg, V.: *Simulation von "Computer-am-Arbeitsplatz"-Systemen 1983*

Simulation von "Computer-am-Arbeitsplatz"-Systemen. München 1983.

Braun, H.; Zierer, H.: *Desktop Publishing 1988*

Desktop Publishing-Perfektion im Büro? Office Management, 36 (1988) no. 1, pp. 50 - 53.

Bretschneider, J.: *Integriertes Rechnungswesen 1983*

Plaut Software M110 für ein integriertes Rechnungswesen. In: Rechnungswesen und EDV, 4th Saarbrücker Arbeitstagung. Eds.: W. Kilger; A.-W. Scheer. Würzburg-Wien 1983, S. 145 - 156.

Brombacher, R.: *Marketing-Informationssystem 1981*

DEMI, Dezentrales Marketing-Informationssystem (Dialogsystem zur Auswahl geeigneter Datenanalyse- und Prognoseverfahren). Saarbrücken 1981 (Veröffentlichungen des Instituts für Wirtschaftsinformatik, no. 28, ed.: A.-W. Scheer).

Buchmann, T. K. H.: *EDIFACT 1988*

Einführung, EDIFACT. In: EDIFACT - Elektronischer Datenaustausch für Verwaltung, Wirtschaft und Transport, 3rd DIN-Tagung 12th and 13th December 88. Ed.: DIN, Herrenberg 1988, pp. 2-3 - 2-29.

Budde, R.; Schnupp, P.; Schwald, A.: *Software-Produktion 1980*

Untersuchung über Maßnahmen zur Verbesserung der Software-Produktion, part 1 (Theoretische Ansätze auf dem Gebiet der Software-Produktion). München-Wien 1980.

Bullinger, H.-J.; Fröschle, H.-P.: *ISDN und Unternehmensorganisation 1989*

ISDN und Unternehmensorganisation. Office Management, 37 (1989) no. 5, pp. 36 - 45.

Chen, P. P.: *Entity-Relationship Model 1976*

The Entity-Relationship Model (Towards an Unified View of Data). ACM Transactions on Database-Systems, no. 1 (1976), pp. 9 - 36.

273

Chen, P. P. (Ed.): *Information Modeling 1984*

Entity-Relationship Approach to Information Modeling and Analysis. Amsterdam-New York-Oxford 1984.

Commerzbank (Ed.): *Handbuch Electronic Banking 1988*

Handbuch Electronic Banking. Frankfurt 1988.

Control Data Corporation (Ed.): *IFPS 1983*

IFPS-TS, Interactive Financial Planning System, User-Information Manual. No. 7607 8900, 1983.

Cordewener, K.-F.: *Kundenbediente Datenstationen 1982*

Kundenbediente Datenstationen als marktpolitische Instrumente des Bankbetriebes. Göttingen 1982 (Göttinger Hefte zur Bankbetriebslehre und Unternehmensfinanzierung, no. 10).

Czech, D. et al.: *Mikroelektronik 1983*

Mikroelektronik im Bankgewerbe. Eschborn 1983.

Date, C. J.: *Database Systems 1983*

An Introduction to Database Systems. Vol. 2, Reading (Massachusetts) 1983.

Davis, G. B.; Olson, M.: *Management Information Systems 1984*

Management Information Systems (Conceptual Foundations, Structure, and Development). New York 1984.

De Marco, T.: *Structured Analysis 1979*

Structured Analysis and System Specification. New York 1979.

Deusch, K.-E.; Freihalter, R.: *Mobile Datenerfassung 1989*

Informationsmanagement im Verkauf mit Hilfe des relationalen Datenbanksystems DB2 und mobiler Datenerfassung im Außendienst. In: Praxis relationaler Datenbanken, IDS Kolleg Fachtagung 1st and 2nd June 1989 Ed.: A.-W. Scheer. Saarbrücken 1989, pp. 99 - 117.

DIN (Ed.): *Schnittstellen 1989*

Schnittstellen der rechnerintegrierten Produktion (CIM) - Fertigungssteuerung und Auftragsabwicklung (DIN-Fachbericht 21). Berlin-Köln 1989.

Dinkelbach, W.: *Entscheidungsmodelle 1982*
Entscheidungsmodelle. Berlin-New York 1982.

Domsch, M.: *Personalarbeit 1980*
Systemgestützte Personalarbeit. Wiesbaden 1980.

Dube, J.; Eisele, R.: *Massenzahlungen 1982*
Massenzahlungen - elektronisch übertragen. IBM Nachrichten, 32 (1982) no. 259, pp. 41 - 45.

Dworatschek, S.: *Datenverarbeitung 1989*
Grundlagen der Datenverarbeitung. 8th ed., Berlin 1989.

Ehrlenspiel, K.: *Kostengünstig Konstruieren 1985*
Kostengünstig Konstruieren. Berlin-Heidelberg-New York-Tokyo 1985.

Eicker, S.: *Telekonferenz 1988*
Telekonferenz. Information Management, 3 (1988) no. 1, p. 39.

Eidenmüller, B.: *Die Produktion als Wettbewerbsfaktor 1989*
Die Produktion als Wettbewerbsfaktor (Herausforderungen an das Produktionsmanagement). Zürich 1989.

Emery, J. C.: *Integrated Information Systems 1975*
Integrated Information Systems and their Effects on Organizational Structure. In: Information Systems and Organizational Structure. Eds.: E. Grochla; N. Szyperski. Berlin-New York 1975, pp. 95 - 104.

EPS Consultants (Ed.): *FCS-EPS 1982*
FCS-EPS Decision Support System Reference Manual. Version 2, 1982.

Frese, E.: *Organisation 1988*
Grundlagen der Organisation (Die Organisationsstruktur der Unternehmung). 4th ed., Wiesbaden 1988.

Galbraith, J. R.: *Organization Design 1977*
Organization Design. Reading (Massachusetts)-Menlo Park (California)-London-Amsterdam-Don Hills (Ontario)-Sydney 1977.

Gansinger, H. et al.: *Smalltalk-80* 1987

Smalltalk-80. Informationstechnik (it), 29 (1987) no. 4, pp. 241 - 251.

General Electric Informations Services Company (Ed.): *MIMS 1981*

The MIMS - System Reference Manual. 1981.

Glaser, H.: *PPS-Systeme 1989*

Zum betriebswirtschaftlichen Gehalt von PPS-Systemen. In: Rechnungswesen und EDV, 10th Saarbrücker Arbeitstagung 1989. Ed.: A.-W. Scheer. Heidelberg 1989, pp. 343 - 369.

Gorry, G. A.; Morton, M.S. Scott: *A Framework for MIS 1971*

A Framework for Management Information Systems. Sloan Management Review, 13 (1971) no. 1, pp. 55 - 70.

Grochla, E.: *Zentralisationswirkungen 1969*

Zur Diskussion über die Zentralisationswirkungen automatischer Datenverarbeitungsanlagen. Zeitschrift für Organisation (ZfO) 38 (1969) no. 2, pp. 47 - 53.

Grochla, E.: *Dezentralisierungs-Tendenzen 1976*

Dezentralisierungs-Tendenzen im Betrieb durch Einsatz moderner Datenverarbeitung. Angewandte Informatik, 18 (1976) no. 12, pp. 511 - 521.

Grochla, E.: *Organisationstheoretische Ansätze 1978*

Organisationstheoretische Ansätze zur Gestaltung rechnergestützter Informationssysteme. Angewandte Informatik, 20 (1978) no. 4, pp. 141 - 149.

Grochla, E.: *Konsequenzen 1982*

Betriebliche Konsequenzen der informationstechnologischen Entwicklung. Angewandte Informatik, 24 (1982) no. 2, pp. 62 - 71

Grossenbacher, J.-M.: *Verteilung der EDV 1985*

Verteilung der EDV. 3rd ed., Zürich 1985.

Gunn, T. G.: *Fertigung 1982*

Konstruktion und Fertigung. Spektrum der Wissenschaft, no. 11 (1982), pp. 77 - 98.

Haberstock, L.: *Kostenrechnung 1987*
Kostenrechnung I. 8th ed., Hamburg 1987.

Hackstein, R.: *Produktionsplanung und -steuerung 1989*
Produktionsplanung und -steuerung (PPS). 2nd ed., Düsseldorf 1989.

Härder, T.: *Datenbanksysteme 1978*
Implementierung von Datenbanksystemen. München-Wien 1978.

Hahn, D.; Lassmann, G.: *Produktionswirtschaft 1986*
Produktionswirtschaft - Controlling industrieller Produktion. Vol. 1 and 2, Heidelberg 1986.

Hansel, J.; Lomnitz, G.: *Projektleiter-Praxis 1987*
Projektleiter-Praxis. Berlin-Heidelberg-New York-London-Paris-Tokyo 1987.

Hansen, H. R.: *Wirtschaftsinformatik I 1986*
Wirtschaftsinformatik I (Einführung in die betriebliche Datenverarbeitung). 5th ed., Stuttgart 1986.

Hansen, H. R.; Amsüss, W. L.; Frömmer, N. S.: *Standardsoftware 1983*
Standardsoftware (Beschaffungspolitik, organisatorische Einsatzbedingungen und Marketing). Berlin-Heidelberg-New York-Tokyo 1983.

Harmon, P.; King D.: *Expertensysteme 1989*
Expertensysteme in der Praxis (Perspektiven, Werkzeuge, Erfahrungen). 3th ed., München-Wien 1989.

Harrington, J.: *Computer Integrated Manufacturing 1973*
Computer Integrated Manufacturing. Florida 1973.

Hausknecht, J.; Zündorf, H.: *Finanz- und Rechnungswesen 1989*
Expertensysteme im Finanz- und Rechungswesen. Stuttgart 1989.

Haverly Systems (Ed.): *OMNI 1981*
OMNI Linear Programming System - User Reference Manual Version 4.1. St. Albans (England)-Denville (New Jersey) 1981.

Hax, A. C.; Golovin, J. J.: *Hierarchical Production Planning 1978*

Hierarchical Production Planning Systems. In: Studies in Operations Management. Ed.: A. C. Hax. Amsterdam-New York-Oxford 1978, pp. 429 - 464.

Hax, H.; Laux, H.: *Flexible Planung 1972*

Flexible Planung - Verfahrensregeln und Entscheidungsmodelle für die Planung bei Ungewißheit. Zeitschrift für betriebswirtschaftliche Forschung (ZfbF), 24 (1972), pp. 318 - 340.

Hedberg, B. et al.: *Organizational Power Structures 1975*

The Impact of Computer Technology on Organizational Power Structures. In: Information Systems and Organizational Structure. Eds.: E. Grochla; N. Szyperski. Berlin-New York 1975, pp. 131 - 149.

Heilmann, H.; Heilmann, W.: *Telearbeitsplatz 1983*

Softwareentwicklung am Telearbeitsplatz - Erfahrungen und Trends aus den USA. Handbuch der modernen Datenverarbeitung (HMD), 20 (1983) no. 110, pp. 95 - 100.

Heinen, E. (Ed.): *Industriebetriebslehre 1985*

Industriebetriebslehre (Entscheidungen im Industriebetrieb). 8th ed., Wiesbaden 1985.

Heinrich, L. J.; Burgholzer, P.: *Informationsmanagement 1988*

Informationsmanagement (Planung, Überwachung und Steuerung der Informations-Infrastruktur). 2nd ed., München-Wien 1988.

Heinrich, L. J.; Pils, M.: *Personalinformationssysteme 1983*

Betriebsinformatik im Personalbereich (Die Planung computergestützter Personalinformationssysteme). 2nd ed., Würzburg-Wien 1983.

Helber, C.: *Gestaltung optimaler EDV-Systeme 1981*

Entscheidungen bei der Gestaltung optimaler EDV-Systeme. München 1981.

Hering, E.: *Software-Engineering 1989*

Software-Engineering. 2nd ed., Braunschweig-Wiesbaden 1989.

Hermes, H.: *Syntax-Regeln für den Datenaustausch 1988*

Syntax-Regeln für den elektronischen Datenaustausch. In: Einführung in EDIFACT, Entwicklung, Grundlagen und Einsatz. Ed.: DIN. Berlin 1988, pp. 7 - 12.

Hofmann, J.: *Aktionsorientierte Datenverarbeitung 1988*

Aktionsorientierte Datenverarbeitung im Fertigungsbereich. Berlin-Heidelberg-New York-London-Paris-Tokyo 1988.

Horton, F. W.: *Information Management Workbook 1986*

The Information Management Workbook (IRM Made Simple). 2nd ed., Washington 1986.

Horvath, P.; Petsch, M.; Weihe, M.: *Standard-Anwendungssoftware 1986*

Standard-Anwendungssoftware für das Rechnungswesen. München 1986.

Hübner, H.: *Integration 1979*

Integration und Informationstechnologie im Unternehmen. München 1979.

IBM (Ed.): *CAPOSS-E 1983*

Capacity Planning and Operation Sequencing System - Extended (CAPOSS-E), Anwendungsbeschreibung, 5740-M41. 1983.

IBM (Ed.): *COPICS (SL & R) 1983*

COPICS-Shop Order Load Analysis and Reporting (SL & R), GH 19-6356-0. 1983.

IBM (Ed.): *Business Systems Planning 1984*

Business Systems Planning, Handbuch zur Planung von Informationssystemen, FNR: E12-1400. 1984.

IBM (Ed.): *Das CIM-Unternehmen 1989*

Das CIM-Unternehmen. Preversion, München 1989.

IEEE (Ed.): *Automation 1983*

Data Driven Automation. IEEE Spectrum, 20 (1983) no. 5, fold-out.

Index Technology Corporation (Ed.): *Excelerator 1988*

Produktinformation zu Excelerator. Cambridge (Massachusetts) 1988.

Ischebeck, W.: *Betriebsübergreifende Informationssysteme 1989*
Betriebsübergreifende Informationssysteme. Information Management, 4 (1989) no. 1, pp. 22 - 26.

Jacob, H. (Ed.): *Industriebetriebslehre 1972*
Industriebetriebslehre in programmierter Form. Vol. 3: Organisation und EDV. Wiesbaden 1972.

Jarke, M.: *Wissensbasierte Unterstützung verteilter Entscheidungen 1989*
Wissensbasierte Unterstützung verteilter Entscheidungen und Modellierungsprozesse. In: Betriebliche Expertensysteme II (Einsatz von Expertensystem-Prototypen in betriebswirtschaftlichen Funktionsbereichen). Ed.: A.-W. Scheer. Wiesbaden 1989, pp. 29 - 54 (Schriften zur Unternehmensführung (SzU), vol. 40, eds.: H. Jacob et al.).

Kargl, H.: *Fachentwurf für DV-Anwendungssysteme 1989*
Fachentwurf für DV-Anwendungssysteme. München 1989.

Kazmeier, E.: *Ablaufplanung 1984*
Ablaufplanung im Dialog - Alternative oder Ergänzung zur Optimierung. In: Operations Research Proceedings. Eds.: H. Steckhan et al. Berlin-Heidelberg-New York-Tokyo 1984, pp. 163 - 168.

Kieser, A.; Kubicek, H.: *Organisation 1983*
Organisation. 2nd ed., Berlin-New York 1983.

Kilger, W.: *Optimale Produktions- und Absatzplanung 1973*
Optimale Produktions- und Absatzplanung (Entscheidungsmodelle für die Produktions- und Absatzbereiche industrieller Betriebe). Opladen 1973.

Kilger, W.: *Plankostenrechnung 1988*
Flexible Plankostenrechnung und Deckungsbeitragsrechnung. 9th ed., Wiesbaden 1988.

Kilger, W.; Scheer, A.-W. (Eds.): *Plankosten- und Deckungsbeitragsrechnung 1980*
Plankosten- und Deckungsbeitragsrechnung in der Praxis. Würzburg-Wien 1980.

Kilger, W.; Scheer, A.-W. (Eds.): *Rechnungswesen und EDV 1983*

Rechnungswesen und EDV, 4. Saarbrücker Arbeitstagung. Würzburg- Wien 1983.

Kistner, K.-P.; Switalski, M.: *Hierarchical Production Planning 1987*

Hierarchical Production Planning - Necessity, Problems and Methods. Bielefeld 1987 (Diskussionsarbeiten der Fakultät für Wirtschaftswissenschaften der Universität Bielefeld).

Kleinrock, L.: *Queueing Systems 1976*

Queueing Systems, vol. II (Computer Applications). New York-London-Sydney-Toronto 1976.

Kneip, L.; Scheer, A.-W.; Wittemann, N.: *PROMOS 1981*

PROMOS (Ein Produktionsplanungs-Modellgenerator-System zur Bestimmung des Primärbedarfs im Rahmen eines PPS-Systems). Saarbrücken 1981 (Veröffentlichungen des Instituts für Wirtschaftsinformatik, no. 26, ed.: A.-W. Scheer).

Korte, W. B.; Robinson, S.: *Telearbeit 1988*

Telearbeit. Office Management, 36 (1988) no. 12, pp. 8 - 15.

Krallmann, H. et al.: *Kommunikationsstrukturanalyse 1989*

Die Kommunikationsstrukturanalyse (KSA) zur Konzeption einer betrieblichen Kommunikationsarchitektur. In: Interaktive betriebswirtschaftliche Informations- und Steuerungssysteme. Eds.: K. Kurbel; P. Mertens; A.-W. Scheer. Berlin-New York 1989, pp. 289 - 314.

Krcmar, H.: *Gestaltung von "Computer-am-Arbeitsplatz"-Systemen 1983*

Gestaltung von Computer-am-Arbeitsplatz-Systemen (Entwicklung von Alternativen und deren Bewertung durch Simulation). München 1983.

Krcmar, H.: *Schnittstellen 1983*

Schnittstellenprobleme EDV-gestützter Systeme des Rechnungswesens. In: Rechnungswesen und EDV, 4th Saarbrücker Arbeitstagung. Eds.: W. Kilger; A.-W. Scheer. Würzburg-Wien 1983, pp. 323 - 350.

Kreuzer, K.: *Datenverarbeitung 1983*

Datenverarbeitung rationalisiert Geldinstitute. Data report, 18 (1983) no. 2, pp. 10 - 14.

Kroeber-Riel, W.; Neibecker, B.: *Computergestützte Interviewsysteme 1988*

Elektronische Datenerhebung (Computergestützte Interviewsysteme). In: Innovative Marktforschung. Ed.: Forschungsgruppe Konsum und Verhalten. Würzburg-Wien 1988, pp. 193 - 208.

Kuba, R. W.: *Projektorganisation 1987*

Computergestützte Projektorganisation. Köln 1987.

Kurbel, K.: *Programmentwicklung 1987*

Programmentwicklung. 4th ed., Wiesbaden 1987.

Kurbel, K.; Pietsch, W.: *Expertensystem-Projekte 1989*

Expertensystem-Projekte (Entwicklungsmethodik, Organisation und Management). Informatik-Spektrum, 12 (1989) no. 3, pp. 133 - 146.

Langer, H.: *Kosteninformationssystem 1980*

AKIS - ein Kosteninformationssystem der Hoechst AG. In: Online-Systeme im Finanz- und Rechnungswesen. Ed.: P. Stahlknecht. Berlin- Heidelberg-New York 1980, pp. 416 - 430.

Leavitt, H. J.; Whisler, T. L.: *Management 1958*

Management in the 1980s. Harvard Business Review, 36 (1958) no. 6, pp. 41 - 48.

Leismann, U.: *WWS mit Btx 1990*

Warenwirtschaftssysteme mit Bildschirmtext. Berlin-Heidelberg-New York-London-Paris-Tokyo 1990.

Lenk, T.: *Telearbeit 1989*

Telearbeit. Berlin 1989.

Liebermann, M. A.; Selig, G. J.; Walsh, J. J.: *Office Automation 1982*

Office Automation. New York-Chichester-Brisbane-Toronto-Singapore 1982.

Lieske, N.: *Vermögen verwaltet 1981*

Wer Vermögen verwaltet, hat viel zu verlieren. Data report, 16 (1981) no. 2, pp. 23 - 28.

282

Limmer, H.: *Chipkarte 1988*

Chipkarte bietet Datensicherheit. Dynamik im Handel, no. 2 (1988), pp. 100 - 102.

Little, J. D. C.: *Decision Calculus 1977*

Modelle und Manager (Das Konzept des Decision Calculus). In: Entscheidungshilfen im Marketing. Eds.: R. Köhler; H. J. Zimmermann. Stuttgart 1977, pp. 122 - 147.

Lucas, H. C., Jr.: *Information Systems 1981*

The Analysis, Design and Implementation of Information Systems. 2nd ed., New York-Hamburg 1981.

Lünzmann, F.: *Roboter 1982*

Integration von 600 Robotern in die Fertigung - Wirtschaftlichkeit und Erfahrungen. In: Rationalisierung. Eds.: W. Kilger; A.-W. Scheer. Würzburg-Wien 1982, pp. 322 - 338.

Maciejewski, P. G.: *Electronic Banking 1989*

Electronic Banking - Stand und Entwicklungstendenzen. Office Banking, no. 1 (1989), pp. 22 - 28.

Mahmoud, S.; Riordan, J. S.: *Distributed Information Networks 1976*

Optimal Allocation of Resources in Distributed Information Networks. ACM Transactions on Data Base Systems, no. 1 (1976), pp. 66 - 78.

Makridakis, S.; Wheelright, S. C.: *Forecasting 1978*

Forecasting: Methods and Applications. Santa Barbara-New York 1978.

Martin, J.: *Application Development 1982*

Application Development Without Programmers. Englewood Cliffs 1982.

McCorduck, P.: *Fifth Generation 1983*

Introduction to the Fifth Generation. Communications of the ACM, 26 (1983) no. 9, pp. 629 - 630.

Meffert, H.: *Marketing Informationssysteme 1975*

Computergestützte Marketing Informationssysteme (Konzeptionen, Modellanwendungen, Entwicklungsstrategien). Wiesbaden 1975.

Meffert, H.: *EDV im Marketing 1980*

EDV-Anwendungen im Marketing. In: Wirtschaftsinformatik III. Ed.: H. D. Plötzeneder. Stuttgart-New York 1980, pp. 29 - 56.

Mertens, P.: *Rechnungswesen 1983*

Einflüsse der EDV auf die Weiterentwicklung des betrieblichen Rechnungswesens. In: Rechnungswesen und EDV, 4th Saarbrücker Arbeitstagung. Eds.: W. Kilger; A.-W. Scheer. Würzburg-Wien 1983, pp. 23 - 36.

Mertens, P.: *Industrielle Datenverarbeitung 1988*

Industrielle Datenverarbeitung. Vol. 1: Administrations- und Dispositionssysteme, 7th ed., Wiesbaden 1988.

Mertens, P.: *Expertensysteme in Funktionsbereichen 1988*

Expertensysteme in den betrieblichen Funktionsbereichen - Chancen, Erfolge, Mißerfolge. In: Betriebliche Expertensysteme I (Einsatz von Expertensystemen in der Betriebswirtschaft - Eine Bestandsaufnahme). Ed.: A.-W. Scheer. Wiesbaden 1988, pp. 29 - 66 (Schriften zur Unternehmensführung (SzU), vol. 36, eds.: H. Jacob et al.).

Mertens, P.; Allgeyer, K.; Däs, H.: *Betriebliche Expertensysteme 1986*

Betriebliche Expertensysteme in deutschsprachigen Ländern (Versuch einer Bestandsaufnahme). Erlangen 1986 (Arbeitsberichte des Instituts für mathematische Maschinen- und Datenverarbeitung (Informatik), Friedrich-Alexander-Universität Erlangen-Nürnberg).

Mertens, P.; Bodendorf, F.: *Methodenbanken 1979*

Interaktiv nutzbare Methodenbanken, Entwurfskriterien und Stand der Verwirklichung. Angewandte Informatik, 21 (1979) no. 12, pp. 533 - 541.

Mertens, P.; Borkowski, V.; Geis, W.: *Expertensystem-Anwendungen 1988*

Betriebliche Expertensystem-Anwendungen - Eine Materialsammlung. Berlin-Heidelberg-New York-London-Paris-Tokyo 1988.

Mertens, P., Griese, J.: *Industrielle Datenverarbeitung II 1988*

Industrielle Datenverarbeitung. Vol. 2: Informations- und Planungssysteme, 5th ed., Wiesbaden 1988.

284

Mertens, P., Plautfaut, E.: *Informationstechnik 1986*
Informationstechnik als strategische Waffe. Information Management, 1 (1986) no. 2, pp. 6 - 17.

Mertens, P., Wedekind, H.: *Betriebsinformatik 1982*
Entwicklung und Stand der Betriebsinformatik. Zeitschrift für Betriebswirtschaft (ZfB), 52 (1982) no. 5, pp. 510 - 519.

Millington, D.: *Systems Analysis 1981*
Systems Analysis and Design for Computer Applications. Chichester 1981.

Müller, E.: *KONSYS 1983*
KONSYS, ein Programm zur Konsolidierung der in- und ausländischen Tochtergesellschaften der VW AG. In: Rechnungswesen und EDV, 4th Saarbrücker Arbeitstagung. Eds.: W. Kilger; A.-W. Scheer. Würzburg-Wien 1983, pp. 508 - 526.

Nassi, I., Shneiderman, B.: *Flowchart Techniques 1973*
Flowchart Techniques for Structured Programming. ACM-SIGPLAN Notices, no. 8 (1973), pp. 12 - 26.

Nastansky, L.: *Tabellenkalkulationsprogramme 1987*
Tabellenkalkulationsprogramme. In: Lexikon der Wirtschaftsinformatik. Eds.: P. Mertens et al., Berlin-Heidelberg-New York-London-Paris-Tokyo 1987, pp. 329 - 332.

Naylor, T. H.: *Corporate Planning 1979*
Corporate Planning Models. Reading (Massachusetts) et al. 1979.

Neibecker, B.: *Apparative Marktforschung 1987*
Apparative Marktforschung (Ein Beitrag zur Werbewirkungsanalyse). Werbeforschung und Praxis, 32 (1987) no. 1, pp. 19 - 24.

Neibecker, B.: *Expertensysteme im Marketing 1989*
Einsatz von Expertensystemen im Marketing. In: Betriebliche Expertensysteme II (Einsatz von Expertensystem-Prototypen in betriebswirtschaftlichen Funktionsbereichen). Ed.: A.-W. Scheer. Wiesbaden 1989, pp. 55 - 82 (Schriften zur Unternehmensführung (SzU), vol. 40, eds.: H. Jacob et al.).

Niedereichholz, J.: *Datenbanksysteme 1983*

Datenbanksysteme (Aufbau und Einsatz). 3th ed., Heidelberg 1983.

Nixdorf (Ed.): *COMET 1978*

Datenverarbeitungssystem 8870/1, COMET 3.2, Programmgenerator CHICO. 1978.

Nomina (Ed.): *ISIS-Software Report 1989*

ISIS-Software Report (Computerprogramme in der Bundesrepublik Deutschland, Österreich, Schweiz). München 1989.

Österle, H.: *Informationssysteme 1981*

Entwurf betrieblicher Informationssysteme. München-Wien 1981.

Olson, M. H.: *Remote Office Work 1983*

Remote Office Work (Changing Patterns in Space and Time). Communications of the ACM, 26 (1983) No. 3, pp. 182 - 186.

Petre, P.: *Customers 1985*

How to Keep Customers Happy Captives. Fortune 2nd September 1985, pp. 42 - 48.

Petri, C.: *Externe Integration 1990*

Externe Integration der Datenverarbeitung (Unternehmensübergreifende Konzepte für Handelsunternehmen). Berlin-Heidelberg-New York-London-Paris-Tokyo 1990.

Picot, A.: *Bürokommunikation 1982*

Neue Techniken der Bürokommunikation in wirtschaftlicher und organisatorischer Sicht. In: Büro-Systeme und Informations-Management. Ed.: CW/CSE. München 1982.

Picot, A., Reichwald, R.: *Kommunikationstechnologien 1978*

Untersuchungen der Auswirkungen neuer Kommunikationstechnologien im Büro auf Organisationsstrukturen und Arbeitsinhalte (Entwicklung einer Unter-suchungskonzeption Forschungsbericht T 79-64). Eggenstein-Leopoldshafen 1978.

Plattner, H.: *Kostenstellenrechnung 1983*

Die Organisation eines interaktiven Planungssystems für die Kostenstellenrech-nung. In: Rechnungswesen und EDV, 4th Saarbrücker Arbeitstagung. Eds.: W. Kilger; A.-W. Scheer. Würzburg-Wien 1983, pp. 89 - 110.

Poensgen, O. H.: *Zentralisation und Dezentralisation 1967*

Zentralisation und Dezentralisation im Lichte dreier moderner Entwicklungen. Zeitschrift für Betriebswirtschaft (ZfB), 37 (1967) no. 6, pp. 373 - 394.

Porter, M. E.: *Wettbewerbsstrategie 1988*

Wettbewerbsstrategie. 5th ed., Frankfurt/Main 1988.

Porter, M. E.; Millar, V.: *Wettbewerbsvorteile 1986*

Wettbewerbsvorteile durch Information. HARVARD manager, no. 1 (1986), pp. 26 - 35.

Pressmar, D. B., Hansmann, R.: *Standardsoftwaresysteme 1978*

Standardsoftwaresysteme zur betrieblichen Kostenrechnung. In: Spezialgebiete der Kostenrechnung. Wiesbaden 1978, pp. 99 - 123 (Schriften zur Unternehmensführung (SzU), vol. 24, ed.: H. Jacob).

Prüsmann, K.: *Standardsoftware 1983*

Auswahl- und Einsatzerfahrungen mit fremderstellter Standardsoftware für die Kostenrechnung bei der Thyssen Industrie AG. In: Rechnungswesen und EDV, 4th Saarbrücker Arbeitstagung. Eds.: W. Kilger; A.-W. Scheer. Würzburg-Wien 1983, pp. 305 - 319.

Reblin, E.: *Stapel- oder Dialogverarbeitung 1980*

Stapel- oder Dialogverarbeitung im Rechnungswesen. In: Online-Systeme im Finanz- und Rechnungswesen. Ed.: P. Stahlknecht. Berlin-Heidelberg-New York 1980, pp. 43 - 55.

Reichwald, R.: *Bürotechnik 1981*

Neue Systeme der Bürotechnik und Büroarbeitsgestaltung - Problemzusammenhänge. In: Neue Systeme der Bürotechnik - Beiträge zur Büroarbeitsgestaltung aus Anwendersicht. Ed.: R. Reichwald. Berlin 1981.

Reuter, A.: *Fehlerbehandlung 1982*

Fehlerbehandlung in Datenbanksystemen (Datenbank-Recovery). München-Wien 1982.

Richter, J. E. & Partner GmbH (Eds.): *ADVIS-Methodenpackage 1981*

ADVIS-Methodenpackage - Softwaretechnologische Methoden im Verbund. Hannover 1981.

Rickert, R.: *Konzeption von Methodenbanken 1982*

Konzeption von Methodenbanken zur Entscheidungsunterstützung. In: Unternehmensplanung und -steuerung in den 80er Jahren. Ed.: H. Krallmann. Berlin-Heidelberg-New York 1982, pp. 164 - 179.

Riebel, P.: *Deckungsbeitragsrechnung 1985*

Einzelkosten- und Deckungsbeitragsrechnung. 5th ed., Wiesbaden 1985.

Rockart, J. F.: *Critical Success Factors 1982*

Current Uses of the Critical Success Factors Process (Proceedings of the Fourteenth Annual Conference of the Society for Information Management). 1982, pp. 17 - 21.

Roemer, A.: *Gemeinsame EDV 1981*

Gemeinsame EDV für die Sparkassen in Niedersachsen/Bremen. Online, no. 3 (1981), pp. 142 - 144.

Röske, W., Gansera, H.: *Strategisches Marketing 1981*

Strategisches Marketing (Ein Vorschlag für ein computergestütztes Marketing-Support-System in den 80er Jahren). In: Datenverarbeitung im Marketing. Ed.: R. Thome. Berlin-Heidelberg-New York 1981, pp. 25 - 97.

Rohrlach, H.-J.: *BfA 1981*

BfA informiert aktuell und schnell. Data report, 16 (1981) no. 6, pp. 10 - 14.

Rosenkranz, F.: *Modell- und computergestützte Unternehmensplanung 1981*

Stand und Perspektiven der modell- und computergestützten Unternehmensplanung. In: Investitions- und Finanzplanung, 2nd Saarbrücker Arbeitstagung. Eds.: W. Kilger; A.-W. Scheer. Würzburg-Wien 1981, pp. 86 - 94.

Schäfer, E.: *Industriebetrieb 1978*

Der Industriebetrieb. 2nd ed., Wiesbaden 1978.

Scheer, A.-W.: *Produktionsplanung 1976*

Produktionsplanung auf der Grundlage einer Datenbank des Fertigungsbereichs. München-Wien 1976.

288

Scheer, A.-W.: *Wirtschaftlichkeitsanalyse 1978*

Wirtschaftlichkeitsanalyse von Informationssystemen. In: Entwicklungstendenzen der Systemanalyse. Ed.: H.-R. Hansen. München-Wien 1978, pp. 305 - 330.

Scheer, A.-W.: *EDV und OR 1980*

Elektronische Datenverarbeitung und Operations Research im Produktionsbereich - zum gegenwärtigen Stand von Forschung und Anwendung. OR-Spektrum, vol. 2, no. 1 (1980), pp. 1 - 22.

Scheer, A.-W.: *Warenwirtschaftssysteme 1982*

Dispositions- und Bestellwesen als Baustein zu integrierten Warenwirtschaftssystemen. Saarbrücken 1982 (Veröffentlichungen des Instituts für Wirtschaftsinformatik, no. 33, ed.: A.-W. Scheer).

Scheer, A.-W.: *Produktionsbereich 1983*

DV-gestützte Planungs- und Informationssysteme im Produktionsbereich. Elektronische Rechenanlagen, 25 (1983) no. 2, pp. 82 - 92.

Scheer, A.-W.: *Wirtschaftsinformatik 1988*

Wirtschaftsinformatik - Informationssysteme im Industriebetrieb. 2nd ed., Berlin-Heidelberg-New York-London-Paris-Tokyo 1988.

Scheer, A.-W.: *Planungs- und Steuerungsfunktionen 1988*

Neues Gewicht für Planungs- und Steuerungsfunktionen. Blick durch die Wirtschaft 29th June 1988, p. 7.

Scheer, A.-W. (Ed.): *Betriebliche Expertensysteme I 1988*

Betriebliche Expertensysteme I (Einsatz von Expertensystemen in der Betriebswirtschaft - Eine Bestandsaufnahme). Wiesbaden 1988 (Schriften zur Unternehmensführung (SzU), vol. 36, eds.: H. Jacob et al.).

Scheer, A.-W. (Ed.): *Betriebliche Expertensysteme II 1989*

Betriebliche Expertensysteme II (Einsatz von Expertensystem-Prototypen in betriebswirtschaftlichen Funktionsbereichen). Wiesbaden 1989 (Schriften zur Unternehmensführung (SzU), vol. 40, eds.: H. Jacob et al.).

Scheer, A.-W.: *CIM 1990*

CIM (Computer Integrated Manufacturing) - Towards the Factory of the Future. 2nd ed., Berlin-Heidelberg-New York-London-Paris-Tokyo 1991.

Scheer, A.-W. in collaboration with Bolmerg, L.; Demmer, H., Helber, C.: *Wirtschaftsinformatik 1978*
Wirtschafts- und Betriebsinformatik. München 1978.

Scheer, A.-W., Bock, M.: *Konstruktionsbegleitende Kalkulation 1988*
Expertensysteme zur konstruktionsbegleitenden Kalkulation. CAD-CAM-Report, 7 (1988) no. 12, pp. 47 - 55.

Scheer, A.-W., Kraemer, W.: *Betriebsübergreifende Vorgangsketten 1989*
Betriebsübergreifende Vorgangsketten und Informationssysteme. CIM-Management, 5 (1989) no. 3, pp. 4 - 9.

Scheer, A.-W., Steinmann, D.: *Themenbereich Expertensysteme 1988*
Einführung in den Themenbereich Expertensysteme. In: Betriebliche Expertensysteme I (Einsatz von Expertensystemen in der Betriebswirtschaft - Eine Bestandsaufnahme). Ed.: A.-W. Scheer. Wiesbaden 1988, pp. 5 - 27 (Schriften zur Unternehmensführung (SzU), vol. 36, eds.: H. Jacob et al.).

Scheer, A.-W. et al.: *Personal Computing 1984*
Personal Computing - EDV-Einsatz in Fachabteilungen. München 1984.

Schellhaas, H., Schönecker, H.: *Kommunikationstechnik 1983*
Kommunikationstechnik und Anwender-Akzeptanzbarrieren (Bedarfsstrukturen, Einsatzbedingungen, Forschungsprojekt Bürokommunikation). München 1983.

Schlageter, G., Stucky, W.: Datenbanksysteme 1983
Datenbanksysteme (Konzepte und Modelle). 2nd ed., Stuttgart 1983.

Schmitz, P., Schönlein, A.: *Optimierungsmodelle 1978*
Lineare und linearisierbare Optimierungsmodelle sowie ihre ADV-gestützte Lösung. Braunschweig 1978.

Schnupp, P.: *Rechnernetze 1982*
Rechnernetze (Entwurf und Realisierung). 2nd ed., Berlin-New York 1982.

Schönweitz, G.: *Bürokommunikation 1989*

Bürokommunikation: Herstellerkonzepte auf dem Prüfstand (1st part: Benutzeranforderungen). Office Management, 37 (1989) no. 10, pp. 42 - 45.

Scholz, C.: *Personal Computing 1989*

Einführung in das Personal Computing. Berlin-New York 1989.

Schulte-Hillen, J.: *Arbeitsmittel 1988*

Arbeitsmittel, kein Zauberkasten. Online, no. 5 (1988), pp. 44 - 46.

Schwetz, R.: *Bürotätigkeiten 1983*

Einfluß kommunikationsfähiger Systeme auf die Bürotätigkeiten und die Büroorganisation. In: Arbeitspapier. Ed.: Siemens. München 1983.

Seibt, D.: *Btx im geschäftlichen Bereich 1986*

Btx-Anwendungsschwerpunkte im geschäftlichen Bereich (Lecture in the cousrse of the seminar: "Gestaltung von Btx-Rechnerverbundanwendungen" 20th and 21st November 1986). Köln 1986.

Seitz, N.: *Warenbewirtschaftung 1982*

Warenbewirtschaftung in Kooperationssystemen: Die V.A.G.-Organisation. Zürich 1982. In: Integrierte Warenwirtschaftssysteme. Ed.: J. Zentes.

Shunk, D. L.: *CIM in den USA 1988*

CIM in den USA. Fortschrittliche Betriebsführung/Industrial Engineering (FB/IE), 37 (1988) no. 1, pp. 19 - 25.

Sinzig, W.: *Rechnungswesen 1989*

Datenbankorientiertes Rechnungswesen. 3rd ed., Berlin-Heidelberg-New York-Tokyo 1989.

Stahlknecht, P.: *Customizen 1983*

Customizen. Informatik-Spektrum, 6 (1983) no. 3, p. 168.

Stahlknecht, P.: *Wirtschaftsinformatik 1989*

Einführung in die Wirtschaftsinformatik. 4th ed., Berlin-Heidelberg-New York-London-Paris-Tokyo-Hong Kong 1989.

Steinmann, D.: *Wissensbasierte Anwendungen 1989*

Konzeption zur Integration wissensbasierter Anwendungen in konventionelle Systeme der Produktionsplanung und -steuerung (PPS) im Bereich der Fertigungssteuerung. In: Betriebliche Expertensysteme II (Einsatz von Expertensystem-Prototypen in betriebswirtschaftlichen Funktionsbereichen). Ed.: A.-W. Scheer. Wiesbaden 1989, pp. 83 - 122 (Schriften zur Unternehmensführung (SzU), vol. 40, eds.: H. Jacob et al.).

Stetter, F.: *Softwaretechnologie 1983*

Softwaretechnologie. 2nd ed., Mannheim-Wien-Zürich 1983.

Synott, W. R., Gruber, W. H.: *Information Resource Management 1986*

Information Resource Management (Opportunities and Strategies for the 1980's). New York 1981.

Szyperski, N.: *Aspekte 1982*

Strategische Aspekte von Office Support Systemen. In: 1st Europäischer Kongreß über Bürosysteme & Informationsmanagement. Ed.: CW-CSE. München 1982.

Telebox 1989

Kommunikation zwischen Telebox und Telex. Office Management, 37 (1989) no. 3, p. 109.

Thome, R. (Ed.): *Datenverarbeitung im Marketing 1981*

Datenverarbeitung im Marketing. Berlin-Heidelberg-New York 1981.

Thome, R.: *Informationsverarbeitung in der Praxis*

Informationsverarbeitung in der Praxis. Landsberg 1986.

Trost, H.: *Wissensrepräsentation 1984*

Wissensrepräsentation in der AI am Beispiel Semantischer Netze. In: Artificial Intelligence, Eine Einführung. Eds.: J. Retti et al. Stuttgart 1984, pp. 47 - 72.

Vorteile im Wettbewerb 1987

Vorteile im Wettbewerb. Btx-Praxis, no. 12 (1987), pp. 34 - 35.

Wagner, H. M., Whitin, T. M.: *Economic Lot Size Model 1958*

Dynamic Version of the Economic Lot Size Model. Management Science, no. 5 (1958), pp. 89 - 96.

292

Warnecke, H. J., Bullinger, H. J., Lienert, J.: *Produktionsbereich 1980*
   EDV-Anwendungen im Produktionsbereich. In: Wirtschaftsinformatik III. Ed.: H. D. Plötzeneder. Stuttgart-New York 1980, pp. 57 - 80.

Wedekind, H.: *Datenbanksysteme I 1981*
   Datenbanksysteme I. 2nd ed., Mannheim-Wien-Zürich 1981.

Wildemann, H.: *Just-In-Time 1987*
   Das Just-In-Time Konzept (Produktion und Zulieferung auf Abruf). Frankfurt 1987.

Wißkirchen, P. et al.: *Bürosysteme 1983*
   Informationstechnik und Bürosysteme. Stuttgart 1983.

Wittemann, N.: *Produktionsplanung 1984*
   Produktionsplanung mit verdichteten Daten. In: Operations Research Proceedings, Vorträge der 12. DGOR-Jahrestagung 1983. Eds.: H. Steckhan et al. Berlin-Heidelberg-New York-Tokyo 1984, pp. 172 - 179.

Wittemann, N.: *Produktionsplanung mit verdichteten Daten 1985*
   Produktionsplanung mit verdichteten Daten. Berlin-New York-Tokyo 1985.

Zacharias, C.-O.: *Lagerverbundsysteme 1982*
   EDV-Einsatz in hierarchischen Lagerverbundsystemen. München 1982.

Zapp, H.: *Computer Integrated Banking 1989*
   Electronic Banking/Computer Integrated Banking (CIB). Die Betriebswirtschaft (DBW), 49 (1989) no. 1, pp. 120 - 121.

Zentes J. (Ed.): *Warenwirtschaftssysteme 1982*
   Integrierte Warenwirtschaftssysteme. Zürich 1982.

Zentes, J. (Ed.): *Kommunikationstechnologien 1984*
   Neue Informations- und Kommunikationstechnologien in der Marktforschung. Berlin-Heidelberg-New York-Tokyo 1984.

Zentes, J.: *EDV-gestütztes Marketing 1987*
   EDV-gestütztes Marketing (Ein informations- und kommunikationsorientierter Ansatz). Berlin-Heidelberg-New York-London-Paris-Tokyo 1987.

Zloof, M. M.: *Office by Example 1982*
  Office by Example. IBM Systems Journal, 21 (1982) no. 3, pp. 272 - 304.

Zwicker, E.: *Dynamische Systeme 1981*
  Simulation und Analyse dynamischer Systeme in den Wirtschafts- und Sozialwis-
  senschaften. Berlin-New York 1981.

Index

A.-W. Scheer, University of Saarbrücken

CIM
Computer Integrated Manufacturing

Towards the Factory of the Future

2nd, rev. and enl. ed. 1991. XII, 287 pp. 149 figs. Hardcover DM 78,–
ISBN 3-540-53667-1

Following a comprehensive justification of the CIM integration principle, this book discusses the current state of applications and new demands arising from the integration principle as applied to the individual CIM components. The interfaces between business and technical information processing are considered in detail.
The main emphasis, however, is on strategies for realization and implementation based on concrete experience. The "Y-CIM information management" model, developed and tested at the author's institute, is presented as a procedural method for implementing CIM and demonstrated using up-to-date examples. In addition to the procedure for developing a CIM strategy, concrete sub-projects are developed which are directed at specific sector or enterprise structures.
CIM developments like design stage cost estimation, use of expert systems and intercompany process chains have proved to be effective CIM components since the first edition of this book and are now treated in the main text. Six German and five American industrial implementations are presented.

A.-W. Scheer, University of Saarbrücken

Enterprise-Wide Data Modelling

Information Systems in Industry

1989. XIX, 605 pp. 450 figs. Foldout in pocket.
Hardcover DM 98,– ISBN 3-540-51480-5

The more the access to EDP-supported information systems is facilitated by user-friendly query languages and evaluation systems, the more the structuring of the database to which these instruments are applied increases in importance. Therefore this book undertakes to "construct" data structures for the functional areas production, engineering, purchasing, sales, personnel, accounting and administration of an industrial company with the aim of supporting planning, accounting, analysis and long-term planning systems.

Springer-Verlag
Berlin
Heidelberg
New York
London
Paris
Tokyo
Hong Kong
Barcelona
Budapest

L. F. Pau, Technical University of Denmark, Lyngby; **C. Gianotti,** Milano

Economic and Financial Knowledge-Based Processing

1990. XV, 364 pp. 67 figs. 12 tabs. Hardcover DM 128,– ISBN 3-540-53043-6

Contents: A Reader's Guide: Introduction: The Strategic Challenge to Banks, Financial Services and Economics. – Basic Concepts. – Applications of Artificial Intelligence in Banking, Financial Services and Economics. – Knowledge Representation. – Artificial Intelligence Programming Languages. – Search and Causal Analysis. – Neural Processing and Inductive Learning. – Technical Analysis for Securities Trading. – Intelligent Information Screens. – Natural Language Front-Ends to Economic Models. – Trade Selection with Uncertain Reasoning on Technical Indicators. – Currency Risk Management. – Reasoning Procedures in Knowledge-Based Systems for Economics and Management. – Appendix 1: Software Codes: Prolog Code for the Tax Adviser. – An Algorithm for Causal and Consistency Analysis. – Prolog NL Parser for Economic Statements. – Appendix 2: Predefined LISP and Prolog Expressions.

M. J. Liberatore, Villanova University, Villanova, PA (Ed.)

Selection and Evaluation of Advanced Manufacturing Technologies

With contributions by numerous experts

1990. VI, 324 pp. 23 figs. 52 tabs. Hardcover DM 120,– ISBN 3-540-52656-0

This book provides a unified treatment of the current state of knowledge concerning the evaluation and selection of advanced manufacturing technologies. A multifunctional perspective is presented, and contributions from management science, accounting, technological innovation, strategic planning, economics, and organizational behavior are included so that a broad-based understanding of the topic can be achieved by the reader.
The book is organized into three sections: innovation issues, methods and applications, and performance measurement.

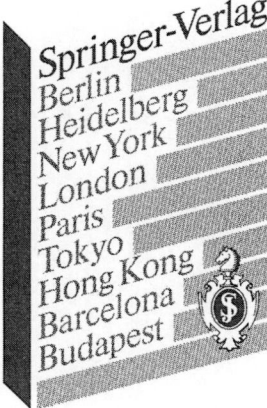

Springer-Verlag
Berlin
Heidelberg
New York
London
Paris
Tokyo
Hong Kong
Barcelona
Budapest